Mummies in Nineteenth Century America

Ancient Egyptians as Artifacts

S.J. WOLFE

with ROBERT SINGERMAN

Foreword by BOB BRIER

McFarland & Company, Inc., Publishers
Jefferson, North Carolina, and London

LIBRARY OF CONGRESS CATALOGUING-IN-PUBLICATION DATA

Wolfe, S. J., 1951–
    Mummies in nineteenth century America : ancient Egyptians as
artifacts / S. J. Wolfe with Robert Singerman ; foreword by Bob Brier.
        p.   cm.
    Includes bibliographical references and index.

    ISBN 978-0-7864-3941-6
    softcover : 50# alkaline paper ∞

    1. Mummies—Egypt.   2. Mummies—United States—
Exhibitions—History—19th century.   3. Mummies—Collection
and preservation—United States—History—19th century.
I. Singerman, Robert.   II. Title.
DT62.M7W65   2009
932.0074'73—dc22   2009030980

British Library cataloguing data are available

On the cover: The red-painted face of the innermost coffin of
Padihershef, the first Egyptian mummy to be commercially displayed
in the United States, 1823 (photograph by David A. Rawson); United
States flag art ©2009 Shutterstock

Manufactured in the United States of America

McFarland & Company, Inc., Publishers
  Box 611, Jefferson, North Carolina 28640
    www.mcfarlandpub.com

To the untold numbers of mummies of ancient Egyptians, in the hope that by "speaking their names" in this book they will live again in the Western Lands.

Table of Contents

Acknowledgments

There are so many of these I felt they belonged in a separate section. I wish I could individually thank everyone who has helped with this project but I fear such a lengthy list would be almost as long as the book. So I have mentioned only the institutions in some cases, and hope my friends and colleagues understand that I really could not list them all by name. Nor could I list every institution—if I have forgotten anyone, I did not do it intentionally.

First, I want to thank my husband, David A. Rawson, for encouraging and indulging me in this pastime. He has served as mentor, driver, technical support, photographer, editor, investigator and researcher. He knows my talks almost better than I do. He's put up with papyrus paintings and artifacts in the bedroom, dining room and living room, as well as bookcases full of tomes on Egyptian topics. He even has planned vacations around mummy collections. He has done so with unfailing good cheer, setting aside his own work to help me with mine. It is truly a labor of love on his part, and this book would not have been written without him.

Second, I must thank Robert Singerman, Judaica bibliographer and former library bibliographer for anthropology, linguistics and Jewish studies at the University of Florida until his retirement in 2006. Robert got me going on historical research by involving me in his own, and when one of our projects engendered this one, plunged into researching mummies with all the passion he has exhibited in every other book on which he has worked. He truly does deserve his place on the title page.

I'd like to thank my colleagues, friends and research fellows, both past and present, at the American Antiquarian Society for all their help, interest and encouragement throughout this undertaking. They found mummy stories for me, brought me pictures, gave me advice on technical questions concerning databases and citation formats. They listened to lunchtime talks, both formal and informal, read parts of the manuscript, offered comments and corrections, digitized illustrations, cheered me on, and in general, were the best support group for which an author could ever hope. I would like to particularly thank Kathleen Haley for her help with the database and for reading and commenting on the first draft of the book.

I'd like to thank colleagues in the field, fellow researchers in the emerging field of "mummyology" who gave me encouragement to work on the history of the mummy as artifact, to explore the modern history of these ancient objects and to write it down so others could learn from it. I am especially indebted to Bob Brier, who so graciously consented to write the Foreword for this book. I would also like to thank Edgar Snow, and Brian Smith for research help in assembling the chapter on the mummies owned by the Mormons, and H. Michael Marquardt for reading and commenting and editing that section of the manuscript.

Many, many librarians, museum curators and directors of historical societies hunted up citations, mailed me copies of requested materials, adjusted permissions fees for reproductions, answered questions about their collections and best of all, said they could not wait for the book to come out. I wish I could name everyone but I can't so I'll just list their institutions (in no particular order): Hay Library at John Carter Brown; Houghton Library at Harvard; Library Company of Philadelphia; Reading Public Museum; George Walter Vincent Smith Art Museum; Massachusetts General Hospital; Warren Anatomical Museum at the Frances A. Countway Library of Medicine; Mutter Museum; National Museum of Natural History; Museum of Fine Arts, Boston; Carlos Museum, Emory University; Metropolitan Museum of Art; Brooklyn Museum; New-York Historical Society; Historical Society, Village of Round Lake; Massachusetts Historical Society; New Hampshire Historical Society; Henry Sheldon Museum; Worcester Art Museum; College of the Holy Cross; College of Wooster; Westminster College; Erskine College; Gardiner Public Library; Warren Public Library; Westbrook Historical Society; Peabody Essex Museum and the Phillips Library; Blunt Library at Mystic Seaport; Beverly Historical Society; Worcester State College; Anna Maria College; Worcester Polytechnic Institute; The Berkshire Museum; Akhmim Consortium; Cazenovia Public Library; Kalamazoo Valley Museum; Hillsdale College Museum; Bridwell Library, Southern Methodist University; and Albertus Magnus College. Special thanks to John Taylor of the British Museum.

A debt of gratitude also goes out to friends, colleagues and attendees at conferences and lectures sponsored by the following organizations—your comments and questions at my presentations made this book what it is: Dublin Seminar for New-England Folklife; Society for the History of Authorship, Reading and Publishing; Society for Historians of the Early American Republic; Archaeological Institute of America; Mormon Historical Association; Northeast Popular Culture Association; New England Historical Association; Maine Old Cemetery Association; Kennebec Historical Society; Washburn Seminar in the Humanities; and MENSA.

I would like to thank my in-laws, Carolyn and Richard Rawson, and sister Linda; friends Martha Gunnarson, Cindy Rinehimer, Shelley Cox, Kathi Kitao, Joyce Forsman and Judy Henry; assorted relatives; and cousins Catherine and Gary Parmentier for listening to me talk about mummies, for attending my presentations, for going to see mummies (even if they didn't want to get too close to them) and for pushing me when I needed it, and for giving me space when I required it.

Very special thanks to George Billias, Alden Vaughan and Mike McGiffert, who grilled me thoroughly over dinner in what could only be described as a dissertation defense on the topic of mummy paper, and who spontaneously awarded me a "Ph.D. by acclamation" in recognition of my erudition on the subject.

I thank Chester Myles, Sydney, Spike and Max for acting as paperweights and "helping" me arrange papers and notes. (A strange new use of the word with which I was previously unacquainted.)

Finally, I'd like to thank my parents—my father, Robert, and my mother, Priscilla, who are no longer with us—who never quite understood my passion for mummies, but who always encouraged me to do my best at whatever projects I undertook. Their continual confidence in my abilities made me the person I am today and I wish they were able to rejoice in my accomplishment in writing this book.

MUMMY, n. An ancient Egyptian, formerly in universal use among modern civilized nations as medicine, and now engaged in supplying art with an excellent pigment. He is handy, too, in museums in gratifying the vulgar curiosity that serves to distinguish man from the lower animals.

> By means of the mummy, mankind, it is said,
> Attests to the gods its respects for the dead.
> We plunder the tomb, be he sinner or saint.
> Distil him for physic, and grind him for paint,
> Exhibit for money his poor, shrunken frame,
> And with levity flock to the scene of the shame.
> O, tell me, ye gods, for the use of the rhyme:
> For respecting the dead what's the limit of time?
> —Ambrose Bierce, *The Devil's Dictionary*

Foreword by Bob Brier

Ask any museum curator what draws people to an exhibition and the answer will probably be either "dinosaurs" or "mummies." It is easy to understand the attraction of dinosaurs. Nothing like a fierce T-Rex to get the adrenalin pumping. The lure of mummies is not quite so easy to explain. I've worked with mummies for forty years and I am still not sure what it is about mummies that fascinates the general public. I think it has something to do with the desire for immortality.

A museum visitor's encounter with a mummy lying in its coffin is rarely a casual one. Staring back at him across three thousand years is another human being. If you had known him thirty centuries ago on the banks of the Nile, you would still recognize him—he still has his curly hair, high cheekbones. Perhaps there's a bit of envy when we see a mummy—it is almost as if he has cheated death. But there's something else.

Our society doesn't talk about death. It's a taboo. That's why we have euphemisms like "The dearly departed" or "He's not with us any more." The Egyptians also had their phrase for death. "He went west." Because we suppress and disguise talk about death, mummies offer a rare opportunity to stare at death—it's OK, it's a museum exhibition, and we're fascinated. For many people the chance encounter with a museum mummy is a confusing experience involving both fear and attraction. It has always been like that. Just read Chapter 1, "An Appropriate Ornament of the Operating Room," to see early Americans' reaction to the first mummy that came to the United States.

Mummies in Nineteenth Century America is a unique and welcome contribution to the field of mummy studies. A scholarly but captivating study of America's fascination with mummies, much of its appeal lies in the details. Who knew that in 1824 a mummy with its coffin cost $350? The Appendices alone are a major addition to our knowledge of how mummies have been received in our not-too-distant past. I have often wondered just how many mummies are in America and which the first were. *Mummies in Nineteenth Century America* provides much needed data to answer these questions. Although the book's focus is backward in time, I predict it will become more and more important in the future.

Mummy studies are soon going to have a central place in modern science. Mummies are like little encyclopedias; if you can read them there is a wealth of information to be gained. Already scientists can determine the city where an ancient Aztec grew up by analyzing the composition of his teeth. (Water is different everywhere and the water you drank when your teeth were developing leaves its signature.) Analysis of ancient DNA is helping paleopathologists figure out how disease-causing organisms have changed over the centuries and this in turn will enable them to predict the future course of the disease's evolution. Thus an ancient Egyptian mummy can help save patients in the future. Soon DNA technology will be advanced enough to enable Egyptologists to answer questions about the relationships between the royal mummies in the Egyptian Museum in Cairo. We still don't know who Tutankhamen's parents were, but DNA analyses may provide the answer. As the general public realizes that Egyptian mummies are not just curiosities, but are also treasure troves of information, they will want to know more about their history. *Mummies in Nineteenth Century America* should be one of the first books to which they turn.

> Bob Brier
> Senior Research Fellow
> C.W. Post Campus
> Long Island University

Preface

This book is not like any other mummy book. It will not tell how mummies were made, nor will it explain the religious and cultural reasons for making them. It also will not address the occupations, social class, or daily life of the persons in ancient times who later became mummies prepared for their passage to eternity.

What it will do is discuss mummies as artifacts in nineteenth-century America—how they got here and what happened to them after they arrived. Because I wish to concentrate on the histories of the mummies themselves, I will mention only in passing the various ethnological and scientific racial theories which the study of mummies engendered during that time period. I will also not discuss at any length the influence of the mummy on esthetics, art, literature, politics and poetry, although I will use the prose and poems of viewers to demonstrate how mummies were perceived by the public who viewed them. In the chapter on the Mormons and their mummies I will focus on the mummies, and refrain from any theological or archaeological speculation on the papyrus which caused Joseph Smith to buy the bodies in the first place. There are whole books written on all of these subjects; some are listed in the bibliography, and others I have detailed in Appendix 2 for supplemental reading if you have a further interest in any of the topics.

The book is divided into seven chapters, roughly in chronological order (at least in their beginnings). For all but one I have used an actual quote from the pertinent chapter as its title. For the odd one out ("Unholy Unrollers") I am indebted to Bob Brier's book on mummies, which used a similar title. I have included four Appendices as well. Appendix 2 I have already mentioned. Appendix 1 is a listing of mummies which arrived in America before 1900 but which I did not include in the narrative. Appendix 3 presents notes on the coffins of the early mummies which arrived in America.

Appendix 4 is an example of how news about mummies spread, using Ward Nicholas Boylston's mummy as an example. I wanted to demonstrate how and why a source about a particular mummy did not always come from a local newspaper. Mummies were big news throughout the nineteenth century and papers copied information across the entire United States. For my purposes, it is lucky that they did this, for oftentimes the originating papers have disappeared or are otherwise not accessible.

Which brings me to another way in which this book is different from most other mummy research projects—it is the result of many hours of research in digital archives, and without them, quite simply, this book could not have come into being. Although I started my work collecting serendipitous snippets of news and descriptions as I researched other topics, the advent of digital archives of newspapers, magazines and books created a very special environment in which I could work more efficiently and effectively and find much more information than I could have found in any other manner. Thank you, Readex, Newsbank, Proquest, Gale, Newspaper Archive, Google and everyone else who digitized things and made them available. I looked at approximately twenty *thousand* digitized citations in order to compile the mummy information used to write this book. All of the information in those citations was recorded in tables in Access, from which I created a database of Egyptian mummies in America up to the present time. It is a prodigious amount of information; at this writing it contains 1,249 entries and represents approximated 560 individuals (or parts thereof). For each entry I plotted twenty-five access points, including linking fields which enabled me to track which mummies went where and when. Some of them were amazingly mobile.

It is my hope that in the near future this database ("Egyptian Mummies in America") will be accessible on Jim Deem's *Mummy Tombs* website (www.mummytombs.com), where I hope it will continue to grow and be refined as new information comes to light and can be added.

My fascination with mummies stems from a chance encounter with a mummiform coffin at the George Walter Vincent Smith Art Museum, in Springfield, Massachusetts, when I was but three or four years old. At the time there were few books on Egypt and mummies for children, and so, being a precocious and prodigious reader, I pored over old *National Geographic* magazines, and badgered the adults in my family to bring me books from the upstairs (adult) library. In this way I learned about the lives and deaths of the ancient Egyptians, but I always wanted to know more. It would not be until I was in college that I would be able to take classes in the subject, refine my interests and actually travel to museums which had mummies in their collections.

My fascination grew and I amassed a huge library of books on Egyptian topics, most of which included at least one mummy. I planned vacations around museums which had mummies and dragged many friends along with me to look at Egyptian collections everywhere. (I have a fond recollection of a dear friend, Lew Perry, who informed me that he was not interested in going to see the mummies at the Museum of Fine Arts in Boston because he had an agreement that he didn't go look at dead bodies and they didn't come and look at him.) I even briefly thought of getting a degree which would allow me to become an archaeologist and work in Egypt, but it was not to be. I graduated instead with a Master of Science Degree in Library Science from the State University of New York at Albany and almost immediately thereafter, began working at the American Antiquarian Society, in Worcester, Massachusetts, which is a research library in pre–1900 American history.

It was there I started working with Robert Singerman on a few bibliographic projects and it was also there that I met David A. Rawson, a fellow from the College of William and Mary, who was researching for his Ph.D. in American history. He became the only research fellow to ever marry a member of the staff, and between him and Robert, I became enmeshed in American history and literature. Alas for my interest in Egypt, I thought, these topics are epochs and continents apart. I remained a determined dilettante, however, and quietly collected articles of interest on the side.

When Robert and I began working on a bibliography of the paper industry in the United States we ran into the whole "mummy paper" story and I decided I wanted to find out more about when and how mummies had come to America. I already knew that the coffin which had so fascinated me as a child belonged to a mummy still extant at Massachusetts General Hospital (and to whom I referred as "my mummy"), but I could not find much written about it, nor indeed, much about the history of mummies in the United States at all. The closest I could come was the research the Mormons had done, and when I looked at that I started to see things which I knew were incorrect. I then contacted various "mummyologists" about this absence of historical material, and they told me that there was indeed nothing much written and that although it sounded like an interesting idea, none of them really had any time to research and write it. So I said to my husband one night during dinner: "Maybe I ought to do something with my mummy." David is a college professor with a lot of non-traditional students, both graduate and undergraduate, and he looked at me and said, "Why not?"

Thus it began. Little did I realize how much interest there was in mummies, and how much people did not know. I started doing presentations and lectures at conferences, museums, libraries and for any group of people who wanted to listen. I was even the research historian for an exhibition of "my mummy," Padihershef, at the George Walter Vincent Smith Art Museum in Springfield in 2003. One year I did six presentations in as many months, and each one was on a different aspect of my mummy research. Every time David and I took our PowerPoint presentation somewhere and I stood up and spoke in front of people, I honed the presentation of my information, adding things which people found interesting and using their questions to refine what exactly was going into my book. By the time I sat down to actually write, most of the rough spots had been smoothed away.

Information poured in, and is still crossing my desk. I have eight filing cabinet drawers filled with "mummy stuff" and am starting on a ninth. I could have easily written a book twice as long as this one had I included everything I have uncovered. Thank goodness I was able to make a chronological and top-ical separation of subjects and concentrate on the mummy as artifact before 1901—the rest is for the next book.

I was privileged during my research to be able to get "up close and personal" with two of the early mummies which came to America, the one which Ward Nicholas Boylston acquired in 1818 and Padihershef, the "Ether Dome Mummy" at Massachusetts General Hospital, who arrived in 1823.

I was able to view Padihershef on the same day that a conservator was coming to check him out before he went on exhibition in Springfield, Massachusetts, in 2003. Jeff Mifflin, the Massachusetts General Hospital archivist, was pleased to introduce me, as it were, to the gentleman whose outermost coffin had so entranced me as a child. As I was helping shift him from his glass case onto an examining table, I was surprised to notice there was no odor from the mummy, except a faint whiff of some unidentifiable spicy smell. His flesh was glossy and tarry-looking, not unlike the color and texture of whole smoked tobacco leaves. His teeth surprised me the most; they were gleaming and startlingly white, bared in a seeming sort of smile. The coffin was vibrantly colored and redolent of wood. I made my usual little obeisance and murmured, "Padihershef, life, power health." The ancient Egyptians believed that to utter the name of the dead was a means of giving that person life in the Western Lands (their version of the afterlife). It's a little ritual I perform for every mummy I meet who has a name. I am not sure why; perhaps it is my way of ensuring their chthonic survival.

Sadly, there is nothing left of Boylston's mummy, save a skull and a wrapped leg. I was able to view the skull through the courtesy of Dominic Hall, curator of the Warren Anatomical Museum in Boston. It lacks its lower jaw and is totally defleshed and has no visible signs that it ever was a mummy. I'm no forensic anthropologist but the more I looked at it and studied it, I came to think it might be female because of its gracile appearance and the lack of prominent brow ridges. Lettering on one side of the skull indicated it had been used at some point as an anatomical model. I wasn't able to really add anything to my knowledge of this mummy by viewing its skull, but as I told the curator, for me, it was as if I had found the Holy Grail.

Poor old mummy—without a name I was not able to perform the magic ritual, but did wish it "life, power health" anyway.

1

"An Appropriate Ornament of the Operating Room"

Padihershef and the Beginnings of Mummymania in Nineteenth-Century America

On Saturday, 26 April 1823, the Yankee brig *Sally Anne* arrived in Boston, under the command of Capt. Robert B. Edes. Onboard her was a most unusual passenger, an Egyptian mummy, one of the first to be brought into the United States.[1]

He was a stonecutter from the city of Thebes, a man named Padihershef, although these facts were not to be known for more than a hundred years, well into the twentieth century. He had died, been embalmed, and been enclosed in two decorated coffins, there to await his rebirth in the Western Lands, according to his religious beliefs. Little could he have dreamed in his most wild imaginings, that he would be uprooted and transported such a far distance as Boston, Massachusetts, or that his arrival and subsequent travels would ignite such an interest that it would become known as "mummymania."

Mummies had already been objects of curiosity and study in England and in France. As early as 1722, William Leetveulier had brought a mummy to England. In 1737 Alexander Gordon published an essay on this and two other mummies. The British Museum installed its first mummies around 1803. The French interest is generally linked to Napoleon's Egyptian campaigns of 1798 and 1799.[2] The publication of *La Description de l'Egypte* (ten folio volumes and two atlases containing eight hundred thirty-seven copper engravings) in 1809 whetted international curiosity about the history and artifacts of the land along the Nile.[3]

The earliest mummy brought to America which has been mentioned in any published source is a mummified hand and arm in a wooden box, presented to the Library Company of Philadelphia in 1767 by the artist Benjamin West, and brought from London to Philadelphia by Francis Hopkinson.[4] It is the left hand of a small woman, covered in "two bandages" with a layer of some resinous substance between the skin and first layer of cloth, and the same

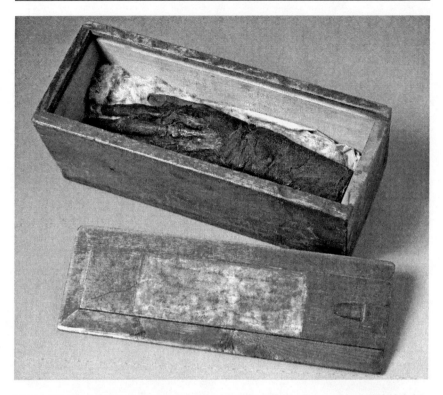

Mummified female hand and arm presented to the Library Company of Philadelphia by the artist Benjamin West. The earliest known mummy or part of a mummy to be imported into the United States (courtesy the Library Company of Philadelphia).

between that layer and the next. The thumb and fingers were separately bandaged.[5] It is still in the collections of the Library Company.

A silversmith by the name of John Germon purportedly imported some mummies (the number is not known) into Philadelphia in 1800. They evidently generated no interest from the public, they received no coverage in the press, and so, being deemed of no immediate financial value to the importer, they were stored in Dock Street below Third Street until 1832, when they were discovered by workers who were repairing the premises. The mummies had long since been forgotten and the workers, unaware of their value, destroyed all of them but one, which was in the hands of a private family in Southwark until at least August of 1848.[6]

In 1816, an infant mummy "stated to be in high perfection" was presented to the University of Pennsylvania by the Rev. Thomas Hall of Leghorn, a former pupil in the College of Philadelphia.[7] Hall also presented the "hand of a delicate female."[8]

An advertisement for Peale's Museum (in the upper rooms of the State

House in Philadelphia) in the 4 March 1817 *Poulson's American Daily Advertiser* noted that the hand of an Egyptian mummy had been recently presented by Dr. Shippen.

Another mummy was reported upon by the Boston *Columbian Centinel* of 16 May 1818:

> Egyptian mummy—In one of the late vessels from Europe, there arrived here a genuine Egyptian mummy, perhaps the first introduced into the United States.—It is in a state of good preservation, and was procured in Egypt by Ward Nicholas Boylston, Esq. in his travels in that interesting and ancient quarter of the globe. He saw it taken from the catacombs at Memphis (Saccara). It is calculated that this embalmment could not have been less than 24 centuries ago, as the most ancient writers mention, that the great art of embalmment had then been lost in Egypt for many ages. We feel indebted to this patriotic gentleman for this addition to the subjects of art and curiosity in our country.

The 6 June 1818 issue of *Niles National Register* was much more succinct. "An Egyptian mummy has arrived at Boston, taken from the catacombs of Saccara." It is not known if the mummy were male or female, or what happened to it after its arrival.

There are no extant broadsides or newspaper accounts which indicated that it might have been exhibited to the public. Perhaps Mr. Boylston kept it in his house, as a curiosity. In England and France it was not unusual for such relics to be displayed, along with other artifacts, in demonstration of the owners' artistic and scientific interests.

This mummy was examined by Dr. John Collins Warren, of the Massachusetts General Hospital, at some point before Padihershef's arrival, for he incorporates a description of it in the article which he wrote about Padihershef:

> The mummy at Roxbury, in the vicinity of Boston, belonging to Ward Nicholas Boylston, Esq., has a fine confirmation of head. This was purchased by the Professor in Egypt and sent to England, where being opened at the custom house, it was so much exposed as to injure the covering, and the flesh has in great

Ward Nicholas Boylston, merchant, member of the Massachusetts Medical Society, he imported the first entire adult mummy into the United States in 1818 (*Medical Dissertations Read at the Annual Meeting of the Massachusetts Medical Society* [Boston: Press of the Daily Advertiser, 1829]. Courtesy American Antiquarian Society).

measure decayed from the bones. The forehead is elevated and large, the jaws filled with fine teeth, not prominent, and the head altogether is the European or Caucasian form.[9]

In November 1819 Boylston gave "relics of an Egyptian mummy" to the American Antiquarian Society in Worcester, Massachusetts, of which he was a member. In August 1820 he gave "a bone and tooth of an Egyptian mummy" as well.[10] The head (minus its ethmoid process) and one of the legs, with many thicknesses of bandages, were donated to the Warren Anatomical Museum by George C. Shattuck in 1859. The museum also had three casts of Egyptian skulls, two from George Gliddon, in its collection.[11]

The American Antiquarian Society divested itself of most of its natural history collections after 1830, and most of those were sent either to the Peabody Museum at Harvard or to the Smithsonian. There is no record at the American Antiquarian Society which delineates the disposition of the mummy fragments. The head and leg are still at the Warren Anatomical Museum, which is part of Harvard Medical School.[12]

In 1821, Commodore Charles Stewart, former commander of the *Constitution*, and a good friend of Titian Peale, strode into Charles Willson Peale's

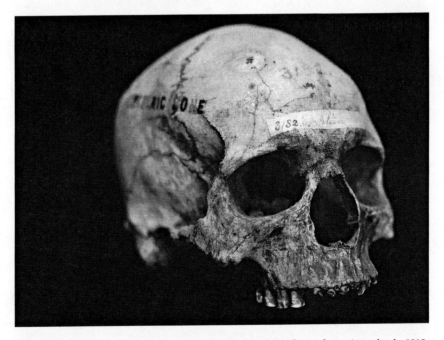

The skull of the mummy which Ward Nicholas Boylston brought to America in 1818. There is no indication it was ever part of an Egyptian mummy. Markings on the skull show it has been used as an anatomical demonstration model (courtesy Warren Anatomical Museum, Francis A. Countway Library of Medicine).

Philadelphia Museum with an Egyptian mummy head and a small animal mummy under his arm, which he presented as gifts to the Museum.[13] This mummy's head had been the object of much speculation, curiosity and ridicule the previous year, owing to its having been identified as the head of Pompey the Great! The identification was the result of the analysis of the Rev. Thomas Hall, at Leghorn, to whom the head and a mummified dog had been given in May 1819, by an Armenian who had just come from Alexandria. The head had been purchased from a slave who had stolen it from a stone coffin which he had discovered while helping to dig a canal from the Nile to that city. The mummified dog had come from a pyramid.[14]

The high preservation of the head and the fine linens and stone vase in which it was contained helped propel the Reverend Hall down the convoluted path of conjecture which led to his claim that the head was that belonging to the great Roman general. Hall's chief source of information was the historian Appian, who stated (according to Dryden's translation) that the head should be interred in Alexandria, and not burned, as was the usual fate ascribed to the relic. He read other historians and found many who related the burial story

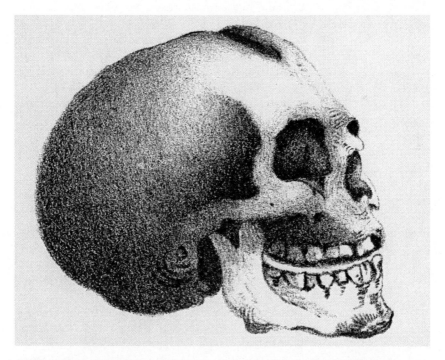

Skull of one of the mummy heads in the collection of the Western Museum of Cincinnati. Possibly the skull given to Dorfeuille by Belzoni (John Delafield, *An Inquiry into the Origin of the Antiquities of America* [New York: J.C. Colt, 1839]. Courtesy American Antiquarian Society).

and so he felt that there was a "high probability" that this was Pompey. The head and dog mummy were then given to William Shaler, the U.S. consul for the powers of Barbary, and sent to America aboard the *Franklin*, under the care of Commodore Stewart. It was then placed on exhibition in the New-York Institution.[15] From there it went to Peale's Museum.

The Rev. Thomas Hall had previously given a baby mummy and a "small hand" to the Philadelphia Medical College—he was considered well respected but easily duped. Numerous articles appeared in newspapers all over the country, most of them ridiculing the idea that this particular mummy was actually Pompey, but a few supporting the idea. The controversy raged for a few months, then died down, with neither side a clear winner.[16]

The Western Museum of Cincinnati was formally dedicated on 10 June 1820. It was begun in 1818 by the efforts of Daniel Drake, William Steele and other Cincinnatians, who assembled a vast collection of shells, fossils, foreign coins, Native American artifacts and "Egyptian oddities."[17] In October 1822, the museum acquired several hundred birds and other objects of natural history, coins, medals and Egyptian and Roman antiquities, as well as the head of an Egyptian mummy, "found in the catacombs of the celebrated Thebes." A number of papyri, votive statues and other *objets d'art* were also added to the collections. More items followed in 1823, including Egyptian and Native American items, but no further mummies are mentioned.[18]

An article in the 11 November 1824 *Cincinnati Emporium* stated that the newly appointed curator of the Western Museum, Joseph Dorfeuille, had "several years since procured from Mr. Belzoni, the celebrated traveler, a number of Egyptian curiosities [including] an embalmed head from the catacombs at Thebes."

Prior to becoming the curator of the Western Museum in 1823, Dorfeuille had been an adventurer of sorts, traveling to distant lands and collecting objects which he then displayed in order to make a livelihood. Dorfeuille promptly incorporated his collection with that of the Museum.[19] In the 13 March 1824 issue of *The Cincinnati Literary Gazette* a "new song" for the Western Museum was printed, to be sung to the tune "Songs of Shepherds in Rustical Roundelays." One of the stanzas related: "Lo here are true mummies of early antiquity, disentombed from the shores of the Red Sea or Nile: but they now look disconsolate, ghastly and rickety, and grin at the visitors more than they smile."

This begs the question of just how many mummy heads did the Western Museum have, one or two? From the poem it would appear there were "mummies" and so it is not unlikely that Dorfeuille acquired a head from the catacombs at Thebes as a gift from Belzoni which he added to the existing head which was donated in 1822. There were untold mummies in the sepulchers at Thebes and so stating that the head was from there is not a distinguishing characteristic. It does not really matter how many the Western Museum had, it had at least one, and for twenty-five cents (children half-price) any Cincinnatian or river traveler or immigrant who went through the city could see everything in the Museum.[20]

There may have been other mummies, or parts of mummies, both animal and human, brought into the United States after this, but no mention of them has yet surfaced. As far as can be ascertained, there were no other human mummy importations into the United States until the spring of 1823 when the *Sally Anne* brought her unusual passenger to Boston.

Bryant P. Tilden and Robert B. Edes addressed the following letter to doctors Warren, Jackson, and Gorham, dated 26 April 1823 and recorded in the *Boston Daily Advertiser* of 3 May 1823:

> Gentlemen: There is now on board the ship Sally Anne, lately arrived from Smyrna, a mummy, sent under the care of Capt. R.B. Edes, to him and myself, to be disposed of as we may think proper, for certain purposes; and as they are of a benevolent nature, and the learned may be gratified in examining the cases, hieroglyphics, &c. &c. we request that it may first be placed under your charge, at the Medical College.
>
> The gentleman who sent it, is Mr. Jacob Van Lennep, to be presented in the name of his commercial house at Smyrna, Messers. Jacob Van Lennep & Co who thus writes upon the subject:
>
> "We have shipped on board the Sally Anne, under the denomination of GUM, a large case, containing a mummy. The British Consul at Alexandria writes me as follows on the subject:
>
> 'I have procured you a mummy, a capital one:—as no good ones, opened, were to be found at Cairo or this place, I commissioned a person going to Thebes to select me one, and I am glad he succeeded in procuring you the best that has been seen for a long time.'
>
> "Capt. Edes takes obligingly under his care this case, under the denomination of Egyptian gum, on account of his men, and we begged to consult you, Mr. Tilden, about presenting it, in some suitable manner, in my firm's name. It will excite some curiosity of the public, and I hope gratify the learned. We have been so much benefited by the Boston trade, we thought of sending you a mummy, thinking it would be acceptable, as I do not recollect having ever seen one in your museums. There are three cases. I think the last one is full of hieroglyphics, and must be opened with caution. We did not open it here, as we were afraid of spoiling it."
>
> If you desire to have the first examination of this mummy, and will be at the trouble of the same, we know of no gentlemen, or place, so suitable as yourselves and the Medical College for the purpose, and it shall be sent to you immediately.
>
> The following plan for appropriating the proceeds which may arise from exhibiting the mummy, is in our opinion a good one—and we trust that the soul, which probably some thousand years past inhabited it, will fully approve of our making use of the same for so benevolent a purpose.
>
> It is to give it to the General Hospital, and let every person who wishes to have an opportunity to see the same, paying the moderate sum of twenty five cents each. The first two hundred dollars that may arise from the receipts, we wish should be paid over to the Boston Dispensary; and all the proceeds afterwards be retained by the hospital, to be given, as the government thereof may see proper, to such poor persons as are destitute or distressed, on leaving this institution, after sickness and confinement.

We believe that the above plan is such a one as Messers. Van Lenneps will cordially approve, and we feel happy in being their friends and agents in this business. Perhaps the suggestion of this small beginning, may be the foundation for a fund, which will relieve many poor in the Hospital, and comfort them with the idea they will not be pennyless on leaving the institution.

Your friends and humble servants,

Bryant P. Tilden, Robt. B. Edes.

The 6 May 1823 issue of the *Salem Gazette* published the following reply from the doctors at the Medical College:

Gentlemen—in compliance with your request, we have received and examined the mummy now in our care at the Medical College, which was sent to you by Mr. Van Lennep, and find it to be in perfect good order. The proposed distribution of the receipts arising from the exhibition, appears to us very judicious, and well calculated to accomplish the liberal intentions of the gentleman who presented it. Yours &c.

James Jackson,

John C. Warren,

John Gorham.

John Collins Warren, in his capacity as a surgeon on the Board of the Massachusetts Hospital, was to have an intimate association with Padihershef almost from the moment of the mummy's arrival in Boston. He wrote:

The trustees of the Hospital, having received the donation, desired me to give a description of it for the general public. The freshness and fine state of preservation of every part, led some persons to suggest it might be one of those fabricated mummies, of which we have heard. These suspicions induced me to examine every thing belonging to it with great care, that I might be able, if it proved genuine, to do justice to the gentlemen who presented it, and to afford the Hospital the fair benefit of its exhibition.[21]

The record of the meeting of Massachusetts General Hospital Board of Trustees for 4 May 1823 shows the following entry:

A letter was received from Bryant P. Tilden, Esq. and Capt. Robt. B Edes enclosing a letter from themselves addressed to Dr. Warren, Jackson and Gorham on the subject of a mummy from Thebes, and presenting the same in the name of Messers. Jacob Van. Lennep & Co. merchants of Smyrna to the Masstts. Gen. Hospital, the first two hundred dollars received from an exhibition thereof to be paid over to the Boston Dispensary and the residue forever to the Hospital.

Voted: to accept the said donation and that Messrs. Lyman and Guild be a committee to present the thanks of the Board to Messers. Tilden and Edes, and through them to Messers. Jacob Van Lennep & Co. of Smyrna.

Voted: that Messers. Parker, Coolidge & Prescott form a committee to take charge of the mummy and make necessary arrangements for and exhibition of the same.[22]

The mummy was promptly placed as "an appropriate ornament of the operating room of the hospital."[23]

According to the Trustees' records of 18 May 1823, "the committee reported that they have committed the thanks of the Board to Messrs. Tilden & Edes & to Jacob Van Lennep & Co. The committee to make arrangements for exhibition of the mummy reported that preparations are in forwardness."[24]

Dr. Warren, acting on behalf of the hospital, contracted with Henry Williams, a Boston engraver, to prepare the mummy ($15.00), make a drawing of the sarcophagus ($30.00) and to make a glass case for holding the mummy ($8.00).[25]

Shortly thereafter, Padihershef was placed on public exhibition at Mr. Doggett's Repository of the Arts, on Market Street in Boston. The Boston newspapers *Columbian Centinel* of 7 May and *Christian Register* of 9 May 1823 ran the following notice: "The mummy—a rare and excellent specimen of mummy has been sent to this city, as a present from the house of Van Lennep & Co. of Smyrna. It is from Thebes; is now at the medical college, and will be in exhibition for the benefit of the Dispensary, and the general hospital."

The Boston publisher, Nathan Hale, was paid $1.87½ for advertising the mummy exhibition, and $1.00 for printing a dozen handbills of the same.[26] The firm of Phelps & Farnham in Boston was paid $1.25 to print one hundred tickets of admission.[27]

At the same time, Warren wrote up a report of the description of his examination of the mummy which he had made for the Massachusetts General Hospital, as well as a general account of embalming, especially for the first volume of *The Boston Journal of Philosophy and the Arts,* published by Cummings, Hillyard and Co. in 1823. It was probably, at that time, the most complete description of a mummy anywhere. Warren wrote "The results of this investigation, together with two

John Collins Warren, surgeon at the Massachusetts General Hospital. Examined Padihershef and wrote the first American treatise on mummies and mummification (portrait collection, American Antiquarian Society. Courtesy American Antiquarian Society).

drawings made from the outer case, I now beg leave to send you for publication in your journal if you find them likely to be in any way useful."[28]

Cummings, Hillyard and Co. accepted his offer, and also published a thirty-four page pamphlet of extracts, with the two plates of engravings, which they marketed as a reprint from the journal.[29] A bill for the artwork, done by the Boston firm of Annin & Smith, shows that the engraving of two views of the coffin of the Egyptian mummy cost $70. The printing of sixteen hundred and twenty-eight impressions cost $16.28, and used eight and one-half gross of paper at a cost of $6.80, making the total $93.08.[30]

As this was an era of scissors and paste-pot editors, other newspapers and journals, such as *Zion's Herald* of 29 May 1823, the *Boston Recorder* of 31 May 1823, and even the Philadelphia *Saturday Evening Post* of 7 June 1823, copied the whole report, or parts of it, for their advertisements and commentaries on the mummy. Included with the reports was an illustration of the outer coffin of the mummy, which was woodcut, This was then later made into an early stereotype plate for the 25 October 1823 issue of the *Minerva* and used in subsequent newspaper advertisements.[31] The records of the Massachusetts General Hospital do not reveal who the artist was for this illustration.

Warren was quite detailed in his observations. He carefully described the coffin thusly:

Engraving of Padihershef's outer coffin, drawn by Henry Williams, and engraved by Annin & Smith (John Collins Warren, *Description of an Egyptian Mummy, Presented to the Massachusetts General Hospital* [Boston: Cummings, Hillyard & Co., 1823]. Courtesy American Antiquarian Society).

The mummy presented by Mr. Van Lennep to the Massachusetts General Hospital was enclosed in a large deal box. On opening this, the outer coffin, or sarcophagus, appeared.... It is a wooden box, seven feet long, and of a breadth proportioned to the length, like the proportions of the human body. The upper part of it is carved, in a very striking and peculiar style, to represent a human head ... covered with a striped cloth or turban, on the upper part of which is painted a globe. The face has the character which has generally been considered as belonging to the Egyptians. The skin is of a reddish colour, the eyes black, nose broad, but not badly proportioned, mouth well formed. The face is broad and short; it has a very agreeable expression, approaching a smile.

He went on for several pages, describing the bands of decorations on the outer and inner coffin, which were shown in the drawings which accompanied the article. Finally, he described the mummy itself:

The mummy is about five feet long, heavy, and solid to the touch. A single cloth of a yellowish colour enveloped the whole body from head to foot, being

Trough of the outer coffin of Padihershef, drawn by Henry Williams, and engraved by Annin & Smith, it depicts the falcon god Re-Harahkte, flanked by the goddess Isis (John Collins Warren, *Description of an Egyptian Mummy, Presented to the Massachusetts General Hospital* [Boston: Cummings, Hillyard & Co., 1823]. Courtesy American Antiquarian Society).

confined closely and neatly to the body by a number of transverse bands of a white colour, under which lay the reliques of corresponding dark coloured bands, so much decayed as to crumble to atoms on being touched. The dark bands were broader than the white, so as to exhibit their edges and produce an ornamental effect; but the colouring substances had caused them to decay,

The lid of the inner coffin of Padihershef (photograph by David A. Rawson).

while the others remained entire. At the feet lay a large heap of beads, composed of green and yellow porcelain, partly connected by threads, whose decay had caused the network to fall in pieces.... As the beads could not be shown in their disconnected state, they have been put together and placed on the mummy, though not in the original form, but as well as circumstances permitted. Some of the beads are still very firm, others crumble on a slight pressure.

In order to examine the state of the body, I cut through the external cloth, where it covered the head, and found a great many turns of bandages about three inches wide, rolled around, to the number of twenty-five thicknesses. The outer cloth and the outer turns of bandage were in fine preservation and considerable strength. They exhibited marks of having been imbued with some glutinous substances, intended to preserve them; and to which is to be attributed the yellow colour. The inner turns were more decayed as they were nearer to the body; those next it were quite rotten, and so closely cemented to the surface as to be separated only by laborious process. The cementing substance is asphaltos, the same in which the body is embalmed. This substance was quite dry, hard, and brittle. Imbedded in it, on the nose, was found a beetle, and near this another small insect, whose character could not be determined.... The skin of the face being exposed, was dry, hard, of a black colour, and in texture readily distinguishable, although deeply imbued with the embalming bitumen. It was wrinkled as if it had been exposed to the actions [of] great heat, or pressure while it was in a soft and yielding state; and the latter cause has produced a distortion of the features, from the right side to the left side. The sockets of the eyes are filled up, the eyelids preserved; but the eyebrows, together with the other hair, is removed or destroyed near to the head, probably by the action of heat; just enough of it remaining however to show that it was not black nor crisped or wooly, but of a heavy brown or reddish brown colour. The teeth are perfect, so far as they can be seen; quite white and shaped like those of the European, contrary to the opinion of some learned men that the Egyptians had the incisor teeth pointed like the canines or dog teeth.... The ears are small, and well filled with embalming substance. The skin of the scalp has the same appearances as that of the face.—Being unwilling to disturb the covering of cloth and bandage, I left every thing on the body in the same state as it issued from the sepulcher of Thebes.... When the bandages were first opened, no great odour issued from the body; but after it had been exposed a few days, a very strong and peculiar smell was perceived, and continued to exhale, until the body was enclosed in a case very tight. The exposure to air did not, however, alter the skin otherwise, than to produce a whitish saline efflorescence on its surface, which consisted of sulphate and carbonate of soda.[32]

According to agreements with Tilden and Edes, reported in the *Columbian Centinal* of 21 May 1823 and the *New England Galaxy* of 30 May 1823, the first two hundred dollars of the proceeds of the exhibition were to be paid to the treasurer of the Boston Dispensary, and the rest of the funds, after expenses, would accrue to the General Hospital. The Hospital would use the money to help poor and distressed people after they had left the Hospital.

The exhibition was a success from its outset. An article on the mummy and an advertisement appeared in the *Boston Patriot & Mercantile Advertiser* under the heading "The Egyptian Mummy" on 21 May 1823.[33] Within two

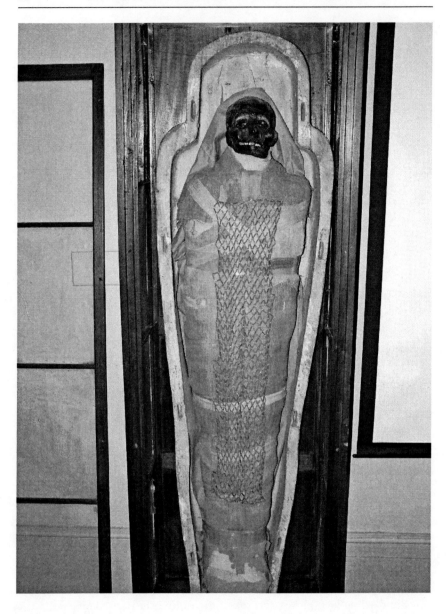

The mummy of Padihershef, showing the faïence bead net which covered the mummy wrappings, and that Warren had found heaped at the bottom of the coffin (photograph by David A. Rawson).

days, it was estimated by the newspapers that five or six hundred people had paid twenty-five cents a head to view this curiosity.

On 26 May 1823, Gideon Snow, chairman of the mummy committee, was able to report that the sum of two hundred dollars had been realized from the exhibition of the mummy and that the money for the Dispensary had been paid over.[34]

Doggett's advertisement in the *Columbian Central* on 28 May 1823 revealed the popularity of the exhibit. "The Egyptian mummy will for the accommodation of the public, be kept open in the future until 9 o'clock in the evening. The room will be illuminated."

On 30 May 1823 the *New England Galaxy* commented: "The Theban mummy. This specimen of the wonderful preservative art of the ancients, and one of the most interesting curiosities ever exhibited here, attracts a crowd of visitors, among whom we gladly see the clergy, literati, legislators, and ladies, with which this city, at the time of election, abounds."

The 13 June 1823 issue of the *Christian Register* reported:

> In the Register of May 9th, we mentioned, that a mummy had been sent to this city, obtained at Thebes; and it was to be exhibited for the benefits of the Boston Dispensary and the Massachusetts General Hospital. The sum of money to be appropriated from the proceeds of the exhibition for the use of the Dispensary has already been paid over to the treasurer of that institution, and the future proceeds are to appropriated exclusively to the very benevolent purposes of increasing the funds of the Mass. Gen. Hospital. The mummy is now exhibiting at Mr. Doggett's Rooms, Market Street. We are informed that it has been visited by upwards of three thousand people.

In his diary for Thursday, 23 September 1823, William Slade, a young man from Sempronius, New York, wrote a description of the mummy and its exhibition at Doggett's, which he saw while he was on a visit to his grandmother in Swansea:

> Walked a little south of the market and saw written over the door "A live ostrich." Inquired if they kept an ostrich there. Said "yes." Asked them the price to see it. The said "9d." Went in and saw it. Said to weigh as much as a middling size man, is 7 feet high. Saw her lay down. Curious looking tent there. Went in and saw the Egyptian mummy, a young lady three thousand years old, lately to arrive from the city of Thebes, the city with its hundred gates. She was found enclosed in two coffins made of sycamore, and on top of each coffin her profile is carved out of wood. The coffins smell very disagreeable indeed. She is said to be a real woman by the doctors who have examined her and no deception. She makes a ghastly and unlovely appearance. Has turned black. Said to be, when alive, red, just the color of the likeness on the coffin.[35]

There was very little public knowledge at this time of the iconography of Egyptian art, the canon of which usually prescribed that men were painted red and women yellow. The red color of the face on the coffin ought to have signified the occupant was male, but the presence of the wig and jewelry con-founded the matter as they were more commonly perceived to be female accou-trements. As it happens, both male and female mummies were equipped with jewelry, or had it represented upon their coffins, and the confusion of female and male proliferated until the decipherment of hieroglyphs made it easier to determine the sex and name of whomever was in the coffin (although this was not always reliable, as will be related in a later chapter).

Padihershef continued to be the chief attraction of Doggett's Repository until the fall of 1823. It is interesting to note that young William got in for nine cents, when the going rate had been twenty-five cents for adults and half that for children. Perhaps Doggett & Co. had decreased the price in order to draw more people. Padihershef's attraction value had dimmed in the wake of such other interesting exhibitions advertised in the *Columbian Centinal* between 23 August and 17 September 1823 such as Peale's *Court of Death*, a painting being shown at Doggett's; the remarkable dwarf, Joseph M. Stevens, who was appear-ing at the New England Museum, a hippopotamus being displayed at the Ton-tine Coffeehouse, the painting *The Dinner Party* by Col. Sargent which was at Mr. Brown's Rooms in the city and the several sightings of a "sea serpent" off of Cape Ann.

Hoping that a change of venue would rekindle interest in the mummy, the trustees of the Massachusetts General Hospital decided to embark on a much more ambitious undertaking. At a special meeting of the Board of Trustees on 16 September 1823, a proposal was made to "hire the mummy for the purposes of exhibition in the southern cities." Mr. Francis and Mr. Guild, in addition to the committee previously formed, were invested with full power to make any arrangements in the name of the Board of Trustees.[36]

On 7 October 1823

> The committee on the subject of the mummy stated that they have made an agreement by which the mummy is leased for one year for exhibition in other cities of the U.S.; also that they have caused to be printed about three hundred copies of a pamphlet containing a description & asked the advice of the Board on the subject of publishing a greater number; the subject was left wholly with the committee.[37]

This printing was probably done by Nathan Hale who had done some earlier handbills for the exhibition. A page of an account with Hale shows the sum of $26.75 spent by the Hospital on 4 October 1823, in connection with printing items for the mummy exhibitions.[38]

Doggett & Co. would be the agents and exhibitors. The mummy would travel by water, as the hospital did not want to trust their delicate money-maker to the vicissitudes of inland travel.[39]

It must be noted here that Padihershef was always referred to as "the mummy." Although the discovery of the Rosetta Stone had started Champol-lion and others down the path of hieroglyph decipherment, it was still next to impossible to translate the symbols. It would not be until 1960, when Dows Dunham, emeritus curator of Egyptian art at the Museum of Fine Arts, translated the hieroglyphs on the mummy and inner coffin in the Ether Dome at Massachusetts General Hospital that Padihershef's name would be known.[40] In retrospect, this is probably a good thing, for it might have been somewhat politically incorrect to refer to the mummy as "Paddy," especially in Boston.

A page from the accounting book of the Massachusetts General Hospital shows the account with Doggett & Co. (through the end of October 1823) as follows: $200 was paid to N. Russell (the treasurer of the Hospital) on 26 May; $400.00 on 6 June; $300 on 3 July and $157.87 on 27 October. They had taken in (as of 1 October 1823) $1,261.96. Their expenses had been $.50 for pasteboard, $.29 for a "book & bills," $6.45 for lamps and tins, $.35 for wickyarn, $.50 for posting handbills, and $2.00 for oil. Doggett's had charged the Hospital $180.00 for four and one half month's rent of their exhibition hall, $5.25 for an extra attendant in the evenings, and $8.75 for W.W. Clapp's advertising bills.[41]

By the middle of October 1823, the mummy and his wooden cases were installed in the passageway leading to the Academy of Arts, in New York City.[42] The price of admission stayed at twenty-five cents. William Grattan printed up a handsome leaflet which was distributed to the visitors. It was a single folded sheet (making four pages all together). The first page bore a marvelous picture of the outer coffin of the mummy (similar to, but not exactly the same as the picture commissioned by the Hospital), with the details of the exhibition flanking it on either side. The second and third pages contained a description of the exhibition, noting exactly what was to be seen there:

> No. 1, is the mummy, enveloped in its numerous bands of linen.... The head was in a similar manner enveloped with linen, having on its nose the sacred beetle. [Warren had unwrapped the head while doing his initial examination for the mummy] A net-work of porcelain beads covers the front. The mummy remains in one half of its sarcophagus, or coffin.... No. 2. The top half of the sarcophagus or coffin, curiously ornamented with figures ... the upper part carved in imitation of a head, with the headdress peculiar to the Egyptians. No. 3 is one-half of the outer sarcophagus.... No. 4 is the upper half or covering of the outer sarcophagus, with a carved head resembling the inner ... not so fresh nor so well-preserved as those on no. 2....

At the head of the description was an advertisement for a brochure, which promised

> A more particular description of the mummy and sarcophagi, with the probable meaning of many of the figures and emblems, by the Rev. Dr. Cumming, of New-York, abridged in part from an elaborate pamphlet by Dr. J.C. Warren, professor of anatomy and surgery in the Harvard University, to which is added an interesting account of ancient Thebes, may be obtained, at a low price, in the exhibition room.[43]

This was also published by William Grattan, and ran to eighteen pages.[44] A brief extract from this pamphlet followed the description of the mummy and

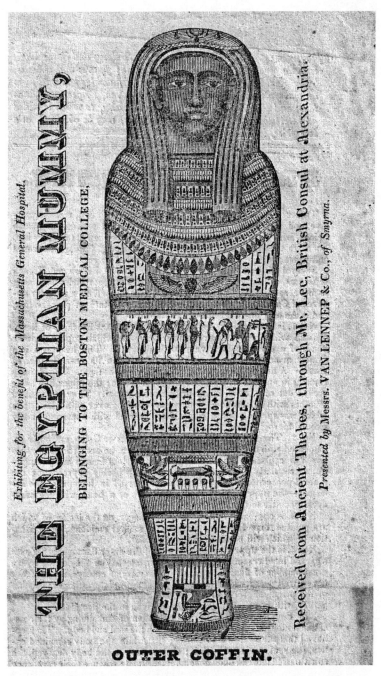

THE EGYPTIAN MUMMY,

Exhibiting for the benefit of the Massachusetts General Hospital,

BELONGING TO THE BOSTON MEDICAL COLLEGE.

Received from Ancient Thebes, through Mr. Lee, British Consul at Alexandria.

Presented by Messrs. VAN LENNEP & Co., of Smyrna.

OUTER COFFIN.

Cover of the four-page brochure which was printed up to accompany the exhibition of Padihershef (*Exhibiting for the Benefit of the Massachusetts General Hospital, the Egyptian Mummy, Belonging to the Boston Medical College* [Boston: Printed by William Grattan, (1823)]).

sarcophagi. At the end of the description was reprinted "Address to the Mummy at Belzoni's Exhibition. By Campbell."[45] Thomas Campbell was not the author of this piece—Horace Smith was. The misattribution of the poem was another error which was perpetuated numerous times throughout the early nineteenth century. The original had been published anonymously in 1821 in *The New Monthly Magazine,* a London literary periodical edited by Campbell. Considering the fact that at the time editors provided a great deal of the content of their magazines, it was natural for American publishers, in copying the poem for their audiences, to attribute the verses to the editor of the original magazine. The poem was to be continuously linked with exhibitions of mummies throughout the nineteenth century, and inspired a number of imitations and even a few parodies. Eventually the correct author was given the credit for the lines, although in a couple of newspapers, the poem is attributed to "Roscoe," which may or may not be a bad anagram of "Horace."

The *Miscellaneous Cabinet,* published in Schenectady, New York, devoted portions of several issues (8 November 1823 to 3 January 1824) to a reprinting of Dr. Warren's article from the *Boston Journal of Philosophy and the Arts.* At the beginning of the article appeared this disclaimer.

> There needs no apology, we trust, for the occupation of a part of our paper by an article so interesting as this: and we hesitate the less because we perceive that the explanation of the figures on the outer case of the mummy which called forth this article, is going the rounds of the newspapers. A cut representing the appearance of the front or top of the outer case accompanies the explanation in the New-York newspapers.

The *Minerva; or Literary, Entertaining, and Scientific Journal* for 25 October 1823 published a shortened version of Warren's article, apologizing that "but our limits will not permit of our making further extractions." The magazine touted the exhibition in terms calculated to appeal to the intelligentsia of the day:

> The rarity and attractions of the object exhibited, will, we have no doubt, induce the curious, and men of science to satisfy themselves by a personal examination. They will then have a more perfect idea of the subject than they can derive from any written description. We are satisfied that the time spent in viewing this unique exhibition, will be doubly compensated by the rational gratification it is calculated to afford.

By the time the article appeared, the mummy had been moved to a new location at the Lyceum of Natural History. The New York *Christian Journal and Literary Register* for November of 1823 published a short article along with this note:

> Through the politeness of the proprietor the publishers of the *Christian Journal* are enabled to insert in this number, the annexed plate, representing the mummy now exhibiting in this city. The description is copied from the papers of the day. We present our readers with a representation [of the outer mummy

case] stereotyped for the *Minerva* ... and now exhibiting at the Lyceum of Natural History in this city.... Having had the curiosity to examine this rare specimen of Egyptian art and mythology, we were agreeably surprised to find that it presented none of those disgusting features, which accompany specimens of preserved human bodies that are to be seen in some of our museums. The present mummy is the only entire one ever exhibited in the United States. And it may be viewed by the most delicate female without exciting the smallest disagreeable feeling.

The proprietors had concerns about their ability to provide a decent description, but were spared the labor by the appearance of Dr. Warren's article in the *Boston Journal of Philosophy and the Arts*. They went on to mention, that, in addition to the aforesaid article, Dr. Warren was preparing a separate work on the "curious art" of embalming.

The spectacle of the mummy inspired at least one poet to pen his thoughts. The following was published in *The National Advocate* for 11 November 1823:

On seeing the winged globe on the breast of the sarcophagus of the Egyptian mummy, supposed to be an emblem of the immortality of the soul:

As flies the earth in her broad circle driv'n;
So wings the soul its airy way to heav'n.
Just as spheres in endless order rise,
In grand procession through empyreal skies;
So sainted spirits soar on wings of fire,
To their august, unchang'd, eternal sire.

The poem comes across as more Christian than ancient Egyptian, probably owing to the general lack of knowledge about the religion of the ancients and the role that the mummy played in their belief in an afterlife.

Doggett & Co. sent a note to the Trustees of the Massachusetts General Hospital on 6 December 1823. "Gentlemen, permit us to ask if you would have any objections to acknowledge the receipts in the public prints of the amount received at New York for the exhibition of the Egyptian mummy in that city. And if you wish it our first-note of seven hundred & fifty dollars we will pay, deducting the interest. Very respectfully ... John Doggett & Co."[46]

Padihershef next traveled a great ways down the east coast to Richmond, Virginia. The 25 December 1823 issue of the *Boston Daily Advertiser* reported: "The Egyptian mummy presented to the Massachusetts Hospital, is now exhibiting for the benefit of the hospital in Richmond." One of the visitors to the mummy there could well have been Edgar Allan Poe [who would make use of a similar curiosity in his short story "Some Words With a Mummy"].[47]

The next port of call was Charleston, South Carolina. In the *City Gazette and Commercial Daily Advertiser* for 24 January 1824, there appears the by now ubiquitous engraving of the outer coffin, under the heading "Egyptian mummy. Exhibiting at no. 26, Broad Street." Accompanying the illustration are excerpts from Dr. Warren's article, and the "Address to the Mummy at Belzoni's exhibition." The editor states that "we noticed a few days since, the exhibition in this city of the Egyptian mummy." After leaving Charleston, Doggett & Co. moved the mummy show to Augusta, Georgia. The arrival was noted in the 6 March 1824 issue of the *Augusta Chronicle*: "Egyptian mummy. This relict of ages long past which has excited so much interest in the northern cities, arrived last evening, in the steam-boat."

The *Augusta Chronicle* of 10 March 1824 ran a long article quoting liberally from Warren's description below the illustration of the outer coffin, noting that the exhibition was at the City Hall. The *Augusta Chronicle* of 17 March 1824 announced that the mummy would be in the court room at City Hall for only two more days, before it was to be removed to Savannah. The price for the exhibition was the highest ever charged, fifty cents (with children, of course, half price). Another article in the same paper commented that "As in its relation to antiquity this subject is one of an interesting nature, we are pleased at learning that it has been numerously attended in Augusta. It may not be amiss to remark, that this day and to-morrow will furnish the only opportunities which may ever perhaps be afforded of viewing so uncommon a curiosity here."

Under the heading "Four days." the Savannah *Georgian* of 25 March 1824 announced that the Council Chamber in the Exchange had been "liberally appropriated" for the purpose of the exhibition, and that the room would be illuminated at night so that the exhibition could be open both in the day and evening. The admission price for adults was fifty cents, but a "season ticket" could be purchased for one dollar.

The *Georgian* announced "Last day!" on 27 March 1824, and also printed the following letter which describes an unknown visitor's reaction to the exhibition:

> The mummy. Extract of a letter, from a gentleman in Charleston, to his friend in Georgia. Dear Colonel—I have just come from visiting the greatest curiosity I ever beheld; it is a young lady only three thousand years old—a somber complexioned lass from Egypt, the land of the pharaohs, the Ptolemies, the pyramids! She is arrayed in a corse [*sic*] cloth, framed on the banks of the Nile, and stands in "a narrow house" decorated with all the taste and science of the most learned people in existence long before the invention of letters. Dark and unlovely are her looks, though she does not actually grin horribly a ghastly smile, her fair, well-set teeth appearing full and undecayed as the everlasting brightness of the star under which she was embalmed. Singular rated girl! Little did she think, when on her dying couch, that she would be exposed to this "undiscovered country" some thirty centuries after her last mortal existence, to the keen gaze of male curiosity, without a sense of shrinking modesty, and serving as a spectacle of curious wonder.

The unknown author of these lines goes on to rhapsodize about Shakespeare, Cleopatra and the future of Charleston and of the world. He must be forgiven his mistake in referring to the mummy as a female—Dr. Warren had unwrapped only the head. This letter was often reprinted as the mummy traveled to different venues.

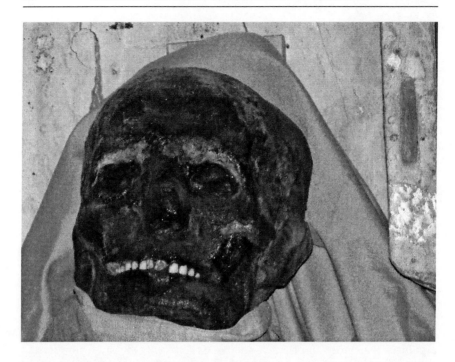

The face of the mummy Padihershef. In life he had been a stonecutter in Thebes (photograph by David A. Rawson).

Padihershef's continuing peregrinations next brought him to Philadelphia. An advertisement in *Poulson's American Daily Advertiser* for 19 April 1824 respectfully informs the public

> The Egyptian Mummy, together with its double sarcophagus or coffin curiously ornamented, received from ancient Thebes, by the Boston Medical College, and exhibiting for the Massachusetts General Hospital in New Hampshire [*sic*], for a few days, at Earle and Sully's Gallery, in Chesnut-Street, opposite the State House. Admittance 25 cents, season tickets 50 cents, children, as usual, half-price.

The Saturday Evening Post of 24 April 1824 carried the illustration of the outer coffin and an advertisement for "the Egyptian mummy now exhibiting at Earle & Sully's, in Chesnut [*sic*] Street, opposite the State House." The article states that the mummy had arrived in Philadelphia the previous week. Again, the press relied upon Dr. Warren's description in order to whet the appetites of the curious. The paper also reprinted the "Dear Colonel" letter which had originally appeared the previous month in the Savannah newspaper. The mummy inspired other contemplative pieces. John Fanning Watson, who was to write in 1830 a history of the city of Philadelphia, penned the following notes about the mummy in his manuscript notes for the history:

This being the first instance of bringing a mummy to this country (A strange visitor from ancient Thebes to visit this rising city and empire) I thus record the facts. Such acceptance shown to this relic justifies the gleanings of which I have made in this way. It proves that their worth to us is caused by the moral associations which they afford. Therefore we feelingly accord with the Post when he asks such questions as-so congenial with our thoughts.

There couldn't develop, if that withered tongue might tell us, what those sightless orbs have seen, how the world look'd when it was fresh and young and the great deluge still had left its green.

Statue of flesh, come prithee tell us! Since in the world of spirits thou hast illuminated what thou hast seen, what strange adventures number'd.[48]

Visitors of all sorts attended the exhibition, as reported in the *Aurora General Advertiser* of 26 April 1824:

On Saturday afternoon, we were present at the exhibition, during which time, a teacher from the Philadelphia Asylum for the Deaf and Dumb entered with almost thirty of his female pupils. They arranged themselves in front of the cases containing the work of antiquity, while their preceptor entered at large into an explanation of the figure, the country from which it came; the process of embalming, &c. all of which, by the astonishment depicted in the countenances of the pupils, they appeared fully to comprehend. The sight was truly an interesting one. We mention this circumstance, thinking it would be advisable for teachers generally to take their classes to the exhibition, as

Stereotype of the outer coffin of Padihershef which appeared in numerous newspaper advertisements and broadsides for the mummy exhibition (*Saturday Evening Post* [Philadelphia], 24 April 1824. Courtesy American Antiquarian Society).

much useful information may by this means, in a few moments, be indelibly impressed upon the youthful mind! At New-York, and other cities, where this curiosity has been exhibited, those who had children under their care, availed themselves of the opportunity of conveying instruction in this forcible manner.

This admonition had some far-reaching effects, for in 1837, the American Sunday School Union, based in Philadelphia, used the illustration of Padihershef's coffin as an illustration for its article on "Mummies" in *The Evergreen*, a book of information and instruction for youth.[49]

The 5 May 1824 issue of *The Gazetteer*, a Philadelphia magazine, rejoiced:

> We have now an opportunity of seeing what we have often heard of—an Egyptian mummy. It has excited a lively interest in this city, and has, in consequence, been numerously visited. The exhibition, we understand, will continue open but one week longer, during which time it is the intention of the proprietor to open in the evening, to accommodate those who have most leisure at that time. As a mere specimen of art, it is an object of rational curiosity, and it would be a reproach to us to suppose that it would not be generally examined. But it is the reflections which it excites, that constitutes its most powerful interest.

Baltimore would be the next venue for Doggett's show. The *Baltimore Patriot* of 28 May 1824 announced the exhibition under the heading "Egyptian mummy."

> It gives us pleasure to inform our readers that Mr. Peale has made arrangements for the exhibition of the Egyptian mummy, which was presented to the Boston Medical College ... we consider it one of the most interesting exhibitions that ever presented itself to the people of Baltimore. It is a lady—probably a princess, for none but persons of distinction were embalmed—and probably some young belle of the family of Pharaoh, who has coquetted with Joseph, or suffered from the plagues of Egypt. Whoever she is, her name and lineage, it is said, cannot be ascertained from her credentials, she is generally allowed to be a young lady of some three thousand years old, and very fond of receiving visits—which we doubt not she will be gratified with to her heart's content.

The *American and Commercial Daily Advertiser* for 15 June 1824, ran this notice, which was followed the next day by a repeat of the notice and the stereotype of the coffin.

> For a short season. The public is respectfully informed that the Egyptian mummy together with its singularly ornamented double sarcophagus, or coffin ... has now arrived, and is exhibiting at the Baltimore Museum, Holliday Street, near the Theatre. The museum is open during the day, and in the course of the evenings the philosophical recreations as usual. Admittance 25 cents, children half price. Season tickets during the exhibition of the mummy $1.

On 18 June 1824 the *Baltimore Patriot* informed its readers that "The Egyptian mummy continues to attract 'crowded houses' at the museum, and, it gives us pleasure to observe, bids fair to remunerate the enterprising proprietor for his exertions to please the taste, and satisfy the curiosity of an intelligent public.... Who would not 'talk a word with this same learned Theban,' on such terms?"

An unknown poet, who signed with only the letter S, penned the following lines for the 23 June 1824 *Baltimore Patriot,* which were inspired by the band of decoration on the coffin which depicted a band of gods and goddesses, inferred to be a court of judgment:

> · To the Mummy.
> I gaze upon thy withered form,
> Thou spectre of the past;
> Where feelings pure and passions warm,
> Did linger to the last.
> The sentence of the awful court,
> Pronounced thy body's doom,
> To hold the mortal shape, and sport
> With time and with the tomb.
> The heavings of life's fitful sea,
> Hath cast thee on the shore—
> A specimen of things that we
> Look'd on as fiction's lore.
> Speak! What art thou? pride's victim, aye?
> That would preserve thy mould
> When all things else meet with decay,
> Wrap'd in oblivion's fold.

On 30 June 1824 the *Baltimore Patriot* ran the following article, which affords a description of the exhibition itself:

> This exhibition has been rendered much more interesting through the politeness of Isaac McKim and John Hoffman, Esqs. in furnishing the Travils [sic] of Belzoni, with colored plates, which may be viewed only in the day time.
> An embalmed cat from Thebes in Egypt; this is one of the deities worshipped by the ancient Egyptians, and frequently found with the mummies in the catacombs—deposited by Professor G.S. Pattison.
> The head of a New Zealand chief: this head is handsomely tattooed ... deposited by Professor G.S. Pattison.
> The museum is brilliantly illuminated every evening.

Rubens Peale, the proprietor of the Museum, had paid John Pendleton, the agent for Doggett & Co., the sum of $650 for the exclusive rights to exhibit the mummy in Baltimore.[50] This was a good deal for Peale, as the mummy's six week stay, from 14 June to 24 July 1824, brought in an almost unbelievable $1,842.00![51] The total cost to Peale was $650 for use of the mummy, $55 for other expenses, $390 for what the museum would have received in any case, leaving him with a tidy profit of $746.00 for a month and a half's work.[52]

Word about the mummy exhibition spread, and engendered not a few misconceptions and confusions over what exactly a mummy was, and what it signified.

The *Saturday Evening Post* of 10 July 1824 cribbed this not entirely tongue-in-cheek editorial from the *Winchester Republican*:

> A wonderful stir has prevailed in town all this week, by flying reports of a mummy in Baltimore. As we happen to be in favour with the women, we were among the first to hear of it, although the buzz was such that neither head nor tail could be made of the matter. All that could be learned for three days was, that the mummy was found in a rock in Baltimore with a black face, eyes wide open, and sixteen fold of twine linen around it. Something mysterious was added about a coffin. One reckoned it was Pharaoh's daughter—another that it was Moses—another that it had dropped out of the air. One said she must send for the pamphlet about it, and gravely hinted that there was a chance for a speculation for the charitable societies, as it would certainly sell well. Things remained in this state for three days, during which time there were numberless inquiries at our office about the mummy—to all which we replied neither yea nor nay—when an old woman solemnly declared she had seen it at David Russel's, and that it was taken to market on Wednesday, and that it was black. The devil! thought I: the mummy at David Russel's! I could stand it no longer, but set out in search; and discovered at last that a gentleman had brought up with him, from Baltimore, a hand-bill, giving a description of the Egyptian mummy now exhibiting in that place—on the front of which bill was a comical figure of said mummy; and this at once accounted for the extraordinary fidgets which seemed to have taken possession of so many of the lineal descendants of our good mother Eve.

Early in August, the mummy was exhibiting in the Senate Chamber of the Capitol Building in Albany, New York. The 13 August 1824 issue of the *Albany Argus* noted the mummy had arrived the previous Tuesday, the 10th. It would not remain long in the city, for it was destined to be heading back down the coast to Rhode Island.

The *Rhode Island American* noted on 31 August 1824: "Among the curiosities of commencement, we notice the exhibition of an Egyptian mummy, at the Court-House.... A similar curiosity is also exhibiting at the Museum, opened by Mr. Greenwood, in this town."

The 1 September 1824 issue of the *Providence Patriot* ran the stereotype of the outer coffin, noting that the mummy would be exhibited in the Assembly Chamber of the Providence Court House for an unstated length of time. The *Providence Gazette* of 1 September noted that the Chamber would be open during the day and illuminated at night. The same paper announced the end of the exhibition on 4 September 1824. On 11 September 1824 the *Newport Mercury* announced that the mummy exhibition at the State House in Providence would be closed at 2 P.M. that day and the mummy removed from town. This was more than likely the final venue for Padihershef's travels as no further newspaper articles have come to light concerning his exhibition at any other localities.

Doggett & Co. were fast losing money in this venture. They reported to the

Trustees of the Massachusetts General Hospital that

> The receipts were very much reduced by circumstances.... Considerable added value was attached to the circumstance of this being the only one in America. The arrival of another shortly thereafter and subsequently of several others, has had the effect of rendering the exhibition less attractive and consequently reducing the income in some places by anticipating the arrival of this mummy. The receipts have with much exertion but little more than balanced expenses.[53]

On 6 September 1824, the Board of Trustees looked over the books of their mummy venture and discovered that "The profits of the exhibition of the mummy are stated to be fifteen hundred dollars. The donation-book, probably deducting certain charges and the payment to the Dispensary make the sum little less than twelve hundred dollars."[54]

The minutes of the Trustees meeting of 26 September 1824 reported

> A communication was rec'd from John Doggett & Co. stating

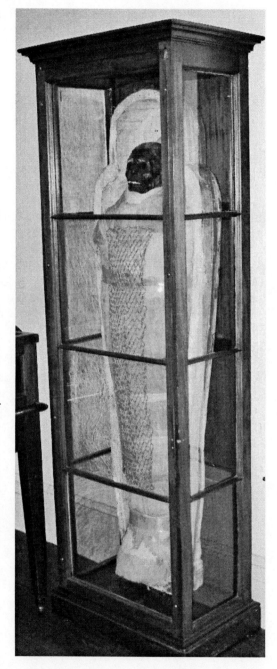

Padihershef in one of the original glass and mahogany cases, standing in the Ether Dome of the Massachusetts General Hospital (photograph by David A. Rawson).

that most of the profits received by them for the exhibition of the Egyptian mummy, after paying to the M.G.H. their notes for fifteen hundred dollars, to be only four hundred & thirty five 95/100 dollars, which they hope will be considered by the trustees as an insufficient compensation for their risk & trouble. An answer of the chairman of the Board ... thereto was also read & approved, & adopted.[55]

There is no extant record of what the chairman's answer was, or any indication Doggett & Co. received any further money from the trustees. Padihershef was returned to the Massachusetts General Hospital, and was reinstalled in the operating theater. There he stood, silently watching over the surgeries, including the famous one on 16 October 1846, the first public demonstration of surgical anesthesia, which gave the room and the mummy the sobriquet "Ether Dome."[56] An accurate, half-size replica of the outer coffin was made by the Franklin Society of Providence, Rhode Island. This eventually wound up in Attleboro, Massachusetts.[57]

In 1870 Padihershef was sent "opened" to the Museum of Fine Arts in Boston. (No notation exists as to when he was returned.) He was sent there again with his inner coffin on 1 July 1885 (the lower part of the outer coffin followed on 14 February 1889, the lid was sent on 26 March 1889). The inner coffin and the mummy were returned to Massachusetts General Hospital and reinstalled in the Ether Dome on 12 October 1896. On 18 November 1931 the outer coffin was returned; this was then offered to the Fogg Museum, which rejected the offer on 19 December 1931. On 17 March 1932, Dr. Coolidge offered to loan the outer case to Mrs. Cordelia S. Pond, curator of the Art Museum in Springfield, where it remains to this day.[58]

Padihershef was reunited with his outer coffin during co-operative exhibitions between the George Walter Vincent Smith Art Museum in Springfield and the Massachusetts General Hospital from December 1984 through January 1985, and again in 2002–2003. The failure of Padihershef to raise a great deal of money for the Massachusetts General Hospital did not discourage the Trustees from honoring Bryant P. Tilden and Captain Edes. At the annual meeting of 1 May 1825 they were elected members of the corporation, as was Jacob van Lennep.[59]

2

"As Cheap as Candidates for the Presidency"

Egyptian Mummies in
Early Nineteenth-Century America

Until the beginning of 1824, Padihershef had been a unique item—the first complete mummy ever to be exhibited to the public in America. This was about to change. The *Boston Commercial Gazette* of 8 January 1824 announced: "An Egyptian mummy was brought in the brig *C. Augusta* [i.e., *Caroline Augusta*], which arrived at this port on Monday, from Trieste."

Larkin Turner, of Charlestown, Massachusetts, was the captain of this brig, and he lost little time in securing testimonials that the mummy was real. The 2 March 1824 issue of the *Salem Gazette* printed the findings of John C. Warren (dated 8 February 1824), and Abraham R. Thompson, M.D., and J. Stearns Hurd, M.D. (both dated 9 February 1824) that the mummy, from all appearances and tests to which they had subjected it, was genuine. Turner was born in Grafton, Massachusetts, in 1781, and had originally been apprenticed to a shoemaker, but at age sixteen, he went to sea and by twenty-two, was a full-fledged captain. He made a success of that career, retired in 1832, and eventually served in the Massachusetts Legislature for two terms, in 1836 and 1837. He declined to run for a third term.[1]

The 11 February 1824 issue of the *Columbian Centinel American Federalist* informed its readers: "The Egyptian mummy from ancient Thebes brought by Capt. Turner, from Trieste; lately mentioned as having arrived in this city; will we understand shortly be exhibited at Doggett's Repository." So while Doggett & Co. were traipsing about the east coast with Padihershef, back in Boston they were exhibiting a second mummy.

The *Independent Chronicle and Boston Patriot* dated 21 February 1824 advertised the mummy with its double sarcophagus would be on exhibit for a few weeks, "open day and evening." The advertisement had been running since the 12th. An article in the *New England Galaxy* of 27 February 1824 displayed an illustration of a mummy case with the accompanying text:

> Another mummy. Capt. Turner, lately arrived at this port, has brought
> another mummy from ancient Thebes, which is now on exhibition at
> Doggett's Repository, Market-Street. We have no doubt, that, in obliging the

proprietor by inserting the representation of one of the sarcophagi, in which it was enclosed, with the accompanying remarks and certificates, we shall also gratify a numerous class of readers, whose residence in the country may deprive them of a view of this relic of antiquity.

Below the illustration are the "certificates of authenticity" attested to by three doctors; J. Stearns Hurd and Abraham R. Thompson of Charlestown, Massachusetts, and John Collins Warren, of Boston.

Evidently Doggett & Co. didn't see any problems with their exhibiting a second mummy for they remained the exhibitors for Padihershef as well as for this one. The arrival and exhibition of this second mummy caused an undisclosed author in Boston (as reported by the *Providence Patriot* of 24 January 1824 and the *New York Mirror* of 7 February 1824) to comment:

> A Boston paper mentions that three persons were tried at the court sitting in that city for disinterring dead bodies. One was fined, and confined to the state-prison. This same paper, we believe, mentions the arrival of another Egyptian mummy, and we suppose the very same jury and judges who convicted and condemned the stealers of dead bodies in Massachusetts, will go and see the mummy, and thus reward stealers of dead bodies at Thebes.

Obviously there were some people who had qualms about digging up the ancient dead for display, but we don't know exactly from what conscience, religious or otherwise, those reservations arose.

The *Salem Gazette* for 23 March 1824 noted that the mummy was in town and referred readers to an article previously published on the 2nd of March concerning the exhibition in Boston, for a view of the coffin. The issue for 26 March 1824 noted:

> Now exhibiting at the Franklin Building, is an object so curious that it can hardly fail to attract general attention. It would be a reproach to the intelligence and science of our town, to suppose that a curiosity so rare, on this side of the Atlantic, and connected with so many subjects of passing reflection, can be passed by. Parents who have children growing up around them, and for whom they are anxiously securing every advantage for improvement, should take them to see an object so well calculated to excite the attention of the youthful mind, and to rouse in it a curiosity for knowing more about antiquity. There would not be a more appropriate introduction to the perusal of Rollin [i.e., Charles Rollin. *Ancient History of the Egyptians; Carthaginians, Assyrians, Babylonians, Medes & Persians, Macedonians, and Grecians*].

The exhibition prompted philosophical contemplation, as recorded in the 29 March 1824 issue of the *Essex Register*:

> In a variety of points of view, this spectacle is worthy the inspection of the curious ... here are the relics of a being that "lived and moved and had its being" on the banks of the Nile, perhaps more than three thousand years ago—who knows but in the days of Joseph and Moses? This withered shred had such sensations, and emotions like our own—it could love as we do—it could give loose the tiniest feelings of friendships. All the purest charities of

life might have dwelt in that bosom—
and its "departed spirit may have
influenced, by counsel or by intrigue,
the most important movements connected with the destinies of a mighty
nation." ... "It would be to consider
too curiously" to develop all the trains
of thought, which this bringing
together of the beings of distant ages
and modern times, the old and new
world, might call up.

An unknown admirer, who signed
only with the initial M penned the following for the 1 April 1824 *Salem Gazette.*

> The Egyptian mummy which had been
> disinterred in ancient Thebes,
> descended the Nile, and crossed the
> Atlantic, has at length been transported
> from Boston to this town. It has
> already attracted hundreds of specta-
> tors among us; and the interest of the
> spectacle is as great as ever. We have
> now an opportunity of seeing what all
> have so much heard of. It is the second
> mummy which has ever reached Amer-
> ica; and itself and its cerements are in a
> fine state of preservation.

The 6 April 1824 issue featured a cut
of the coffin and noted that the exhibition
would "positively close tomorrow evening."

From Salem the mummy show would
journey only a short distance to Newburyport, where the 6 April 1824 *Newburyport
Herald* reported: "We learn with pleasure
that the Egyptian mummy ... which has
excited so much attention in Boston, is to
be exhibited in this town for a few days,
and will probably be open for public
inspection on Saturday next [i.e., the
10th]."

**The inner coffin of the mummy imported in 1825 by Captain Larkin Turner, of
Charlestown, Mass. (*New-England Galaxy* [Boston, Mass.], 27 February 1824. Courtesy American Antiquarian Society).**

It was on display for about a week, according to the 17 April 1824 *Portsmouth Journal of Literature and Politics* which noted that the exhibition was due in Portsmouth. New Hampshire, in about a week's time. That this occurred was borne out by the 24 April 1824 issue of the *Portsmouth Journal of Literature and Politics*, and the 27 April 1824 issue of the *New Hampshire Gazette* which reported on the mummy. According to the advertisements in those newspapers, the exhibition was at the Portsmouth Franklin Hall, and admission was the usual 25 cents—children half price. A season ticket could be bought for 50 cents.

On 19 May 1824 the *Hampshire Gazette* ran the woodcut of the mummy and noted: "We have seen no particular description of the mummy itself. We are informed that the proprietors of this interesting relic of ancient times, intend to exhibit it in Northampton [Massachusetts], in the course of the coming summer or autumn. It will probably excite more admiration than any of the modern belles."

The residents of that Western Massachusetts town were doomed to disappointment, for there is no record that it, or any other mummy, ever was exhibited there. The mummy was returned to Doggett's Repository in Boston "For a few days only" as advertised in the 29 May 1824 *Independent Chronicle and Boston Patriot*. The article had been running since the 24th.

In June of 1824, Ethan Allen Greenwood, proprietor of the New England Museum in Boston, purchased the mummy, and noted in his diary: "18th. Got ready to go to Portland.... Bought the mummy & put her on board.... 19th.... Last Friday I bought the Egyptian mummy together with the cases &c for $350.00. 23d. Got out bills for the mummy exhibit."[2] E.G. House, printer at Merchants Hall, Boston, made up a handsome broadside to accompany the mummy. In elaborate letters the sheet proclaimed "Egyptian mummy, from the catacombs of Thebes." It contained the same illustration of the mummy case which had adorned the advertisement in the newspaper, included a brief description of the mummy and its case, and Dr. Warren's certificate of authenticity. The mummy was described as "The mortal remains of a lady of very high rank, as none but the rich were embalmed in this style."

Large letters near the bottom proclaimed "It will be open for exhibition at _____" leaving a space for the local exhibitor to fill in his name and address. Admission was twenty-five cents, the same as Padihershef. Children (as always) were admitted half-price.[3]

How anyone could tell the sex of the mummy is a good question, for only its face and right hand were uncovered, and no one had attempted to decipher the inscriptions on the sarcophagus. Neither could it be known if the mummy were of high rank or low. It was not uncommon for exhibitors of exotic treasures to inflate any or all of the attributes of the objects in their shows. Proclaiming an object to be "royal" or of other high rank could only enhance its

The façade of Ethan Allen Greenwood's New England Museum. Turner's mummy as well as the mummies from the *Peregrine* were exhibited in a special room upstairs in this building (Abel Bowen, *Bowen's Picture of Boston, Or, The Citizen's and Stranger's Guide to the Metropolis of Massachusetts* [Boston: Lilly, Wait & Co. and Lorenzo H. Brown, 1833]. Courtesy American Antiquarian Society).

attractiveness to the general public who did not often get the chance to view such an exalted personage, whether alive or dead.

A little eight-page booklet was also produced to accompany Capt. Turner's Theban mummy on its exhibition tour. The cover depicts the outer mummy case framed in the words "Egyptian mummy to be exhibited at," followed by a blank space for inserting the locale. It contains a description of the mummy, Dr. Warren's certification, extracts from the *Commentary on the Holy Bible* by Adam Chase (librarian to the King of England), a description of Egyptian funeral ceremonies and embalming, and of course, the "Address to the Mummy at Belzoni's Exhibition."[4] There is nothing in the pamphlet which tells where it was printed, or who printed it, or when it was printed. The cut is the same as on House's broadside, and although the text of the description is different, it is not inconceivable that this too, came from his press.

Under the headline "An Old Lady" the 22 June 1824 issue of daily *Eastern Argus* announced:

> A lady arrived in this town yesterday for the purpose of a short visit to this metropolis, who, though not very remarkable for her beauty, is certainly venerable for her age. She is supposed to be nearly three thousand years old, and was an inhabitant of the city of Thebes. In short she is no other than the famous mummy, which has resided in Boston for some months past. She is now at the Portland Museum where she will remain a short time for exhibition. Those who have the curiosity to see a human body which has been pre-

served for thousands of years, can now be gratified by calling at the museum. The sarcophagus, in which the subject was originally enclosed, accompanies it, and is really a curiosity. We just stepped in and made our bow to her ladyship yesterday before our paper went to press, and regret that we had not time to describe the peculiarities of her costume.

In the 29 June 1824 issue of the weekly *Eastern Argus* the proprietor of the Portland Museum informed the public that he had "at considerable expense" arranged for the exhibition of the mummy, sarcophagi and "envelopes." The public was solicited to call early so as not to miss the spectacle.

Greenwood exhibited the mummy in Portland, Maine, until at least early July, as the Portland Museum announced in the 5 July 1824 issue of the weekly *Eastern Argus* that for the celebration of Independence Day, not only would it be "decorated in handsome style, and brilliantly illuminated in the evening" but that the mummy was still being exhibited in connection with the museum. An article in the 12 July 1824 weekly *Eastern Argus* discussing whether or not the mummy was genuine referred to the mummy "now exhibiting in this town." Another article in the same issue informed the public that this was the final chance to see the mummy "before its final removal from the New England states."

Down in Providence, Rhode Island, on 1 September 1824, the new Providence Museum, 65 North Main St, opposite the Baptist Meeting House, was opened by Greenwood on the premises formerly run by Mr. Wilder as a hotel. According to an article in the 12 September 1824 Providence *Independent Inquirer and Commercial Advertiser* the Museum would be:

> Conducted on the principles of the best regulated museums, and the collections in the various productions of nature, though small at present, will be rapidly increased. Portraits of distinguished characters will hereafter form a conspicuous place. Among the present, is a very fine full length portrait of Washington. There is also a handsome collection of wax figures, and great variety of miscellaneous curiosities. Although their beginning is small, the proprietors hope the public will find it worthy of patronage. Admittance 25 cents, without distinction of age. Season tickets $2. Gentlemen and lady $3.— Family not exceeding five persons $5.

Sharing top billing with the father of our country was Captain Turner's mummy from Thebes. That was not the only thing the mummy was sharing— the Massachusetts General Hospital mummy was being exhibited at the Court-House during this same time period.

The *Independent Inquirer* of 16 September 1824 billed Greenwood's mummy as being "one of the most perfect ever discovered" and stated that for some time it had been exhibited in Boston, where it had been viewed by several thousands. "Certificates of genuineness and antiquity (as given in the opinion of several of the most learned men in New-England)" were also on display. Admittance (normally twenty-five cents) was hiked to fifty cents for the duration of the exhibition.

On 7 October 1824, the *Independent Inquirer* proclaimed "Last week of the Egyptian mummy ... previous to its final removal from the New England States." Greenwood's diary does not mention this mummy again.

On 15 June 1824 the ship news column of the local weekly paper *Independent Chronicle and Boston Patriot* included the following information: "Brig *Peregrine*, Clark, fr Gibraltar, via Plymouth, with salt, wine, specie, &c.... The P. has two mummies on board." Quite obviously mummies were eminently newsworthy if such information about them preceded their actual arrival in port. The 17 June 1824 issue of the *American Statesman & City Register* recorded their arrival.

> The brig *Peregrine*, [Captain] Clark, from Gibraltar, arrived here on Tuesday, brought two mummies, fresh from Thebes, and of undoubted antiquity. At this rate the flesh of mummy will be as cheap as that of dogs. The market is already glutted; a few more of these Egyptian carcasses, with a mermaid or two, and the stock of our museums will be as cheap as candidates for the presidency.

The *Providence Gazette* of 23 June 1824 repeated this and appended a query. "Will not some 'learned Theban' ere long take a hint from the statute book of this country, and have a law enacted, making it penal for persons to violate the sanctuary of the dead?" This echoes the sentiments of the unknown Boston writer earlier in the year. Again, we do not know the grounds for the objection, only that the writers did not approve of the practice.

According to the 22 June 1824 *Baltimore Patriot*, "the market must now be overstocked at five." Four of the five would be the Massachusetts General Hospital mummy, Turner's mummy, and the Peregrine mummies. The fifth mummy is as yet unrevealed—Boylston's mummy was presumably no longer fully extant, and so number five remains, at least at this writing, an unrecorded one. It is not stated for whom the mummies which had arrived on the *Peregrine* were imported, nor has information come to light which reveals if (or where) they were exhibited after their arrival, but by March of 1825 they had been purchased by Greenwood. He noted in his diary: "[1825] Mar. 1st. Began to unroll the mummy & had good success. Dr. Fisher & others assisted."[5] [May] 21st. Prepared the mummies for exhibition ... June 1st. Mummies beginning to attract."[6]

The three mummies at the New England Museum were described by Bernhard, Duke of Saxe-Weimar Eisenbach who visited them in 1825:

> The mummies were brought last year in an American vessel from Egypt. One was in the same condition in which it had been taken from the coffin, except the cloth had been taken from the face. The two others were more or less uncovered; their coffins were well preserved. I was astonished to see the fresh colours of the figures painted on them. One of the mummies had two coffins, whence it is inferred that she was a person of high rank.[7]

An undated broadside from the New England Museum, but probably printed in 1825, has illustrations of the three mummy cases on exhibition at the museum, with the note: "Not being adapted to the tastes and wishes of all, they are placed in a separate apartment, to which the admission is 25 cents. Open day and evening."[8]

Greenwood's hopefulness about the popularity of the mummies was clearly not shared by others, for the *Boston Medical Intelligencer* of 12 July 1825, observed:

> Although we are perfectly aware the public has been completely satiated with the sight of and conjectures about mummies, we cannot omit calling the attention of our professional brethren towards the subject, once more. In the New-England Museum, there is one room exclusively set apart for mummies, which, besides the speculations afloat respecting the probable time of their burial, &c., are, and always will be, objects of wonder and curiosity to physicians.

This may have influenced Greenwood to exhibit the mummies at other venues outside of Boston. It may have also influenced him to dispossess himself of Turner's mummy, as there exist no further records which link that mummy to Greenwood. The latest notice found which mentions three mummies is an advertisement for the New England Museum in the 23 May 1825 issue of the *Boston Commercial Gazette*.

One of the issues continually plaguing mummy exhibitors was the presence of "doubting Thomas" people who questioned the legitimacy of the artifacts. Most mummies were accompanied by written testimonials warranting the authenticity of the bodies. Reports of faking mummies were often circulated in the newspapers, such as this one from the *New York Statesman* of 12 July 1824 (which was repeated in many newspapers for months afterwards): "Mummies—who'll buy—A gentleman who doubted the genuineness of the mummies exhibited in this city and other cities some time ago, has made some inquiries of his correspondents abroad: and has received for answer, from a gentleman in the south of France, than any number of Egyptian mummies can be supplied from the town at 150 francs ($30) each."

In November 1827, Greenwood collected the requisite certificates and testimonials of authenticity from John Collins Warren and others, preparatory to sending the pair of mummies from the *Peregrine* on tour. In January 1828, they were at Mr. Pattee's Hall (which was connected to a tavern) in Warner, New Hampshire. Greenwood claimed that "Having seen and examined all the Egyptian mummies, except one, ever brought to this country, I consider them as real Egyptian mummies, and in as good preservation as any I have seen. The bandages were removed from the female mummy by me, in the presence of several of the faculty and other learned persons, who were unanimously satisfied of their genuine antiquity."

The original broadside printed for the exhibition of the mummies has admittance 25 cents, children half-price. This has been amended, in manuscript, on the broadside for the Warner exhibition, to indicate admission would

Broadside from the New England Museum, showing, from left to right, Turner's mummy and the two mummies from the *Peregrine* (*Three Mummies from Egypt at the New England Museum, 76, Court-Street, Boston* [Boston: s.n., 1825]. Courtesy Massachusetts Historical Society).

be 12½ cents for everyone.[9] At the end of the year, according to the 8 December 1828 *Essex Gazette,* the mummies were on exhibit in Captain Turner's hometown of Charlestown, Mass. It is not known if he or his family went to view them.

The *Portsmouth Journal and Rockingham Gazette* dated 1 November 1828 invited its readers to see:

> Ancient natural curiosities. To be exhibited for a few days only, at Franklin-Hall, Congress Street—to be open Monday next.
> The inhabitants of Portsmouth are respectfully informed that there will be exhibited as above two Egyptian mummies, accompanied with their sarcophagi.... The mummies have been examined carefully by Docts. Warren, Ingalls, and Dexter of Boston, and certificates given by these gentlemen of their belief in the genuineness.... One is a male, probably of high rank and advanced in life, of large size and strong features. The other is a female, and from the splendour of the sarcophagus, (the brilliancy of the colouring which is remarkable) was probably of high standing....
> Admittance 12½ cents.—Doors open from 8 A.M. to 6 P.M.

The reduction in the usual admittance charge of twenty-five cents possibly indicates a slight decline in interest of viewing mummies, even the spectacle of viewing two at the same time.

It is interesting to note that the mummies are described as male and female, when Padihershef had been erroneously described as female. There are no obvious external characteristics on the coffins to denote this, and so it may be that the iconography had become better known by this time. The *Connecticut Mirror* for 14 February 1829 announced: "A male and female mummy, with their sarcophagus will be exhibited at the Hartford Hotel, from 12 o'clock on Saturday, the 14th inst. until sunset and on Monday the 16th. from 8 o'clock A.M. until 9 o'clock P.M."

In 1839, after Greenwood suffered financial losses, the museum and its contents were sold to Moses Kimball, who at the time had a museum in Lowell, Massachusetts.[10] Shortly thereafter, Kimball moved his museum operations to Boston, opening the Boston Museum and Gallery of Fine Arts on 14 June, 1841[11] (see ill. p. 46). A catalogue from the Museum for 1842 lists only two mummies, a male and a female, in case twenty-eight.[12] In 1893, Kimball's family donated parts of the museum collections to various other museums in the city. The *Peregrine* mummies most likely went to the Peabody Museum at Harvard, and from there possibly made their way to the Smithsonian museum.[13]

Turner's mummy (once it disappeared from Greenwood's collection) was certainly, if nothing else, peripatetic, for notices about its exhibition show that it traveled extensively—throughout Connecticut, New York State, Pennsylvania, Maryland and Washington, D.C. Although most of the advertisements carry the information that the mummy had been brought from Trieste by Captain Turner, the name of the exhibitor is not mentioned.

An advertisement for Scudder's Museum in New York in the *New-York*

American for 24 February 1825 advises prospective viewers of the mummy "The exhibition of this wonderful antiquity will positively close on Saturday next." An article immediately below this one informed readers that "In order to present better advantages to visitors of this wonderful antiquity, tickets have been left for sale at the principal hotels, bookstores, and public places." The mummy was described as having had one of its hands unwrapped, and as this tallies with the description of Turner's mummy, it is most likely this is the mummy which was on display.

A copy of the broadside which E.G. House had printed in 1824 shows the mummy to have been exhibited at Richard Pearson's in Lyme, Connecticut. However, the date has been mutilated, and so it cannot be ascertained when it was exhibited in that city, except that it must have been between 1824 and 1829. Quite probably it was in 1827, for the *Middlesex Gazette* of 25 April 1827 noted that a gentleman was now exhibiting a mummy in Middletown, Connecticut and Middletown is about twenty-five to thirty miles from Lyme, either by road or by river.

The 6 September 1827 issue of the *Rochester Daily Advertiser* noted under the headline "Egyptian Mummy" that: "The wonderful presentation has returned to this village and is now exhibiting in the room formerly occupied by the Collector's Office near the canal on Exchange Street. Adm. twelve and a half cents. Open days and evenings." From the insertion notice at the bottom of the article, the advertisement had been running since 18 August. The exhibition lasted until at least mid–October, for the advertisement was still running in the 13 October 1827 issue of the newspaper. No information has come to light as to the earlier exhibition of the mummy in Rochester.

Lambdin's Museum in Pittsburgh also exhibited the mummy in 1827, but the exact dates are not known.[14] The *Hagerstown Mail* of 5 December 1828 published the woodcut of the coffin and informed the citizens of that town and the vicinity: "An Egyptian mummy will be exhibited at Daniel M. Schnebley's Tavern, Hagerstown, on Monday and Tuesday Dec. 8th & 9th 1828.... N.B. It will be exhibited in Williamsport on Wednesday the 10th, Funkstown on Thursday, the 11th, Boonsboro' on Friday the 13th, inst. Admittance 12½ cents—children half price."

The *Daily National Intelligencer* on 15 January 1829 informed the public that the mummy was at Gadsby's Hotel, Pennsylvania Avenue, in Washington, D.C. "for a few days and evenings." According to the same paper, dated 23 January 1829, the mummy was at the National Hotel. The 19 February 1829 issue of the *United States Gazette* advised, in an advertisement which had been running since the 13th of that month: "The ladies and gentlemen of Washington, are respectfully informed, that an Egyptian mummy will be exhibited for a short time on Pennsylvania Avenue, between 9th and 10th Streets."

The 6 May 1829 issue of *The Lycoming Gazette* noted: "The inhabitants of Lycoming County are respectfully informed that an Egyptian mummy is now exhibited at the home of P. Vandervelt, Jr., in Williamsport, Pennsylvania, where it will remain until Friday evening next.... It will be exhibited at the house of R.W. Dunlap, in Muncy, in this county, on Saturday and Monday next." Admission was 12½ cents for everyone.

The 1 January 1830 issue of the *Pittsburgh Gazette* ran the plate of the coffin with the following notice. "The proprietor of the Pittsburgh Museum [James R. Lambdin] on Fifth Street, would inform the citizens of this city, that he has added to his collection of curiosities, an Egyptian mummy, which will remain a few days—no additional charge.... The proprietor flatters himself that the eye of the curious will be highly gratified in viewing it."

The following advertisement appeared in the 8 July 1830 *Baltimore Patriot*.

> Exhibition of the Egyptian mummy, at the Washington Museum, no. 95 Baltimore Street. At the request of a number of the medical faculty of the city, the proprietor has consented to remain two days longer. These venerable remains of antiquity presents [*sic*] to the eye of the beholder a striking picture of three thousand years, and is unquestionably the greatest curiosity ever offered to an American public.... Open from 9 A.M. to 10 P.M.

No further information has come to light regarding this mummy or its fate. It was probably either Turner's mummy or Lee's mummy, which also arrived in 1824 and with which it is easily confused unless coffin illustrations are present. or the testimonials are mentioned.

Façade of Moses Kimball's Boston Museum. The mummies from the *Peregrine* were exhibited here as well as their coffins (Sarah W. Lander, *Spectacles for Little Eyes* [Boston: Walker, Wise and Co., 1862]. Courtesy American Antiquarian Society).

On 10 August 1824, the *New York Evening Post* ran an illustration of an elaborate mummy case. Under the drawing appears the following letter, addressed to Captain Larkin Lee, and dated at New-York, 1 August 1824:

> Sir—When you first announced to me the arrival of a human mummy, from Egypt, I made an overture immediately for its particular and careful examination. At that time, the body was entirely covered by the cloth and bandages of embalming. These were opened in the presence of the most respectable witnesses, at the College of Physicians; and the disclosures afforded satisfactory evidence of genuineness.—My attending friends, and myself, were highly gratified by the fair opportunity we enjoyed of inspecting such a curious piece of antiquity:—and if I was to express an opinion to my fellow citizens, it would be in the form of an exhortation, for them to view this rare and real production, without delay.
>
> Accept my thanks for the addition you have made to our stock of rational information. [Signed] Samuel L. Mitchell.

Below this was an attestation of the authenticity and curiosity value of the mummy, signed by Valentine Mott, J.D. Jacques, N.H. Dering, and Wm. Js. MacNeven.

Mitchell wrote a brief description for the *New York Daily Advertiser* which was quoted in its entirety by the 22 July 1824 *Baltimore Patriot*:

> Captain Lee, who arrived a few days since at this port from Leghorn, brought out an Egyptian mummy in complete preservation, except where it had been cut open by an Italian Custom House officer who suspected it might contain contraband goods. It was opened and examined by Dr. Mitchell in the presence of a number of the trustees, professors and students of the college and other gentlemen, and proved to have been subjected to the ancient mode of embalming, swathed in bandages and cased in two wooden coffins, formed like those which have been recently exhibited in this city, and painted in water colours, with hieroglyphic and mythological figures. The wood of which they are formed is cross grained and knotty or gnarly, fastened together with pegs; and from the awkwardness betrayed in smoothing the surfaces and in closing the seams, it might be judged that some of the mechanics arts were not very far advanced.
>
> We have not room to enter more fully into the description, and shall content ourselves with the following statement furnished by Dr. Mitchell. "The hair was entire upon the scalp, not crisped but straight, not coarse but exceedingly fine—of a chesnut brown colour, mixed with a few scattering white stragglers, showing that the lady had lived long enough to be going gray. The sunken eyelids retained their eye lashes, which were plainly distinguishable. The lips were regularly closed; and on being separated a little, allowed the teeth of the lower jaw to be seen, in a perfectly white and sound state. The nose was entire, though somewhat flattened by pressure. The whole complexion was black, entirely perhaps, or at least in a great degree occasioned by the antiseptics, aromatics and conservatories with which the body had for so many ages been enveloped. The bones of the skull were apparently as compact as ever; and the ears were plainly distinguishable."

An accompanying article on another page makes it clear this mummy is not to be confused with that of the one from Massachusetts General Hospital:

> The mummy.—The representation of the sarcophagus inclosing [sic] the mummy, inserted in another column, is not the same as that which we gave last summer, and which then was exhibiting at the Academy of Arts; but the coffin of another mummy brought direct from Egypt, and which, it will be seen by the certificates of several scientific gentlemen in this city, is as genuine as its predecessor. It possesses this advantage over the former, that the figures on the upper part and sides are far more numerous, which renders the exhibition interesting even to those who examined the first. From the circumstances of more labour and expense having been bestowed on the body and its envelope, it is inferred that the person when alive (believed to have been a female) belonged to some rich and distinguished family in Egypt.

The mummy was to be exhibited from 8:00 in the morning until 9:00 at night, at 328½ Broadway, "nearly opposite the Hospital." Admittance was the usual 25 cents, with children admitted at half-price.

Sometime after 4 September 1824, a brochure was made up for the exhibition of this mummy, similar to the ones which had been printed for Padihershef and Turner's mummy.[15] It was produced by Ephraim Conrad, of New York, and cost 3 cents.[16] The first page is a woodcut of the sarcophagus, surrounded by the words "The Egyptian mummy with its sarcophagus." Opposite this is a description of what is in the brochure. "The works of the old world, the wonder of the new. An Egyptian mummy, taken from the king's tombs at Thebes, in Upper Egypt, together with the following antiquities, collected from the ruins of cities in Egypt, Nubia, Abyssinia and Persia, imported into N. York by Capt. Larkin T. Lee."

The eight-page pamphlet contains the letter quoted in the *New York Evening Post*; a long, minute description of the sarcophagus and the mummy; an article from *The Minerva*, describing the acquisition of the mummy; the increasingly ubiquitous "Address to the Mummy;" and a list of the antiquities which accompanied it. The description of the mummy begins with a very small history of embalming as it related to the Biblical Joseph and continues:

> This present article is offered as an EGYPTIAN MUMMY. It was procured from a catacomb, or excavation in the mountainous rocks of Thebes, high up the Nile.... Upon the plain statement of its transportation down the river to Alexandria, and thence to New-York, by way of Leghorn, its genuineness might be safely rested; but there are other matters and circumstances upon which every beholder will be enabled to form an independent, and it is believed, a satisfactory opinion.
>
> The COFFIN or CASE first claims the attention of visitors; who are invited to examine it particularly, as to the following points: 1. The wood, which is different from any that the western world affords. 2. The roughness of the joints and seams, probably anterior to the invention of the plane. 3. The connection of the parts by tree-nails or wooden pegs, in an age prior to the knowledge of iron nails or screws. 4. The covering of the sides with lime-wash or crust of calcarious carbonate, to hide the roughness of the implaned boards. 5. The painting of the figures of natural objects, such as the scaraboeus or

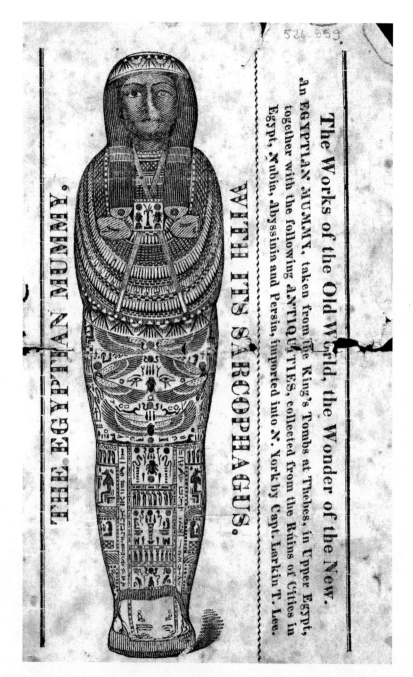

THE EGYPTIAN MUMMY.

WITH ITS SARCOPHAGUS.

The Works of the Old World, the Wonder of the New.

An EGYPTIAN MUMMY, taken from The King's's Tombs at Thebes, in Upper Egypt, together with the following ANTIQUITIES, collected from the Ruins of Cities in Egypt, Nubia, Abyssinia and Persia, imported into N. York by Capt. Larkin T. Lee.

Elaborately painted coffin of the mummy brought from Livorno by Beverly ship captain Larkin Thorndike Lee. The man who had charge of the exhibition of the mummy absconded with both the artifact and the money it earned as an attraction (title page of *Works of the Old World, the Wonder of the New* [New York: E. Conrad, 1824]. 52L-359, Department of Printing and Graphic Arts, Houghton Library, Harvard College Library).

sacred beetle, and of emblems or hieroglyphs in water colours, before it was
known how to grind paints in oil.

This is formed evidently for receiving and preserving the embalmed body in
an erect or standing posture; the embalmed subjects not being extended hori-
zontally, or laid on their backs, as in our way of disposing of the dead. Every
coffin, with its body, is understood to have occupied its own niche; and what,
according to our method, is the lid, so with them the door of the coffin. It is
on this account that the ancient position is observed in this exhibition.

The BODY itself next merits consideration; and presents the following views
to the beholder. 1. The many folds and wrappers of cloth with which it is
enfolded or shrouded. 2. The dusky colouring derived from the embalming
materials, the composition of which is unknown to the moderns. 3. The conversion of the scalp and of the face by an incorporation of the embalming materials
with the skin and flesh, into the black mass, called in the strictness of language,
mummy. 4. The perfect condition of the hair, of a bright chesnut or auburn
color, turned somewhat gray, but straight and fine and perfectly free from crisp-
ing or frizzling. 5. The admirable soundness and whiteness of the teeth.

The proprietor respectfully assures his fellow citizens, that the lower as well
and upper parts of the body, on examination, gave evidence of the complete
change of the flesh to mummy. But the bones every where were found as
sound and entire as if the person had not been dead a twelve-month.

It is impossible to ascertain who the individual was. If we were sufficiently
acquainted with the painted symbols and emblems, we might probably read
the biographical story.

At present we can go very little further than from the female face, carved
upon the lid or door, to conjecture that it was a woman; and from the skill,
learning, labour and expense, bestowed both upon the body and its envelope,
to add another supposition, that she must have been a member of a rich, considerable, and distinguished family.

From this last part of the description, and from the note to Captain Lee,
it may be speculated upon that the mummy was partially unwrapped or uncovered during its examination by the learned men of the institution. Most likely
they uncovered the face and hands, and possibly even parts of the body and
lower limbs. There is no evidence of a complete removal of burial linens, as
the mummy was later unwrapped before an audience. It would have been quite
easy for the learned men to feel the mummified flesh beneath the wrappings
and so make the claims in the article.

The next part of the pamphlet contained a small biography of Alexander
Grant, the person responsible for procuring the mummy and for the collection of Egyptian artifacts which also formed part of the exhibition.

Alexander Grant, Esq. is one of the modern travellers who has penetrated into
the high regions watered by the Nile, and even visited Nubia and Abyssinia.
His researches are more recent than that of Mr. Salt and Mr. Belzoni. His travels into the eastern countries, as far as Persia, were continued for twelve suc-
cessive years, and of these, five were devoted to exploring the banks of the
Nile, from its disemboguement towards its source. This gentleman having
been favoured with health, fund, zeal and good fortune, collected a great body
of antiquities in the places he visited.... It was through an acquaintance with

Mr. Grant, that Captain Larkin Lee obtained a knowledge of his travels and adventures....

The mummy now offered for the inspection of the curious, was obtained by Mr. G together with several others, from the catacombs, or repositories of the dead, in the neighbourhood of Thebes. There the bodies of the individuals belonging to rich and great families were deposited in standing postures, within niches excavated with immense labour in the rocks and mountains. The coffin, with its door, thus resembled a small house or sort of sentry-box, for containing the corpse with its cloths, bandages and wrappers, and with all the materials employed for embalming. Thus preserved, the body, with its shroud and case, might endure, or rather has continued, in all probability, for several thousand years; and is at this day, a specimen of the once fashionable, but now neglected art of preserving carcasses from corruption, and at the same time, a monument of the labour, skill and expense attendant on such a method of treating the dead....

But this piece of antiquity is not all. Mr. Grant has furnished a collection of articles, which further illustrate the history of that peculiar people. These he found, as he was occupied with a company of thirty labourers, in ransacking the ruins of Thebes.

This last reference to "ransacking" is enough to cause a collective shudder in the ranks of present-day archaeologists. "Scientific archaeology" was decades in the future; most so-called archaeologists at this time were little better than treasure seekers. The much-touted Belzoni was no more than a former circus strong-man turned inventor, who had gone to Egypt to sell a water wheel contraption, and who had returned with mummies and artifacts which had been looted, and in some cases, literally blown out of their resting places by explosives. Sir Flinders-Petrie, generally regarded as the father of "modern" archaeology, was not even born until 1853.

Grant did try and impose some sort of rational order on the items in the exhibition. The pamphlet continues:

He has arranged them in several groups, so they may be understood with the least possible difficulty, by the student. Indeed, the person who possesses the great and invaluable work of Father Montfaucon on the explanation of antiquity, and the representation of sculptures ... may now behold the originals, instead of engravings.... Here are things from the king's tombs at Thebes ... a tableau of offerings to the god Osiris, cut from the temple of Dendera ... two dozen and more idols in wood and stone, covered with hieroglyphics; several heads of men and deities in granite and marble; and a piece of papyrus, in good condition ... eighteen separate lots of curious things belonging to former ages ... among them is a speculum, or mirror, in gold, from Memphis, with a handle to it, as used before the invention of looking-glasses; human figures in bronze; ancient Egyptian beads; beetles carved in granite and serpentine; nilometers; Masonic emblems of the pyramids ... and a multitude more, some known, and others of dubious meaning, on which the rational enquirer will be enabled to exercise his taste and judgment.[17]

Shortly after this, Lee arranged with a Mr. Bishop to exhibit the mummy and its accompanying collection of artifacts for him and his New York partner Ebenezer Fisk. Fisk wrote to Lee (who had returned to his home in Beverly, Massachusetts) on 11 January 1825: "Respecting the mummy. Mr. Bishop got no place to remove it to until yesterday. From the time you left, up to yesterday, he has paid over to me $13.81. I have not advertised the mummy yet. Thought I would wait until Mr. Bishop got it placed in some convenient situation. He has taken a room n. 11 near the park, Chatham Street."[18]

Shortly after this, Lee went to sea again and died in 1825, off the coast of West Africa, of "anxiety." He was fifty-four years old, having been born in Beverly, Massachusetts in 1780. His body was returned to Beverly and he was buried on 2 August 1825.[19] His heirs and executors tried without much success to locate Bishop and the mummy, so that they could settle Lee's estate.

On 25 October 1825, Ebenezer Smith wrote to John Dike (both of whom were involved in business ventures with Lee):

> Enclosed is what Mr. Fisk wrote to me concerning the mummy—he mentioned further to me that there was not much dependence to be placed in Bishop. His notes in New York was worth but little or nothing—the obligation he gave Capt. Lee not to leave New York with the mummy was without any date and was an excuse for him that he cared nothing about it for is [sic] was good for nothing.[20]

On 9 December 1825 Fisk wrote to Robert Rantoul (one of a committee appointed to help settle Lee's estate):

> I have been endeavouring to see Mr. Bishop in whose care Capt. Lee left the mummy. He left New York last March with the mummy to be about four weeks and then return to the city. He sent me one half the income of the exhibition of the mummy while he was at Newark, New Brunswick, Elizabethtown, Princeton and Trenton. From there he went to Philadelphia. On his arrival there he wrote me he should be there about a month. I wrote him several times to come to N. York but got no answer. I wrote to one of my friends in Philadilphia [sic], who ascertained that he had been there but could git [sic] no other intelligence of him, since which I have seen nothing from him for the mummy nor any communication.
>
> About six weeks since I heard he had been in New York, by diligent search and inquiry I found his wife, who refused to give me any correct intelligence of him, nor the mummy. I have repeatedly called on his wife, some times she would say he is gone to Albany. Other times in the country. & at other times she did not know any thing about him. I have called a number of times since I received your letter [of 25 November] but could not see his wife. A little girl told me he was gone to sea. I have left word repeatedly for Bishop when he came in town to come and see me but he never made his appearance.
>
> What is to be done I am unable to say. I have consulted my friends here they think the business looks rather dark. I did think of having the papers with some attorney, but have not, fading in hopes I should get sight of Bishop, and I thought it might be spending money and get no recompense.
>
> I have recv'd $82.62 for the one half of the income of the mummy since Capt. Lee left New York. I have often requested him [Bishop] to pay some on the note Capt. Lee left with me, but have not seen one cent.[21]

The mummy was exhibited in Trenton during the second week in March 1825 at the United States Hotel.[22] Then, according to the *Saturday Evening Post* dated 7 May 1825, the mummy, which had just arrived in the city, was on exhibition at Jesse Sharpless's Pennsylvania Museum "for a short time."

Ebenezer Fisk wrote one last time in December to unnamed persons in Beverly concerning the mummy. He had obviously been in contact with Bishop, who had sent him some money, but was again derelict:

> Tell Capt. L.T. Lee's family or Samuel Lovett [Lee's brother-in-law] that the mummy is in Pensilvania [sic], and has been there for several months for the first two months I saw about $20—since that have seen nothing. I have wrote & sent by persons several times for Bishop to come and bring the mummy to N. York, but I have not seen him neither has he wrote me for two months but has wrote his wife after & told her he was coming next week & next week it is out of my power to leave my business. If he doth not come soon I shall send some person to him if it will not cost too much.[23]

By all appearances, Bishop absconded, and there is no further extant correspondence which reveals what happened to him. An advertisement for the Pennsylvania Museum, no. 272 Market Street above the upper Market, Phialdelphia, appeared in the *Aurora and Franklin Gazette* for 3 May 1826, touting: "Late additions—an Egyptian mummy, with its sarcophagus, and other antiquities, from Thebes, upwards of 3000 years old."

The insertion date at the bottom of the advertisement shows that the mummy had been in the museum since at least 14 April. Lee's mummy was the only one at this time which was accompanied by antiquities or curiosities, and so this is most likely his mummy. It is not clear if this is still a traveling exhibition or if the owner of the museum, Jesse Sharpless, had actually purchased the mummy, and, after displaying it in his own museum, was sending it out on tour.

In 1827 the mummy was in the Louisville, Kentucky, Museum, as reported by the *Focus* of 5 June 1827:

> Museum. Main Street. The Egyptian mummy with its sarcophagus! Upwards of 3000 years old. Taken from the city of Thebes, in upper Egypt, together with other curiosities, found with her and imported into New York by Capt. Larkin T. Lee, and has been examined by Samuel Mitchell, Valentine Mott, and a number of other physicians, and pronounced by them to be a genuine mummy.... The mummy, &c will continue until the 12th instant, when they will be removed to Cincinnati. Admittance 50 cents—children 25 cents.

The 22 August 1829 issue of the *Saturday Evening Post* ran an advertisement for the sale of Sharpless's Washington and Pennsylvania Museums. Listed among the exhibits was the following: "The Egyptian mummy, and accompaniments, 3000 years old, brought by Capt. Larken [sic], of New York, and attested genuine by Dr. Mitchell, and others. This single article would insure a fortune if carried through the western and southern states."

This is clearly Capt. Lee's mummy; how or where or when or from whom Sharpless acquired it is not known, although he had exhibited it at least twice earlier at the Pennsylvania Museum, in 1825 and again in 1826. Obviously the provenance was a bit fuzzy by this point in time as it is referred to as Capt. Larken's mummy. Nor is it known who purchased the mummy and what happened to it subsequently.

These early mummies excited tremendous interest, and the articles and notices concerning them were published not only in local newspapers, but were copied repeatedly in many other newspapers all over the country. Mummies were clearly newsworthy, and people flocked to see them whenever and wherever they were exhibited. They inspired poetry, philosophical reflection and an interest in the physical evidences of ancient history, all parts of the phenomenon we now call "mummymania." Sadly, almost all of them (with the exception of Padihershef and Boylston's mummy) seem to have disappeared somewhere in the nineteenth century, gone, without a trace.

3

"An Exceedingly Dry Company"

Exhibiting Egyptian Mummies in Nineteenth-Century America

The successful exhibition in the early 1820s of mummies such as Padiher-shef and Turner's and Lee's mummies enticed others to import them and put them on the lecture and show circuit, or to display them in museums and other venues.

One such entrepreneur was George Barclay of New York, who obtained two mummies from Egypt through the agency of John W. Kearney, United States consul at Trieste. These arrived early in 1826, and were accompanied by the following letter as recorded in the *Mercantile Advertiser* of 15 February 1826.

> I have sent by the *Hannibal*, two genuine mummies on which you may depend, they were brought to Treaste [*sic*] by a very respectable man from Grand Cairo in Egypt, who saw them removed from the places of original deposit. I took every pains to ascertain his character and the result was a per-fect conviction that these mummies are not only genuine, but of very great antiquity.

Barclay placed the mummies on exhibition at Peale's Museum and Gallery of Fine Arts, Broadway, across from the Park. According to the 14 February 1826 *New York Evening Post* the museum was open all day and brilliantly illu-minated all evening. Admittance was the usual twenty-five cents, with children, as usual, half-price. A yearly ticket to the museum for a family was ten dol-lars, and for an individual, five dollars. A ticket could also be obtained by a gentleman, which allowed him to bring a lady each time, for ten dollars.

Shortly after their arrival, Rubens Peale, proprietor of the museum, bought the mummies himself, much to the dismay of his father, Charles Willson Peale, who worried that the revenue gained from their exhibition would be very slight and not worth the amount paid for the mummies.[1]

By April 1827 Peale had sold one of the mummies to a trio of gentlemen from upstate New York. Messers Frederick Boughton, Ira Curtis, and Ebenezer G. Holt exhibited the mummy, which was in a curious, distinctive, "block-headed" coffin, at Ithaca, New York. The mummy was accompanied by a certificate of authenticity from Rubens Peale, detailing the manner of its acqui-sition, and certificates of authenticity from Drs. Stevens and Post. Samuel L.

Mitchell also contributed a letter about the mummy, commenting that it had pleased him that such a relic had arrived in America, and that his "fellow citizens might receive at home the instruction which such preparations are capable of affording to the Biblical scholar—the curious historian, and the learned antiquarian."[2]

A.P. Searing & Co. of Ithaca printed up an eight-page brochure to accompany the exhibition. It was quite similar to the brochures which had accompanied earlier mummy exhibitions. The first page was a plate of the coffin, with "Will be exhibited at" printed lengthwise along the side, and a blank space left for the insertion of the exhibition venue. Inside were the aforementioned certificates, and a description of the mummy:

> The mummy retains its form and features very perfectly. It is wrapped in thirty-five folds of the twined linen of Egypt, mentioned in the Scriptures. The envelope is removed from the face, breast, one hand, and the toes. It is of a dusky colour, derived from the embalming materials, and not the original colour; the hair is sandy and perfectly strait [sic]. The coffin is of sycamore wood, covered within and without with an Egyptian cement, on the front of which are painted various forms of idols, worshipped by the Egyptians, together with an epitaph of the person in hieroglyphicks, such as were used previous to the invention of letters. It is impossible to determine the antiquity for a certainty, but it is reasonable to conclude that it must have been entombed previous to the destruction of the city of Thebes, which all writers on the subject make nearly three thousand years since and some, three thousands and two or three hundred.

Following this were extracts from the commentary on the Holy Bible by Adam Clarke, a discussion of embalming, a notice from a Paris newspaper of 12 March 1827 (copied from a New York paper) about the unwrapping of a mummy in Paris; the ubiquitous "Address to a Mummy at Belzoni's Exhibition," and a piece entitled "A Few Reflections Suggested by a View of the Egyptian Mummy," signed by the pseudonymous Brotos:

> While beholding this ancient relick of mortality, my thoughts involuntarily reverted back to the period when it was the residence of an immortal spirit— to the time, when this now distinguished mass of deformity, animated by a living principle, played her part in the theatre of life. She may have been born in affluence, and enjoyed all the advantages which wealth and power could command.—She may have been the idol of her parents and the delight of her friends.—She may have been beautiful, accomplished, and, among the proud daughters of Thebes, the proudest. But what is she now? Whence has fled the lustre of those eyes which betrayed the secrets of the heart? Whence those animating smiles which played upon the lips, and spoke the inward pleasure of the soul? Death chased them away, and that form so delicate and graceful; the object of so much attention, was delivered to the embalmers, to be prepared for the long sleep of the tomb. After the season of mourning was accomplished, the body was deposited in the caverned rock, where it slumbered an hundred ages; and is then brought forth and exhibited to the world as the silent representative of other times. A thousand interesting thoughts crowd

upon the mind as we look back to the time when Thebes stood on the plains of Egypt in all its pride and glory; Where now is Thebes? Where her splendid palaces, whose halls echoed to the song of pleasure and the mirthful laugh? Where the busy population that thronged her spacious streets? Where are her princes and nobles? Where her statesmen, and warriors? Where her bands of armed men? And where are her massy walls, her lofty battlements and her hundred gates? They have been swept away by the hand of time. Ages have rolled away since "the city of the sun" veiled its splendours in darkness.

While these inquiries are passing rapidly through the mind, the solemn question arises, where now is the spirit that fled from this ruined tenement, three thousand years ago? What is its mode of existence? Does it retain all its faculties of thought, and consciousness? Does it increase in knowledge and power? If so, how great must be its capacity for happiness or suffering. With what indifference does it look upon the affairs of this world—the petty trifles which harass and agitate the majority of mankind! What is the vain, pomp and glory of this world to her? They affect her not—and have not for three thousand years—nor will they while eternity rolls.

Though hundreds may gaze with stupid wonder upon the body which was hers on earth, yet how few will follow the immortal past into the invisible world! How few will cast a transient thought upon that never-dying principle of our natures, which thinks, and feels, and acts beyond the grave? How very soon will those who now look with curious eyes upon this relick of the tombs themselves become its tenants? How soon will the honours, the pleasures, the riches, and grandeur of earth fade from the eye and vanish in eternal night? What then will be the hopes and fears, the joys and disappointments of this life three thousand years to come? Who can mark the soul's flight across that trackless ocean which knows no bound? Who desires its intellectual progress? Who tells the sun of its joys, or the aggregate of its miseries?

Look again at this ancient remnant of mortality. What was it once? The residence of an immortal soul. What is it now? A senseless lump of clay; and such, in a short period, reader, shall we be. What folly then to waste a whole life in pampering and decorating a body that must shortly return to dust? Could we but know ourselves as God knows us—could we perceive the feebleness of our frames, and the slight tenpur [sic] by which we hold our lives, the awful scenes which await us on the other side of the grave would occupy every thought, and nerve to action every faculty of the mind; could we call back again the soul, which once animated this body, from its unseen state, what intelligence would it bring? Would it disclose any new truths, or make a clearer demonstration of the realities of the dread world, than is already revealed in the book of God? If we hear not Moses and the prophets, neither shall we be persuaded, though one rose from the dead.[3]

After Ithaca, the mummy went to the Franklin House in Buffalo for an unknown period of time in July. The proprietor announced that "an opportunity of witnessing a mummy may not soon occur again," and it probably didn't.[4]

The *Rutland Herald* of 1 January 1828 ran an illustration of the coffin and noted:

The ladies and gentlemen of Rutland and its vicinity are informed that an Egyptian mummy, together with its coffin, will be exhibited at the house of

Mr. Abbott, in East Poultney, Vermont, on Tuesday, the 1st; at Mr. Greeno's in Fairhaven Wednesday, the 2d; at Mr. Moulton's in Castleton, on Thursday the 3d, and at Mr. Gould's, in Rutland, on Friday, Saturday and Monday, the 4th, 5th, and 7th of January 1828.... Tickets 12½ cents—to be had at the bar. Hours of exhibition from 9 A.M. til 9 P.M.

Presumably the exhibition was not open on Sunday out of deference to the Sabbath. A similar advertisement was in the *Vermont Republican and American Yeoman* on 8 February 1828, and listed the following venues: "Mr. Websters, in Hartland, on Monday the 11th—at Mr. Peite's, in Windsor, on Tuesday and Wednesday, the 12th and 13th—at Mr. Stevens, in Claremont, on Thursday and Friday, the 14th and 15th—and at Mr. Hassma's in Charleston, on Saturday and Monday, the 16th and 18th of February 1828."

Tickets and location for purchase were the same as in the earlier advertisement, and again, the exhibition was not open on Sunday. Quite possibly all of these locations were taverns, which would normally be closed on the Sabbath.

On 8 August 1828 the *Saratoga Sentinel* announced that the mummy would be on view at Bailey's Congress Springs Hotel

EGYPTIAN MUMMY.

PLATE OF THE COFFIN.

From the *Edinburgh Encyclopedia.*—"Embalming, as an art, was carried to great perfection by the Egyptians; it was conducted by persons specially initiated in it, and performed at a costly charge to the survivors. So long as the body remained entire and undisturbed, they believed that the spirit would re-animate it after the lapse of thousands of years.

A. P. SEARING & Co. PRINTERS, ITHACA.

Curious coffin of the mummy which was sold by Rubens Peale to a consortium of gentlemen, the occupant of which was destroyed by rowdy students who were attempting to discern the authenticity of the mummy (*Egyptian Mummy* [Ithaca, N.Y.: J.P. Searing & Co., (1827)]. Courtesy American Antiquarian Society).

"for a few days only." The advertisement had been inserted on the 5th. Tickets were 12½ cents and could be had at the bar.

In 1828 it was exhibited at a public house in Rennselaerville, New York, where it met with a terrible fate. Eight young men, some of them medical students, out of a desire to prove that the mummy was genuine, determined to dissect the mummy. At about midnight they broke into the establishment, subdued the attendant "with no easy hand" and "hurried her mummyship down the stairs with more haste than the gravity of the situation could at all justify." After that escapade, the mummy disappeared, and not even fragments were recovered. In 1829, Messers. Curtis, Boughton and Thorn (who had replaced Holt) brought a suit of trover against the young gentlemen, to recover the monies which they would have earned had they been able to continue their exhibition of the mummy, which had been producing a net income of eight dollars a day. The courtroom battle devolved on whether or not the mummy was "property," and if so, who owned it? The defense argued that the only person who could properly claim the mummy was its last, lineal descendant, and moreover, it was a human body and could not then be considered to be property, and as such, it had no intrinsic value and was worth nothing. The prosecution countered with letters from Peale, the original examining physicians, and others, advancing the argument that although the body was human, it was as much property as were any physicians' anatomical specimens. The defense responded that if that were the case, then it would have to be proven that the mummy's direct descendants had sold the body! The prosecution crowned the argument by pointing out that as the Pasha of Egypt had become the administrator general of all the catacombs in Egypt, where the mummy had been buried and discovered, he was therefore quite legally within his rights to sell off the contents, which he had done in conveying the mummies to Henry Barclay.

Judge Duer and the jury returned a verdict for the plaintiffs, in the amount of twelve hundred dollars, plus the legal costs of the suit.[5]

As a curious sidelight, the 13 March 1835 issue of the *Christian Advocate and Journal* ran an article about the mummy currently exhibiting at Peale's Museum (in New York). The cut of the coffin is the same illustration as was printed on the brochure and in the advertisements for the mummy destroyed at Rensselaer, and so the question must be asked—was the mummy sold to the Ithaca group actually destroyed, or did it reappear back at Peale's Museum? Peale did have another mummy, but according to advertisements for his museum in the *New York Commercial Advertiser* for 21 and 24 February 1832, the mummy on exhibition was "decidedly the finest ever brought to this country" and was enclosed in a double coffin. More likely than not, the printer of the magazine happened to have that cut handy and used it, oblivious to (or unconcerned by) the fact that it wasn't correct.

A curious advertisement in the Massachusetts *Lynn Mirror* of 7 June 1828

announced the exhibition of a different mummy in that city, probably beginning around the end of May:

> A mummy, discovered in a cave in Upper Egypt by the distinguished traveler
> Belzoni. The box which contained it, the ornaments, &c. are worth examining.
> The scientific antiquarian and lovers of art will examine it with intense curios-
> ity. The simple beholder will be gratified. All will see the perfection of the art
> of embalming, an art acquired by the Jews during their captivity in Egypt,
> often mentioned in the Old Testament, but is now lost wholly to the world.
> This mummy must have been in existence more than three thousand years. It
> cost the proprietors a large sum, and is now offered for examination, at the
> White Store, east end of Market Street. Admittance 12½ cents. Children half
> price.... On Monday next the mummy will be removed to the Mechanics Hall,
> in Woodend, where it will remain one or two days for the convenience of visi-
> tors in that neighborhood, and then it will be removed to the Lynn Hotel, for
> exhibition.

One enraptured viewer penned the following observations detailed in
another article elsewhere in that same newspaper:

> The mummy—there is a strange feeling of admiration and astonishment—an
> undefinable compound of pleasure and pain—that pervades breast, on behold-
> ing this relic of by-gone ages. It seems as if a new perception were imparted to
> the mind—new emotions arise—and thoughts, which never filled the senso-
> rium before, come thronging upon us. It is as if a strange key were given us by
> some shadowy being, and we were permitted to open one of the secret apart-
> ments of nature, that had been kept locked for centuries, and to view the dark,
> and awful, and shuddering contents. I have seen beauty and deformity—I have
> looked on life in all its loveliness, and death in its calmness and serenity, and
> in its revoltingness and dread—I have watched the coldness creeping through
> the warm veins of infant innocence, and the bright, the lovely, the intelligent
> eye, turning glassy, and losing its endearing consciousness—and I have seen
> the foe of animation lay his benumbing hand on the strength of manhood—I
> have beheld the fairest of God's works an object from which the eye turned
> away with revoltingness and tears, while the injunction of the poet to the vain
> beauty arose to my recollection—"tell her, that, paint an inch thick, to this
> must come at last"—but never did I experience such sensation as when my
> eyes first fixed on this inhabitant as were of another world. I stood beside a
> being who had probably lived three thousand years ago—a being who had
> walked on the banks of the Nile, before Rome had been founded, or David
> ruled over Israel—an inhabitant, it may be, of Thebes, the city of one hundred
> gates—or a sister of the artist who formed the statue which resounded at sun-
> rise—or a daughter of one of the kings who built the pyramids. Perhaps it was
> the maiden who protected the infant prophet from the destruction of the
> Nile—or the enamored Zuleika herself, who laid her hand on the Hebrew boy.
> Was it a reality—did she stand there before me?—or had my existence passed,
> and was I no longer a denizen of earth, and surrounded by animated and
> breathing forms....
>   When Mr. Belzoni visited Egypt, he informs us that he discovered deep cav-
> erns in the earth, of several hundred yards in extent, the sides of which were
> filled with mummies, piled on cases one above the other.... This mummy
> which is now exhibiting in this town, was obtained in Egypt, and purchased by

several gentleman at extended expense. The box, or case which contains it is of plank, in a perfect state of preservation. The corners are regularly dovetailed, and the top was fastened on with wooden pins. The body was enveloped by several hundred yards of coarse linen cloth, of a dirty yellow color, which tears easily. The head was enclosed in a painted mask, on which the eyes, ears and nose were guilt [sic]. There are various other paintings around it—on some of which are women represented in the attitude of prayer, and on others various animals. There were found about twenty small ornaments of cornelian and other stones.

The mummy itself is the greatest curiosity. It is enclosed in a glass case, in an upright position. It is entire, with the hands crossed on the breast, and perfectly black. The head is well formed, the teeth sound, and the feet bare with an appearance of delicacy. The whole object however serves to impress the beholder with sensations of the most solemn and awful kind.

Belzoni was a name familiar to most people who had any interest in Egypt, as he had been one of the first explorers of that country and had made a name for himself as a quondam archaeologist having failed as an hydraulic engineer. (One must consider that looting statues, blasting into pyramids with explosives and having rows over the ownership of artifacts was common archaeological practice at the time.) He had discovered many mummies in his adventures and there is nothing in his writings, nor in this description which can determine which one of them is this particular exhibit. Indeed, it is entirely possible that the proprietors, needing to excite interest in their property, made up the Belzoni provenance.

This mummy being exhibited in Lynn presents something of a mystery. It does not correspond to any of the mummies known to be in America at this time. All of them were enclosed in mummiform coffins,

EGYPTIAN MUMMY.

A MUMMY, discovered in a Cave in Upper Egypt by the distinguished Traveller Belzoni. The box which contained it, the ornaments, &c. are worth examination. The scientific antiquarian and the lovers of art will examine it with intense curiosity. The simple beholder will be gratified. All will see the perfection of the art of embalming, an art acquired by the Jews during their captivity in Egypt, often mentioned in the Old Testament, but is now lost wholly to the world. This mummy must have been in existence more than three thousand years. It cost the proprietors a large sum, and is now offered for examination, at the White Store, east end of Market Street. Admittance 12½ cents. Children half price.

Lynn, May 31st.   22

ON Monday next the Mummy will be removed to the Mechanics Hall, in Woodend, where it will remain one or two days for the convenience of visitors in that neighbourhood, and then will be removed to the Lynn Hotel, for exhibition.

June 7th

Advertisement for the exhibition of a mummy purportedly excavated by Giovanni Belzoni (*Lynn Mirror* [Lynn, Mass.], 7 June 1828).

while this coffin appears to be a box, or rectangular receptacle. Moreover, none of the mummies previously mentioned was described as having a gilded mask over its face, a fact which would have been duly noted and reported. The mummy also seems to have been completely unwrapped. Its sex is not known, although the writer appears to believe it was female. No further advertisements for this mummy (using the Belzoni reference and the cartonnage mask as points of identification) have been located at this point in time and so there can be no determination of what happened to it after its exhibition in Lynn.

Rubens Peale exhibited a mummy at his Baltimore Museum in March of 1829, but it is not clear from the advertisements in the *Baltimore Patriot* from 16 to 27 March 1829 which mummy is being exhibited. The exhibition began on Monday the 16th and on the 27th the headline announced "The last two days of the Egyptian mummy." Either Turner's mummy or Lee's mummy could have been in Baltimore at this time, or Peale could have sent his New York mummy to Baltimore—there are no clues of any sort in the advertisement, and no accompanying illustrations. Because the mummy appears to be a "traveling show," it was probably hired just for that particular appearance.

Peale's Museum and Gallery of Fine Arts (also known as the New York Museum) and the American Museum of John Scudder were two of the earliest public institutions of this type in New York. Scudder, originally an itinerant organ-grinder, had begun displaying his collection of curiosities in 1810. It had occupied three locations during its lifetime and was, in the 1820s, housed in a building he had designed especially for it, on the corner of Ann Street and Broadway. Peale's Museum, established in 1825, was at 252 Broadway, opposite the Park. Both museums were taken over by P.T. Barnum in 1841, and he concentrated the exhibitions at the American Museum location.[6]

Scudder's collections were "well arranged and beautifully displayed in four spacious saloons, each 100 feet in length." Peales's Museum consisted of four spacious apartments, arranged in order of "natural history and all its branches"; a large and valuable collection of paintings; a cosmorama, and a gallery of wax figures, shells, minerals, and miscellaneous curiosities.[7] No gallery guides or descriptions survive which report how the exhibitions had been arranged in those museums and so there is no way to tell exactly how the mummies had been displayed by Peale and Scudder. Indeed, it cannot be ascertained whether or not the mummies even existed at the time the museums were acquired by Barnum. The book *Sights and Wonders in New York* (New York: J.S. Redfield, 1849) has an illustration on page 14 of a mummy in its coffin, head and upper torso exposed, while the remainder of the body is still wrapped with narrow longitudinal strips, including a wide vertical band down the center, crossed by eight horizontal bands, and two diagonal bands which form a criss-cross just below the folded arms of the mummy. The coffin has a smooth, rounded top. This drawing, supposedly of Barnum's American

Museum mummy, does not seem to correlate to descriptions of either of the mummies in the earlier museums (see ill. p. 65).

To further muddy the identification waters, an undated catalogue of the American Museum has two illustrations, one of a mummy and coffin in a glass case in the Sixth Saloon, and another drawing of a mummy in its coffin.[8] The mummy in the Sixth Saloon, although indistinct, bears more of a resemblance to the drawing in *Sights and Wonders in New York* than it does to the more detailed drawing, especially as it appears to be in a coffin with a rounded top. The other drawing of the mummy shows a partially unwrapped mummy, head and upper torso and arms, but the bandaging pattern is quite different, numerous horizontal bands with a criss-cross pattern down the front, consisting of six crosses, secured with seven horizontal bands across the diagonals. The top of the coffin has a rectangular "crown" above the rounded head portion. These are the earliest known examples of portrayals of the actual mummies themselves, not merely the coffins. Indeed, in each of these illustrations, the coffin serves only as a backdrop. The question is, how accurate were the drawings? (See ill. pp. 66–67.)

What the catalogue does do is give some idea of how the mummy was displayed and what sorts of things might be found near it. It is not unreasonable to assume that Peale and Scudder displayed their mummies in a similar fashion.

In any case, the catalogue lists only one mummy, and that, according to the 29 July 1865 issue of *Harper's Weekly*, was destroyed in the fire which consumed the building on 13 July 1865. The *Times* of 14 July 1865 had a rather different description, as it listed all of the exhibits which had perished in the conflagration, and quite precisely mentions three mummies:

> Who can forget, be he man or boy, the startling effect produced upon him by the three men of Egypt, whose blackened skulls and grinning, ghastly faces stuck offensively out from the top of funereal wrappings? These dead men, or women, as the case may have been—dead any reasonable number of thousands of years—whose gay and festive lives were spent perhaps in the halls of a royal pharaoh, or who, perchance, did their best to make bricks without straw, in the day of the fat and lean kine; about whose necks the fond caressings of love were hung, or, perchance, the noose of infamy; at whose death bitter tears of regret were shed; whose bodies were wrapped and swaddled in cloth, and dipped in tar, and stuffed with preservatives and laid away securely for the great day of days; and whose spirits have since roamed the paths of an eternal world, knowing the secrets of the infinite. We can imagine the tender regard with which sensitive spirits observed the mournings of their mundane relatives, and the satisfaction with which they noticed the good places selected for their long sleep. We can likewise see in our mind's eye the awful indignation experienced when the vandal hand of intrusive Yankees pulled from the dust-covered shelves the entombed, mummific remains, and rudely tore off the covering from the face, playfully pulled the lock or two of hair on the top of the cracking skull, and finally shipped them off to BARNUM. With what agony of soul these spirits, of just men made perfect, or perchance of wicked and unhappily located sinners, have watched the exposure of the feeble and scarred

articles; how they have groaned, as old ladies have said "oh, law," and young boys have expressed a desire to furnish them with spit-ball eyes, and how often they have wondered whether they would be able at the day of universal resurrection to find their friends in Egypt at a moment's notice. Poor perturbed spirits; perhaps they had settled all these points and were resting secure in the promise of some inherited ethereal express company, only to be rudely awakened from their ease by the startling cry of "FIRE!" They are gone, and though they may have walked with Moses, or danced with Miriam, or feasted with pharaoh, or supped with the earliest descendants of persecuted Ham, they are no longer preserved but powdered mummies, and the sacred dust of Egypt now mingles with the dirt of Broadway and the cinder of Barnum's. The inhabitants of the oldest country in the world are crushed by the heated falling bricks of the curiosity shop of the earth's latest infant.

Whatever their antecedents or provenance had been, it was no longer significant. The mummies had been lost in the fire, and it did not matter from whence they had come to the museum. The author of the article is sensitive to the double tragedy of these ancient relics—first removed from their original resting place and subject to the curious, and possibly profane, scrutiny of strangers, and then to be utterly destroyed along with their hopes of an afterlife of any sort.

At the same time Barnum was exhibiting mummies among his myriad curiosities, Henry Abbott was conducting a small museum which contained his own personal collection of Egyptian artifacts. Born in 1812, Abbott became a physician in the service of Mohammad Ali, and over the period of twenty years' residence in Cairo amassed a large collection of artifacts for which he had spent the sum of one hundred thousand dollars. This being a tremendous amount of money, he was urged by his friends to smuggle the collection out of Egypt and sell it in New York, as the prohibition on removing antiquities from the country (in effect since 1835) had made Egyptian artifacts desirable to American buyers. By unknown maneuverings and machinations, Abbott and the collection arrived in New York in 1853, but no one was interested in purchasing a collection consisting of over eleven hundred items. Abbott was persuaded to open his own museum, which he did, with some misgivings. The museum was located at various spots along Broadway, including the Stuyvesant Institute.[9]

Abbott issued a catalogue in 1853 of the collection at the institute, it ran for seventy-two pages, and was illustrated with examples from the collections. Sixteen human mummies or parts of mummies are listed throughout the catalogue, including, among others, the mummy of a dwarf; the skull of a female mummy with plaited hair; the leg of a female wanting the foot which had been amputated; a "very handsome mummy, supposed to be a female"; and "a mummy in a very splendid case." Numerous hands and feet, gilded and unadorned are also mentioned, as well as mummy cases and parts thereof. The collection was also noted for its three Apis bull mummies, which were considered quite rare[10] (see ill. p. 68).

Walt Whitman, who had a great interest in Egypt, was a frequent visitor to the collection, and became friendly with Abbott. He wrote in an article for *Life Illustrated*

> You enter the corridor leading to the Egyptian Museum from the gayest and most crowded part of Broadway, and ascending a flight of stairs to the second story, pass into a suite of three large halls, with back windows—halls with great contents—halls dim, dreary, silent, eloquent. Two or three visitors stalk about without noise—for this is not a popular or vulgarly attractive exhibition. Perhaps you even find yourself the solitary gazer amid these wonderful relics.

After a long dissertation upon the history and culture of Egypt, Whitman continued

> Then there are the great mummy cases, some of them with the lids off, and the cerements partly torn away, disclosing the mummy, black with the pitchy substances used in embalming. There are three large mummies of the sacred bull, Apis; this animal had some reference to their worship, which is now lost. There are also mummied cats, lizards, ibises, and crocodiles.[11]

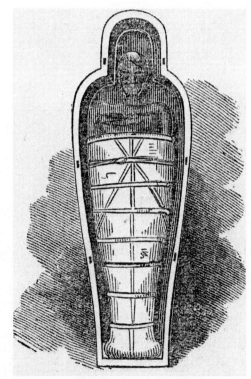

The 9 March 1853 issue of the *Brooklyn Eagle* printed these comments from an unknown author:

> How the strutter up Broadway, as he steps into one of the museums and looks at the Egyptian mummies there on exhibition, laughs at these old fogy representatives of a defunct people who have left but a few of their notions in the shape of pyramids, obelisks, and mummies, to tell the present world that they once lived. Well, have we any specimens of art among us that shall exist as long as there [*sic*] pyramids and mummies, and shall not the dwellers on the earth some thousands of years

A drawing of the mummy in Barnum's American Museum. The bandaging pattern is different from the two shown in the catalogue of the museum and so it is not known if this is an accurate representation or not (*Sights and Wonders in New York* [New York: J.S. Redfield, 1849]. Collection of the New-York Historical Society).

hence not laugh at us and our ephemeral follies, if, indeed, we be not utterly forgotten? The fact is, we are not such philosophers as we pretend to be, and a little calm reflection will convince us that the ancients were not such fools after all.

Another visitor to the collection wrote in the 24 November 1853 issue of *The Independent*:

Here are what are called a handsome mummy and a very handsome mummy, and a magnificent mummy, but I am not savant or amateur enough to see any beauty in a mummy; but the colors of the hieroglyphs are very brilliant, and all the figures are in wonderful preservation. On a piece of a covering of a mummy is the figure of an Israelite, bound and placed on the sole of a sandal as a mark of contempt. What a verification of Bible history; indeed this is the place for the infidel and the skeptic to come and ponder, to believe and tremble!

The museum venture was not much of a success, and soon Abbott was again offering the collection for sale. An article in the 24 October 1853 *New York Daily Times* signed by a group of fifty-four public-spirited men announced:

Egyptian antiquities—To the public. In view of the fact there exists among us no national institutions, such as have long been established in the principal cities of other civilized lands, for the permanent deposit of works of art, antiq-

Barnum's Sixth Saloon, showing a mummy in its coffin in the glass case on the left. The mummy is surrounded by numerous other Natural History specimens (Barnum's American Museum, *Catalogue or Guide Book of Barnum's American Museum, New York* [New York: s.n., before 1865?]. Courtesy American Antiquarian Society).

No. 803.--Case—Egyptian Mummy from Thebes, three thousand years old, enclosed in case of sycamore wood ; Russian soldier's Cap and Helmet from Sebastopol ; Musket and Scotch Claymore, from Balaklava.

No. 804.—Case—Different kinds of Coral, from all parts of the world.

No 805.—Case—Sandwich Islands Cap, or Helmet, and a War-Horn, with enemies' hair attached ; Hand Shields, of New Zealand ; Feejee Fishing-Line ; War Canoe Ornament, of the Sandwich Islands ; Breast-Plate ; Mask, and Stilts, of the natives of Sandwich Islands ; Plane used upon the Congo river, Africa ; Horse-shoe, overgrown in a tree ; Indian Hut, Fish-Line, &c.,

Mummy.

The Mask.

of the Sandwich Islands ; Burned Peas, found over the remains of

Drawing of the mummy and its case in the Sixth Saloon of Barnum's American Museum. It is not known if this is an exact representation. It does not match the drawing of the mummy in the Sixth Saloon (Barnum's American Museum, *Catalogue or Guide Book of Barnum's American Museum, New York* [New York: s.n., before 1865?]. Courtesy American Antiquarian Society).

uity, and natural history—the undersigned ask leave to call the attention of their fellow citizens to the opportunity now afforded to secure for this metropolis, as a nucleus or basis for a museum of arts and sciences, a collection of Egyptian antiquities of great rarity, unrivaled completeness and permanent value. The articles of which it is composed were gradually obtained during a residence of twenty years in Egypt, by the proprietor, Dr. Henry Abbott.... For several of the specimens large prices have been offered, but the proprietor has wisely declined breaking the unity of the entire series; and as it is not expected that any individual will purchase the whole, we earnestly desire to retain it as a public benefit.

They tried to raise by subscription the sixty thousand dollars for which Abbot was asking, in the hopes of placing the collection in the Cooper Institute. However, only twenty-six thousand dollars was raised and there the attempt languished until 1859 when the New-York Historical Society became interested. By dint of vigorous fund raising, including the distribution of circulars and subscription lists, and the arrangement for a series of lectures on ancient Egypt, all but five thousand dollars of the remaining thirty-four thousand of the original asking price had been raised and paid over to Dr. Abbott when he died in 1859. The remaining sum was soon paid to his executors, and on 1 December 1860, the greatest Egyptian collection in America was purchased by the Society, and was on view by 2 April 1861. It remained there for a number of years, when it was lent to, and finally transferred to the permanent ownership of the Brooklyn Museum.[12]

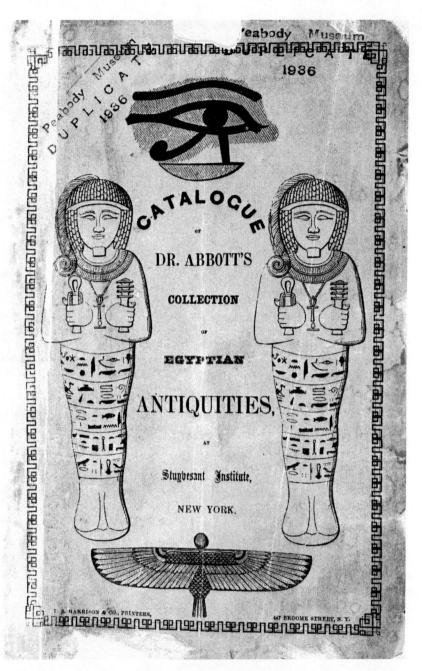

Cover of the catalogue to the Abbott Collection of Egyptian curiosities. The collection included several mummies and numerous parts of mummies, including hands, feet and heads (Abbott Henry, *Catalogue of a Collection of Egyptian Antiquities the Property of Henry Abbott, M.D. Now Exhibiting at the Stuyvesant Institute* [New York: J.W. Watson, 1854]. Courtesy American Antiquarian Society).

Museum displays of mummies in other parts of the country were not all of such high a caliber as was the Abbott collection. The 25 December 1847 issue of *Friends' Review* described the mummy at the Philadelphia Academy of Natural Sciences as:

> The body of a priest who died several hundred years before Christ. The form of the body is very perfect, and a string of beads around the neck is almost complete, showing their form and colour; the body is wrapped in its original shroud of the deceased.... That the poor frail tenement, after having been interred, and perhaps entirely forgotten for ages, should thus be again introduced upon the earth, in something of its original form and appearance, carries the mind back to the time when it, like ourselves, existed a created being; and what a tide of associate ideas succeed! The pages of history, both sacred and profane; are open to our view; numerous incidents which then occurred, are remembered, with delight, and although the projecting bones, the shriveled skin, and hardened and contracted flesh, may not be a most agreeable object to look upon, yet it may not prove an unprofitable one.

In 1852 the Academy of Natural Sciences of Philadelphia displayed its collection of four human mummies (three Peruvian; one Egyptian in its original sarcophagus, which had been presented by John L. Hodge in June 1846), a mummified calf, two hawk, six ibis and thirty-two serpent mummies, all the gift of George Gliddon, "in a closet, opening on the passage to the stairs, at the south-east extremity of the principal hall."[13] A mummified child from Thebes, the gift of J.H. Slack, was added sometime before 1858, for it appears in the catalogue published in the 1858 proceedings of the academy, as do two mummies "contents unknown" also from Thebes, again a gift of George Gliddon.[14] The child mummy is probably the same as the one which caused quite a stir (around 1977) when it was discovered in a storage area at the academy. Affectionately known as "Annie," she has been on display there with Petiese, the mummy of the priest, and is now being studied by the Akhmim Mummy Studies Consortium. Another mummy, collected by Charles Huffnagle, was added to the collection in 1885.[15]

According to articles in the *New York Times* of 26 and 28 June 1885 the estate of Dr. Charles Huffnagle, late consul-general to British India, were auctioned off by Henkel & Co.'s Auction House. Among the goods being offered were

> A mummy case containing the remains of the daughter of a high priest of Horas [*sic*], who passed away about 1,400 B.C. or near the time of the Exodus of the Israelites from Egypt. Dr. Huffnagel [*sic*] obtained the mummy in 1847 from the great pyramid at Saccara. The auctioneer vainly tried to obtain a respectable bid for the ancient case. He ran it down as low as $800, and then came to the conclusion that there was no person present to whom a mummy was a crying want.

Before this the mummy had been on exhibition at Col. Joseph H. Wood's Museum and Art Gallery, in 1872, and the Memorial Hall Museum at Fairmount Park in Philadelphia in September 1881; the coffin was offered for exhibition at the Macon Art Exhibition in March 1882 by Huffnagle's brother, George, who had inherited the collection. He noted "the body had returned to dust, with which a few bones, has been removed by us from the casement."[16]

In Washington, D.C., the National Institute, situated in the Patent Office Building, was located in a "large and magnificent hall" with a colonnade and entablature across and under the great arch which admitted light from the dome. Visitors turned right upon entering the room and passed between parallel rows of numbered cabinets. Case 37 held skulls of all sorts from mastodons, birds and mammals. The lower shelf contained porpoise skulls, a large ox horn from Missouri, and human skulls and mummy heads from around the world. In addition were "Egyptian mummies, partly uncovered; one is quite black, the other has rather a brownish appearance; has a full set of teeth, and are double all around."[17]

The mummy with the double set of teeth was one of two which the actor Junius Brutus Booth purchased in 1834 from a traveling mummy show, and which he had presented to John Varden for his museum.[18] (There will be more about these mummies in a subsequent chapter.)

Varden had opened the commercial "Washington Museum of Curiosities" in 1829, but was driven out of business by the free National Institute which started up in 1840. He promptly sold his collection, including the two mummies to this museum and became its assistant curator.[19]

The museum was rearranged sometime prior to 1857 and the mummies were moved to a new location, case 78, in the north side of the West Gallery. This time they did *not* have to share their accommodations.[20]

Otis T. Nason, in an article for the July 1885 *Chatuaquan*, referred to the mummies in the National Museum as "an exceedingly dry company" and mused: "It is hard to tell how they got into such outlandish boxes and mountings. There they stand, nailed and screwed into narrow white boxes, side by side, with mouths open, as if Pompeian convulsions had seized and embalmed them by instantaneous mummification just as the curtain was falling on a grand duet."

Nason referred to "two mummies." The National Museum had the two Varden mummies, but, according to the *Green Bay Advocate* of 2 February 1848, the museum had also received two mummies from the United States Exploring Expedition. The museum catalogues refer to the mummies has having come from Varden, in which case, they were male. It is not known for sure to which mummies Nason was referring, as an article in the *Macon Telegraph and Messenger* of 24 July 1881 refers to the mummies as a male and a female. The National Institute was absorbed into the National Museum of Natural History at the Smithsonian but there are no records indicating that these mummies are now part of that collection, and so are to be considered among the lost.[21]

In 1872 the Museum of Fine Arts in Boston was the recipient of a magnificent collection of Egyptian antiquities from C.G. Way. This collection had been assembled by an Englishman, Sir Robert Hay and purchased by Samuel Way, who left it to his son C. Granville Way, who in turn presented it to the Museum. The collection included four complete sets of mummies and coffins; those of Penu (Pennu), Nes-Ptah, Tabes (Ta-Bes) and Ankhpefor, all of which are still in the collections of the MFA.[22]

In an extract from George Bryant Woods "Woods's Essays, Sketches and Stories," in the May 1873 issue of the *Atlantic Monthly*, the writer describes an early look at the Way collection, which was in temporary storage at the Athenaeum while a new wing was being built at the museum:

> As one enters this chamber, peopled with numerous remains of so distant an antiquity, the effect is quite that which hitherto one could only encounter in visiting museums abroad. Here are ponderous mummy cases of wood, with a pair of hands sculptured on the front, standing upright against the walls between the glass cases filled with smaller relics. Other mummy-cases, made of matting richly figured over with bird and beast and hieroglyphic shapes, lie near, under glass, with the gilding slowly scaling from their faces, in dignified decay.

Appleton's Journal for 13 June 1874 reported the following under the heading "Boston art:"

> Beautiful mummy cases. Two or three of these cases are intact, painted and gilded, as when they were taken from the tombs. To afford an idea of the method of embalming, one or two more of the cases are opened, disclosing the cotton-wool in coarse locks, and in still another case is the revealed figure of the mummy, brown and dry as a herring, but with no more disclosure of the skeleton of the form than there is in life. A curious little hand in one case has been detached from a mummy, delicate and slender, more beautifully modeled than is common, but resembling in its present state the dry hand of a monkey.

In 1895 the museum received another mummy, Nes-Mut-Aat-Neru, from the Egypt Exploration Fund. She, with her nest of coffins, is still on display at the MFA.[23]

Another museum of a different color opened in Chicago in 1886. Charles Frederick Gunther (1837–1920), a candy and confectionary maker who had invented the caramel, built a six-story wholesale candy factory and retail store at 212 South State Street, which incidentally, had a museum upstairs. Visitors were invited to view numerous relics from the Civil War, the "skin of the serpent that tempted Eve in the Garden of Eden" and an Egyptian mummy whose label read "Pharaoh's daughter who discovered Moses in the bulrushes."[24]

Gunther issued a pamphlet with the title "Chicago's Royal Princess of the Ancient Pharaohs" in which he claimed that the Princess was from the cache of royal mummies discovered at Deir-el-Bahri in 1881, but does not tell how he came by this extraordinary treasure. The pamphlet contained an illustration of the outer coffin, a rumination on the wonders of beholding a princess in Chicago, a short dissertation on embalming, H.D. Raunsley's poem "The Mummy of Sesostris," and the inevitable Smith's "Address To a Mummy of Thebes." This wonder of ancient Egypt could be seen *free* at Gunther's new confectionary store[25] (see ill. p. 74).

Eugene Field penned the following tribute to the mummy in the *Chicago Daily Times* (republished in the 21 April 1889 *Rocky Mountain News*):

> To Gunther's Mummy.
>
> I can but ask thee who and what thou art:
> Where thou wert born; will thou reveal the mystery?
> What in life's ancient drama was thy part?
> Hast thou done ought of which we read in history?
> Thou canst not answer. Death gives his embargo
> Even though thy mumminess is in Chicago.
>
> Didst thou see little Moses on the Nile?
> Perchance it was thy sister by the water,
> Or it might be thyself, that gave the smile,
> And made the rescued "son of pharaoh's daughter?"
> But why these questions? We may never know
> The mysteries of three thousand years ago.
>
> For thou wert rich and noble; high and proud;
> The greater would speak to thee with bated breath
> How haughty thy demeanor to the crowd
> That whispered of thy beauty. Yet in death
> We look upon thee to thy mystic rest,
> In this enchanted city of the west.
>
> Say, didst thou hear the angry pharaoh's words
> When he refused to let the Hebrews go?
> Didst thou behold the rigor of his lords
> Who wrought the Israelites such bitter woe?
> Thou art a woman; it might be thy part
> To mollify the hardness of his heart.
>
> Perhaps from dreams of love and visions gay;
> Thou wert aroused by walls on every hand,
> On that dark morn of which we read to-day
> When God's own angel went throughout the land,
> Through every house, through every home he sped,
> Striking the firstborn sons of Egypt dead.
>
> 'Tis not unlikely that thy love might be
> A noble chief in pharaoh's army found;
> One of the host who dared to cross the sea,
> And in its falling, folding waves was drowned.
> Perhaps it broke thy heart, if thou wert dutiful,
> For certainly thou hast been young and beautiful.

What was this land of ours when thou wert dwelling
In pharaoh's palace by the flowing Nile?
Were not the wondrous oracles foretelling
About the land on which the god would smile,
Where kings would be unknown as rulers singly,
But where all men should rule because so kingly?

Yes, I would have thee, princess, if thou wouldst
Tell me of olden days in accents pleasant;
And I would have thee, also, if thou couldst
Give me thy thoughts about the wondrous present:
Say, are those days in which we live and die,
Better and nobler than the days gone by?

Did ever poet sing in flowing rhyme,
Or prophet utter in charactured tone,
Of a strange people in a distant clime,
Speaking a language that was then unknown?
And didst thou, princess, dream that thou wouldst be
In future ages here among the free?

Didst ever dream of this our land afar?
Did some lost art reveal the wondrous west?
And did its future, shining like a star,
Awaken hope in many a troubled breast,
That, chafing in the old and narrow plan,
Aspired to better days for man as man?

Princess, farewell! Thou canst not answer me;
Thy name, thy lineage, are all unknown.
And yet perchance thy soul, redeemed, may be
Who knows, beside a brighter, greater throne
Than that of pharaoh. Nor will thou deplore
Thy resting place in a Chicago store.

Gunther and Field were neither the first nor last to claim kinship of a mummy with Moses, although in this case, there was more than a little temptation and justification to do so, as the Deir-el-Bahri cache had included the mummy of Rameses II, generally regarded at that time as the pharaoh of the Exodus. In 1888 Gunther and Chicago insurance man William Gray purchased the infamous Libby prison, and brought it back to Chicago where it was reassembled and opened in 1889. Gunther moved all of his museum collection to the new locale, which was demolished in 1897.[26] The mummy eventually became part of the Field Museum collection, and is still part of the collection.[27]

The 18 February 1887 *New York Times* informed its readers that the Metropolitan Museum of Art had purchased twenty Egyptian sarcophagi, complete with mummies, ranging from the Eighteenth Dynasty to the Byzantine epoch. They had been obtained by Louis P. di Cesnola, the museum's director, with the help of Gaston Maspero, director-general of the Boulaq Museum of Egypt-

The coffin of the mummy Charles Gunther exhibited in his candy store, and which he billed as "the princess who saved Moses" (Charles Frederick Gunther, *Chicago's Royal Princess of the Ancient Pharaohs* [Chicago: (s.n., 1886?)]. Courtesy Brown University Library).

ian Antiquities, in 1886. The Metropolitan exhibited the mummies in 1888, upon its reopening on the 27th of November of that year. The *New York Evangelist* of 25 October 1888 reported that a preview of the installation revealed:

> The mummies are in the elaborate painted and ornamented cases in which they were resting when discovered in Egypt. A number, from the inscriptions and ornaments found upon them, are undoubtedly all that now remains of some of the proud members of the ancient Egyptian royal families, while others, though not of royal stock, evidently belonged to families high in rank and estate. One of the mummies when found was within three distinct cases or coffins, all of them richly colored and decorated. Another is especially interesting because of some very handsome beadwork found upon it. A great number of variously colored beads have been artistically arranged to represent a mask and a human face. They were so placed that there was much difficulty in removing them from the mummy wrappings without breaking the design, but the delicate operation was finally successfully accomplished.

Ripley Hitchcock, in a piece entitled "New York's Art Museum" which he wrote for the December 1889 issue of *Frank Leslie's Popular Monthly*, described some of the mummies as follows:

> Khousou is only a mummy, but in his day he was evidently a man of wealth and consequence, an Egyptian Vanderbilt or Astor. His present estate will tempt the moralizer. At his death he was embalmed, closely swathed in linen bandages and placed in a case which was put inside of others, and made practically air-tight; yet time has treated Khousou badly. His feet are in ashes, and his face, after three thousand years or so, does him no credit. He rests beneath a painted mask surrounded by representations of hair. The inner caskets usually contain beads, gold ornaments and records of the dead. Khousou's outer casket is the richest of all. It is profusely decorated in colored relief upon a dark green ground. The convex cover grows larger until we reach the arms,

which are represented as carved in low relief. The model of the face is surrounded by the hood-like head-dress. The decoration, done in a composition of plaster and fibre, painted and varnished over, show portraits of the Egyptian divinities, and other strange figures. On the casket of Khousou's neighbor Iunofirte are scenes from the life of the deceased, who is represented as a young and beautiful woman. But, alas! this availed her nothing, for iconoclastic explorers ruthlessly disrobed the mummy and found that Iunofirte was of small stature and great age. Nevertheless something was left of her wealth of fine golden hair, and perhaps the admiration of that was some solace to poor Iunofirte's shade. Even in death she was not safe. The "nothing of the dead save good" was not written for her, and the innocent fictions of her mummy-case were exposed at last.... About them are other ancient Egyptians wrapped in cloths, covered with painted masks and decorated coffin-lids.

An undated article from the *Boston Transcript* was quoted in the 2 November 1892 issue of *The Indiana Progress* and describes the mummy of "Princess" Iunofirte even further:

> She is done up in a remarkable and unusual way, being wrapped in a sort of basket of papyrus reeds outside of the usual linen bandages. The top of her coffin is a carved and painted board, one in low relief, and representing her as she was in life., with white gown and costume complete. Every detail of her person is carefully represented, even to her dainty almond-shaped nails.

Khousou, or Khonsu, as the mummy is known today, is actually a female, and has been on long-term loan to other institutions, including the Peabody Museum of Salem, Massachusetts, and the University of Rochester. The remainder of the mummies are still in the collection of the Metropolitan.[28]

According to the 12 March 1893 *Philadelphia Inquirer,* the Museum at the University of Pennsylvania was informally opened on the 11th, at a tea hosted by Mrs. Cornelius Stevenson, curator of the Egyptian section and Mrs. John Harrison, chairwoman of the Egyptian section. One of the highlights of the new museum was an Egyptian mummy. A drawing in the *Philadelphia Inquirer* of 8 December 1895 shows the collection of the University of Pennsylvania arrayed in a line, standing on their feet (see ill. p. 77).

The larger mummies and cases were purchased from the Egyptian Museum by Mrs. John Harrison, from Brugsch Bey, curator of the Egyptian Museum in Cairo. One of these, Nefer-ii-ne, was discovered at Akhmim. She was loaned to the Reading Public Museum in 1930, and they purchased her in 1949 (see ill. pp. 78–79). The two small mummies may be the ones imported in 1887 by Thomas Lowrey, which were admitted "free of duty," and which were subsequently given to the Gresham School sometime before 1902.[29] The others are still in the collection of the University of Pennsylvania.

Throughout the nineteenth century, the concept of "museum" was a loose one. Some were larger versions of the cabinets of curiosities so popular in previous centuries, wherein were displayed objects of every sort with no sort of systemic or systematic organization. Others were depositories of art and/or natural history. Many of these early museums considered it was part of their mission to educate their visitors. Exhibits were arranged in order to inculcate knowledge, not merely to stimulate the curiosity. Each type had its own particular charm, and some combined elements of both in order to both entertain and instruct. There was always a balance to be struck so that patrons would be enticed to return. Exhibitions had to change for there were few people who would pay over and over again to always see the same things they had seen before. Lectures and special exhibitions filled some of this need, but there was always the fear that too much entertainment would cheapen the institution and turn it into nothing more than an idle amusement rather than an opportunity for edification.

Then there were the pure curiosity shows, the so-called dime museums. They functioned, for the most part, as repositories for human and natural history oddities, alive and dead, which were displayed to satisfy the morbid or prurient curiosity of their visitors. Some, such as the popular (as opposed to medical) "museums of anatomy" which sprung up all over the United States, offered their clientele, almost exclusively male, frank and sometimes prurient glimpses of both male and female bodies. The line was finely drawn sometimes, whereas legitimate medical anatomy museums were intended to serve as repositories of clinical and medical specimens for the edification and use of members of the medical profession (i.e., the Mutter Museum, which actually has two mummy skulls from the Hyrtl skull collection, acquired from Vienna in 1874[30]), many of the popular museums were run by men who claimed to be physicians, and who offered "anatomy" lessons, as well as advice on marital relations and various types of disorders of the male and female reproductive systems.[31]

One of these was the Pacific Museum of Anatomy and Science (for gentlemen only) which opened in San Francisco in 1865. According to an illustrated advertisement in the November 1865 *Puck,*

> This magnificent collection has been culled from the first schools of anatomy in the world, and contains innumerable preparations of every portion of the human frame; also, full length figures which dissect into the most minute proportions. Prominent among them is the life-like "Florentine Venus," which takes into seven hundred pieces. Here may be seen every nerve, artery, muscle and bone of the wonderful creation, "The house we live in." ... The evils resulting from tight lacing are shown, and illustrated by a full-length, truthful, and life-like figure, proving the prejudicial affects frequently following this absurd practice. The Egyptian mummies, five in number, curiously show the customs of by-gone ages.

The mummies were described in the museum's catalogue only as having been "brought from the East by Captain Grant, and presented to Dr. Jordan." There is no attempt to explain them or to discuss embalming, they exist here merely as curiosities.[32] The Pacific Museum (and its mummies) were destroyed in the San Francisco earthquake of 1906[33] (see ill. p. 81).

Another of these "for gentlemen only" museums was the Great European Museum, which was located at 708 Chestnut Street in Philadelphia. According to an advertisement in the 6 May 1894 *Philadelphia Inquirer*, this museum featured "freaks, monstrosities and mysteries of existence," the anatomical Venus, as well as Egyptian mummies.

The 17 July 1876 *Chicago Daily Tribune* offered the following description of the Chatham Street Side Show under the heading "All for ten cents":

> On the northwest corner of Dearborn and Randolph Streets, in a vacant lot, stands a tent, decorated with the most remarkable specimens of the painter's art. The tent itself is not large, but its surroundings, the indices to the contents, are fearful and wonderful. The miraculous creations, in very red paint, are described by the legend below to be the Aztec Children, the last of their race, while close beside them is a figure of a mummy, who, if she walked in ancient Thebes, must have carried a newspaper route.... Beside the snake was a glass case containing a very bad piece of paperwork and labeled "a mummy." It was a fearful fraud.

Although this dime museum was located in a tent, some had more permanent spots, even if were for only a few years. E.M. Worth's museum collection was one of these. The 21 February 1882 Williamsport, Pennsylvania, *Gazette and Bulletin* noted that "an Egyptian infant, a devil fish, and a musty mummy and a few other nice little things" were the chief attractions at Worth's Museum, New York. Worth next shifted west and opened the Great Chicago Museum, which boasted in its 1885 catalogue "The only stripped mummy on the conti-

EGYPTIAN MUMMIES.

A Case in the Sepulchral Hall of the Egyptian Museum of the University of Pennsylvania. These Mummies Range From the XXIIld Dynasty (900 B. C.) to the Ptolemaic Period. The Superb Mummy Case on the Right Was Presented by Mrs. John Harrison, Who Obtained It in Egypt From H. Brugsch Bey. From Earliest Times the Egyptians Mummified Their Dead. The Process Continued to A. D. 500. The Art Reached the Highest Point at Thebes During the XVIIIth and XIXth Dynasties. When Spices and Aromatic Substances Were Used and the Skin of the Bodies so Prepared As to Retain a Slight Color and a Certain Flexibility.

The exhibition of the newly acquired mummies at the University of Pennsylvania museum (*Philadelphia Inquirer*, 12 March 1893. From Early American Newspapers an Archive of Americana Collections, published by Readex [Readex.com], a Division of NewsBank, inc.).

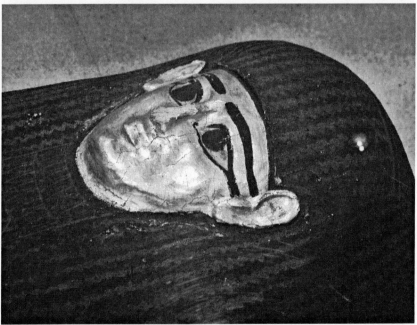

Top: The mummy of Nefer-ii-ne, showing the cartonnage coverings which were laid on over the wrappings. *Bottom:* Face of the coffin of Nefer-ii-ne, a mummy excavated at Akhmim, formerly belonging to the University of Pennsylvania Museum (both photographs by David A. Rawson. Courtesy Reading Public Museum, Reading, Pennsylvania).

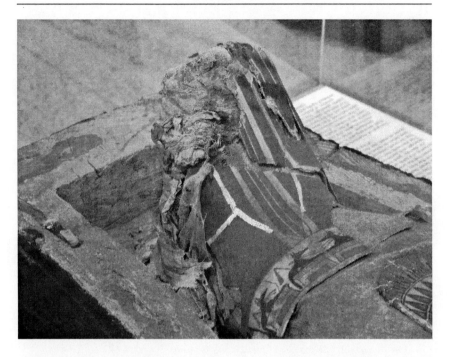

Cartonnage foot cover on the feet of the mummy of Nefer-ii-ne (photograph by David A. Rawson. Courtesy Reading Public Museum, Reading, Pennsylvania).

nent, the wrapping, some hundred yards of linen, being entirely removed. In this specimen the hair, eye-lashes, teeth and nails are remarkably perfect. The scarabee or beetle placed over the left eye of the mummy by the owner contains the name Amon."[34]

According to a note in the 12 August 1888 *Brooklyn Eagle*, Worth moved his collection back to New York in 1888 and opened the Palace Museum.

At some point during this time period he also owned E.M. Worth's American Museum. An undated carte-de-visite from this museum shows a man's hand holding a tiny coffin, in which there is a child mummy, unwrapped, arms folded over its chest. The edges of the coffin are carved in a curious undulating wave pattern. The name of the museum is stamped on the back of the photo, as well as a note "Egyptian child mummy from Thebes, over 3,000 years old." There is also an advertisement for a T. Meehan, manufacturer of looking glass and picture frames, Boston, Mass., which probably was the location of the museum. Another carte-de-visite from the same museum is that of a stripped mummy, tied with bandages across his chest, pelvis and knees, standing upright in a plain wooden box. The adult mummy is no doubt the same as the one described as being at the Great Chicago Museum. The baby mummy's provenance is unknown.[35]

An article in the 5 October 1875 *Atlanta Constitution* announced"Geo. Johnson is here with his mermaid and mummy."

The 18 May 1883 *Atlanta Constitution* carried an obituary of this same George Johnson, a man who had made his living between circus, sideshow and dime museum. His final business venture was the Menagerie on Broad Street, which featured a "stuffed lion, tiger, mermaid, a mummy, etc. which brought him a living." He moved back to Decatur Street after a few years, and was badly beaten up and knocked on the head, which led to his decline and death. His stuffed collection was then scattered to parts unknown.

The *Syracuse Standard* of 31 January 1886 recorded that "Captain Paul Boyton made a failure of his New York 'Ship' and the place, together with the captain's collection of rare and curious things, including armor, rare coins, old-steel engravings, water color paintings, mummies, shells, minerals, and the rubber suit in which the captain made his famous voyages were to be sold at auction."

Boyton took this museum venture failure in stride, and announced he was off to document the entire length of the Amazon River. Another dime museum which moved about was the Boston Museum, which, as far as can ascertained, had no connection with that city at all. It appears to have rented halls or building for its venues.

On 31 March 1889 *The Atlanta Constitution* recorded the following:

> The Boston Museum, located at the corner of Pryor and Decatur Streets, opened yesterday at 2 P.M., and did a land office business up till a late hour last night. Three times during the evening the manager came to the door and announced that no more tickets would be sold until some of the people inside could get out. The collection is large and carefully selected. The collection of mummies is among the largest in the United States, comprising the three classes of Egyptian, Aztec and Peruvian.

The 25 April 1889 *Knoxville Journal* claimed the Boston Dime Museum had been showing there since the previous Saturday and that the price of admission was a "mere bagatelle when the attractions are considered." The 28 April 1889 issue of the same newspaper announced that new attractions would be added for the coming week. The exhibition closed on 4 May 1889, with a special matinee for women and children, according the *Knoxville Journal* for that date.

An unnamed museum in the Bowery, New York City was described in the *Brooklyn Eagle* of 19 October 1890:

> I wandered into one of those places, following on the heels of a fair sized crowd. There was such a magnificent display of pictures in front of the building that quite a number of people were induced to enter. The lithographed signs and photographs outside advertised dancers, women bicycle riders, a swimming contest of women and a dozen or two more features of prominence.... Within the fraud of it all was amazing. There were three rusty chairs,

an alleged Egyptian mummy and a small cigar case in the "museum." Inside the case was a dead rattlesnake. A few cheap photographs of views of Niagara Falls, were at the other end of the room.... Down stairs there was a little stage and some chairs and on the stage a feeble variety performance.

This description probably sums up the appearance of most of these little shows, a lot of ballyhoo on the outside to attract the attention of passersby, and dubious wonders within. The mummy may not have been real; there is no way of telling. An advertisement for the New World's Museum, formerly the Academy of Music, which featured a devil child, alligator boy and an Egyptian mummy appeared in the 21 and 23 February 1890 *Fort Wayne Gazette.* A similar collection of oddities in a museum which had just opened in the Eddy Block was reported by the Warren, Pennsylvania, *Evening Democrat* on 17 August 1893.

Some folks found these entertainments were not always diverting and amusing, as one disgruntled observer wrote in the *Evening Democrat* on the following day (18 August, 1893):

This wouldn't soothe anything. There is music that hath charms to soothe the savage, and there is also music that would drive a savage to distraction. A good example of the latter class is thrown upon the breezes near the corner of Second and Liberty Streets every afternoon and evening where the mummy and illusion man is gathering in the sheckles. If the man who runs that "conostrophy" gets out of town alive it will be solely because his saw-filing apparatus has so enervated people that they lack the energy to indict him.

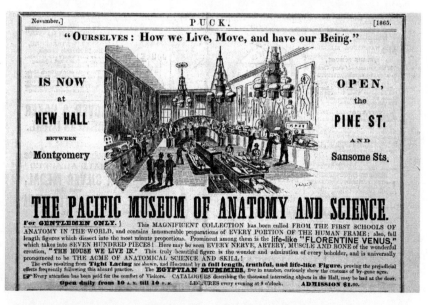

View of the interior of the Pacific Museum of Anatomy (for men only) showing the types of exhibits, including several cases of mummies (*Puck* [San Francisco, Calif.], November 1865. Courtesy American Antiquarian Society).

BARNUM'S ADVANCE COURIER.

This image of a wrapped mummy comes from an advertisement for P.T. Barnum's Circus, 1873 (courtesy American Antiquarian Society).

The most difficult mummy exhibitions to document and trace are those which were shuffled about from place to place, as part of traveling sideshows and circuses. They often left little impact on their viewers, and very little is known about from whence the mummies in them came, how they were exhibited, if they were, in fact, real, and what happened to them after their traveling days were over. Although there is a strong oral tradition of mummies being part of circus sideshows, there is an appalling lack of documentary evidence.

Of course the first name which comes to mind in connection with both mummies and circuses is that of P.T. Barnum. From at least 1851 through 1853 the mummy with the oddly shaped coffin which is pictured in the catalogue of the American Museum was on tour as part of the "Museum of Wonders" attached to his Asiatic Caravan, Museum & Menagerie.[36] In 1870, Barnum wrote to his friend Moses Kimball, proprietor of the Boston Museum and Gallery of Fine Arts: "Have you got an Egyptian mummy in your museum that you will sell? If not, can you tell me where I can buy one?"[37]

An article in the 8 April 1871 *New York Clipper* under the title "Circuses. The Tenting season of '71" which describes the amount of detail which goes into organizing and conducting a circus, lists a "3,000 year old mummy" among the exhibitions, indicating that Barnum managed to obtain one, although not from Kimball's Museum.

An undated broadside (possibly as early as 1871) with the title "P.T. Barnum's Museum, Menagerie, Caravan & Hippodrome" includes a crude drawing of a two swaddled mummies, one large, one small. There is also a vignette of two mummy coffins at the head of the broadside; a small one with striped headdress and horizontal bands of decoration, its hands apparently crossed on its breast, and a larger coffin, which appears to be a garment wrapped about the body, with the hands angled, and containing a single vertical line of decoration.[38] The drawing of the two mummies is repeated in an advertisement for the circus in the *Prairie City Index* of 6 September 1872. One is possibly the mummy of a child, it is hard to tell. And it is not known if either of these mummies is the same as the ones depicted on the 1871 broadside (see ill. pp. 84–85).

Mummies (plural) are again mentioned by the 6 September 1872 *Prairie City Index* as being part of Barnum's great show:

> With its six separate colossal tents, its one thousand men and horses, one hundred thousand curiosities, a hundred first-class artists ... three trains of forty cars each—in fact with the largest and most attractive combination of startling wonders ever known, will exhibit is Des Moines, on Saturday, Sept. 7th, 1872, giving three entertainments—morning, afternoon and evening. Special trains at reduced fares will run to convey passengers who wish to visit the mammoth exhibition.

P.T. Barnum's Advance Courier for 1873 shows on p. 6 a conglomeration of wonders which attend his circus. Among them is the figure of a mummy, with horizontal bands of wrapping about the chest. Whether or not this is an actual image of the mummy in the show cannot be ascertained, but it is a different image from others Barnum had used in previous advertisements (see ill. p. 82).

The 27 June 1871 *Fort Wayne Daily Sentinel* announced that Warner's Museum, Caravan, Menagerie and Circus would be in that town, and that its attractions included Egyptian mummies. Under the heading "Horrible scene" the *Little Rock Daily Republican* of 16 October 1872 reported on a performing hippopotamus which had run amok through the circus ring and caused an ensuing ruckus amongst the menagerie and sideshow. Many of the caged animals were inopportunely freed, including the big cats, who attacked, killed and devoured some of the sideshow inhabitants while an elephant amused himself by "knocking the stuffing out of the 'Egyptian mummies.'" The hyperbole involved in the gruesome recitation makes the article somewhat suspect as a true source of information about circus or sideshow mummies, but as the evidence garnered to date is so meager, it is presented here for the readers' amusement, if for no other purpose.

On 17 November 1872 the political editor of the Columbus, Georgia *Daily Sun* reported on the unnamed sideshow at the Opelika Fair, where he had spent two days in viewing the sights:

> The Egyptian mummy—"three thousand years old!!!" This was a sight. If Cleopatra were no better favored (and this eyeless, noseless thing may have been the queen that "age could not wither her, nor custom stale her infinite variety,") we would not have any ambition to rival Antony in her affections. "That skull had a tongue in it and could sing once." Did this body cost no more the breedings' but to bring money? To what base uses we may return! A curious, scientific doctor, who was familiar with human bones, but somewhat

skeptical, was present. He quietly opened his knife and proceeded *secundum artum* to dissect the mummy and see if it were a sure enough Egyptian! Artemus [the barker] objected, and at one time we thought there would be a fight or a foot race between the curious age of science and the enraged showman. It was agreed to leave the issue with the brainless skull, but it was silent and still refuses to answer. Even if it would respond, it might be in a language which perished centuries before either Homer and Virgil sang the Greek and Latin.

According to the *Brooklyn Eagle* of 27 September 1873:

In the town of Ilion, a great traveling show once tarried and held forth, greatly to the admiration of the people for miles about, being quite as good as a holiday in the country whenever a circus or anything of the kind makes its advent in town.

Among the many who went to see it was Aunt Tappy Jones, everybody's aunt, by the way. She was greatly delighted with everything, especially the curiosities. These she examined with enlarged eyes until she reached the mummy, and she seemed to be somewhat disappointed when she found it was dead. She dwelt upon this for some time, but finally she exclaimed with a sigh: "Wal, we've all got ter die once," and turned away without observing the smiles of the bystanders.

The *Janesville* (Wisconsin) *Gazette* for 7 November 1874 reported the following convoluted lawsuit tried before the Circuit Court, involving J.H. Tay-

Drawing of the two mummies which accompanied Barnum's Museum, Menagerie, Caravan and Hippodrome. Possibly the mummies of an adult and a child (detail from *P.T. Barnum's Museum, Menagerie, Caravan and Hippodrome* [New York?: P.T. Barnum, between 1871 and 1881?]. Courtesy Connecticut Historical Society).

lor, O. Brooks and A. William Porter over the contents of a traveling show. Taylor claimed ownership based on a transfer to him by Porter. Brooks, however was also a creditor of Porter's, claimed that the property belonged to him and that Porter had not had the right to give it to anyone else. The circumstances were related as follows:

> The property in question was used in the management of a show run by Mr. Porter and a partner of his, and consisted of two wagons, five horses, a fat boy, an Egyptian mummy and numerous monkies. The show enterprise proved a failure, and wholly collapsed in Pontiac, Illinois, by reason of the death of the fat boy and of the Egyptian mummy, as well as the extreme scarcity of the fractional currency.

The case had already been tried in the justice court and was being appealed in the circuit court. A trial was ordered, and court adjourned until the following Monday. The final disposition of the case is not known.

The 29 September 1879 *Wheeling Register* noted that the Parkersburg Fair would have an Egyptian mummy on exhibition but that they "suspect it is a base imitation of the original, being some merchant who refused to advertise."

Mummy jokes were rampant in the latter half of the nineteenth century, and so it is not uncommon to find these little announcements turned into something of a "groaner" on occasion. The 15 September 1886 *Davenport Gazette* reported: "An Egyptian mummy was on exhibition at the State Fair, but as business was dull the owner of the defunct could not pay his bills, con-

Coffins of the two mummies which accompanied Barnum's Museum, Menagerie, Caravan and Hippodrome on its performance circuit. Not known if the depictions are accurate (detail from *P.T. Barnum's Museum, Menagerie, Caravan and Hippodrome* [New York?: P.T. Barnum, between 1871 and 1881?]. Courtesy Connecticut Historical Society).

sequently the landlord levied on his mummyship, and at present a king of three thousand years standings is being held to satisfy a grasping landlord's claim to fame."

The editor of the San Jose *Daily News* saw an opportunity to make a bit of fun, and he changed the article a little on 26 September 1886: "An Egyptian mummy on exhibition at the Iowa State Fair has been seized by a landlord in payment for the owners' board bill and the owner now complains that his exhibit is a dead loss." Although the humor does add a little fillip to the base news, it can make it difficult to judge whether or not there is an actual event being portrayed. A case in point is the following poem from the 5 May 1887 *Dallas Morning News*:

> The circus at Butte.
> Dakota Bell.
>
> We kinder calculated—that's Bill an' Ike an' me
> We'd all got down to Sentinel Butte and hev a sort of spree;
> The day the Greatest Show on Earth were thar in one big tent.
> We judged 'twere something in our line so nattur'ly we went.
>
> Inside we struck a table with a cur'ous sort of creeter.
> An' a sign as said his name were Pharaoh Salt Peter.
> An' that he was a 'Gyptian king as long ergo went hence—
> The show had got the mummy at stupendous expense!
>
> We stood an' sized it up erwhile, when Ike turned 'round and said
> "It 'pears to look erbout to me 'sif this gentleman were dead.
> An' as Im cor'ner I 'low without no further fuss,
> We'd better stop and kinder see what killed the ornery cuss."
>
> Then Bill remarks: "I reckon it'u'd be a good idee."
> An' I chimes in with: "A inquest would just erbout hit me."
> An' then we sot upon the corpse of Pharaoh Salt Peter,
> An' fixed a reg'lar verdick in surprisingly short meter!
>
> "Whereas, the P.S. Peter, being that layin' as dead's a stone,
> Therefore this jury finds he croaked by causes quite unknown."
> We 'lowd that fifty dollars were what the job were worth,
> an' collected from the treas'rer uv the Greatest Show on Earth.

There are numerous variations on the mummy and coroner (or judge) story and so it is difficult to tell if this is just a humorous poem, or if the arrival of the circus in Butte were real, and served merely as an excuse to dredge up the hoary old tale, and set it in verse in an attempt to wring even more silliness out of the vernacular language and doggerel rhyme. Even the pharaoh's name makes the story suspect, but as before, it is included here on the off chance it does document (albeit in an absurd way) a real circus mummy. The Texas State Fair of 1891 included a sideshow with "mummies, skeletons and freaks of nature" as reported in the 19 October *Dallas Morning News*.

The 3 May 1894 *Philadelphia Inquirer* reported on every circus owner's nightmare under the heading "Frightened the Freaks:"

> Fire, freaks and shrieks excited North Broad street yesterday morning, and half the people of that quarter thought the "greatest show on earth" was gone. The blaze licked up the tent of a side show to the circus, the tent covering the freaks belonging to Thomas Derr and managed by George West.
>
> Mr. West was resting peacefully near his six-legged cow, eight-legged horse, pig-faced baby and a mummy when he felt uncomfortably warm blasts of air. He flung the mummy out, drove out the too-many-legged beasts and rescued the nervous pig-faced baby. All the beasts were badly frightened and some were scorched. The fire engines were able only to add to the commotion too late to turn water on the flames that got started from no one knew where and consumed the tent and straw. The showmen restored their tent for $200 and exhibited their freaks yesterday as before. The animals were only singed a little.

The South Carolina State Fair of 1897, as reported in *The State* of 10 November 1897, not only had a plethora of Clemson College–related events and horse racing, but also a midway with numerous attractions, including a photo gallery, a fortune teller, panorama and, of course, a mummy.

Of all the types of fairs and exhibitions which would entice the public to view the exciting and new, or the strange and exotic, none were more calculated to do so than the great "world's fairs" of the nineteenth century.

"From Egypt to the Centennial Exhibition, Philadelphia" proclaimed the headline on a broadside advertising the mummy belonging to Dr. Jabez Lamar Monroe Curry and which was going to be on exhibition in Cook, Son & Jenkins's Work's Ticket Office at the Fair. Curry had obtained the mummy while literally on a "Cook's tour" of Egypt. The mummy and case had been presented years earlier by the Khedive to the Prince of Wales, who in turn had presented it to an American gentleman who had interpreted for him. Curry bought it from this gentlemen and loaned it to Cook's for the exhibition.

The mummy had been removed from its damaged coffin and placed in a glass case. The face and hands were unwrapped, and the top of the cranium was visible, as well as "brown, jagged, half-disintegrated teeth." The body was covered with a black skin, and looked more "like a skeleton that had been dipped in melted pitch and left out to dry." The linen wrappings were coarse, tattered, half rotten and of a dirty yellow color.[39]

In December 1876 a banquet and reception were held for the mummy and Dr. Curry, and the mummy was placed in the new Richmond College Museum. Her name was deciphered in 1897 when James Henry Breasted visited the college and read the hieroglyphics, pronouncing her "Thi-Ameney-Net," daughter of Nesy-Amon and Ru Ru (or Lu Lu).

Richmond College underwent several remodelings and moves, during which time Ti-Ameny-Net spent time in various college departments and offices. Richmond College eventually became University of Richmond and the mummy in still at that institution.[40]

The Chicago World's Fair (or to give its proper name of the World's Columbian Exposition) of 1893 provided a more interesting exhibition of mummies, albeit facsimiles, in the "Cairo Street and Turkish Village." They were wax replicas of some of the mummies found in the Dier-el-Bahri cache in 1881, and included some of the most famous pharaohs. According to Demetrius Moscana, the Egyptologist in charge of the temple exhibition, the display included "Huhor, Pinozeme, Rameses II, and his father Seti I, Thothmes III, and Ahrons." Each was in a coffin which was an exact replica of the original one in which the mummy had been found.[41]

After the fair Isaaq Benyaker exhibited the "street" and the mummies across the United States. They were going to the San Francisco Midwinter Fair, but there is no evidence that they ever arrived there. He was still touring with his exhibition as late as 1898 when the "Streets" were broken up and dispersed to various locales.[42] The whereabouts of these facsimile mummies has not as yet come to light.

P.T. Barnum had offered $100,000 to exhibit at the fair (and other venues afterwards) the actual bodies of Rameses II and his daughter (popularly believed to be the pharaoh of the Exodus and the real princess who rescued Moses from the bulrushes) but his prospectus was declined. And Alexander Tagliaferro, a citizen of Alexandria, had offered the sarcophagus of Cleopatra as well as pulverized bones which he claimed were hers, but as they were not proven to be authentic, they too did not make it to the fair.[43]

One of the continuing issues which bedeviled all the mummy exhibitions right from the first was the questioned authenticity of the objects themselves. For the early exhibitions this was almost always countered with certificates from physicians and other experts, which declared the mummy real and genuine. These were prominently displayed with the mummy and reported in the newspaper articles and included in the brochures.

However, Muhammad Ali's decree of 15 August 1835, which effectively banned the export of Egyptian antiquities for almost 50 years,[44] did produce a scarcity of real mummies, and more and more of the ones in the less "respectable" types of exhibitions became suspect.

Periodically articles appeared in the newspapers, decrying the practice, such as the following from the 27 April 1838 issue of the *Hagerstown Mail*: "Some Yankee it is said, is hoaxing the people of Columbus, Ohio, by exhibiting ready made mummies, formed by burnt cork, and filled with sand to give them weight."

The Milwaukee *Daily Free Democrat* of 1 August 1853 claimed that the mummy attached to the menagerie then visiting in that town had been "manufactured in New York." Other Milwaukee newspapers of the same date indicate this was Barnum's circus and menagerie, and so the mummy on which aspersions were being cast was actually one of less suspicious ones on the circuit.

An article in the New York *Galaxy* dated July 1869 asserted:

> The fabrication of Egyptian mummies is carried on in Paris on a very high scale. One man, alone, has manufactured no less that 800 "relics" of the Ptolemaic era for provincial museums. This outdoes Barnum even in his own line. The export business of counterfeit mummies extends over half the globe, even to Egypt itself, whence they return to Europe with a sort of genuineness. A skull, two fillets of veal; a dog's skin and some linen bands, suffice for all that was mortal of a Cheops, a pharaoh, a Ptolemy, or a Cleopatra. How this takes the romance out of the fine lines by Horace Smith to a mummy:
>
> "And thou hast walked about, how strange a story!
> In Thebes's streets, three thousand years ago."

The 19 April 1884 issue of *Texas Siftings* ran a long article under the heading "Monstrosities to order" in which a manufacturer of fake curiosities, including mermaids, mummies and alligator boys, described his vocation and explained how such items were of interest to the general, inquiring public, and how easy it was to dupe them.

Part of the problem, to be sure, was the general condition of any real mummies in any sort of traveling show at this time period. How many had been roughly tumbled about in boxes packed in wagons or on trains, packed and unpacked with unprecedented frequency, dropped, banged about, exposed to all sorts of dust and dirt and who knows what else along the way? Even the most sturdy specimen was likely to look quite bedraggled and forlorn after all of this, and so there is no doubt that people, when confronted with a dirty pile of old cloth with a bone or two here and there, might have been suspicious—especially if it bore little or no resemblance to the splendid painting on the outside of the tent or building within which it was displayed.

Perhaps the most egregious exhibition of mummies during the latter half of the nineteenth century was the use of them for advertising purposes, having nothing at all to do with ancient Egypt, Bible history or indeed any other rational correlation. On 22 May 1873 the *Boston Daily Advertiser* ran an advertisement which read: "The Egyptian mummy. Barnum can't have it, for Brewster bought it, and you can see it in his front window, 486 Washington Street. Mr. Brewster has also for sale a fine collection of preserved fish, crabs, &c., just brought from Algeria." From Boston city directories, it appears that Mr. Brewster was an importer of fancy goods. It is not clear from this advertisement if Brewster intended to sell the mummy or if he were using it only as an attraction. The provenance and disposition of the mummy are unknown. The firm of Kurtz & Norris inserted a small advertisement in the 16 December *Ans* (Athens, Ohio) *Messenger* of 1880, which exhorted its readers to "Go and see the mummy at loan exhibition, 3.000 years old."

Much later, during the 1890s, another spate of mummies in advertising appeared in locations ranging from Wisconsin to Massachusetts. It is not at all clear if this same mummy is being used over and over, for there exists no image of it and the descriptions are less than enlightening. If it is the same mummy, then some unnamed, enterprising showman certainly got a lot of distance out of, and exposure for, his curiosity. The 3 June 1891 *Sandusky Daily Register* reported: "An Egyptian mummy, 3,000 years old is attracting much attention at the J.L. Hudson Clothing Store. Farmer Hicks, the manager, says it will remain on exhibition only this week and those who wish to see the curiosity should 'call early and avoid the rush.'" The mummy's attraction was short-lived, for on 12 June 1891 the newspaper announced: "A black bear snare drummer has taken the place of the mummy as an attraction in the windows at J.L. Hudson's clothing store."

On 20 October 1892 the *Portsmouth* [Ohio] *Times* informed its readers that "One of the most ghastly advertisements ever sprung on the public is that in the show window of W.L. Reed & Co., purporting to be a genuine Egyptian mummy 3,000 years old." Under a print entitled "Bringing the mummies from the Rameseum" the Race Clothing Manufacturing Co. advertised in the 10 April 1893 *Decatur Daily Republican* the following: "Always wishing to please our many friends and patrons we are able this day to show what few have seen, an Egyptian mummy, over three thousand years old. This curiosity will be on exhibition for a few days only, but we have at all times the largest and best selected stock of clothing and gents' furnishing goods that is on exhibition in the city."

By the following week the mummy (if it is indeed the same one) was in Omaha, in the window of Hayden Brothers, as reported by the 18 April 1893 issue of the *Omaha World Herald* under the headline "Throngs have seen it." The article also included a long extract from *World Herald Encyclopedia* concerning mummies and mummification.

The mummy certainly was peripatetic for on 30 June 1893 *The Marshfield* (Wisconsin) *Times* reported: "The Egyptian mummy in Luemle's show window draws large crowds of spectators. It is genuine."

The Stevens Point Journal of 15 July 1893 informed its readers that "B.H. Kohorn, proprietor of the Banner Clothing Store has lately been receiving a variety of curiosities, which he has placed on exhibition in the windows and interior of his store. This week the attraction has been an Egyptian mummy. It has attracted considerable attention and is a rare curiosity."

Schaul Brothers Clothing Store displayed an Egyptian mummy which was "more interesting than pretty" as reported in the 22 December 1893 *Hornellsville Weekly Tribune*. *The Salem Daily News* dated 10 March 1894 announced that the Golden Eagle Clothing Store in Salem, Ohio, would have an Egyptian mummy in their window "next week." *The Hornellsville Daily Tribune* recorded another mummy show on 4 May 1894, under the title: "A Curiosity. In the Howard Shoe Store on Main Street is a mummy from the World's Fair, exhibited in his front window."

It is hardly likely that this shoe store had one of these fake mummies, as Benyaker was still touring with them until 1898; and so it is difficult to know exactly what mummy it did have. The mummy may have been Native American or Peruvian, both types of which were also exhibited at the Columbian Exposition. Or the store owner may have had the traveling mummy which had already been once to Hornellsville the previous year and wanted to make this one seem different in order to attract visitors.

There was an Egyptian mummy in New York State at the time as evidenced by this advertisement in the 28 May 1894 *Middletown Daily Argus*: "A stranger from the tombs of Egypt. If you have never seen any of those wonderfully preserved bodies of the Egyptian dead, then it is worth a long journey to see the mummy which rests in our window. It is a strange sight, so are the goods in the opposite window, where the descriptive card is placed. Stranger, because of the low prices. Look at both. Isaac Lipfeld." Unfortunately, there is no indication as to the type of business run by Mr. Lipfeld.

From New York State the mummy traveled to Massachusetts, where the *Fitchburg Daily Sentinel* of 27 July 1894 reported: "Ferdinand & Austin have on exhibition at their store an Egyptian mummy more than 3,000 years old. The mummy is valued at $1100 and is owned by a New York party." This is the only information which is given in any of these advertisements about the actual owner of the mummy, although even in this case he is not named.

The mummy moved on, and was quite an attraction in the mill town of Lowell, Massachusetts. *The Lowell Daily Sun* announced on 6 August 1894:

> A valuable curio was placed on exhibition in O'Donnell & Gilbride's window today, immediately upon its arrival in this town.
> It is nothing less that an Egyptian mummy, and the claim is made that it is 3000 years old. It is attracting the attention of everyone who passes, and wrapped in its embalming clothes, it is certainly a queer looking object. The mummy was discovered at Dayrel Bahree, near the plain of Thebes, in Egypt.... The mummy will remain on exhibition during this week only, and will undoubtedly serve to attract thousands of people to O'Donnell & Gilbrides's windows. Next week this enterprising firm proposes to provide another grand attraction, which will also be placed on exhibition in the window on Merrimack Street.

The Lowell Daily Sun of 9 August 1894 states: "A man who has watched the crowd that stops to look at the Egyptian mummy in O'Donnell & Gilbride's window says that on a conservative estimate fully 13,000 people stop to see it each day." On 13 August 1894 a large advertisement ran in *The Lowell Daily Sun* under the headline "The Egyptian mummy transferred."

> By special request of hundreds of our patrons, the exhibition [*sic*]will be continued one week more, positively ending Saturday, July 18th, at 10 P.M.
> Owing to the fact that many people were unable to get close enough to our mammoth show window to view to their entire satisfaction the wonderful curios, and having had many complaints from people who were crowded from

the sidewalk by the tremendous throng that congregated, we concluded to put a special exhibition room on the second floor of our store, wherein the mummy will be exhibited this week, and where the opportunity is sufficient to accommodate at least one thousand persons at one time. We therefore extend a convivial invitation to every person in Middlesex County to visit the exhibition room during this week, and see the Egyptian mummy.

NO ADMISSION FEE CHARGED. NO NECESSITY TO BUY GOODS.

Everyone is welcome to view the curio at their leisure. This week affords the last opportunity to Lowell people to see in their own city the greatest historical curio of the age. O'Donnell & Gilbride. Importers and retailers of dry goods, carpets and furniture.

One has to wonder at how much actual business was brought in by the mummy, although it must have been substantial for the store to keep the mummy another week and put it on special exhibition where even more people could see it.

A rival mummy was exhibiting in Hartford, as reported in *The Hartford Courant* of 8 August 1894. "An ancient curiosity. The Egyptian mummy, 3,000 years old, in Gemmill, Burnham & Co.'s show window is viewed daily by crowds of the curious. It is causing considerable jealousy in the hearts of some women who cannot lace so tightly around the waist. They gaze at Mrs. Mummy, grit their teeth, and then take up a couple of links in their lacing apparatus."

An advertising mummy was still touring as late as 1895—*The Kansas City Star* reported in its 12 April issue for that year "A Lamarr business house sports a $1,100 Egyptian mummy." *The Emporia Daily Gazette* of 23 April 1895 announced:

The Star Clothing Store is exhibiting in their window a quite dead person, in fact that he or she has been dead these 3,000 years. It has been placed in the north window where large crowds view it with interest.

The mummy is supposed to be the body of an Egyptian woman and to be about 3,000 years old and is valued at $1,100. It came by express from the east yesterday and will be on exhibition perhaps ten days. It is a queer looking object, wrapped in the remains of the grave clothes—hard, dry, shriveled and wrinkled. The teeth, the hair and the skin, even the folds of cloth wrapped around her body are remarkably well preserved and speak well for the Egyptian art of embalming....

It is one of the most interesting articles ever exhibited in the city and as an advertising medium cannot be excelled. It will prove profitable to those who study history and show to what lengths wide awake hustling merchants will go for the good of their firm.

One merchant even managed to insinuate a mummy and his clothing store into his run for election in a debating society. *The Herald* of Syracuse, New York, ran a story in its 26 July 1885 issue about Dr. Riley V. Miller, and his aspirations to become the president of the North American Debating Club. According to the newspaper account:

He read a paper that, from the admiration it aroused, makes his election an almost foregone conclusion. The subject of the essay was "Did the Ancient Egyptians Wear Pants?" The essayist showed by abundant historical quotations and by photographs of the pyramids that the ancient Egyptian did not wear pantaloons. He also exhibited an Egyptian mummy, and asked his hearers if they could detect any symptoms of pantaloons on him. Mr. Miller then traced the decadence of the Egyptian power and proved conclusively that it was because they didn't wear the garments so familiar to male Syracuseans, and advised his hearers to purchase pantaloons at once of the latest style and fabric. He carefully avoided making any allusion to his own firm and their stock of ready made clothing, and this touch of diplomacy was regarded as particularly shrewd.

Sadly, there seems to be very little information on the source or disposition of these mummies, nor have any descriptions or pictures been located.

Some mummies served in much nobler (or at least less commercially crass) causes. In 1863 the Rochester, New York Ladies' Hospital Relief Association held a Christmas bazaar to benefit the medical care of wounded soldiers during the Civil War. Among their amusements was a "side show," made up of "various stuffed birds and animals, with a preserved mummy, a live monkey and a black cat." The side show made between sixty and eighty dollars for the association, chiefly owing to George Darling's description of the contents of the side show, including presenting the mummy as "a fine living specimen of a silver gray Whig."[45]

St. Ann's Church exhibited a mummy of unrecorded origin at their charity bazaar as reported by the *Brooklyn Eagle* on10 December 1869. On 26 August 1891 the *Tacoma Daily News* reported that the mummy which had been loaned by Allan C. Mason to the ladies of Mason Chapel had earned $170 towards lifting the debt on the chapel. The Lincoln, Nebraska, *Evening News* for 7 May 1892 contained an article stating that Mr. & Mrs. C.J. Ernst had imported a "number of Egyptian mummies" at great expense, and they were exhibited at their Lincoln, Nebraska home, at a party for twenty-one new members of Grace Lutheran Church. This may be one of the few recorded instances of an American unwrapping party, of the sort more frequently seen in England, although the instance of its being attended by a church group make it much more likely that the mummies were of historical biblical interest.

In 1893 the 5 May issue of the *Dallas Morning News* announced that Frank N. Ford of McKinney, Texas, offered to loan his mummy "who might have been related to Cleopatra" for the celebration of the first steamboat to navigate the Trinity River. The 19 April 1895 issue of *The Daily Northwestern* contained an article about a mummy's hand, used by Mrs. Ramsay to illustrate "Old Mortality" at a "library and tea for young society ladies in Oshkosh." According to the 14 February 1896 issue of the *Bismarck Daily Tribune,* "the mummy of Rameses II, direct from the pyramids of Cheops, and so natural that old-timers will recognize him at a glance," was exhibited at a "sideshow" at the Mother Goose Social, at the Bismarck Atheneum. Although it was most certainly not Rameses II, it may have been an actual mummy or it may have been a fake, made up as a prop.

The 11 December 1898 *Brooklyn Eagle* reported on plans for the Graeco-Roman Festival at the Thirteenth Regiment Armory (to benefit an unnamed charity), which included a series of Oriental (Japanese, Egyptian, Persian and Turkish) rooms, one of which would contain a mummy loaned by Dr. Charles West.

Numerous mummies and mummy parts also served as props and illustrations for Egyptological lectures given by various travelers. One of these was William C. Prime, who showed an entire mummy (sex unknown), plus mummified feet, hands, and the head of a lady with beautifully braided hair and another head covered with cloth resembling silk from Abbot's collection after his 1857 trip to Egypt (chronicled in his travel book *Boat Life in Egypt and Nubia*).[46]

Close on his heels was George W. Samson, who exhibited an unknown number of mummies, as specimens of the art of embalming, during a course of six lectures delivered at First Baptist Church in Washington, D.C., sometime between 1859 and 1870, when he was president of Columbian College.[47] In 1874 Dr. Bogert exhibited the head of a mummy at the semi-annual meeting of the Queens County Medical Society as reported *Brooklyn Eagle* of 9 November 1874. The *Wheeling Daily Register* of 23 April 1878 recorded that F.S. De Hass, lecturer on "Around The World in Seventy-Five Days" exhibited a mummified hand as part of his lecture in Wheeling, West Virginia.

As has been demonstrated in the preceding accounts, mummy exhibitions during the nineteenth century ran the course from the sublime to the ridiculous—from exquisitely mounted displays to tawdry shadows of ballyhoo. But no matter where or how they were shown, their audiences reacted. Some reactions were humorous, inspiring jokes, puns, or other types of witticisms, such as this one which an anonymous "Visitor to the Curiosities" penned in the 14 July 1824 *Baltimore Patriot* after viewing Padihershef:

> I was very much gratified in visiting Mr. Peale's Museum, for the purpose of seeing the mummy. After which I went to see Mr. Taylor's Museum, corner of Camden and Charles Streets, which is not so well known, and was very much pleased with his large collection of natural and artificial curiosities, among which, is the gun of Robinson Crusoe, presented by the late Samuel Cole, Esq. and is thought by some to have been used by one of the Egyptian mummies.

For many people, the mummies invoked thoughts of religious history and were perceived as very tangible links to persons and events mentioned in the Bible. Others connected mummies with historical personages such as Cleopatra and the Ptolemies. This was not discouraged by many showmen; in fact, it enhanced their exhibitions by providing a ready-made context for the viewer.

Others were caught up in the idea that these dessicated bodies were once alive, and that they were maybe not so different in their hopes and fears as people were in the present day and age. The *New York Mirror* published the following on 22 September 1827 under the title "Reflections on the Mummy:"

They have been into the chambers of the dead—they have disinterred an inhabitant of the grave—she is brought to light—a lovely woman of Egypt— she is brought to light, after reposing three thousand years in darkness, but not to life; it is a resurrection before the appointed time—her sleep is not out; her slumbers are not over; the hand of death is yet heavy upon her. Still we feel her to be strange company; she seems to speak, though dumb. What are all those efforts to preserve from decay this mortal frame? Those bands of linen; those gums and spices; those embalming preparations, so artfully devised? They tell us of the dread of annihilation; they speak of strong feelings of the soul, the powerful desire for immortality; and strengthen the belief in a future life, but showing how strongly the God of nature has implanted the desire in our breasts. What more do we learn?—beads—a necklace—aye—it was a female—these were her ornaments! Then the female character has not changed. Woman was vain three thousand years ago. She had finery—trin- kets—beads! That is illiberal. She desired to please. She was lovely, and her friends delighted to see her charms heightened by ornaments. The desire to render one's self agreeable, is it not praiseworthy?—Ha! Ha! Is it laughter! or is it the sound of the trumpet? Hark! Behold—both!—the sound of the trumpet, and the shouts of joy—the gay laugh—the trampling of steeds—the rolling of wheels—give token that from her hundred gates Thebes is sending forth her warriors to battle. See them pass under the window of the fair maiden. She is decorated to bid him farewell, whose footsteps make her heart flutter like a captive bird—she stands ready to wish him honour and victory, and a safe return. He bows his head to the neck of his gallant steed—kisses his hand— dashes the briny drop that steals in his eye—a thousand tumultuous passions throng his breast. She smiles through her tears, and waves her white handker- chief from the window!—where is Thebes, and where her countless multi- tudes? Nothing of all her pride, and power, and greatness, but his poor mummy left! Behold this virgin, now exposed to the vulgar gaze. How would she shrink at the thought! How supreme the folly of attempting to arrest the course of nature! The world and its joys are false—all hopes of mortal immor- tality are false. We are all vanity. "Dust thou art, and unto dust thou shalt return."

Finally, there were those who espoused the sentiments expressed in this article in the 9 October 1891 issue of the *Aberdeen Weekly News*—and which are surely echoed by some people today:

Scientists are beginning to object to the exposure of mummies to the public gaze and to feel that after all these old kings were human beings, and that exposing their bodies, not for scientific reasons, but to satisfy mere curiosity, in even after so many thousand years, is desecration of the dead. It is proposed that after mummies have been photographed, studied, and measured scientifically they shall be wrapped up again, hermetically sealed in leaden coffins, and walled up in one of the chambers of the great pyramids. For pub- lic use casts would do just as well.

4

"The Leg of Pharaoh's Daughter, the One Who Saved Moses"

Egyptian Mummies in the Mormon World

In July of 1835, Joseph Smith, the Mormon prophet and patriarch, obtained some papyrus rolls and some Egyptian mummies from Michael Chandler, an entrepreneur who had been exhibiting the artifacts in Kirtland, Ohio. This simple statement belies the incredibly complex and sometimes incomprehensible story which lies behind it. It is a tale full of adventure, intrigue, theft, murder, at least one riot, body snatching, desecration, mistaken identity, humbug, showmanship, bravado and sheer *chutzpah*. It has all the good elements of a Greek tragedy, with a smidgeon of humor tossed in here and there, along with a cast which would be the envy of any soap opera. It spans three continents, several European countries, the United States and Canada. It began several thousand years ago, and may not be over yet.

The easiest place to begin is with Chandler's own version of the story, which Smith included in the *History of the Church*:

> The records were obtained from one of the catacombs in Egypt, near the place where once stood the renowned city of Thebes, by the celebrated French traveler, Antonio Sebolo [*sic*], in the year 1831. He procured license from Mehemmet Ali, then Viceroy of Egypt, under the protection of Chevalier Drovetti, the French Consul; in the year 1828, and employed 433 men four months and two days (if I understand correctly) Egyptian or Turkish soldiers, at from four to six cents per diem, each man; entered the catacombs June 27th, 1831, and obtained eleven mummies. There were several hundred mummies in the same catacombs, about 100 embalmed after the first order and placed in niches and two or three hundred after the second and third orders and laid upon the floor or bottom of the grand cavity. The last two orders were so decayed that they could not be removed and only eleven of the first, found in the niches. On his way from Alexandria to Paris, he put in at Trieste, and, after ten days illness expired. This was in the year 1832.
>
> Previous to his decease he made a will of the whole to Mr. Michael Chandler, (then in Philadelphia, Pa.) his nephew, whom he supposed to have been in Ireland. Accordingly the whole were sent to Dublin, and Mr. Chandler's friends ordered them sent to New York where they were received at the custom house in the winter or spring of 1833. In April of the same year, Mr. Chandler paid the duties and took possession of his mummies. Up to this time they had not been taken out of the coffins, nor the coffins opened. On opening

the coffins, he discovered that in connection with two of the bodies was something rolled up with the same kind of linen and saturated with the same kind of bitumen, which, when examined, proved to be two rolls of papyrus previously mentioned. Two or three other small pieces of papyrus with astronomical calculations, epitaphs, etc., were found with other of the mummies. When Mr. Chandler discovered that there was something with the mummies, he supposed or hoped that it might be some diamonds or valuable metal and was no little chagrined when he saw his disappointment. He was immediately told, while yet in the custom house that there was no man in the city who could translate his roll; but was referred by the same gentleman, (a stranger) to Mr. Joseph Smith Jr., who, continued he, "possess some kind of power or gifts, by which he had translated similar characters."[1]

Joseph Smith inserted an editorial comment in the ongoing tale.

I was then unknown to Mr. Chandler, neither did he know that such a work as the record of the Nephites had been brought before the public.

From New York he [Chandler] took his collection on to Philadelphia and obtained the certificate of the learned (see Messenger and Advocate, p. 235) and from thence came on to Kirtland, as before related in July. Thus I have given a brief history of the manner in which the writings of the Fathers, Abraham and Joseph have been preserved and how I came into possession of the same—a correct translation of which I shall give in its proper place.[2]

As interesting as this story is, there are some parts of it which do not always hold up under close scrutiny, or historical record.

The first problem occurs with the name of the supposed procurer of the mummies. In Smith's original accounts it is recorded as "Sebolo." This name did not correspond to anyone known to have been excavating in Egypt during the time period. Parley P. Pratt, who published the translations of the papyrus as the *Book of Abraham*, in the *Millennial Star* in 1842, recorded the name as "Lebolo."[3] This appears to be the correct spelling, as there was an Antoine (or Antonio) Lebolo working in Egypt in the early decades of the nineteenth century.

Antonio Lebolo was born in Castellamonte, Piedmonte, 22 January 1781.[4] By 1817 Lebolo was in Egypt and working for Bernardo Drovetti. He worked for Drovetti for several years, probably through 1821 or 1822.[5] During the 1820s he often served as Drovetti's host to visiting dignitaries. At the time, Lebolo was living in a small cave above Gurnah, not far from the Rameseum, where he had carved "Lebolo 1820" on a large pillar on the east side of the temple.[6]

By 1821 Lebolo was no longer excavating, and was instead engaged in buying and selling artifacts and exotic animals in Cairo and Alexandria.[7] Ernst August Burghart bought a collection from him in 1821 which went to the Kunsthistorisches Museum in Vienna. Among other items the collection included artifacts from "three mummies in double enclosed coffins." It was probably also at this time Lebolo sold what is called "The Soter collection" to several museums in Europe (including the British Museum, the Bibliothèque Nationale, the Louvre, the Berlin Museum, and other collections in Turin,

Leipzig, Florence, Leyden, and Cairo). This collection of late Greco-Egyptian pieces was unearthed by Lebolo's men in Thebes, and was named after the family who had originally owned the objects. The artifacts, including twelve or thirteen mummies, were welcomed by Western scholars, who could read their Greek inscriptions.[8] Decipherment of the hieroglyphs would not be accomplished until Champollion's work in 1822 and 1824.[9] There is no complete count of how many mummies Lebolo dug up or paid others to dig up for him, nor are there any records showing how and when he disposed of them.

In 1822 Lebolo left for Europe, and his name appears in the Trieste newspaper *Dell' Osservatore Triestano* dated 12 October 1822, in the column listing recent arrivals and departures.[10] From 1822 through 1825 Lebolo was doing business between Egypt and Europe. In 1823 Lebolo traveled between Venice and Trieste with Bernardino Drovetti, the consul-general's nephew.[11] Lebolo was back in Cairo in 1825, but returned to Castellamonte in late 1825 or early 1826, where he led a fairly flamboyant lifestyle, and worked in the grocery and real estate business. He also lent out large amounts of money.[12]

There is no evidential support for Chandler's claims that Lebolo had obtained the excavating *firman* in 1828 and discovered the mummies in 1830.

On 17 November 1829, Antonio Lebolo drew up a will in Castellamonte, Piedmont.[13] He died in Castellamonte (not Trieste, as stated by Chandler) several month later, either on the 18th or 19th of February (he died overnight), 1830, aged forty-nine.[14] There was no mention of mummies in his will, nor of any Irish nephew named Michael Chandler. If it had not been for the listing of a picture of Drovetti in the contents of the estate, it could have been argued that this was not the correct man.[15] However, a legal paper in the archives at Turin, in which Giovanni Metua, the guardian of Lebolo's minor children, turned over a special power of attorney to Pietro Lebolo (the eldest son, who had been separately provided for in the original will), states that Metua had given eleven mummies, originally belonging to Antoine Lebolo, to Albano Oblassa in order for Oblassa to sell them and liquidate the property for the heirs.[16]

It cannot be discerned exactly when Lebolo brought these eleven mummies from Egypt, for no documents have as yet been located which give this information. Shippers were reticent about the nature of the contents of their goods, and so manifests often contain only generic information, such as the number of boxes or crates without specifying the contents. However the Albano Oblassa Shipping Company, which shipped goods back and forth from Trieste to Egypt (and other places throughout the world), had been in business for several years prior to 1822 and remained in business several years after 1831. As Oblassa was given the charge of selling the mummies, it can be supposed that the mummies were shipped during their tenure. Whether the mummies had been stored in Egypt or in Trieste, or in another hitherto unknown place cannot be ascertained.[17]

In 1833 another document was issued in Turin transferring special power of attorney from Pietro Lebolo to Francesco Bertola, and assigning Bertola the authority to claim the eleven mummies and other antique objects "located in various boxes" belonging to the deceased Antonio Lebolo, who had consigned the boxes to Albano Oblassa of Trieste. Oblassa had sent the mummies and artifacts to New York, to the "house of Mr. M'Led and Quellerspie of Meetland and Kennedy." Bertola was further given authority to sell the mummies and artifacts to whomever he thought would pay the amount the procurator decided, and then make sure the money got back to Lebolo's family and heirs.

Francisco Bertola had left Castellamonte and moved to Philadelphia. His son, Francisco Jr., became authorized to deal with the two New York firms of "Maitland & Kennedy" and "McLeod & Gillespie," who had charge of the eleven mummies and sundry other boxes of Egyptian goods. By the time young Bertola received the go-ahead to follow through on shipping costs, customs duties and other charges relative to the mummies' arrival in New York, Michael Chandler had had the mummies for at least six months.[18] There are no extant records showing that Maitland & Kennedy and/or McLeod & Gillespie ever offered the mummies and artifacts for auction or sale. There are also no records which show for certain when the mummies actually arrived in New York, although they were being displayed in Philadelphia by 3 April 1833. With all of the arrangements which would have to be made concerning customs duties, shipping costs, exhibition and advertising fees, even though it was only a day's sail from New York to Philadelphia, it is doubtful that the mummies arrived any earlier than March, 1833.[19] Chandler does not mention having any artifacts and so it is not known what happened to them. Presumably they were sold, but there is no extant record of the transactions.

No documentation has been found which substantiates Michael Chandler's claim to being the nephew of Antoine Lebolo. Nor is it known how he learned of the mummies or purchased them. He may have had connections with one or another of the shipping firms, but that has not been verified. What is known is that Michael Chandler was born in Ireland around 1797. His daughter Catherine, his fifth child, has been listed in various census reports as being born in Ohio, Pennsylvania or Canada, in 1829; so it is logical to assume Chandler was in the United States around that time. Census records of his remaining seven children show their birthplace as Philadelphia. In any case, Chandler left job and family to go about showing the mummies and papyrus for profit, selling an occasional mummy along the way if he needed ready cash.[20]

Although I will refer to Chandler as being the exhibitor of the mummies, his name does not actually appear in any of the newspaper articles about the collection from Philadelphia, Baltimore, Lancaster, Harrisburg, Pittsburgh or New Orleans, or in any of the advertising for the show until it reaches Hudson, Ohio. It will be assumed then, until evidence surfaces to the contrary, that

Chandler was the exhibitor based on his story that he retrieved the mummies in New York.

An 1844 letter written by Mormon apostate Joseph Coe, who had once been financial assistant to Joseph Smith, and who had loaned the church $800 to help them buy the mummies and papyrus, claimed Chandler was only an agent for a consortium of men in Philadelphia. In fact, Coe claimed that Chandler was the object of a lawsuit by these unnamed men to recover costs from him. (The suits intimated that Chandler had not been a very astute businessman.) The mummies had been valued at $200 or $300 in Philadelphia; Chandler had sold them to the Mormons for $2400. Moreover, his exhibition expenses had exceeded income by about $1550, despite his selling off seven of the mummies along his way West. Chandler's backers obviously felt they had been swindled and were suing to recover damages. This does not square at all with Chandler's assertions that he had received the mummies in Lebolo's will.

Furthermore, from 1 October through 10 October 1853, the prominent Philadelphia maritime merchants William Craig and Winthrop Sargent were plaintiffs in a continuing series of lawsuits against Chandler to the amount of some $6000.[21] Unfortunately the court records do not state the nature of the merchandise or services which had engendered this debt. Craig and Sargent were involved in factoring all sorts of goods and also in leasing oceangoing vessels. Perhaps these two men were part of a consortium which had underwritten Chandler's acquisition of the mummies, and who had hoped to reap large monetary rewards from their exhibition.[22]

A totally different story of Chandler's acquiring the mummies was reported by N.L. Nelson in *The Academic Review* of March 1885. In his account, Nelson says that Chandler had received four mummies, from his uncle, a "certain English Minister Plenipotentiary."[23] There has been no evidence as yet discovered which supports Nelson's statements, and so it is generally accepted that Antonio Lebolo discovered the mummies and that they came into the possession of Chandler either as Lebolo's heir or through Lebolo's heirs and that the mummies numbered eleven, according to the legal records.

The first notice of the mummy exhibition appears in the *Philadelphia U.S. Gazette* for 3 April 1833. The advertisement was repeated fifteen times between then and 23 April 1833:

> The largest collection of Egyptian mummies ever exhibited in this city, is now to be seen at the Masonic Hall, in Chesnut [sic] Street above Seventh.
>   They were found in the vicinity of Thebes, by the celebrated traveler Antonio Lebolo and Chevalier Drovetti, General Consul of France in Egypt.
>   Some writings on papirus [sic] found with the mummies, can also be seen, and will afford, no doubt, much satisfaction to amateurs of antiquities.
>   Admittance 25 cents, children half price. Open from 9 A.M. till 2 P.M., and from 3 P.M. to 6.

The *Philadelphia U.S. Gazette for the Country* of 8 April 1833 and *Atkinson's Saturday Evening Post* of 13 April 1833 exhorted their readers to come to the city and see the marvels: "We must ask attention to the exhibition of mummies at the Masonic Hall. These old folks, who flourished perhaps when Moses and Aaron were little boys, deserve some public attention. The rolls of papyrus, the hieroglyphics, the wrappers and other appliances are all exceedingly interesting."

The *Daily Chronicle* ran a slightly different advertisement on 3 April 1833. "Now exhibiting at the Masonic Hall, Chesnut [*sic*] Street above Seventh, a large collection of Egyptian mummies and other antiquities, found in the vicinity of Thebes, by the celebrated traveler Antonio Lebolo, under the protection of Mahomet Ali, Viceroy of Egypt."

The 9 April 1833 *Philadelphia Daily Intelligencer* reported:

> A collection of nine bodies, said to have been found in the vicinity of Thebes, by the celebrated traveler Antonio Lebolo, and the Chevalier Drovetti, the General Consul of France, is now to be seen at the Masonic Hall, in Chestnut Street, above Seventh. Besides these, several rolls of papyrus, obtained at the same time, are also exhibited. From the appearance of the mummies they must be of considerable antiquity.

None of the previous articles mentions the number of mummies, and only nine mummies are mentioned in this article. The *Saturday Courier* of 20 April 1833 further confuses the issue: "The ten Egyptian mummies now exhibited at the Masonic Hall, have been inspected by several gentlemen competent to judge them; and are pronounced to be genuine specimens of the relics of those who 'walked about in Thebes's streets, three thousand years ago.'"

Either someone could not count or one or more of the mummies were not always on display, or Chandler was selling them off. If there were eleven, ten or only nine, it was in any case, the largest collection of mummies to have been as yet exhibited in America, all at one place, at the same time. Chandler's choice of the Masonic Hall as the venue for his collection was inspired, for some of the Freemason's rituals had strong Egyptian roots.

The 16 April 1833 issue of the *Philadelphia Pennsylvanian* gives the first corroboration that Chandler had opened at least one of the mummies in New York. "The mummies, now exhibiting at the Masonic Hall, are said by competent critics, to be veritable. They are well worth a visit. One of them was, while in New York, stripped of its envelopes, it being supposed that valuable ornaments might be upon it. The search ended in disappointment of course."

According to notices in the *Philadelphia Gazette* from 10 May to 3 June 1833 the exhibition had been moved from the Masonic Hall to the Arcade, located at "No. 9, East Avenue, downstairs, opposite Mr. Kerr's china store." By this time there were probably only nine mummies remaining, as evidenced by the advertisements which appeared in the 20 May 1833 *Philadelphia Daily Chronicle* and the 25 May 1833 *Philadelphia Saturday Courier* for the exhibition:

> Nine mummies, found not long since in the vicinity of Thebes in Egypt, are being exhibited in Philadelphia. The reservoirs of this species of curiosity seem to grow more abundant the more they are drawn upon. Seven years ago, Mr. Peale of the New York Museum gave $1800 for one of these specimens, which may now be obtained for less that a fourth part of the sum. A strange market, indeed, for the proud land of the pyramids to come to? Its mummies would seem to be worth more than its men.

These articles reinforce the idea that there were only nine mummies remaining at this time, and using their calculations, each mummy was worth about $450.00.

At some point during the mummies' stay in Philadelphia, two were purchased by Samuel G. Morton, for his skull collection, and it may be that they were purchased that spring, although they were not dissected until December. The mummies are listed in his catalogue of the collection as:

> 48. Juvenile mummy, female, about eight years of age, from the Theban catacombs. Dissected by me, before the Academy of Natural Sciences, Dec. 10, 1833. S.G.M. [and] 60. Head of a female Egyptian mummy, brought from the catacombs of El Gurna, near Thebes, by the late Antonio Lebolo, of whose heirs I purchased it, together with the entire unwrapped body; the latter I dissected before the Academy of Natural Sciences, on the 10th. And 17th. Of Dec. 1833, in presence of eighty members and others.[24]

Although Morton does not explicitly say in the catalogue that he bought the juvenile female mummy, no. 48, from the same source as no. 60 (the heirs of Antonio Lebolo), it is almost certain the two mummies both came from the same seller, for there was no other source for mummies in the area at that time. Interestingly, Morton does not name Chandler as either the agent or one of the heirs. It just happens that Chandler was the only person at that time and place who had a plethora of mummies; and, as has been demonstrated, he had begun with eleven and now had nine. The math works.

Later on, in a paper delivered in 1846 before the Academy of Natural Sciences which detailed his 1833 dissections, Morton commented: "In the year 1833, I purchased of the heirs of the late Senior Le'Bolo [sic], a dilapidated mummy from Thebes, of which I prepared the skeleton, now preserved in the Anatomical Museum of the University of Pennsylvania."

He goes on to add in a footnote: "I have reason to believe that this cranium which I obtained separate from the rest of the mummy, belonged to another Egyptian skeleton subsequently procured from the same source."[25] Morton's description of the poor condition of the mummy raises the question of how came the relic to be in such a sorry state?

Chandler stated that the coffins had not been opened before they got to New York, and that he had opened them, hoping to find treasure, but found only papyrus rolls, and those on just two of the mummies. Chandler himself reported he had been disappointed when he opened the mummy coffins and found no diamonds or precious metals. His knowledge of ancient Egypt seems to be selective, for he told Smith that the mummies Lebolo found were embalmed according to the first and second orders and that only mummies of the first order had been taken as the others were too damaged to be moved. The orders of embalming had been first described by the Greek historian Herodotus, and he mentioned three "orders."[26]

Chandler had obviously read or learned this from somewhere, but he was not knowledgeable enough to know that the Egyptians didn't make much use of diamonds in their funerary jewelry. Presumably Chandler would have had some sort of "patter" which he used in order to effectively exhibit the mummies. There were any number of books available which Chandler could have read, including Belzoni's accounts of his experiences, Thomas Pettigrew's tome on mummies, or even the records of Napoleon's conquest. John Collins Warren had written articles about several mummies. So there was information available.

Census records have shown that Chandler was an immigrant Irish farmer. So how likely is it that he had access to these types of things, or, more to the point, would have read them? If he did *not* read them, who gave him the information? These readings would have also pointed out the best places for finding jewelry on mummies—most notably in the form of necklaces and bracelets around the throats and wrists, and amulets near the heart and on the abdomen as well as other places. It may be that Chandler was aware (or had been made aware) of this and had searched the bodies, causing damage in the process. From the advertisements it is evident that at least the heads of the mummies had been unwrapped but there is little more to be gleaned about the rest of their wrappings.

None of the advertisements for Chandler's mummies show depictions of the coffins or mummies, as had many of the earlier mummies exhibited in the 1820s and 1830s, and so it is difficult to know if there were any cases or what the mummies themselves looked like. The only drawing of any of the mummies which exists is an engraving of the skull #60 (number 6) on plate X in Morton's *Crania Ægyptiaca*[27] (see ill. p. 106). Morton's collection eventually went to the Academy of Natural Sciences where it remains to this day.

Chandler's possibly sketchy knowledge of mummies and Ancient Egypt was certainly bolstered by the actions of seven medical "experts from Philadelphia" who examined the mummies and pronounced their authenticity. Chandler promptly had a "Certificate of the Learned" printed up into a placard which he placed in the mummy exhibition. The placard was an unsolicited testimonial, and Chandler obviously intended to make the best use of it. It read:

> Having examined with considerable attention and deep interest, a number of mummies from the catacombs, near Thebes, in Egypt, now exhibited in the Arcade, we beg leave to recommend them to be the observation of the curious inquirer on subjects of a period so long elapsed; probably not less than three thousand years ago. The features of some of the mummies are perfect in

expression.—The papyrus, covered with red or black ink, or paint, in excellent preservation, are very interesting. The undersigned, unsolicited by any person connected by interest to this exhibition, have voluntarily set their names here-unto, for the simple purpose of calling the attention of the public to an interesting collection, not sufficiently known in this city.

The "certificate," similar to the ones signed by physicians which accompanied earlier mummy exhibitions, was signed at first by John Reedman Coxe, M.D., Richard Harlan, M.D., J. Pancoast, M.D., William P.C. Barton, M.D., E.F. Rivinus, M.D. and Samuel G. Morgan [sic], M.D. W.E. Horner added a postscript. "I concur in the above sentiments, concerning the collection of mummies in the Philadelphia Arcade, and consider them highly deserving the attention of the curious."[28] There is no Samuel G. Morgan, M.D., listed in Philadelphia city directories for the time; this is most likely a spelling or transcription error for "Morton."

Chandler admitted freely that he did not find the jewels for which he had hoped, but that he had found papyrus rolls in two of the mummy coffins. He could not know if they had any value, for he could not read them. In spite of his claims of being told in New York that Joseph Smith might be able to read the ancient writing, Chandler was not in much of a hurry to seek out the Mormon prophet.

By July of 1833, Chandler and six of the mummies were in Baltimore, at the newly remodeled and re-opened Baltimore Museum.[29] The *Baltimore Gazette and Daily Advertiser* and the *Baltimore American and Commercial Daily Advertiser* carried the following notice by J.E. Walker, manager of the Museum, beginning on 20 July 1833 (and continuing through 16 August):

> The citizens are respectfully informed that the manager has received from the vicinity of Thebes, that celebrated city of ancient Egypt, six strangers, illustrious from their antiquity, count, probably, an existence of at least one thousand years anterior to the advent of our blessed Saviour, and contemporaries; if so, of the first sovereigns of Israel, viz: Saul and David. They are by no means insignificant aspirants to public patronage. In the present day, in a country unknown, and where transatlantic ancestors, at that period wrapt in the gloom of idolatry and paganism, what singular and interesting points of history could they not unfold, connected with those early periods of the world, were the vital spark, so long at rest, permitted to resuscitate their slumbering remains. But surely none could view these truly singular remnants of *Auld Lang Syne*, without being carried retrospectively to those far distant periods of antiquity.

The question of numbers of mummies in the exhibition again rears its ugly head, for two days later, on 22 July 1833, the *Baltimore American and Commercial Daily Advertiser* ran a column copied from the *Philadelphia Daily Chronicle*—written by the pseudonymous Pythagorus:

> I had yesterday, a solemn, silent intercourse with eight or ten foreigners from the vicinity of Thebes. I cannot but hope that curiosity may lead all who can

spare 25 cents to see these fragments of mortality. How far, 3,000 years hence, any remnant of those, who may look upon these Egyptian mummies, may exist to call into notice the curious speculation of the living; it may be well to think of. The pouting lip, the bright and scornful eye, the panting bosom of the present beauty, will probably be more fleeting than the actual remains I now exhort my fellow citizens to contemplate and think upon.

The original ending date for the exhibition at the Baltimore Museum was 14 August, as advised in the *Baltimore Gazette and Daily Advertiser* of 10 August 1833. "The exhibition of the Egyptian mummies will close on Wednesday evening, the 14th instant." For some reason the exhibition was extended two more days and "positively closed" on 16 August 1833 as recorded in the same paper for that date.

From there, the exhibition went to Lancaster, Pennsylvania, where the *Lancaster Journal* for 30 August 1833 informed its readers that the exhibition was at Mr. Rohrer's Hotel, East King Street. By 9 September 1833 they were at the Masonic Hall in Harrisburg, staying through the month. Then off again to Pittsburgh for four weeks during October and November.[30] According to the 25 December 1833 issue of the *Cincinnati Advertiser and Ohio Phoenix,* six Egyptian mummies were at the Western Museum in Cincinnati, the advertisement having been inserted on the 24th.

The *Daily Louisville Public Advertiser* of 10 January 1834 announced: "The public are respectfully informed that six Egyptian mummies have arrived and will be at the Louisville Museum for a few days only. Open for exhibition from 8 o'clock in the morning till 9 at night." The mummies stayed there until at least the 24th and may have stayed a few days longer.[31] The actor Junius Brutus Booth, who was in town at the same time, purchased two of the mummies. He wrote to his father:

> I have just purchased two Egyptian priests of the god Apis (mummies) and hire them for exhibition at the museum, for which I receive 12 dollars per week. Perhaps this is as good an investment as some of the stock in some of the more tottering banks at this juncture. They (the priests) are in good preservation and yet neither eat nor drink; they are direct from Thebes and have only been in the union 4 months.[32]

One of the mummies was notable for having two rows of teeth.[33] Booth probably began exhibiting the mummies as soon as Chandler had left the city. He was still exhibiting them in February as shown in an advertisement in the *Daily Louisville Public Advertiser* for the 17th of that month and continued his exhibition until at least 16 April 1834.[34]

Booth had eventually intended the mummies to be sent as gifts to the Hermitage for General Jackson, but upon being informed that they were very rare items, he was persuaded to give them instead to John Varden, who was collecting specimens for a national museum in Washington. They were subsequently deposited in the museum at the Patent Office.[35] As explained in a

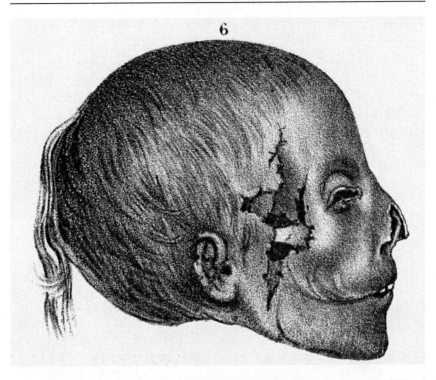

Skull number 6. This is the only known depiction of any of the mummies exhibited by Michael Chandler (Samuel George Morton, *Crania Aegyptica* [Philadelphia: Pennington, 1844]. Courtesy American Antiquarian Society).

previous chapter, the mummies followed the progression of that museum all the way to the Smithsonian.

According to *The Bee* for 28 April 1834, the remaining four mummies were exhibiting at the corner of Chartres and St. Louis Streets in New Orleans. They remained in New Orleans until the first week of May, and their whereabouts from then until 16 February 1835, when they show up with Chandler in Hudson, Ohio, are still a mystery.[36] No newspaper accounts, handbills, or other advertising paraphernalia or ephemera have been located which refer to Chandler and his mummies during this time period.

Counting down from the eleven in New York, Morton bought two in Philadelphia, there were six in Baltimore, and Booth bought two in Kentucky. That leaves seven mummies. Only four are mentioned as being with him in Hudson. Somewhere along the line between Philadelphia and Baltimore, three mummies "went missing." Interestingly enough, in the spring of 1834, Col. David C. McKinstry opened a museum in Detroit with three mummies. These were later destroyed by a fire in 1842.[37] There is no proof that these were some the mummies Chandler had, but as the numbers match up nicely, it is strong circumstantial evidence. Oliver Cowdery would later record in the *Messenger and Advocate* that Chandler reported the seven missing mummies had been purchased for private museums.[38]

The arrival of Chandler and the mummies was noted by David Hudson, the town founder's son, in his diary (entry for February 1835): "At Baldwin's store today, I saw a handbill, giving notice that there was to be an exhibition of mummies at the Mansion House of L. Edgerly." In an entry dated 19 February 1835, Hudson wrote: "Exhibition of mummies—there was an exhibition of four mummies at Mr. Edgerly's tavern on Monday, Tuesday, and Wednesday. I went in to see them yesterday. They were ghastly looking objects, and the sight of them was not desirable."[39] Unfortunately, no copies of the handbill seem to have survived.

The *Cleveland Daily Advertiser* of 26 March 1835 recorded a visit from Chandler and the mummies to that city:

> Egyptian mummies.—Our limited room will not at present permit an extended description of these remarkable posthumous travelers who are now in this village; but we cannot forbear calling upon those of our citizens who have not yet seen these ancient specimens of humanity, to visit them before they are removed which we understand will be in 3 or 4 days. The exhibitor permits as free an examination of them as is consistent with their preservation. Specimens of the ancient method of writing on papyrus, found with the mummies, are also shown by Mr. Chandler, whose intelligent conversation adds much to the interest of the exhibition. The collection is offered for sale by the proprietor.

This is the first notice seen in which the mummies are actually offered for sale. The article also points out that Chandler's patter was "intelligent," hinting that he had knowledge of the customs and manners of the ancient Egyptians.

At Chandler's invitation, a reporter from the *Cleveland Whig* attended the show and detailed in his paper under the line "A Rare Exhibition" on 27 March 1835:

> We accepted the invitation of Mr. Chandler to visit last evening his exhibition, just opened at the Cleveland House, of four Egyptian mummies, purporting to have been obtained from Thebes, by the celebrated traveler Lobelo [*sic*]. The announcement of such an exhibition, is very apt to bring with it the suspicion of impositions; as much probably from its rarity in this "back-woods country," as from the state of advancement which has attained in the arts of humbuggery and deception. But we have no hesitation in saying, that a very slight examination of these relics, will convince any one there is no deception about them, and there are in truth before him, the bones and sinews, if not the flesh and blood, of four ancient beings of his own race, whose frames have survived the decay of some two thousand years. The relic forms are of three males and one female—of mature age, and two of them at least, evidently far advanced in life at the period of their deaths. The first sight of them produces sensations by no means pleasant—but those feelings soon give way to others of a different character, and the more you contemplate them the more interested you become. Curiosity immediately becomes excited; a variety of queries passes through the mind—which are by no means solved by contemplation. What

nation were they of? At what age and where did they live? What were their names? Their circumstances? Their occupation? Were they slain in battle—or died they a natural death by the "visitation of God?" What was the leading trait in the character of that old man, whose arms repose in a cross over his breast? Has he not truly what the phrenologists call an "intellectual head" Imagination perhaps is better than science to solve the question. And that female too—the mother of Agamemnon, for aught that appears—her aged head still retains the hair that graced it in youth—The peculiar features that distinguish the sex in our day, are distinctly preserved in this withered form. This train of thought becomes richer as it advances; and the visitor before he is aware of it, will become absorbed in meditation and awe. There will be no mirth in that hall—or if there is, it will be forced and unnatural. An involuntary feeling of solemnity and awe will reign in its stead. We speak from experience.

The exhibitor will relate and illustrate incidents which add much the interest of the exhibition. There was found deposited in the arms of the old man referred to above, a book of ancient form and construction, which, to us, was by far the most interesting part of the exhibition. Its leaves were of bark, in length some 10 or 12 inches and 3 or 4 in width. The ends are somewhat decayed, but at the centre the leaves are in a state of perfect preservation. It is the writing of no ordinary penman, probably of the old man near whose heart it was deposited at the embalming. The characters are the Egyptian hyeroglyphics [sic]; but of what it discourses none can tell. That probably, like the name of the author, and of the figure before you, will never be unfolded. There is also another book, more decayed, and much less neatly written—its character and import involved in like mystery.

There is no concealment about this exhibition, the spectator is allowed to examine as critically as he pleases; and in this respect it is much more satisfactory than any similar exhibition we ever witnessed. We are not apt to speak favorably of the thousand and one performances and exhibitions with which we are annually afflicted—which have a tendency to excite the worst passions of youth, and lead many into habits of profligacy. But that of which we have been speaking, we consider an exception to their usual character, and tendency. Mr. Chandler will remain at the Cleveland House a few days; and visitors to his interesting exhibition are taxed the moderate fee of 25 cents.

This was followed by the ubiquitous "Address to the mummy at Belzoni's exhibition, London" which was featured in most of the earlier mummy exhibitions in the United States. It is interesting to note that Chandler's mummies had by now been unwrapped sufficiently for observers to know the sexes and ages (in opposition to former exhibits who may have had just their heads and one or more hands revealed). Chandler obviously allowed visitors to touch both the papyrus rolls and the mummies, which no doubt contributed to their general disrepair. None of the advertisements in any of the cities has mentioned coffins or sarcophagi, and so it is not possible to say if the items still existed and what form they took. By this time, the mummies were, for all intents and purposes, close to being naked.

Another description of the four remaining mummies in the Chandler collection was printed in the *Painesville Telegraph* for 27 March 1835:

Mr. Editor,—the history of the ancients is replete with grandeur & curiosity, and who is there so callous, as not to be excited with sufficient curiosity to traverse with interest, all the dark labyrinths of pagan lore and long gone by usages. History, indeed, calls to mind spirits which have long since been traversing the golden works of the celestial world; but how much more are we reared to them, when we can commingle with bodies spiritless, who traversed this earth, thousands of years ago, as we now do, possessing passions and wants, ambition, avarice, and superstition like ourselves. Could we but look forward beyond the dark curtain of time and see the mighty changes, which will transpire for thousands of years to come, we should be lost in amazement. The past is wonderful although very incomplete; yet we are daily obtaining new light from the researches of scientific antiquarians. The discoveries which have been hidden from the world about 1800 years are truly interesting. The habits, manners, and customs of those once inhabited cities are plainly inferred from the appearance of charred dwellings and other edifices for public purposes—their amphitheaters and temples of Isis, holy utensils and baths &c. &c.

But the most interesting of all antique subjects is the opening of the catacombs of Egypt where human bodies are found in a complete state of preservation or nearly so. How, or by what agency those bodies were preserved, or for what object is wholly an enigma. Many have conjectured that the doctrine of the resurrection was embodied in the Egyptian religious faith, and others again suppose that the practice of embalming their dead originated in their abhorrence to decay—but all is speculation. Curiosity has frequently prompted us to visit and critically examine mummies which were found in the catacombs near Thebes, and to realize that I was viewing one of my own species who had lived like myself and been a member of a community three or four thousand years ago, produced a sensation like that of associating with people from another world.

I received a short description from a friend in Cleveland of four mummies that are now exhibiting in that place which may not be uninteresting to some of your readers. A. Gardner.

There followed a letter in the form of a newspaper article:

Dear sir: I send you a description of four mummies, now exhibiting in this place [i.e., Cleveland]. They were found in June, 1832—three miles from Thebes, 236 feet deep in a catacomb or vault 94 by 18 feet in the clear. Some stones described by the finder 32 ft. long, 8 high and 5 feet wide, evidently belonging to Mount Leyben, to which there are strong indications of a railroad. The stones were put together with a cement and exhibited superior workmanship.

Some of the bodies stood in niches of the wall; a row of bodies, however, laid on the bottom 8 feet deep (reversed,) more or less decayed. This statement of the owner is accompanied by good authority.

No. 1—4 feet 11 inches, female—supposed age 60; arms extended, hands side by side in front; the head indicating motherly goodness. There was found with this person a roll or book, having a little resemblance to birch bark; language unknown. Some linguists however say they can decipher 13–36, in what they term an epitaph; ink black and red, many female figures.

No. 2—Height 5 ft 1 1–2 inch; female, suppose age 40. Arms suspended by the side; hands brought into contact, head damaged by accident; found with roll as no. 1, filled with hieroglyphics, rudely executed.

No. 3—Heighth [sic] 4 ft 4 1–2—male, very old, say 80; arms crossing on the breast, each hand on its opposite shoulder; had a roll of writing as no. 1 & 2; superior head, it will compare in the regions of the sentiments with any in our land; passions mild.

No. 4—Height 4 ft 9, female. I am inclined to put her age at about 20 or 25; others call her an old woman; arms extended, hands by her side; auburn hair; short as girls at present in their new fashion. Found with her a braid of hair, three strans [sic] of the color of that on her head and 18 inches long. The head approximates to the form of the orang outang. The occipated and bazillar regions very large; the head indicating a person of the lowest grade of human beings. Slander, fight, and devotion to the passions were undoubtedly peculiar traits in her character. They were enveloped in linnen [sic] saturated with gum, the qualities of which are not well understood. A thousand yards are supposed to be used on each body; 186 thicknesses have been counted on one of them. They are covered so as to preserve the exact form of the body and limbs. No. 3 and 4; the envelope is mostly stripped off; on 1 and 2 it is some broken. 1, fine linnen [sic]; no 2, coarse; no. 3, very coarse; no. 4, very fine. The bodies evidently were reduced before winding. The man, no. 3, whose cerebral organization indicates a mind able to guide the destinies of a nation, is enveloped in the poorest and coarsest linnen [sic], while the woman, no. 4, whose head indicates a disposition which may well be represented as the demon of society, was in the most careful manner enveloped in the finest linnen [sic] and with a much greater proportion of gum. Is not this circumstance an intimation to us that rank was not according to merit—that superiority in station did not follow from superiority of mind, but from extraneous circumstances.

It is interesting to observe in these individuals the external indications of disposition which at this day build up and pull down society; that these relics of another and unknown age were once animated with life, and actuated by passions, hopes and fears, as we now are. How pleasing to contemplate that aged man, by rules that will not deceive, in the active exercise of those sentimental powers of the mind from which the hope of immortality springs. In such minds there is light—in such minds a nation will find prosperity, and society an anchor. But how sad to contemplate the history of that young female (no. 4)—revenge and hate indignant frown upon her brow.

The love of property is not indicated on either of their heads as being in any proportion as strong as with us. Did they not hold property in common? And is not this remark applicable to Indians? Farmer.

The confusions multiply. The first account identifies the mummies as three males and one female, all of "mature age," and at least two of them veritable ancients. The second account calls for one male and three females, one very aged, two in middle years, and one obviously younger than the others. This seems to indicate that it was difficult to tell exactly of what sex or age the mummies were.

The reporter says that Chandler's story is "backed by authority," but it does not reveal the nature of that authority. This is the first time the burial spot and the mummies in it have been so graphically described in any of the advertisements for the exhibition. It also intimates that Chandler did have a source of information about the mummies and where they were found and that he used this when he told Smith the story of the mummies. This source has not survived and so it cannot be checked for veracity. As with so much else in this complicated story, it is difficult to isolate what is true from what is probably conjecture or hyperbole. It was very common for mummy entrepreneurs to exaggerate the social status of their mummies in order to inflate the interest factor. Many were described as royal (princes, princesses, kings, etc.) or else as highly placed religious officials. Chandler could have easily made up the account of the dig from unrelated readings as it would be important to tell a good story about these relics of antiquity. It is just as likely that he was told the story about the mummies from whomever had hired him to tour with them. Or he may have been repeating family history, if he were indeed Lebolo's nephew, as he claimed. There is nothing extant which can verify this.

"Farmer" is most evidently a devotee of phrenology, and applies his observations to the mummies' physiognomies and makes certain deductions then about their state in the social hierarchy based on their characters as he perceives them. In the absence of any other discernable distinguishing features, this is probably as good an analysis as any one could make at that time.

Near the beginning of summer, Chandler made his way to Kirtland, Ohio, where Joseph Smith and his band of followers had made their homes. Again, there is confusion in the dates of his arrival. Oliver Cowdery wrote that Chandler had arrived on the last of June or first of July. The *History of the Church* stated that Chandler arrived on 3 July, but Cowdery's date is substantiated by a letter from W.W. Phelps to his wife on 19 and 20 July 1835. Phelps wrote:

> The last of June four Egyptian mummies were brought here, there were two papyrus rolls, besides some other ancient Egyptian writings with them. As no one could translate these writings, they were presented to President Smith. He soon knew what they were, and said they, the "rolls of papyrus," contained the sacred record kept of Joseph in Pharaoh's court in Egypt, and the teachings of Father Abraham. God has so ordered it that the mummies and writings have been brought to the Church.[40]

Chandler registered at the Riggs Hotel and made plans to exhibit his mummies and papyri. He had his "Certificate of the Learned," the document signed by the Philadelphia medical men, and he also had a placard which he placed in the exhibition:

> Egyptian antiquities. These mummies, with seven others, were taken from the catacombs of Egypt, near where the ancient, and we may say, almost unparalleled city of Thebes once stood, by the celebrated French traveler Antonio Lebolo; at a great expense under the protection of the French consul, by consent of Mehemet Ali, the viceroy of Egypt. It is to be noticed that several hundred mummies, differently embalmed were found in the same catacomb, but only the eleven in a state to be removed. The seven have been sold to gentlemen for private museums, and in consequence are kept from the public.— They have been exhibited in Philadelphia and Baltimore, to crowded

audiences; in the latter place, although only engaged for two weeks, the exhibition was prolonged to five weeks, with attraction. Of all the relics of the ancient world that time has left, the mummy is the most interesting. It is a well known fact, recorded in both sacred and profane history that men were embalmed, which science has attracted the learned for ages. All other antiquities are but the work of man, but mummies present us with the men themselves—they are the personages, preserved in human form, for the gaze and attraction of people who are occupying down the stream of time centuries from those—they have certainly been conspicuous actors in those mighty scenes of which the history of Egypt is full. An hundred generations have passed away, and new empires have began [sic] since this flesh was animated— since these eyes were bright, and this tongue was eloquent, and the heart beat within this breast. These strangers illustrious from their antiquity, may have lived in the days of Jacob, or Moses, or David, and of course some thousand years have elapsed since these bodies were animated with the breath of life! History records the fact, that the higher class concealed their knowledge from the lower, in figures and hieroglyphic characters—A few of those, upon papyrus, used by the Egyptians for writing, will be exhibited with the mummies.[41]

Once settled at the hotel, Chandler sent several messages to Smith hoping to arrange a meeting. Smith had other plans for the first meeting time, but eventually he did meet the Mormon prophet, the man to whom he had been directed in New York, almost two years previously, as someone who might be able to translate the language on the rolls of papyri.[42]

When Joseph Smith examined the papyri, he became convinced that he had sacred writings of some of the patriarchs, including Abraham and Joseph. He decided he should purchase the papyrus rolls and offered to do so. But as Orson Pratt reported:

The Prophet Joseph having learned the value of the ancient writings was very anxious to obtain them, and expressed himself willing to purchase them. But Chandler told him he would not sell the writings unless he could sell the mummies, for it would detract from the curiosity of his exhibition. Mr. Smith inquired of him the price, which was a considerable sum, and finally purchased the mummies and the writing, all of which he retained in his possession for many years; and they were seen by all the Church saw proper to visit the house of the Prophet Joseph and also by hundreds of strangers.[43]

The reported cost of the mummies ranged from "about $2000" to $2400. The bill of sale confirms the cost to be the latter. It was a tremendous amount of money, and many of Smith's followers in Kirtland were not wealthy and were already short of cash because of construction of their Temple. There are conflicting stories as to how the money was raised and who raised it. Interestingly enough, the money was not raised solely by the church. Joseph Coe explains in his 1844 letter to Smith:

I have for a long time been anxious to receive some communication from you in relation to my interest in the mummies, etc. but having failed hitherto of learning anything satisfactory on the subject I have not thot [sic] proper to drop you a line as the most ready means of exchanging sentiments on this subject. Permit me to here sketch the history of the purchase etc. in order to bring the subject fresh to your recollection. When the subject of purchasing that concern came up I was somewhat involved and unable to sustain a heaver burthen [*sic*] any great length of time, but having all confidence in the unity of the collection, and being assured by yourself that the burthen [*sic*] would be but temporary; that the profits coming from the work when translated would be more than adequate to the defraying all the expense which might accrue by the purchase. I therefore managed the business in relation to the purchase with the same confidence that I had previously done business which I thought would result in the good of the church. Previous to closing the contract with Chandler, I made arrangements with S. Andrews for to take one third part and your self & Co. one third leaving one third to be borne by myself.[44]

Joseph Coe and Simeon Andrews each raised $800.00, while Joseph Smith raised the remainder with the help of the church members, and other townspeople, for the mummies and the papyrus had an effect on everyone who saw them.[45] One non-church member who saw the mummies in Kirtland observed:

The Mormons have four mummies, and a quantity of records, written on papyrus, in Egyptian Hieroglyphics [*sic*], which were brought from the catacombs near Thebes, in Egypt. They say the mummies were Egyptian, but the records are those of Abraham and Joseph, and contain important information respecting the creation, the fall of man, the deluge, the patriarchs, the book of Mormon, the lost tribe, the gathering, the end of the world, the judgment, &c. &c. This is as near as I can recollect it; if there is an error I hope some of the Mormons will point it out, and I will recall it. These records were torn by being taken from the roll of embalming salve which contained them, and some parts entirely lost but Smith is to translate the whole by divine inspiration, and that which is lost, like Nebuchadnezzar's dream, can be interpreted as well as that which is preserved; and a larger volume than the Bible will be required to contain them.[46]

Smith now had his sacred writings, and he hoped he could devote much time in the coming years to their translation.

The mummies became an attraction unto themselves, and Smith exhibited

The Mormon prophet, Joseph Smith. He bought four mummies from Michael Chandler in order to obtain the papyrus which accompanied them, writings which he was convinced were the words of the patriarchs (*Jos. Smith the Martyr*. Portrait Collection, American Antiquarian Society. Courtesy American Antiquarian Society).

them, as well as the papyri., although they were not always displayed together, and not always at Smith's house. On 25 October 1835, a Mr. Goodrich and his wife saw the mummies at Dr. F.G. Williams' house and viewed the papyrus rolls separately.[47]

Some visitors were in awe and some were not. The *Cleveland Whig* of 31 July 1835 was certainly less than kind. Under the heading "Another humbug" the paper reported:

> We are credibly informed that the Mormons have purchased of Mr. Chandler three of the mummies which he recently exhibited in this village, and that the prophet Joe has ascertained, by examining the papyrus through his spectacles [a reference to the "seer stones" which Smith used to help translate the golden plates], that they are the bodies of Joseph, and King Abimelech and his daughter. With this shallow and contemptible story, Williams [President Frederick G. Williams of the First Presidency] has commenced traveling about the country, and will, no doubt, gull multitudes into a belief of its truth. Surely one half of the world are fools.

The number of mummies is incorrectly reported as being three in this account; the people out West evidently had as much trouble counting as did the Philadelphians. This is also most likely the account which prompted Oliver Cowdery to pen this apologetic which was printed in the *Messenger and Advocate* and later incorporated in the history of Joseph Smith that became the *History of the Church.*

> The public has been excited of late by reports which have been circulated concerning certain Egyptian mummies and ancient records which were purchased by certain gentlemen of Kirtland, last July. It has been said that the purchasers of these antiquities pretend that they have the bodies of Abraham, Abimileck the King of the Philistines, Joseph who was sold into Egypt, etc. etc., for the purposes of attracting the attention of the multitude and gulling the unwary, which is utterly false.
> Who these ancient inhabitants of Egypt were I do not at present say. Abraham was buried on his own possession.... Abimeleck lived in the same country and for ought we know he died there and the children of Israel carried Joseph's bones from Egypt.
> The record of Abraham and Joseph found with the mummies is beautifully written on papyrus with black and a small part of red, ink or paint, in perfect preservation.
> The characters are such as you find on mummies—hieroglyphs, etc., with many characters or letters like the present (though probably not so square) form of the Hebrew without points.[48]

The *Cincinnati Journal and Western Luminary* dated 25 August 1835 records that the mummies went on a short tour after they had been acquired by the Mormons.

> Last summer a man came to Kirtland and brought the Mormons four Egyptian mummies. The exhibition exactly struck their fancy. All the Mormons flocked to see the wonderful sight; and Joseph deciphered some of the hieroglyphics,

and made known in writing the name and character and antiquity of some of the mummies;—this was additional proof of his divine inspiration. The man continued with them a week; and then a command was given them to purchase the whole which they did for $2400. The mummies were soon sent out for exhibition by one of their apostles, but being unsuccessful, he brought them back to Kirtland, and threw them aside. There is reason to believe, that many who come here with high expectations, have met with sore disappointment.

On 17 February 1836, Joseph Coe was given responsibility for the mummies and the papyri. He hired a room at John Johnson's inn, where they might be put on display, and money gained from their exhibition. Coe was admonished to take special care of the manuscripts. By August 1836 the precious documents had been moved to Smith's "translating room," the west room on the top floor in the Kirtland Temple. They were joined some time later by the mummies.[49]

But all was not Paradise in Kirtland, and by January of 1838 many of the former faithful had fallen away, and things were deemed to be so troubled, that on 12 January 1838 Joseph Smith and Sidney Rigdon fled Kirtland and headed for Missouri. The apostates had turned on their former religious leaders with all sorts of persecutions, including devastating lawsuits which stripped the faithful of their properties. The mob swore to take the mummies and the papyri and burn them. They obtained an execution on them for $50.00, but for a while Lucy Mack Smith and others managed to keep the relics safe. However, the enemies of the Church, notably Warren Parish, the former confidential secretary of the Prophet, did eventually gain possession of the treasures.[50]

Eventually the papyrus rolls and the mummies were rescued, and hidden in the house of William Huntington, whose daughter Zina slept at night in her bed, under which were hidden the mummies in their sarcophagi. The Huntingtons were soon driven out of Kirtland, and headed for Missouri., turning the antiquities over to another family. In late 1837, Edwin Wooley, a Mormon convert from Rochester, Ohio, made a trip to Kirtland to meet Smith. He found things in chaos, and Smith gone. He did learn, however, that Smith's father was in New Portage, Ohio, with the Huntingtons. Wooley persuaded the elder Smith to return with him to Rochester, and the Prophet's father did so, but not before hiring a wagon to carry the mummies and the papyri with him.

There is no record of the whereabouts of the mummies for the next year or two. The history of Samuel Wooley, (as claimed in his diary) noted that in 1838 he had helped transport the mummies and papyri to Far West, Missouri. On 24 May 1838, William Swartzell, a disenchanted former church member and author of an anti–Mormon pamphlet, recorded in his diary that he had seen "Joseph Smith's box of mummys [sic]" at Richmond Landing, Missouri. In light of these recollections, it is probable the mummies were as much on the run as were the Mormons themselves.

The fleeing Saints finally found a sanctuary at a spot they named Nauvoo, in Illinois, and commenced to settle there. The papyri eventually found their way to this new town, and Smith hoped once again to have enough time to devote to working on his translations. While in Nauvoo, the mummies were displayed at three different sites. The first was on the second floor of Joseph Smith's log cabin. Elizabeth Clements Kimball described her visit to the mummies: "The mummies were kept in the attic where they wouldn't be destroyed and in those days there weren't any stairways in the houses such as we have now, and in order to get to the attic one had to climb a ladder which was straight up along the wall." She was worried about the ladder but managed to make the climb. The mummies frightened her, but Smith encouraged her to touch them, telling her that if she did, she would never be afraid of the dead.[51]

Another account appeared in an article entitled "A Glance at the Mormons," which was widely disseminated and republished. It appeared in the 16 July 1840 *Boston Courier*, attributed as being "from the *Alexandria Gazette*," no copy of which has been as yet located. The article was republished in Philadelphia on 22 July 1840 in *The North American and Daily Advertiser*, and on 25 July 1840 in *The Friend; a Religious and Literary Journal*. The *Supplement to the Courant* in Hartford, Connecticut, reprinted it on 29 August 1840, and the Illinois *Quincy Whig* did the same on 17 October 1840.

> [Smith] conducted us, as our request, to an upper room, where he drew aside the curtains of a case, and showed us several Egyptian mummies, which we were told that the church had purchased, at his suggestion, some time before, for a large sum of money.
>
> The embalmed body that stands near the center of the case, said he, is one of the pharaohs who sat upon the throne of Egypt; and the female figure by its side was probably one of the daughters.
>
> It may have been the princess Thermutis, I replied, the same that rescued Moses from the waters of the Nile.
>
> It is not improbable, answered the Prophet, but my time has not yet allowed me to fully examine and decide that point.[52]

The identity of the mummies was still a mystery. Someone had identified them as the remains of Abraham and Joseph, or King Abimelech, prompting Oliver Cowdery's apologetic which was mentioned previously. In this report, the author attempts to correlate the female mummy to an Egyptian female in the Bible, in this case, the princess who rescued Moses in the bulrushes. Smith does not either confirm or deny this. He does, however, refer to one of the mummies as a pharaoh. This was probably the male mummy, which had been described as having its arms crossed on its breast and its hands resting on opposite shoulders.

As in Kirtland, there was some question as to how many mummies there were. Catherine Hulet Winget visited Nauvoo in the fall of 1840, in order to attend a conference. She went to Smith's house and recalled that he had three Egyptian mummies in his room.[53]

William I. Appleby visited the Prophet in Nauvoo in June 1841, and wrote:

Viewed four mummies, one male and three females brought from Ancient Thebes in Egypt ... the male mummy was one of the ancient pharaoh's [*sic*] of Egypt, and a priest, as he is embalmed with his tongue extended — representing a speaker. The females were his wife and two daughters, as a part of the writing has been translated, and informs us who they were, and whose writings it is, and when the mummies were embalmed, which is nearly four thousand years ago.[54]

Eudocia Baldwin Marsh wrote a long manuscript account, "When the Mormons Dwelt among Us," and recalled that while visiting the Mansion House, they were told that they could see the mummy exhibition "for a small sum." They were ushered into a room where Smith's mother stood, "a trim looking lady in a black silk gown and gloves." Mrs. Smith then used a long stick or wand to point to the mummies, describing them as "Old King Pharaoh, of old Egypt himself, with his wife and daughter." When asked how she knew this, the Prophet's mother replied that her son had received a revelation from the Lord in regard to the mummies. Another visitor, Jerusha Walker Blanchard, recalled playing with her cousins in Smith's house. Her favorite hiding place was an old wardrobe which contained the mummies, whom she recalled as being "the old Egyptian king, the queen and their daughter."[55] Both of these accounts refer to three mummies, one of them male, the others female.

On 19 February 1843, a girl by the name of Charlotte Haven visited the Smiths, and left this account of another visit to the mummies, who were at that time residing in their second Nauvoo home, the cabin of Lucy Mack Smith, the Prophet's mother:

Madame Smith's residence is a log house very near her son's. She opened the door and received us cordially. She is a motherly kind of woman of about sixty years. She receives a little pittance by exhibiting the mummies to strangers. When we asked to see them, she lit a candle and conducted us up a short stairway to a low, dark room under the roof. On one side were standing half a dozen mummies, to whom she introduced us, King Onitus and his royal household,—one she did not know. Then she took up what seemed to be a club wrapped in a dark cloth, and said "This is the leg of pharaoh's daughter, the one who saved Moses."[56]

Charlotte refers to a half-dozen mummies, but this is probably incorrect. There are no records of the appearance of the coffins, or even that they still existed— if they were mummiform, then they could have looked like more bodies, especially in a dimly lit room.

Another account was included in a letter of LaFayette Knight, 21 December 1843: "I went into his [Joseph Smith's] house and had a comfortable chat with him, and then examined the four mummies one of which his Mother told me was King Onitus, on whose breast was found the writing of Abr[a]ham It being as they say, the astronomy taught by him."[57]

The Pharaoh now has a name, "Onitus," and obviously one of the mummies is in sad shape if Mrs. Smith can disengage her leg in order to show it off. If this mummy were so shabby, perhaps it was not often displayed upright, as the others seem to have been. If it were recumbent in a box, it could be easily overlooked, leading visitors to recall seeing only three mummies. Even Smith's son had trouble remembering how many mummies there were. He recalled that there were two cases of mummies, in a larger case, and that there were five bodies, one much smaller than the others.[58]

Again, one of the female mummies is described as being the princess who saved Moses. There seemed to be a need for people who saw and exhibited the mummies to link them to such Biblical personages if they could. The princess who saved Moses was familiar to almost every person who had owned or read the Bible, and if her body could be displayed, well then, it would be likely to invite more visitors to see it. There was no way to prove it was the body and no way to disprove it, either.

The sex of the mummies seems to have settled on only one male, and the rest female, although it was not uncommon for the genders to be confused. At the time little was understood about Egyptian iconography or art. When the first mummies were exhibited in America, there was constant confusion as to their sex, even if the mummies' heads were unwrapped. The presence of wigs and jewelry seemed to predispose the idea that the bodies were female.

Almost all of the visitors agreed upon one thing—the mummies were not attractive. In his reminiscences Christopher G. Crary wrote, "They were not very pleasing objects to look up—fried skeletons and as black as coal tar. Whether this was from age, the materials for embalming, or were real Negroes, I could not tell."[69] By September 1843 Smith had found himself unable to support all his visitors and company, and so the Mansion House was built as an hotel to house visitors. The mummies were then moved there, readily available to anyone who wished to see them.

Another visitor penned this account of the exhibition, as published in the 16 May 1844 St. Louis *Evening Gazette:*

> On approaching the home of the Prophet one notices a sign above the left side of the door on which the words "Ancient Records—Egyptian Mummies" are painted in large letters. We were mystified as to what this singular announcement might mean, though we had firmly resolved not to be amazed at anything we might behold in Nauvoo and especially in the Prophet's house. During our conversation with the Prophet we mentioned this sign and asked its meaning. Thereupon he rose and led us into a room opposite the public parlor, where several females were variously engaged. Two of them were young and pretty; a third, who was rather elderly, was introduced to us as the Prophet's mother. A single syllable about the "antiquities" was enough to loosen the tongue of the old lady in a flood of words hardly to be expected from one her age and dignity. Obviously this was one of her favorite topics, or perhaps it was the only one on which she had expended time or thought or on which she could express an opinion.

Opening the folding doors of a wardrobe, she showed us four blackened, ghastly looking Egyptian mummies, from which emanated a peculiar odor of balsam that can hardly be as agreeable to the olfactory nerves of a lady as the perfume of the herbs with the help of which the "mortal is made immortal." There they stood, the dry and shriveled hulls of those, who, perhaps four thousand years ago, walked about the sands of Egypt as dwellers in an ancient Nile city. What a flood of associations is called for by these old relics if one thinks for a moment about their origin and history! Century after century has passed: revolution has followed revolution; conquerors and kings, dynasties and kingdoms, succeeded each other, and written their histories in fire and blood, and come to exist—yet here, in the new world, thousands of miles from the spot of their birth and burial, and thousands of years after they saw the light of today, then exchanged the palace for the grave, these human hulls still remain, hardly less mortal than the spirits which once occupied them.

The main features of these mummies were fairly well preserved, even a certain amount of expression remained on their faces—an expression of pain, or at least an expression which is painful to behold. The lips are entirely shriveled, but they were sufficiently parted to expose the teeth, which in two or three of the mummies appeared to be quite sound. The limbs and extremities were dried down to the bone. Fragments of the fine linen in which they had been embalmed stuck to these parts and the heads and breasts of the mummies. On the head of one there even remained a small quantity of fire-red hair. The skulls were small, and would seem shrunken, if that were possible, like other parts of the body. In addition to the mummies that were intact, there were some fragments of others, including a limb of that Pharaoh's daughter who rescued Moses when he had been exposed to the crocodiles in the bulrushes of the Nile. The mummies themselves, we were told with the same assurance, were great monarchs, pharaohs, kings, and queens of Egypt! Two were in perfect condition, but the other two were badly mutilated. The skull of one was fractured and a piece of the chest had been torn from the other.

The mutilations were further described by young Mary Ann Hubbard, who visited in June 1844.

One afternoon it was raining very hard, and your uncle proposed that we should go down to the basement and see some mummies, the notice saying that one of them was that of Pharaoh's daughter. The exhibition was kept by Joe Smith's mother, who received us kindly and explained the history of the long dead laid out for inspection. I did not feel so solemn as one would have expected, for the old woman was all the time committing murder (of the King's English). The principal mummy had lost most of her fingers and toes, as they had been stolen for relics.... When we had seen and heard enough, we prepared to go. We had bought a Mormon Bible and I had thanked Madam Smith for showing the relics, when your uncle unexpectedly inquired the charge, and paid the old lady for her polite attentions. I forget how much he paid, but I was sorry to have wasted my politeness in thanks.[60]

Josiah Quincy, who was to go on to become the mayor of Boston, visited Nauvoo in the spring of 1844, on his own mission to examine and understand Smith and his by now, quite controversial flock of believers. He traveled in the company of Charles Francis Adams, son of John Quincy Adams, and he published the following report:

"And now come with me," said the Prophet, "and I will show you the curiosities." So saying, he led the way to a lower room, where sat a venerable and respectable-looking lady. "This is my mother, gentlemen. The curiosities we shall see belong to her. They were purchased with her own money, at a cost of six thousand dollars," and then, with deep feeling, were added the words, "and that woman was turned out upon the prairie in the dead of night by a mob." There were some pine presses fixed against the wall of the room. These receptacles Smith opened, and disclosed four human bodies, shrunken and black with age. "These are mummies," said the exhibitor. "I want you to look at that little runt of a fellow over there. He was a great man in his day. Why, that was Pharaoh Necho, King of Egypt!"

As Smith ushered his guests out, he told them "Gentlemen, those who see these curiosities generally pay my mother a quarter of a dollar."[61]

There is no record which tells how Smith connected the name "Necho" with any of the mummies. However, Necho II, of the Twenty-sixth Dynasty, reigned 610–595 B.C.E. He is one of the pharaohs to whom a real connection can be made with Biblical history, as his name appears in the Second Book of Kings.[62] He was the pharaoh who opposed King Josiah and conquered Megiddo. He imposed a ruinous tax on Jerusalem, and battled disastrously with Nebuchadnezzar II. He was buried at Sais, near the Delta,[63] which makes him quite firmly *not* one of the mummies, as it is generally agreed that they had come from the Theban Necropolis, which is far up the Nile.

The name Onitus is not immediately recognizable as any of the late ruling pharaohs. Justification for the use of the name comes from an odd manuscript of Smith's, with the title "Valuable Discovery of Hidden Records That Have Been Obtained From the Ancient Burying Place of the Egyptians." It is a thirteen-page booklet, containing Egyptian texts, apparently copied from the papyrus rolls. On one of the pages appear the words "Katumin, princess, daughter of On-i-tas King of Egypt, who began to reign in the year of the world 2962. Katumin was born in the 30th year of the reign of her father, and died when she was 28 years old, which was the year 3020."

Using the date 4000 B.C.E. as the beginning point (the traditional date for the fall of Adam), that gives a date of 1038 B.C.E. for Onitas's reign.[64] That would make him Dynasty 21, which sported two groups of Pharaohs. One was the family of high priests at Thebes, one of whose rulers, Piankh, would later become famous as the priest who oversaw the reburial of many of the great pharaohs in the Deir el-Bahari cache. The other pharaohs ruled from Tanis simultaneously.[65] None of the names of the kings or their family resemble either Onitas or "princess" Katumin. John A. Wilson, professor of Egyptology at the University of Chicago, made some studies of this booklet and other documents, (including one which became known as "Facsimile no. 2"), and despite poor quality reproductions, thought he discerned the names "Sheshonk," and "Amenhotep."[66] There were a number of Pharaohs whose names were Sheshonq, beginning with Sheshonq I, 945–924 B.C.E. and ending with

Sheshonq V, 767–730 B.C.E. (Dynasty XXII and XXIII).[67] The Amenhotep pharaohs were of Dynasty XVIII, which also included the Thuthmoside kings, Hatshepsut, Akhenaten, and Tutankhamun. The tombs of many of these have been located in the Valley of the Kings, or at Amarna and many of the mummies have also been located. It is extremely doubtful that the mummy to whom Joseph Smith referred as the king, was any of these.

Modern research has narrowed the site of Lebolo's digs to the Valley of the Nobles, near Thebes. Acting on the leads given in the various reports of Lebolo's activities, Pit Tomb 33 has been put forward as a logical candidate for the site of his depredations, but there is again, no concrete proof that this was the site. Pit Tomb 32 has also been proposed, and this has the added attraction of having Lebolo's name carved on the ceiling of the tunnel passage.[68] In any case, it is highly unlikely that a pharaoh of Egypt was buried in any of the pit tombs. In the lack of any surviving coffins, or mummy wrappings, the names and identities of the mummies must still remain a mystery.

Joseph Smith died on 27 June 1844, leaving behind his mummies and papyrus. His mother exhibited them for a time, using the money she made to support herself and her remaining son, William. In 1846, William mentioned the mummies in two letters to James J. Strang, who, with some others, had broken from the mainstream Church and were part of a rival group. He was making arrangements to move his aged mother and the mummies and papyrus away from Nauvoo. William had been excommunicated by Brigham Young and the Quorum of Twelve Apostles, and was trying to establish himself with the apostates. Possession of the mummies and scrolls would help his cause.[69]

There is an account which states William displayed the mummies and writings during a lecture series he gave while living near Galesburg. The story also claims that William, having become stranded somewhere along the Illinois River, sold the mummies and papyrus with the understanding he could repurchase them, which he never did. Brigham Young was told on 31 January 1848, "William has got the mummies from Mother Smith and refuses to give them up." This account is very confusing, for they were in Lucy Mack Smith's possession when she died, 14 May 1856. Her daughter and son-in-law, Emma Smith and Lewis C. Bidamon, and Joseph Smith III sold them less than two weeks later.[70]

A bill, dated at Nauvoo City, 25 May 1856, conveys the mummies and the papyrus to Abel Combs:

> This certifies that we have sold to: Mr. A Combs four Egyptian mummies with the records of them. Thes [sic] mummies were obtained from the catacoms [sic] of Egypt sixty feet below the surface of the earth, by the Antiquarian Society of Paris, & forwarded to New York & purchased by the Mormon prophet Joseph Smith at the price of twenty-four hundred dollars in the year eighteen hundred thirty-five they were highly prized by Mr. Smith on account of the importance of the records which were accidentally found enclosed in the breast of one of the mummies. From translations by Mr. Smith of the records

these mummies were found to be the family of Pharo King of Egypt. They
were kept exclusively by Mr. Smith until his death & since by the mother of
Mr. Smith notwithstanding we have had repeated offers to purchase which
have invariably been refused until her death which occurred on the fourteenth
of this month.[71]

Here again is some confusion—neither Chandler nor Lebolo is mentioned, only
"The Antiquarian Society of Paris." Drovetti, Lebolo's employer, was the French
consul-general, but to identify him with the society is really stretching the point.

This bill of sale negates the claims that William Smith (who was certainly
involved with the mummies one way or another) transferred them to Isaac
Sheen (who would become the editor of the *True Latter-Day Saints' Herald*,
an organ of the Reorganized Church of Latter Day Saints) who in turn transferred them to the Chicago Museum.[72] Combs had bought the mummies and
papyrus in May of 1856. By August he had sold two of them to Wyman's St.
Louis Museum which placed the following advertisement in the *Daily Missouri
Democrat* of 2 August 1856.

> A combination of exhibitions! Third story, Wyman's Hall, (opposite the
> courthouse): This establishment is now open for exhibition, under the man-
> agement, and for the benefit of Mr. J.P. Bates, practical naturalist, and con-
> tains FIRST—the finest and most unique collection of birds, quadrupeds,
> reptiles, fish and other illustrations of natural history in the west, and unri-
> valled for its choice and rare specimens, (about 2,000 in number), and the
> style and beauty displayed in their preparation and arrangement.
>
> SECOND—the greatest geological wonder in the world, the cetacean saurian
> ophidian monster, Zeuglodon Macrospondylus, of Muller, discovered by Dr.
> Koch, in Alabama, a complete skeleton 96 feet in length, and set in natural
> position.
>
> THIRD—two mummies from the catacombs of Egypt, which have been
> unrolled, presenting a full view of the records enclosed, and of the bodies,
> which are in a remarkable state of preservation.
>
> FOURTH—Vance's great collection of panoramic views of towns, cities, and
> places of note in California—about 200 in number, and exhibited to thou-
> sands of persons in New York, at a charge of 25 cents.
>
> FIFTH—a fine collection of minerals, fossils, shells, choice paintings and
> curiosities.
>
> Admission fee to the whole 25 cents—and refunded if satisfaction is not
> given. Open every day (Sunday's excepted) from 9 AM, to 6 PM, and on Tues-
> day and Saturday evenings from 7 to 10 P.M. Contributions solicited and care-
> fully preserved. Taxidermal work executed as usual.

The editor of the paper encouraged readers to visit the exhibition in his column of amusement notices: "Lately, we observe a new attraction, consisting
of a pair of mummies from the catacombs of Egypt, which are a great novelty
in these parts, and should be seen by all."

In the 13 May 1857 issue of the *Daily Missouri Democrat* an article appeared
which intimates that there was doubt about the integrity of the exhibition.
"Some of the brethren have had the hardness to deny that these were the patri-

archal manuscripts and relics. But an unanswerable confirmation of the fact has lately occurred; certain plates issued by the elders as facsimiles of the original having fallen into Mr. Wyman's hands, which plates are also facsimiles of the hieroglyphics in the museum."

The brethren mentioned could have been either from the mainstream or the apostate group, it is not known which. But evidently their protestations continued, as about a month later, on 12 June 1857, the paper ran a second notice about the veracity of the identification of the antiquities.

> The Mormon Prophet's mummies—not long since, we stated that the mummies and accompanying Egyptain [sic] manuscripts at the museum were the identical mummies and manuscripts formerly purchased by Smith the Mormon Prophet. They were purchased by the proprietor of the museum from Mr. A. Combs, who bought them at Nauvoo City on the 26th of May, 1856. In a work published by "the saints" is a facsimile of the manuscripts with the information added that they were written by the great Jewish patriarch, Abraham himself. Doubt having still been expressed that they were the prophet's mummies, etc., we now append the certificate with which the sale of them to Mr. Combs was accompanied.

The "certificate of the sale" was an edited and printed copy of the original written document. The financial and travel arrangements which enabled the St. Louis Museum to purchase the artifacts from Combs have not been disclosed. There is the possibility that Combs had brought the mummies via riverboat or a "floating palace" of amusements, as such a thing was advertised in the newspapers two weeks before the Museum announced it had the mummies. An exhibition was held at the steamboat landing on 7, 8 and 9 August 1856, and according to the *Daily Missouri Democrat* of 2 August 1856, was touted as having one hundred thousand relics from Egypt, Greece, Rome, Pompeii and Herculaneum.

The question arises of why only two of the mummies were sold to the museum. It is possible that the price for the four of them was too high. The floating palace of amusements may have bought two of them. Combs may have decided to keep two and sell them elsewhere. Or, it is possible, only two of the mummies were in decent enough shape to sell. The events which had transpired with the Mormons since Smith had bought the mummies were not the most optimum conditions for these ancient relics. They had been moved numerous times, and not in cushioned crates but more likely jostled about in the backs of springless wagons. The mummies had been unrolled in search of treasures, and one had a damaged face and another, or maybe the same one, had a detached leg. They were stored up under the eaves of hot dusty attics, allowed to be handled by visitors and in general subjected to any number of damaging conditions.

The St. Louis Museum was founded in 1843 when Edward Wyman established a school there. He had hired J.P. Bates, who billed himself as a "practical naturalist" to manage the museum. Bates had traveled the world in search of unusual specimens of natural history, most likely preparing the specimens himself for exhibition, for he had advertised his taxidermy trade in museum advertisements.[73] On 3 July 1863 a startling notice appeared in the *Daily Missouri Democrat*: "The St. Louis Museum will positively close on Saturday the 11th inst. And it is being moved to Chicago." The announcement was signed: J.P. Bates manager.

The *Chicago Tribune* of 6 July 1863 was pleased to note: "We make the announcement with pleasure that, through the liberality of two of our public-spirited citizens, the St. Louis Museum has been purchased, and will soon be removed to, and permanently located in, this city. This museum is much the largest in the west, and in several of its features the choicest one in the United States." On 10 August 1863, after what may have been a sneak preview of the museum for the media, the *Chicago Tribune* announced that the museum contained "The two mummies which in the hands of Joseph Smith were made to give a revelation and still bear the original tablets with the cabalistic or Coptic characters thereon."

The museum opened to the public on 17 August 1863. The collection occupied two floors. One of the chief drawing cards was the Zeuglodon skeleton. On the upper floor was an exhibition of fine paintings, and in a hall at the rear a panorama of London was unrolled nightly, for the additional fee of fifteen cents. The museum also boasted sixty-two cases of exhibitions in six different departments. There were thirteen cases of insects, a case of American birds' eggs, four cases each of sea shells and minerals; five cases of miscellaneous objects, twenty-seven busts, fifty-eight assorted specimens not in cases, models of the Parthenon and the United States Capitol, and of course, the mummies.[74]

The museum was located on Randolph Street, between Clark and Dearborn Streets, and was open every day and evening from 8 A.M. to 10 P.M. Admission was twenty five cents.[75] An amusing story about the mummies was printed in the 3 September 1863 *Chicago Times*:

> What an old lady thought about mummies. An old lady at the museum a day or so ago, coming suddenly upon a case containing two Egyptian mummies was extremely horrified at their exhibition without clothing of any kind, and showed symptoms of an intention to hold her nose until assured that, notwithstanding the long interval since their decease, no disagreeable odor was emitted. She was not long in betraying still greater ignorance by remarking to the young girl who accompanied her, "Sairy them critters is of African descent true as preachin, and that accounts for their not being buried like white folks and Christians." "These are mummies, Madame," remarked a gentleman who stood nearby, endeavoring to control his inclination to laugh heartily at the old lady's speech. "Wall," returned she with renewed indignation, "I don't keer whose mummies they be, it's a tarnal shame to have human beings dug up and made a show of, even if they be niggers. But it's just like them poky southerners to beat their colored brothers to death and then stick them in the ground with nary a stitch of clothing on to hide their nakedness."

On 26 October 1863, the *Chicago Times* referred to the artifacts as "mummies, horribly shriveled things."

Joseph H. Wood had started in the mercantile business, but having always been drawn to a study of nature, he opened a museum in Cincinnati in 1849. He built a new building for the museum in 1852, but soon thereafter took his collection of curiosities, both human and otherwise, on a tour of the United States and West Indies. Not satisfied with this, he turned a steamboat into a floating museum, and traveled for two years along the western rivers, before again arranging to take a show on the road, this time to Cuba. From there he and his troupe toured Europe as a combination menagerie and museum. That venture lasted about three years, when he returned to Chicago and the museum business, buying the Chicago museum from Wyman on 25 January 1864. He spent only a few years running the museum, expanding its collections. He then retired to Adrian, Michigan, but soon returned to the museum business in Chicago.[76] Upon his return to the museum business he changed the name of the museum to "Wood's Museum."[77]

The title page of the museum's 1868 catalogue boasted "A complete guide to the Chicago Museum, including a description of the wonderful antediluvian monster, the great zeuglodon, catalogue of birds, quadrupeds, fishes, reptiles and insects; microscopes, stereoscopes, cosmoramas, philosophical instruments, minerals, shells, mummies, models and curiosities. Admittance, twenty-five cents."[78]

The papyri and the mummies were described inside:

> Egyptian mummies. These mummies were obtained in the catacombs of Egypt, sixty feet below the surface of the earth, for the Antiquarian Society of Paris, forwarded to New York, and there purchased, in the year 1835, by Joe Smith, the Mormon Prophet.... The body of one is that of a female, about forty; the other, that of a boy about fourteen. They were kept by the Prophet's mother until his death, when the heirs sold them, and were shortly after purchased for the Museum.
>
> The art of embalming is, in a measure, lost, and its details are not known or practiced as among the ancients. With the poor it was a very simple process, and the principle articles used were salt and asphaltum. The rich spent large sums in embalming the dead, using the most costly spices and perfumes. The practice was not confined to Egypt; several examples have been found in the western states of this country, showing that it was in use to some extent among the aborigines.[79]

At this time, the museum was part and parcel of a theater, which Colonel Wood was also managing. He sold the whole parcel to Mr. Aiken, one of his actors, in October 1867, bought it back in March 1869, resold it to Aiken in October 1869, and the name was changed to Aiken's Museum. It was changed back to Wood's Museum in June 1871 when Wood resumed control.[80]

During that time, many faithful went to Chicago to see the mummies and papyri. There was even an article about the museum in the *Salt Lake City Direc-*

tory and Business Guide for 1869 describing the mummies. Joseph Smith III of the Reorganized Church of Latter Day Saints recalled seeing the mummies in 1871.[81]

On 8 October 1871, "late last night, when we were all in bed, Mrs. O'Leary hung a lantern in the shed" and the cow kicked it over, and the rest is history. The fire broke out at 8:45 P.M. on the west side of Chicago, and jumped the river by midnight. Ninety minutes later, it consumed Wood's Museum. According to a newspaper account the only thing which was left was a silver mounted revolver. Wood supposedly erected a sign which read "Col. Wood's Museum, Standing Room Only"[82] (see ill. pp. 128, 130).

Wood declared he was bankrupt, and left the city for Philadelphia, opening "Col. Wood's Museum Gallery of Fine Arts and Temple of Wonders" at Arch and Ninth Streets, on the premises of the minstrel house of Carncross & Dewey, in 1872.[83] A catalogue from the museum, dated 1872, lists only one mummy, in case XV, described as "Egyptian mummy, taken from a tomb at Sahara [i.e., Sakkara] by Dr. Charles Hufnagle [*sic*], enclosed in an encasement made of a composition, and modeled in form of body, richly ornamented with hieroglyphics."[84]

This mummy as well as other items in the collection were only on loan to the museum by Charles Huffnagle (as was related in an earlier chapter). The listing of objects auctioned from Dr. Huffnagle's collection matches numerous items listed in the 1872 Wood's Museum catalogue and so removes any doubt about that mummy's identification. As with Wood's Chicago Museum, this one also contained a theater. A broadside from the museum, dated 9 June 1873, advertised "mummies" and a "petrified human body" among other curiosities.[85] Wood closed his Philadelphia venture in 1878, the same year in which he sold a collection of Egyptian antiquities, including four mummies, to the Niagara Falls Museum.[86]

Thomas Barnett, an Englishman, had begun the Niagara Falls Museum as a cabinet of curiosities. He moved to the Canadian side of the Falls in the early 1820s.[87] In 1854, his son Sydney made the first of three trips to Egypt. He would make two more, one in 1860, in the company of the Quebec physician, Dr. James Douglas, and a third in 1861. In the course of these trips, Sydney purchased four mummies and other Egyptian antiquities, which he brought back to the Museum. Among these was "an Egyptian warrior ... the finest in the world—there is not one in any other collection which is so perfect in preservation."[88] This is probably the mummy touted as "General Ossipumphnoferu" in the later Niagara Falls brochures (see ill. p. 133).

Douglas had been to Egypt several times, and on his trip with Sydney, he found him a fine mummy, in double cases, for which he paid the sum of seven pounds.[89] These mummies became a stellar attraction of the museum.

William Howard Russell painted this very unflattering view of the museum in his *My Diary North and South*, published in 1863:

> It was distressing to find that Niagara was surrounded by the paraphernalia of a fixed fair.... Close by the remnant of the "Table Rock," a Jew (who, by the

by, deserves infinite credit for the zeal and energy he has thrown into the collections for his museum), exhibits bottled rattlesnakes, stuffed monkeys, Egyptian mummies, series of coins, with a small living menagerie attached to the shop in which articles of Indian manufacture are for sale. It was too bad to be asked to admire such *lusus naturae* as double-headed calves and dogs with three necks by the banks of Niagara.[90]

On 1 May 1878, Barnett's chief rival, Saul Davis, purchased the museum and immediately spent $40,000.00 on new exhibits, including artifacts and mummies from "Wood's Chicago Museum."[91] The question which comes to mind immediately is which Wood's Museum, and what collection? The Museum in Chicago had burned to the ground in 1871. The next year, Wood had opened a similar Museum in Philadelphia, with one mummy (not one of the Mormon ones; and which was only on loan to him) and then in 1873 advertised "mummies"—type not explained—prior to the Niagara Falls Museum buying his collection, which included Egyptian objects and at least four mummies.

From where did Wood acquire at four mummies? There are no museums in Philadelphia at the time which are selling mummies. There are no newspaper reports of traveling shows selling mummies. But there is Abel Combs, who was living in Philadelphia, as evidenced by entries in the city directories, where from 1875 to 1892 his business was listed as "lamps" or "artist." He had bought the four mummies from Joseph Smith's heirs, and had sold, as far as can be documented, only two of them. Perhaps he kept the remaining two, and sold them in the mid–1870s to Wood in Philadelphia. After all, Wood had already had two from the same batch.

In 1967, the Mormon Church acquired eleven pieces of papyrus from the Metropolitan Museum of Art in New York, papyrus which had once been the property of Joseph Smith. They had been given to the Museum by the descendants of Comb's housekeeper, to whom he had left them as a legacy.[92] Obviously, Combs had kept some of the papyrus he had bought—it is only a short step then to admit the possibility that he had also kept the remaining two mummies. That still only accounts for two of the four mummies which Wood supposedly sold as part of his collection.

In 1887 the museum property was requisitioned by the Canadian government, in order to use the land to build a public park.[93] Davis was paid $102,000 for the museum and other properties, minus the value of the museum's collections and interior furnishings. Davis promptly shifted his operations to the New York side of the border, where it changed hands a number of times, finally winding up in the hands of the Sherman family in 1942.[94] In 1958 the Americans decided to build a park on the site of the museum, and so it moved back to Canada, where it stayed until its dissolution in 1999 when the mummy collection was bought by the Michael C. Carlos Museum at Emory University.[95]

A circa 1961 catalogue of the Niagara Falls Museum lists seven mummies,

One half of a stereograph view of the ruins of Col. Wood's Globe Theater and Museum (*Views in Chicago & Vicinity Before and After the Fire* [(Chicago): P.B. Greene, (1871)]. Courtesy American Antiquarian Society).

several of which are described as follows: "General Ossipuphnoferu, the famed warrior who served with the mighty King Tuthmosis III (circa 1450 B.C.) ... the vizier Osissupthfe, priest of Tuthmosis I (circa 1530 B.C.) ... Princess Amen-hotep ... was the daughter of King Amenhotep II (circa 1408 B.C.) ... her sister-in-law, Septhnestp, a wife of her brother, King Amenhotep IV (circa 1370 B.C.)."[96] Inasmuch as Amenhotep IV is more familiarly known as Akhenaten, husband of the famous Nefertiti, this last has to make one wonder from whence this information came, for none of it is correct.

The website for the Niagara Falls Museum has the following information about the mummies (and the coffins) from the collection, under the headings of "The mummies," and "The coffins."[97] There are discrepancies on the pages between which mummies are in which coffins and so I have separated them for the sake of clarity, as I am not at all sure which set of identifications is correct.

Mummy 1 appears be a bearded male from Roman times (ca. 990–960 B.C.E.).

Mummy 2 appears to be a young woman from Graeco-Roman times.

Mummy 3 appears to be a male of uncertain age.

Mummy 4 is an adult female.

Mummy 5 is the mummy generally known as Ossipumphnoferu, and he is not from the age of Tuthmosis III, but rather from the Roman period (ca. 30 B.C.E. to 400 C.E.), according to the style of mummification and the fabric in which he was wrapped, as well as his red hair and beard (see ill. pp. 134, 135).

Mummy 6 is an adult woman with braided hair, who suffered from scoliosis, and who died young. She had been identified as "Princess Amenhotep" but she may actually be one of the original inhabitants of coffin 7 and 8 (twenty-first to twenty-sixth dynasty) and her name is Iaw-tays-heref. [A candidate, as is Ossipumphnoferu, for the mummy which James Douglas helped to procure].

Mummy 7 was originally identified as the wife of Amenhotep IV (Septhnestp), but proved instead to be a male, between thirty-five and forty-five years old, with his arms crossed upon his chest. [This mummy has since been putatively identified as Rameses I and returned to Egypt].

Mummy 8 is the mummy of a child, possibly four years old at death. It is coated with a bituminous coating and has patches of gold leaf pressed in.

Mummy 9 is also a child's mummy, about one and one half years old. Both legs had been amputated. The style of bandaging suggests a Graeco-Roman dating.

None of the mummies appeared to be in coffins which were their own.

Coffin 1 is a XXI dynasty male coffin.

Coffin 2 is probably a late XXI dynasty coffin, original made for the chantress of Amon, Tahat.

Coffin 3 is also XXI dynasty, and most likely was made for a male, although the beard, hands and feet are missing.

Coffin 4 is ostensibly a woman's coffin from the XXI dynasty, at least in regards to the lid. It fits poorly with its bottom, which contains some imagery associated with a male occupant. Thus the two parts may not be a match.

Coffin 5 is that of a woman, and could date from dynasty XVIII to XIX.

Coffin 6 is that of a child, late dynasty XV to XXVI. An old museum label with the name "Hori" is identified with this coffin.

Coffin 7 and 8 are the inner and outer coffins of Iaw-tays-heref, daughter of the Lady of the House, Tadist, and of the wab priest Padikhnumdjuty. Over the years several different mummies have been photographed within these coffins, further muddying the waters of who was who in the Niagara Falls Museum.

One half of a stereograph view of the ruins of the Globe Theater, which also housed Col. Wood's Museum. Two of the mummies formerly owned by the Mormons were incinerated along with the building (*Great Fire in Chicago, Oct. 9, 1871* [Chicago: Lovejoy & Foster, (1871)]. **Courtesy American Antiquarian Society).**

Coffin 9 belonged to Nespakashuty, overseer of the singers of the god Min, and dated from between the XXV and XXVI dynasties.

Under the heading "Artifacts" appear a mummified female head, which had originally been labeled as the wife of Seti I. She has golden patches on her skin which suggest a Roman date for her. Also listed in this section are a mummified hand and foot.

Needless to say, all the shifting back and forth across the border did the collection no good, and in the course of the mummies' peregrinations, the bodies and their coffins and any labels have gotten thoroughly mixed up. It is possible that some of these mummies might be those which Joseph Smith had. The descriptions of the mummies which Joseph Smith bought are vague, and are hard to reconcile with the Carlos mummies Because there are no extant provenance nor acquisitions records for the collections at the Niagara Falls Museum it is doubtful there will ever be a certain identification.

There are so many variables and so many coincidences it is difficult to know what fits in where. It was mentioned earlier that Dr. John Wilson had thought he identified the names Sheshonk and Amenhotep in connection with the papyrus which had been found with the mummies. In the Niagara Falls Museum, there was a small female mummy, mouth agape, with a damaged face, and braids of hair. Although of probable Dynasty XXI date, she had been labeled by the Niagara Falls Museum at some point in time as "Princess Amenhotep, daughter of Amenhotep II."[98] One of the Mormon mummies was described as "female, supposed age 40, arms suspended by the sides, hands brought in contact; head damaged by accident; found with a roll as no. 1, filled with hieroglyphs, rudely executed." Is it possible that this is one of the missing "Mormon" mummies? (See ill. p. 136.)

5

Unholy Unrollers

"Scientific" Interest in Egyptian Mummies in Nineteenth-Century America

Almost any book about mummies will detail the process by which it is believed these artifacts were fashioned. Basically, highly wet organs (intestines, liver, spleen, and lungs) were removed, the body was dried out, and then wrapped in numerous layers of cloth, with or without resins, unguents, amulets and jewelry tucked inside. Wrappings could be very simple, or could involve individual "bandaging" of fingers, toes, extremities, and so on. Often the penis was wrapped erect. The head was usually wrapped separately as well, and then the entire body could be padded out and swaddled even further, covering all of that. The end result, under all of the layers of preservations, was often something which looked quite human, and which somehow generated the desire to know more about it.

Nearly everyone who came in contact with mummies had a curiosity about what was inside both the coffins and the bodies. The reasons varied widely, from ethnological studies to treasure hunting to morbid curiosity. But whatever the instigation, mummies were unwrapped in order to find out what was inside. In some instances it was a "parlor amusement," done at someone's home, after dinner. Other times it was a medical or scientific study, performed before an audience which could have included both lay and professional people.

Numerous unwrappings had taken place in England and continental Europe, beginning as far back as 1718. The pace accelerated after Napoleon's conquest of Egypt and mummies began flooding into England and France. Thomas Pettigrew, Augustus Granville, and Samuel Birch, were among the foremost "scientists" who engaged in this practice, as were Emil Brugsch and Gaston Maspero, who did most of their work in Egypt in the latter half of the nineteenth century. Mummy unwrappings were highly publicized and American newspapers and magazines avidly reprinted and recounted the details to their fascinated readers.[1]

The practice of mummy unwrapping in America started small, with often only the face or maybe a hand being fully uncovered, as in the case of Padihershef or Turner's mummy. But that soon progressed to full-fledged removal of the wrappings and exposure and examination of the dessicated flesh and bones inside. On 14 December 1824, the first public unwrapping of a mummy

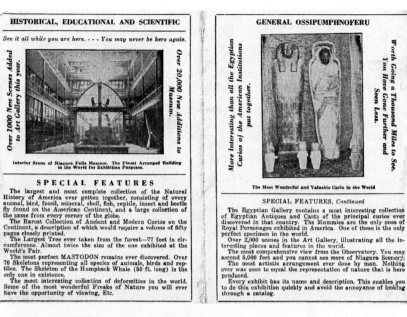

Brochure from the Niagara Falls Museum showing the interior of the museum and a view of the exhibition of the mummy known as Ossipumphneferu (Niagara Falls Museum, *Visit Our Niagara Falls Museum Tower and Art Gallery* [Niagara Falls, N.Y.: Niagara Falls Museum, between 1901 and 1928?]).

in America was done before a small audience at New York City's Castle Garden. The Philadelphia *Gazetteer* of 22 December 1824 reported:

> The mummy was on Tuesday opened ... it appeared to be wrapped in twenty-six fold [*sic*] of linen, which by age, had been firmly matted together; but upon placing the knife at the head, and with difficulty cutting a straight line to the feet, the casement was easily separated from the body, which was found to be in a hard, black and perfectly dry state. The bones were hard, the flesh rather soft, the arms, hands and fingers, were in a perfect state, and in a natural position by the side of the body. A large quantity of glutinous substance was found within the body, which on burning was of an agreeable odour. No doubt can now remain that the mummy exhibited, was entombed three thousand years ago; and by the pains taken in embalming it, that it was the body of a female of no inconsiderable importance.

The January 1825 issue of *The Christian Journal and Literary Register* gives the following account of the same historic event:

> Unclothing the mummy. The ... operation of unclothing the body took place at Castle-Garden, on the 14th instant, in the presence of several gentlemen of the faculty. The following certificate, taken from the *Evening Post* of the 27th, must prove satisfactory to the most obstinate skeptick [*sic*]:—New-York, Dec. 14, 1824. Having been invited by the proprietors of the Egyptian mummy, recently exhibited in this city, to aid in separating the bandages, and to disen-

robe the body of its funeral investments, in order to remove all doubts of deception, and to ascertain the contents of the sarcophagus—we certify that we did assist in this operation, on the 14th day of December, 1824, at Castle-Garden, in the city of New-York, in the presence of a numerous concourse of respectable citizens. The bandages were cut through the back, and though they adhered to the body, they were gradually separated, and the corpse exposed completely to view. It was in a state of dryness and preservation, that left no doubt on the mind, that it was a genuine mummy, of great antiquity, preserved by the Egyptians. There were 25 folds of linen cloth wrapped around the body, and between the folds were the powder and spices of aromatic gums; the cavity of the body was also filled with the same. From this exposure it is ascertained that the individual was a female, and probably between 25 and 30 years old when embalmed.... Samuel Akerly [and] Valentine Mott.

The mummy which was unwrapped was most likely Capt. Lee's mummy, as it was the only one which corresponds to the description or which was in town at the time.

As noted in an earlier chapter, Ethan Allen Greenwood also unwrapped some of his mummies, at least partially. Twenty-six coverings had been removed from Turner's mummy, and it was esti-

Ossipumphnoferu, possibly the magnificent "warrior mummy," in a double coffin, which James Douglas helped Sydney Barnet obtain for the Niagara Falls Museum (*Niagara Falls Museum News* [Niagara Falls, Canada], September 1960).

mated that forty or fifty more remained. The face and right hand were completely exposed and "very perfect." The female mummy from the *Peregrine* had been entirely unrolled, and found to be in perfect preservation. Seventy-two layers of wrappings were removed, disclosing an incision on her left side, large enough to insert the hand and arm. The cavity had been filled with gum and other preservative substances. The body was covered with a "coat of black varnish or gum, very like gum asphaltum." The hair was described as perfect and about eight inches long. Her male companion had been relieved of at least twenty coverings, exposing his bald head, feet and one hand. Greenwood estimated that at least fifty more layers of wrappings remained.[2]

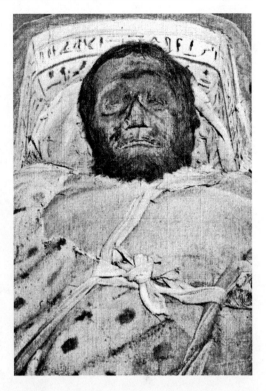

The face of the mummy Ossipumphnoferu. His red hair and beard indicate he was probably not a native Egyptian (*General Ossipumphneferu* [Chicago, Ill.: Curteich, n.d]).

The *Rhode Island American* of 10 June 1825 reported that: "James L. Hodge, a merchant of Philadelphia, has just received, by the ship *America*, an Egyptian mummy, which has been submitted to the inspection of a number of physicians, and declared to be one of the most perfect ever brought into this country." The name is in error; this is John L. Hodge, who later donated the mummy to the Academy of Natural Sciences in 1854.

The *Berks and Schuylkill Journal* of 11 June 1825 cribbed the following description of the dissection of Hodge's mummy from the *National Gazette*:

> The sarcophagus is formed of the two pieces or trunks of trees, sufficiently hollowed out to admit the mummy.... At one end of the mummy case is sculptured a head and face of the Grecian character, which bears, however, but little resemblance to that which it is intended to represent. The case is coated on all sides with a calcareous cement, over which is firmly adherent a canvas of a close and strong texture. On this are painted hieroglyphical ornaments, which are supposed by some antiquarians to exhibit a history of the individual over whom it is placed....
> Upon removing the sarcophagus, the mummy presented itself enveloped in

fine cotton bandages, applied in the most curious, exact and methodical manner.... These bandages are surrounded by a network of beads, of a variety of colors. Over the breast is wrought with the same materials a rude representation of the scarabeus....

In order to obtain a view of the face, breast, and one arm, an incision was made through the envelopes on the right side of the mummy, extending from the top of the head to the lower false ribs. After removing twenty or thirty layers of the bandage, the remainder was so firmly agglutinated by a bituminous substance that much difficulty was experienced in proceeding with the development. As the bitumen was reduced by heat and age to the condition of carbon, no liquid could be applied which would prove a solvent of this substance. By cautious perseverance, however, the gentlemen succeeded, by the use of knives, in exposing such parts as they had originally intended. The prominent thyroid cartilage, the beard, and the general character of the features, furnish abundant evidence of its being male.

It appears to be in a

The mummy identified as "Princess Amenhotep" in the Niagara Falls Museum. This mummy is possibly one of the "lost" Mormon mummies (*Niagara Falls Museum News* [Niagara Falls, Canada], September 1960).

perfect state of exsiccation, exhibiting nothing, literally, but skin and bones. Judging from the prominence of the anterior part of the nasal bones, we might infer it to be the remains of a Hebrew. It is difficult, however, to form an opinion of the whole contour of the nose, as the cartilaginous part of it is compressed on a level with the upper lip, by the firmness with which the bandage was applied over the face. The beard on the chin is the eighth of an inch long, and is of brownish hue, occasioned, perhaps, by being in contact with the bitumen. The natural eyeballs have been removed, and those of ivory substituted; and the anterior parts of which are painted a correct representation of the corneae and pupils. The crown of the head is bald, but crisp hair, strongly adhering, is observable behind the ears....

When the body is fully exposed, other objects of interest will doubtless be discovered.

The medical inspection was the usual one to ensure that the mummy was not a fake. This possibility was always in the minds of some observers, as a wit penned in the 15 June 1825 issue of the *Norwich Courier*: "Another mummy has recently been imported into Philadelphia. The mines of these learned Thebans seem to be prolific in these ancient treasures, and will probably engage in a dangerous competition with the manufacturers of these articles."

A public unwrapping of the two mummies bought by Rubens Peale from George Barclay was advertised on 2 March 1826 in the *New York Evening Post*: "Egyptian mummies—The scientific and curious are respectfully informed that the two mummies lately received will be examined and partly unwrapped, by several of the most respectable physicians of this city, at one o'clock on Friday, 3rd instant, in the lecture rooms of Peale's Museum. N.B. On this occasion, children cannot be admitted."

On 6 March 1826 the *Mercantile Advertiser* advised: "The public is respectfully informed, that according to notice the two Egyptian mummies were partially unwrapped in the presence of a respectable audience of ladies and gentlemen on the 3d inst. by Dr. Stevens and Dr. Post, and are now replaced in the museum for the inspection of the curious, exhibiting the numerous folds of linen which surround the body." One of these two mummies was the one which would be sold to the Ithaca, New York consortium, and subsequently destroyed by the rowdy medical students. The other, described in the *New York Evening Post* of 7 January 1827, was in a double coffin.

David Marks, a minister of the Gospel, wrote in his memoirs concerning this mummy:

> The next object was an Egyptian mummy, five feet and two inches in height. It was taken from a catacomb at Thebes. The body was enveloped in sixty-eight thicknesses of linen, the most of which had been removed from the face. The features were regular, the skin nearly black, and the hair a little curly. It was enclosed in a sarcophagus (a sort of coffin) of sycamore wood, which was covered with hieroglyphics. Strange feelings passed over me while gazing at this relic of antiquity. How far it was from the thoughts of those friends who embalmed this body, that it would ever find its way across the mighty ocean,

and in the New World be a wonder upon which many should gaze. After all, how vain is the effort of man to perpetuate his memory. While the tenement in which the soul dwelt a few brief years is preserved from decay, the name of the individual has been forgotten for centuries. And while acres of catacombs have been discovered, it is said that the present inhabitants of Egypt, instead of reverencing the respect of their ancestors for the dead, are using the mummies for common fuel. Surely, the "glory of man is as grass."[3]

This mummy (as well as its museum setting) was shuffled through several owners as Rubens Peale tried to keep from floundering financially. However, he finally gave up the New York Museum in 1842 to his landlord, and from thence it was purchased by P.T. Barnum. Presumably the mummy then perished in the 1856 fire which destroyed Barnum's American Museum.[4]

The *Boston Commercial Gazette* of 30 January through 13 March 1827 ran the following advertisement:

> Egyptian antiquities. For sale, just received from Egypt, via Gibraltar, by the brig *New Castle* 4 mummies, one with a double sarcophagus, extremely rich in hieroglyphics, 6 embalmed animals; 1 Isis, containing a mummy, pedestal, and base relief.... One of the human and one of the animal mummies have been opened by scientific gentlemen, and found to be in an uncommonly fine state of preservation.... For particulars apply to no. 13, India-Wharf.... The publisher of the following papers are requested to insert the above advertisement, ... and forward their bills to the Commercial Gazette Office for payment, viz: Noah's New York Advocate, Philadelphia National Gazette, and Baltimore Patriot.

The 9 February 1827 issue of the *Baltimore Patriot* reported further on the unwrapping in addition to running the advertisement as requested:

> A very interesting collection of Egyptian antiquities have lately been received here from Alexandria, which we understand were ordered to this country by the Pacha of Egypt.—There are four mummies, one of which, has been opened by Dr. Warren. in presence of a number of other scientific gentlemen, who pronounce it the most interesting specimen of antiquity that has been seen by them either in this country or Europe. The opened mummy is of a female of 25 or 30 years old, as all the teeth are in fine preservation.—The physiognomy if uncommonly distinct, and the foldings of 45 thicknesses of cloth have been developed, exposing the hand and arm of the figure, and showing the outline to great advantage. The cases of sycamore wood, especially the inner one, are uncommonly rich in those hyroglyphics [*sic*] which it is known are painted on these coffins. On the concave side, the colors are as bright as if they were recently laid on. There is a strong presumption that the other mummies are in equal good order.

If Warren left any notes on this unwrapping, they have not as yet come to light, and that is all which is known for sure about this group of mummies.

Some unrollings were certainly less than scientific. The 26 February 1827 Cooperstown, New York, *Watch-Tower* published the following, taken from the 4 February issue of the *Savannah Georgian*:

> The ship *Spermo*, M'Pherson, from New York, bound to New Orleans, was totally lost on Alligator Reef, coast of Florida, about four weeks since. A part of the cargo was saved and carried to Key West. Among the articles saved was what was said to be an Egyptian mummy, but smelling bad it was unrolled, and after stripping it of a multitude of folds of fine linen, nothing was discovered but a skeleton with the neck dislocated. The smell was so offensive that the collector ordered it to be burnt.

The origin of this mummy is not known, nor is the name of the collector.

On 26 January 1832 John Scudder, proprietor of the American Museum, Broadway, New York proudly announced in the *New York Commercial Advertiser*: "This day added. The Egyptian mummy, recently received from Thebes, In Egypt. It is a great curiosity and well worthy of the attention of every man of science and discernment. This mummy was taken from one of the most remarkable catacombs, and is considered to be very old. It is enclosed in its sarcophagus or coffin, ornamented with numerous hieroglyphics."

Scudder had previously displayed Turner's mummy, in February 1824, and was in rivalry with Rubens Peale, who also had a museum and mummy in the city at this time. Scudder knew the value of a dead Egyptian as well as anyone and so he obtained one of his own. Although its provenance has not been determined, it is touted as being "recently arrived from Thebes." (As opposed to the same old one which Peale had been exhibiting since 1826! By the same token, it cannot be either Turner's mummy or Lee's mummy, as they were not "recently arrived," unless the attribution was false in order to lull observers into thinking this was an entirely new mummy.)

Thinking that the mummy in itself was not that great a draw, Scudder announced in the 5 March 1832 issue of the *New York Commercial Advertiser* that the mummy "Which is nightly drawing crowds of visitors ... is to be examined and dissected on Wednesday next. It will, however, be exhibited in its present state until then. Those who wish to procure tickets, would do well to apply early, as 50 tickets will only be sold." (This also argues against it being Lee's mummy, as that one had already been unwrapped and dissected in 1824.)

The 12 March 1832 issue of the same paper put forth the following order and rules to be observed under the heading "Public dissection of the Egyptian mummy":

> 1st. Every gentleman to procure tickets of the lower door keeper.
> 2d. No gentleman will be allowed to leave his seat on any account.
> 3d. All questions will be directed to the superintending operator.
> 4th. No ladies admitted.
> After the dissection, the body will remain in state, for the gratification of the curious. Ample arrangements have been made.

The public, in this case, obviously did not include women (or presumably, children). Also, there was no mention of whom was going to perform the unwrapping.

The 13 March 1832 *Adams Sentinel* (of Gettysburg, Pennsylvania) took a slightly disparaging view of the whole spectacle:

> A trite affair.—The learned doctors of New York, are about to dissect a three-thousand-years-old mummy, from Egypt, who has had lodgings at the Museum in that city for some time past. He is said to be an old aristocrat, according to his dress; the marks of which decide he was never a plebian. He is to be undressed and opened on Wednesday next. The old gentleman has not had a change of linen for thirty centuries. Thus the physicians of this Yankee world, are about to proceed to the demolition of a form, which has been spared for ages by all the worms of Nile.

The body of the mummy "lay in state" at the museum following the dissection. According to the 13 March 1832 *New York Commercial Advertiser*, there was no extra charge to view this. The *Genesee Farmer and Gardeners Journal* for 21 March 1832 reported:

> The female mummy in the possession of Dr. Scudder, of New York, was examined a few days since at the museum in the presence of seventy or eighty spectators. The wrappers, about a hundred in number, were removed. An elliptical incision was made round the chest, and the front part of the body lifted up. The odor from the materials used for embalming was then very powerful. There can be no doubt of the antiquity of this curiosity.

The following description of an unrolling is taken from the 1 December 1838 issue of the *Boston Weekly Magazine*.

> One of the mummies brought from Egypt by Com. Elliott [of the *U.S.S. Constitution*] and presented to the Washington Medical College of Baltimore, was disengaged from its bandages on the 20th inst. As we learn from the Baltimore Athenaeum, in presence of the class of medical students, and a numerous company of scientific gentlemen and theologians.
>
> The mummy was enveloped in ample folds of cotton cloth, of several degrees of fineness, the outer layers having been placed transversely to the body, and the interior being longitudinally disposed, from the head to the feet. It was mostly of a dark color, approaching that of oxidated iron, but a part of these cerements was found, which still retained the delicate softness, the whiteness and purity which it originally had, though twenty centuries of sepulture have passed over it. Some of it was so decayed that it crumbled to dust when it was taken away from the body.... When the whole of the cloths had been taken away, amounting to 50 yards, the bones and remaining softer parts were exposed, the former perfectly preserved by the antiseptic character of the embalming materials. The tendons, ligaments, and some remnants of muscular fibre, remained attached to the larger joints, but so dessicated, and altered in color that an anatomists eye alone could detect them. It was the skeleton of an individual about five feet six inches high; the bones of the lower limbs were perfect, part of the bones of the pelvis and spinal column were absent. The skull was examined also, ... contained one or two ounces of dried embalm-gums, as myrrh, benzoin and olibanum.

On 26 November 1838 the *Boston Daily Advertiser* advised its readers that the "skeleton mummy" given by Commander Elliott to the Washington Medical College was to be unwrapped by Dr. J.H. Miller. who had unwrapped the other mummy. The article listed numerous Egyptian artifacts Elliott had donated, including a mummy head.

As far back as Dr. Warren's description of Padihershef and Ward Nicholas Boylston's mummy, unwrappers commented on the features of the face, the color of the hair, shape of the nose, and so on. The budding science of ethnology was just at this time beginning to articulate theories about the races of men, and how they developed. One of these theories was polygenesis, which postulated that each race of mankind had developed from the different sons of Noah. Ham, who had been cursed after seeing his father drunk and naked, was the supposed ancestor of the blacks. There was also strong urge to substantiate the idea of the superiority of the white race, and to prove that the blacks were inferior, chiefly in their mental capacity. The dark demeanor of the mummies might lead one to believe they had been black, hence the common remarks about the color being caused by the "bitumen" and the comments about the texture of the hair and the fineness of the features. It seemed vital to these early scientists to prove that the magnificent culture of the ancient Egyptians had not stemmed from the black race of mankind.

One of the foremost researchers in this field was Samuel George Morton, who amassed a collection of one thousand and thirty-five skulls from all over the world, of which at least one hundred and thirty-seven were Egyptian mummies (see ill. p. 144). Most of these had come to Morton through the good graces of George R. and W.A. Gliddon, A.C. Harris, and Charles Pickering. The collection was eventually purchased by the Academy of Natural Sciences and filled sixteen cases.[5] Morton wrote about just the Egyptian skulls in *Crania Ægyptiaca; Or, Observations on Egyptian Ethnography.* This was first published in volume thirteen of the transactions of the American Philosophical Society, and then re-published as a monograph, replete with twelve plates of engravings of mummy heads and skulls, in 1844. The skulls are described in great detail, including their origin, cranial capacity (which Morton had measured by filling the vaults with lead shot, then measuring the volume of the shot), and any distinguishing characteristics. Morton states at the beginning that the physical characteristics of the ancient Egyptians were variously ascribed by different scientists to "Jews, Arabs, Hindoos, Nubians and Negroes."

Morton had obtained most of these mummies as heads or skulls only, and it is not known how many he actually unwrapped to expose the features beneath—none of the ones depicted on the plates show any vestiges of their cerements[6] (see ill. p. 145).

Dr. Locke, of the Ohio Medical College, was moved to write about his experiences in viewing this collection, under the heading "Mummy-land" in the *Cincinnati Gazette*, which was reprinted in the 7 May 1841 issue of the *Daily Missouri Republican:*

Dr. Moreton [*sic*] and the cabinet of skulls.... A case 7 feet high and 20 feet long, containing the skulls of all ages, from an ivory pate which had been alive two months ago, to the crumbling relic of an American mound, and even the black, skinny *capites* from the pyramids of Egypt, embalmed, bandaged, and deposited more than three thousand years since. yet still they speak and tell some curious tales ... see my skull, it was once filled with thoughts and cubic inches of brains—and my hair, it is silky brown, long and in graceful undulations. Another still speaks of departed beauty, and calls upon gallantry to commiserate the ravages of three thousand years.... And who wert thou with the large face, and the diminutive brain? I was an idiot, and the embalmers, to preserve my character, have left my mouth open, and my teeth protruded. My face was as vacant in the streets of Cairo, as it is now in the mummy case.

Josiah Clark Nott and George Gliddon considered themselves disciples of Morton, and relied heavily on Morton's research for their book *Types of Mankind; Or, Ethnological Researches Based upon the Ancient Monuments, Paintings, Sculptures, and Crania of Races; And upon Their Natural, Geographical, Philological and Biblical History*,[7] a book which was so hugely derogatory in regards to the black component of humanity, that it is still castigated as being racist.

Morton did dissect two bodies before eighty members of the Academy of Natural Sciences, in Philadelphia—a juvenile female, about 8 years of age, from Thebes, on 10 December 1833, and another female from El Gurna, on the 10th and 17th. Presumably they joined that collection, although Morton did keep back the skulls for his own research.[8]

George Robins Gliddon was born in Devonshire, England in 1809, the son of John G. Gliddon, who later became U.S. consul at Alexandria. He was taken to Egypt at an early age, and later himself became U.S. vice-consul in Egypt (at Cairo). In 1842 he came to America where he lectured on Egyptian archaeology at Boston and Lowell, Massachusetts, as well as across the country as far west as St. Louis. He published several works about ancient Egypt, *Otia Aegyptiaca, An Appeal to the Antiquaries of Europe on the Destruction of the Monuments of Egypt*, and *Ancient Egypt, Her Monuments, Hieroglyphics, History and Archaeology, and Other Subjects Connected with Hieroglyphical Literature*.[9]

In 1845, Gliddon unwrapped an adult male mummy in Baltimore, during a course of lectures he was giving in that city. The mummy had been part of the Egyptian collection of Mendes Cohen.[10] Cohen was a Jewish-American collector of Egyptiana, who lived in Baltimore. In 1832 he took a voyage up the Nile, made numerous purchases of antiquities and brought nearly seven hundred items back to America. He placed his collection at the disposal of Gliddon during his Baltimore lectures. After Cohen's death in 1847 the collection passed into the hands of his nephew, who then donated it in 1884 to Johns Hopkins University.[11] By that time the mummy was no longer part of the collection and its fate is not known.[12]

In November 1849, Gliddon obtained the transparent *Panorama of the Nile* and brought it from England to New York, from whence he intended to exhibit it throughout the principal cities of the United States.[13] In the handbook he listed some of the Egyptian antiquities which would accompany the panorama, among them "four unopened human mummies, besides crania of ancient Egyptians, and several highly finished mummy cases ... animal mummies of every variety"[14] (see ill. p. 146).

In 1850, while Gliddon was exhibiting the *Panorama* in Boston, he offered to conduct an unwrapping of one of the mummies which accompanied the exhibition. Two versions of the proposal were issued, one "Printed for private circulation among Mr. Gliddon's friends" and another which announced: "Mr. Gliddon, having to make many arrangements before he can announce the opening of the mummy, requests that parties who feel disposed to subscribe should forward their names to him on or before the 18th May" (see ill. p.148).

Below this were illustrations of two coffins and two mummies, described as the:

> Unopened mummy of ANCH-ph****; "Daughter of the High Priest of Thebes—Got-Thoth-I"—who lived between B.C. 1200 and B.C. 1500—say about the time of Moses, or above 3.200 years ago. [and] Unopened mummy of GOT-MUT-AS-ANCH; "Daughter of a priest and scribe of Thebes"—who lived between B.C. 650 and B.C. 1000-say about the time of Solomon, or above 2,900 years ago. (These mummies may be seen at the "Panorama of the Nile.")
>
> After delays of five years, which include twenty-five months spent in two personal visits to the museums of Europe, Mr. Gliddon has succeeded in bringing to the United States, two highest class Egyptian mummies. He proposes to open one in Boston, and the other in Philadelphia....
>
> A few remarks will serve to give an idea of the difficulties, apart from the remote chance of procuring, at this day, an intact specimen from the Arabs, encountered in bringing a mummy of this high character, from Thebes to Boston.
>
> In 1845, Mr. Gliddon intimated from Paris to his friend Mr. A.C. Harris, the most influential resident in Egypt, his desire to possess a series of funereal antiquities to illustrate his lectures in the United States. The letter fortunately overtook Mr. Harris during one of this gentleman's archaeological visits at Thebes, where accident enabled him to obtain this admirable mummy, at the mouth of the tomb, "in perfect condition." It was conveyed in his own yacht to Alexandria, with a dozen other human mummies collected at Thebes, Abydos, and Memphis, intended for Mr. Gliddon.
>
> In 1846, after fruitless efforts to ship them, four were sequestered at the Alexandrian Custom-house; Mohammed Ali, since 1835, having forbidden then exportation of antiquities by any but agents of European powers. An official application made by the United States Consul to the Vice-Roy failed; and in 1849 these four mummies were found to have perished through the damp of the Custom-house. Happily Mr. Harris had preserved the most valuable specimens, the ones above figured, at his own residence.
>
> In 1848, on Mohammed Ali's superannuation, permission to export Mr. Gliddon's collection was refused by Ibraheem Pasha. On his death in 1849, Mr. Harris's personal claims upon the courtesies of the government, obtained leave

from Abbass Pasha; and the above mummy, with two of inferior order, was forwarded to Liverpool; where the influential compliance of Messers. Baring Brothers obtained their transshipment to the United States, free of examination at the quarantine and Custom-House. At New York, similar facilities were accorded to Mr. R.K. Haight; and after five years of disappointments, Mr. Gliddon received this specimen last November. The honorable names mentioned in this note suffice to show a few of the obstacles overcome, apart from time, labor and expense, in procuring the opportunity now offered in Boston. Other details will be given in the proposed lectures; but from the opening of a black mummy of his superior rank, the best archaeological curiosities may be expected in jewelry, trinkets, and papyri, no less than a beautiful sample of the ancient art of embalming.[15]

The 16 May 1850 issue of the *New Hampshire Patriot and State Gazette* noted, in an article attributed to the *Boston Transcript*: "An Egyptian mummy, 3500 years old, will be opened at the Tremont Temple in this city on the 1st of June, by Mr. Gliddon, the celebrated archaeologist, assisted by some twenty-five of the most eminent physicians of our city." The *Christian Register* of 18 May 1850 announced:

> Unrolling a mummy. Mr. Gliddon, the Egyptian traveller, who is now lecturing in this city and exhibiting his *Panorama of the Nile* and various curiosities, illustrative of the past history and present condition of Egypt, offers to open one of the mummies in his collection, if a suitable subscription can be raised.
>
> This mummy is the body of the daughter of a high priest of Thebes who lived more than 3,000 years ago, or about the time of Moses. It is one of the most valued specimens of the curious art of embalming, and its market value is said to be about $1,500. Mr. Gliddon proposes to devote three lectures to the work of opening and explaining this mummy, if the needful number of subscriptions can be obtained. The plan is, to secure 300 subscribers, at five dollars each, which will entitle the subscriber to four tickets of admission to each of the three lectures to be given in connection with the opening of the mummy.

Samuel George Morton, scientist and ethnologist, collected the largest assemblages of skulls in the United States for use in determining his theories on race and origins of man (portrait collection, American Antiquarian Society. Courtesy American Antiquarian Society).

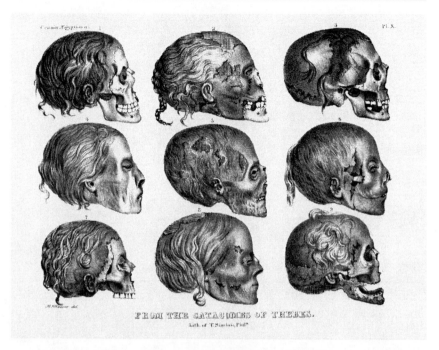

"From the Catacombs at Thebes." Engravings of some of the mummy heads in the collection of Samuel George Morton (Samuel George Morton, *Crania Aegyptica* (Philadelphia: Pennington, 1844). Courtesy American Antiquarian Society).

The *Scientific American* of the same date ran a similar announcement, concluding with:

> The process of unrolling the body is to be conducted under the supervision of several of our most distinguished surgeons and physicians. A larger number of our wealthy and influential citizens have already given their names to encourage this curious and interesting undertaking, we cannot doubt that the requisite subscriptions will be obtained so soon as a general opportunity is offered to our citizens to express their interest in this enterprise.

The *Hartford Daily Courant* reported on 29 May 1850:

> The subscription to the exhibition of the mummy by Mr. Gliddon, in Boston, being so nearly completed, it has been resolved to unroll it on the mornings of the 3d, 5th, and 7th of June. There were three hundred tickets to be sold at five dollars each, each ticket being entitled to four seats. About two hundred and fifty have been sold. These are all entitled to reserved seats. Single tickets for each lecture, at fifty cents each, will be sold, but the buyers must take their chance for an accommodation. Mr. Gliddon will accompany the unrolling with interesting lectures on the history &c. of Egypt, and will exhibit some great novelties in the way of books and plates, hitherto unknown to the public. The mummy has already been taken out of its outer coffin or case, and it remains now only to detach it from the inner envelope and the folds of linen

THE

NILE,

Pharaonic, Persian, Ptolemaic, Roman, Byzantine, Saracenic, Memlook, & Ottoman,

ITS ANCIENT MONUMENTS, ITS MODERN SCENERY,

AND THE

VARIED CHARACTERISTICS OF ITS PEOPLE, ON THE RIVER, ALLUVIUM, AND DESERTS,

EXHIBITED IN A

GRAND PANORAMIC PICTURE,

EXPLAINED IN

ORAL LECTURES,

Embracing the latest Researches, Archæological, Biblical, and Historical,

AND ILLUSTRATED BY A GALLERY OF EGYPTIAN ANTIQUITIES, MUMMIES, &c.,

WITH SPLENDID TABLEAUX OF

Hieroglyphical Writings, Paintings, and Sculptures.

By GEO. R. GLIDDON.

LONDON:
JAMES MADDEN, 8, LEADENHALL STREET.

Price—Two Shillings.

Cover of the *Hand-book to the American Panorama of the Nile*, indicating that mummies and other Egyptian artifacts were on display at the Panorama. Although printed in London, this hand book also served during the American tour of the Panorama (George R. Gliddon, *Hand-Book to the American Panorama of the Nile* [London: James Madden, 1849]).

in which it is swathed. The body has been ascertained, by the hieroglyphics on the outer case, to have been that of a female, the daughter of a high priest or scribe of Thebes. Her name, imperfectly ascertained, was ANCH-ph*****. Mr. Gliddon thinks the evidence is strong that the body is more that 3000 years old. The Boston Transcript says the style of the hieroglyphics, and well known fashion of embalmment render it probable that this lady lived between the XVIIIth and XIXth dynasties, say between B.C. 1200 and B.C. 1500. For aught we can assert to the contrary, she may have witnessed the 10 plagues of Egypt, or mourned the loss of brothers, sons or cousins, drowned in the Red Sea! The doubts as to her epoch will be solved on opening her coffin. All the wealth, fashion, beauty, science and literature of Boston, Cambridge and Roxbury, will be represented at these interesting meetings. Seventeen of our highest medical and scientific gentlemen form themselves into a committee to superintend the process; and their learned remarks will enhance the educational value of the exhibition.

The *Courant* concludes the article with its own observation that: "Barnum is undone in his own province, and unless he can get up another Joyce Heth, may as well succumb."

On 4 June 1850 an anonymous poet penned the following, which was published in *The Boston Daily Atlas* of 7 June 1850:

The mummy at home.
(Written for the Atlas.)

Long, long ago, three thousand years before the "good old time,"
There lived a young and joyous maid in Egypt's burning clime;
Around his cherished darling, clung a father's hopes and fears,
And the sunshine and dew were hers—a mother's smiles and tears.

Fair grew the child, and ripened soon to lovely womanhood,
And 'mid the brightest of the land in virgin beauty stood,
While the rosy light of love revealed that soon the garden's pride,
Transplanted to another's bower, would bloom and blush a bride.

Alas for human happiness! 'twas then as it is now,
The fairest flowers are the first beneath the storm to bow:
Dark is the dawn of that young life—dimmed is the lover's smile—
He weeps upon the broken stem of the lily of the Nile.

Faint through the rolling ages, we hear the anguished cry,
And onward swell the tears that flowed till misery's springs were dry,
While her pure and spotless memory, in frankincense and myrrh,
"Smells sweet and blossoms in the"—pitch—'tis all that's left of her.

Now for that lover, so forlorn, that broken-hearted youth,
No fiction shall my page adorn, but plain, unvarnished truth;
Ere twelve short moons he dried his eyes, forgot his lady gummy,
And wooed another, who in turn, was maiden, wife, and mummy.

Three thousand years and more are fled—a strange, unthought of race
Is dwelling in what was to her a quite unheard of place;

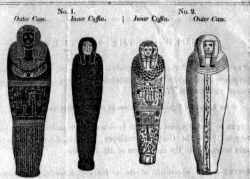

PROPOSAL.

MR. GLIDDON, having to make many arrangements before he can announce the *Opening of the Mummy*, requests that parties, who feel disposed to subscribe, should forward their names to him on or before the 18th May.

	No. 1.				No. 2.	
Outer Case.	*Inner Coffin.*		*Inner Coffin.*		*Outer Case.*	

Unopened Mummy of ANCH-ph * * * *; "Daughter of the *High Priest* of Thebes—GOT-THOTH-I."— who lived between B. C. 1200 and B. C. 1500—say about the time of Moses, or above 3,200 years ago.

Unopened Mummy of GOT-MUT-AS-ANCH; "Daughter of a *Priest* and *Scribe* of Thebes "—who lived between B. C. 650 and B. C. 1000—say about the time of Solomon, or above 2,900 years ago.

(THESE MUMMIES MAY BE SEEN AT THE "PANORAMA OF THE NILE.")

After delays of five years, which include twenty-five months spent in two personal visits to the Museums of Europe, Mr. GLIDDON has succeeded in bringing to the United States *two highest-class Egyptian Mummies.*

He proposes to open one in Boston, and the other in Philadelphia. It is the one represented above, *Fig.* No. 1, which, as the more ancient and valuable specimen, he has preserved intact for the former object.

To accomplish it in a manner satisfactory to his friends and the public, best calculated to insure attention to the scientific results of the experiment, and at the same time compensatory to himself, Mr. GLIDDON submits the following sketch of a *Programme*, while soliciting on the part of his friends their co-operation and counsel.

The commercial value of so rare a specimen as *Fig.* No. 1, is about £300—in the Museums of Europe.* This estimate, $1500, would be reimbursed to him, were 300 *Subscribers* obtained, at $5 each, to THREE LECTURES on the "Art of Mummification among the Ancient Egyptians."

* A few remarks will serve to give an idea of the *difficulties*, apart from the remote chance of procuring, at this day, an intact specimen from the Arabs, encountered in bringing a Mummy of this high character, from Thebes to Boston.

In 1845, Mr. GLIDDON intimated from Paris to his friend Mr. A. C. HARRIS, the most influential resident in Egypt, his desire to possess a series of funereal antiquities to illustrate his Lectures in the United States. The letter fortunately overtook Mr. HARRIS during one of this gentleman's archæological visits at Thebes; where accident enabled him to obtain this admirable Mummy, at the mouth of the tomb, in perfect condition. It was conveyed in his own yacht to Alexandria, with a dozen other human Mummies, collected at Thebes, Abydos, and Memphis, intended for Mr. GLIDDON.

In 1846, after fruitless efforts to ship them, *four* were sequestrated at the Alexandrian Custom-house: MOHAMMED ALI, since 1835, having forbidden the exportation of Antiquities by any but agents of European powers. An official application made by the United States Consul to the Vice-Roy failed; and in 1849 these *four* Mummies were found to have perished through the *damp* of the Custom-house. Happily Mr. HARRIS had preserved the most valuable specimen, the one above figured, at his own residence.

In 1848, on MOHAMMED ALI'S superannuation, permission to export Mr. GLIDDON'S collection was refused by IBRAHEEM Pasha. On his death, 1849, Mr. HARRIS'S personal claims upon the courtesies of the government, obtained leave from ABBASS Pasha; and the above Mummy, with two of inferior order, was forwarded to Liverpool; where the influential complaisance of Messrs. BARING BROTHERS obtained their transshipment to the United States, free of examination at the *Quarantine* and *Custom-house.* At New York, similar facilities were accorded to Mr. R. K. HAIGHT; and after five years of disappointments, Mr. GLIDDON received this specimen last November. The honorable *names* mentioned in this note suffice to show a few of the obstacles overcome, aside from time, labor and expense, in procuring the opportunity now offered to Boston. Other details will be given in the proposed Lectures; but from the opening of a *black Mummy* of this superior rank, the best of archæological curiosities may be expected in *Jewelry, Trinkets,* and *Papyri,* no less than a beautiful sample of the ancient art of embalming.

1850

The broadside Gliddon had printed announcing his lectures and mummy unwrappings in Boston (*Proposal* [Boston: s.n., 1850]. Courtesy American Antiquarian Society).

And Britain's honored Queen is throned in that most favorite spot,
Which now is called old England—and was then—the powers knew what.

From those far shores adventurous feet have wandered to the land,
Where the crocodile and ibis in mummied glory stand,
And eager hands have bartered gold for Egypt's buried daughter,
To bring her to the western world across the flowing water.

Three days (a magic number) she now holds a matineé,
For fate decrees that strangers her cerements rend away;
Each throbbing heart in stillness waits, till gliding from her case,
The Ancient and the Modern are meeting face to face.

Like her own goddess, veiled she attends, before our wondering gaze
And on her shrouded form once more, behold the sun's warm rays;
Leave her awhile in mystery—'tis fit that she should keep
Her solemn watch one little day, ere we invade the sleep.

Young antiquity, we welcome thee! In silent eloquence
Thou speakest to our spirits, though dumb to ear of sense,
And still thou shalt embalmed be in every memory, while
We think with awe-struck wonder on the maiden of the Nile.

Unwrap the clinging vestments—lo! She bursts upon the sight,
With the jewels on her dusky form, like stars upon the night;
She lived, loved and died, and was forgot—her history is told—
And it is now then as it was, before the days of old.

The first lecture was described in the 3 June 1850 issue of the Boston *Daily Evening Transcript*:

> Opening of the mummy. Quite a large and intelligent audience assembled at the Tremont Temple this forenoon to witness the opening of the mummy-case imported by Mr. Gliddon, and to listen to Mr. G's instructive explanations. On the platform were the venerable T.H. Perkins, Rev Dr. Sharp, professor Agassiz, Doctors Hayward, Channing, Holmes, Lewis, Wyman, Jackson, Cabot, Bigelow and other scientific and distinguished gentlemen. The body of the hall and the galleries were well filled with an assemblage, of which many were ladies.
>
> The cases of sycamore wood, ornamented with hieroglyphics, were placed horizontally upon a stand; and while Mr. Gliddon discoursed upon the Nile and the pyramids of Giza and the receptacles where mummies were found, an officiating carpenter took off his coat, and, with a small saw, proceeded to saw the case lengthwise. After this has been done on two sides—an operation which occupied about half an hour—it was ready to be taken apart for the disclosure of what it might contain. This was done by Mr. Gliddon and his assistants in view of the whole audience. The mummy came out in beautiful condition, as if it had been deposited in its case but yesterday instead of 1500 years before the birth of Christ. It came out swathed in linen, smooth and but slightly discolored by the lapse of time. On the front covering were a series of hieroglyphics of a fresh slate color, as distinct as as [sic] if they had been just painted. A burst of applause and a murmur of surprise from the audience showed the sensation, which the exhibition produced.

> As the lady thus brought before the public, was, according to the inscrip-
> tions on her sarcophagus, a person of rank, and the daughter of a high priest,
> it was naturally expected that the interior of the case (which, by the way, was
> in a wonderful state of preservation) would reveal some ornaments, jewelry,
> trinkets, &c., of value. But this expectation has not thus far been gratified.
> Probably the interior folding, which will not be disturbed till Wednesday, will
> reveal some curiosities of this nature, as well as some specimens of papyrus,
> and a "scarabæus" or papyrus book of the dead usually deposited with the
> Egyptian dead. The audience seemed highly interested, and we doubt not that
> the second lecture on Wednesday will show an increased attendance.
> Among the incidents "not set down in the bill" was the unrolling of the
> mummy of a white ibis, at which Professor Agassiz presided.

During the lectures Gliddon had exhibited the skull of a girl, from Samuel
G. Morton's collection, and another skull and foot, to demonstrate the different types of embalming and had displayed in glass cases, mummified animals,
including a calf, ram, jackals, serpents, crocodiles, an ibis and a cat.[16] The lectures and unrolling continued on Wednesday and were duly reported by the
Daily Evening Transcript of 5 June 1850:

> There was a much larger attendance today at the second levee of the Egyptian
> lady, introduced to the Boston public by Mr. Gliddon. After an explanation of
> the hieroglyphics on the exterior fold of linen, Mr. G. placed the mummy in
> charge of the committee of scientific gentlemen, appointed for that purpose,
> and they proceeded to unwrap the numerous bandages, in which it was
> swathed. This operation occupied about half an hour, and resulted in the dis-
> covery of a papyrus or book of the dead, such as was usually deposited with
> corpses by the Egyptians, and a scarabeus, or winged beetle, which Professor
> Agassiz pronounced a very perfect specimen. The papyrus, ante-dating the
> period of the sojourn of the Israelites in Egypt, was not in a state to unroll, as
> to prevent its crumbling in the operation. It must first be carefully mois-
> tened....
> After the bandages had been taken from the greater part of the mummy,
> which was unrolled today, it was displayed to the audience. But the mode of
> embalming this specimen had been peculiar—being by dipping the body in
> boiling bitumen, so that the face looked as if carved out of anthracite coal.
> Some of the learned medical gentlemen on the platform disputed the sex of
> the mummy, and for a moment doubt was thrown upon the accuracy of Mr.
> Gliddon's reading of the hieroglyphical inscriptions. But this doubt was soon
> dispelled by one of the most distinguished of our anatomical professors, who
> very satisfactorily showed that the position of the hand had led to the erro-
> neous supposition invalidating Mr. Gliddon's statement.
> During the operation of unfolding the linen bandages, a fine resinous dust
> was raised, which set many of the audience to sneezing. The mummy having
> been unswathed was placed, together with the articles found on the person, in
> a glass case for the inspection of the curious. On Friday Mr. Gliddon will lec-
> ture on the whole subject; and this promises to be the most interesting of the
> three exhibitions.

"Mr. Gliddons last lecture" was recorded in the *Daily Evening Transcript*
of 7 June 1850:

There was another good attendance at the Tremont Temple to-day to hear Mr. Gliddon's closing remarks upon the mummy; and the development which a further examination has revealed. After a very clear and satisfactory account of the processes, by which the date of embalmment is fixed, he stated that the hieroglyphics on the leathern cerements across the breast of the present mummy gave the name of the king, in whose reign it was embalmed, and thus the period, at which the subject lived, could be ascertained within a few years. The date in this case was 900 years before Christ.

A revelation, which excited no little surprise and amusement was now made. The mummy was not the body of a priestess, but of a man. The fact was very satisfactorily established by the medical gentlemen who had examined it. Mr. Gliddon remarked that mistakes would occur in the best regulated families, but in this case he was very certain that the mistake occurred 3000 years ago at Thebes, and was not in his reading of the hieroglyphical inscription. He explained how naturally, in an establishment, where hundreds of bodies were undergoing the process of embalment [sic], the ticket might have got slipped, and a mummified man found himself in the coffin intended for a priestess. His explanation was so ingenious and satisfactory that the audience received it with a burst of applause.

One has to admire Gliddon's quick thinking to ameliorate the fact that he had not unwrapped a priestess, but instead had uncovered a body "exhibiting in its fossil state the erected unequivocal mark of its sex."[17] One also has to wonder at the ineptitude of the gentleman who had demurred at the original questioning of the sex of the corpse and who had insisted that the mummy's hand could be mistaken for male genitals!

Donald Grant Mitchell penned the following witty view of the entire affair in *The Lorgnette: Or, Studies of the Town. By an Opera Goer*:

Following close upon the opera, the Egyptian princess has created one of the periodic fevers of Boston. It was not allowed to the people of our town to be the patrons of such a learned, and antiquarian exposition, as belonged to the unwrapping of the mummy. The enthusiasm of our sister city amounted even to romance, and poets made anticipatory sonnets to the Theban princess. Boston prudery forgot its blushes in the presence of so old and august a belle, and came prepared to witness the unclothing of the high-priestess, without a veil.

The company was worthy of the interest of the subject. Scientific men, the erudite Agassiz, and the accomplished Bigelow, with a host of others, were proud to lend their aid to the unfolding of that mystery, which, for the time, was to throw into the shade the lectures of a Hudson, and the antithesis of a Parker. Day after day, the enlightened assemblage gazed upon the rapidly diminishing envelopes, occasionally forgetting their dignity in an operatic bravura, and only restraining a shower of bouquets upon both lecturer and princess, when it was discovered that the mummy was a man! Dr. Bigelow blushed, and Professor Agassiz put his hands in his pockets.

But the Bostonians are too well taught, and too erudite to be surprised; the metamorphose astonished no one; and the old, withered, bituminous Theban was as much a thing of course in the progress of their inquiry, as a north-easter to their summer, or a mystery to their faith. Had it been even a dipped, bituminous crocodile, there would have been those present, who would have

FIG. 268.

FIG. 269.

Inner Shell.

Outer Case.

Inner and outer coffins of Got Thoth Aunk, the mummy Gliddon claimed to be female, and which he unwrapped in Boston in 1850 (Josiah C. Nott, *Types of Mankind* [Philadelphia: Lippincott, 1854]. Courtesy American Antiquarian Society).

foreseen it from the beginning, and who would have taught Mr. Gliddon his hieroglyphics.

Upon the whole, the result was effective; it has given an admirable topic for disquisition on mysteries in general, by the Town and Country Club. The theologians are put on alert; and they will lack their accustomed ingenuity, if they do not draw from the contradiction of the mummy case, to the mummy included, a new argument against the authenticity of the Gospels. The metaphysicians, too, possessed of the bare fact, that an undoubtedly Egyptian princess, bore every appearance of a man, will easily base upon it some new theory of objective philosophy, for publication in Mr. Brownson's Review. The Historical Society of our town will, without my suggestion, see the propriety of putting in a claim for the scattered leaves of papyrus, and the leathern belt strapped around the old Theban. A paper should, of course, be prepared, to be read at the next monthly meeting, showing with historical accuracy, and with what might have been on the papyrus if it had been longer, as well as indulging in a few moral reflections upon leathern belts and bitumen.[18]

The newspapers had a field day, reporting on the gaffe with glee. *The Boston Daily Atlas* of 11 June 1850 published this unsigned rhyme, which had been written on 8 June, after the "mistake" had been revealed:

The Mummy not "at home"
Written for the Boston Atlas

The worm is in the shroud and the serpent in its skin,
The young birds in their nests, their mothers know they're in;
And when fair Anch T's father had given beyond a doubt
His daughter to Osiris, could he guess that she was out?

Say, when he paid the fee, to the tune of—what's the pitch—
Three hundred or a thousand? To mummify the witch,
And sent her to her long repose among the chilly rocks—
How could he know, alas! That she was in the—yes, wrong box?

The nigerensis lilium! where was she in that hour
When sacrilegious hands made way into her bower?
Her bower—is not that hers which love has consecrated,
And paid for—(make a note of)—the price that it was rated?

Was that her pitch? I mean did she come up to five feet, four?
Which overtops Britannia's queen by inches three or more—
Why question? there's one comfort—if Sphinx is overbold,
His appetite is not so good as it was held of old.

Of flowers, queen! and taller than the rest by half a head—
Unless this bed of her's were a Procrustean bed;—
I wonder, had she chanced to look on that translated phiz,
If she guessed what "Mister wight" her lawless tenant is!

Was he of speakers who affect the metal of a saw?
Was he a priest who loved the church but didn't love the law?

Was he a lawyer, who, on looking at her case,
Found it would suit him to a T, and so took Anch T's place?

Was he of that bold breed who take your good umbrella,
And leave a broken-ribbed, old, cotton for its fellow?
A fair—yes, fair for them—exchange, being no robbery—
And patch their ugly morals up with such like cobblery?

Well, patience priestly lady—three thousand years and more
Have snowed the world—and you may well forgive the trespass hoar.
Murder will out—'tis like a cloud of pure Egyptian dark,
That, down our bald today, comes tumbling like a lark.

The world is towards its prime, and we're wiser in some ways,
Than were your handsome neighbors in old Egyptian days;
Take this, then, from your friend, when your souls return dear dummies,
Trust instinct and not learning for finding out your mummies.

The *Barre Patriot* of 14 June 1850 was much more kind.

The explanations furnished by Mr. Gliddon as to the cause of this untoward
event were deemed satisfactory by the audience. No one pretends to implicate

FIG. 267.

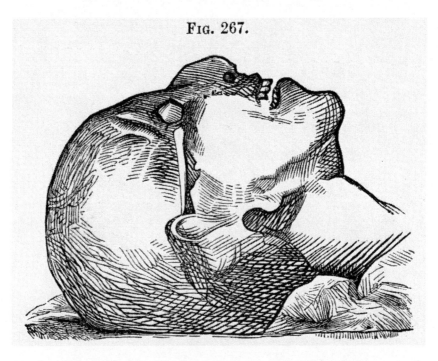

Drawing of the head of Got Thoth Aunk, the mummy Gliddon had erroneously
claimed to be a "priestess" (Josiah C. Nott, *Types of Mankind* [Philadelphia: Lippincott, 1854]. Courtesy American Antiquarian Society).

Mr. Gliddon in the deception, and all agree in thinking him as much deceived as any one of his audience. He has in his possession another mummy which he proposes to open in Philadelphia. We hope his second attempt may meet with better success than his first.

The *Christian Register* of 15 June 850 was equally as forgiving:

It was certainly not Mr. Gliddon's fault any more than it was ours, or the mummy's own, that it turned out not to be a "lady of the Theban aristocracy." Nor yet a "priestess," nor even any lady at all, but a plain man—male altogether. A mummy it was indubitably,—an authentic, intact, veritable, dried, packed and preserved mummy. Mr. Gliddon affirms that a certain writing on one of the bandages gives him ample reason to be satisfied that this much mistaken and abused person died and was dipped in bitumen and buried about nine hundred years before Christ. With all possible respect for the learned gentleman's erudition, we must be excused for holding our faith in these matters, after the recent disappointment, in a somewhat easy and non-committal attitude. It seems to be generally supposed that the undertakers at Thebes got a little confused some day, whether from hurry, or "excess of wine" and so put a man's body, after inscribing it with a female name and hieroglyphics, into a woman's coffin. A precise explanation of the facts would probably be about as difficult a matter as a complete analysis of the various motives that drew together the immense and highly entertained assembly in the Tremont Temple at the unrolling.

On 17 June 1850 the *Hartford Daily Courant* printed the following: "The Boston correspondent of the Springfield Republican says that he has ascertained the true name of Gliddon's mummy, to be *Spurious Mummius*, the intimate friend of one of the Scipios."

Even more staid and serious magazines, such as the *Scientific American* of 22 June 1850 could not resist the chance to take a cheap shot at the embarrassed lecturer:

That mummy. Well, our Boston scientific friends have paid the piper in the $5 ticket, to see Gliddon's mummy unrolled. It was a most wonderful mummy that—the virgin priestess of a great priest who dwelt in Egypt 1900 years before our blessed era. Well it was worth $5 to see such a character revealed from amid her swaddling bands of linen and what not. How important was the subject, how intricate the wrappers?—more mysterious than a Boston one, truly. Three days—yes, three long days were occupied in the unrolling process. How eloquently Gliddon discoursed upon the subject—the age, the glowing virgin beauty of the within, as she long, long ago used to sing by the banks of the Nile. We can imagine the interest that was excited in the countenances of that intelligent and select audience, as Gliddon approached the last wrapper and exclaimed, "Behold the hour is at hand." There she was, the ancient maiden of the delta, the long hid, the long desired to be gazed upon; but alas! for the changes of time upon this human race, she was a man—yes, a man! Some felt shockingly disappointed; but why should they? Perhaps it was no mistake at all. The sexes may now be misunderstood by us. The Egyptian women may have been men. There was Semiramis and the old Amazons. That is surely some evidence to prove this assertation. We therefore think that Mr. Gliddon had no right to say, that a mistake happened in the mummy family.

The *Home Journal* dated 29 June 1850 reported:"The opening of the mummy at Boston has been dramatized. Another theater in that city has a piece founded on the same event, called 'Taken In, and Done For.'" On 20 June 1850 *The Pittsfield Sun* added that "The Boston Post says that one of Mr. Gliddon's patron's declares that although the mummy turned out to be man, he still considered it to be a dam-sel." The racial specter even reared its ugly head to add to the tumult, as recorded in the *North Star* for 27 June 1850:

> Were the Thebans Negroes—There has been a wonderful fuss over a mummy at Boston lately. It is described as very ancient, and was supposed to be a princess or priestess of Thebes in her glory.—Great parade and ceremony has been made as to the unrolling of the mummy. It has been done with much care and regard to the highly excited literary taste in Boston, and in regard to the science of mummy-making, as well as the presumption that jewels, or manuscripts, might be found entombed in this relic of mortality.
>
> Before the unrolling of the antiquated thing, we had many literary strictures and lectures from the learned, in Boston and about, in regard to the genealogy of the Thebans, of whom the mummy was supposed to be a royal relic. One important point was, to make out, that the Thebans, were a different race from the poor black creatures that mope now about the ruins of the city of a hundred gates. Oh! no. It would be bad taste enough to be paying great respect to the corpse of a nigger, if it be royal. We were assured therefore, by the learned doctors, that the Thebans were not Africans, but a nobler race, and had none of the peculiarities of niggerdom. Although this did not quite agree with Herodotus, and their contemporary historians, nevertheless the learned were sure it must be so.
>
> Well, the poor old mummy, was at length stripped of its swaddling clothes, and disemboweled, and furnished evidence of little else than it was a veritable "he nigger" after all. A humbling relic enough of Theban royalty, learning and renown.

The mummy debacle became national news. By July of 1850 the word had reached as far as Madison, Wisconsin. The 9 July 1850 *Wisconsin Express* presented a humorous description of the proceedings which not only made fun of Gliddon, but also the pretensions of the haughty Bostonians who witnessed the event.

> The Boston Mummy.
> Lately in the town of Boston,
> All the wise and great were lost in
> Transcendental admiration,
> At a startling publication,
> In which all the world was bidden
> By the famous Mr. Gliddon,
> To behold a dame Egyptian,
> Great and rich, by his description,
> From the garments disencumber'd
> In which, she for centuries slumber'd.

All the wise of modern Athens
Gather'd round the pitchy within's
In the folds of which lay hidden
The fair dame of Mr. Gliddon.
Holmes, the funny bard physician,
Had a prominent position,
And the knowing dentist Wyman
And some more of Boston's high men
Sat respectful—sapient finders
Of the truth from calcin'd grinders—
They can prove the mummy's entity,
These great dentists of identity.
Parsons sober, wise professors
Join'd this band of grave undressers,
Sapient heads in wigs and glasses,
And, without them, sage Agassiz,
There were hosts of modest ladies,
For the best one not afraid is
To behold this model maiden
Of her linen all unladen.

Then began the great undressing,
Gliddon all the time professing
To know all about the history
Of this dried-up female mystery.
She a lady was of station,
In the old Egyptian nation—
A priest's daughter, for he, Gliddon,
Read her name and sex the lid on.
Three whole days the process lasted,
But the Athenians would have fasted
Three whole weeks, without appearing
Of the business to be wearying.
On the sages went, unfolding,
Eager, breathless for beholding
The mysterious Theban beauty.
While the process was progressing,
Gliddon learned was addressing
Sage remarks explanatory
Of the Egyptian lady's story;
Telling too of all experiments
In unrolling mummies' cerements,
And of treasures sometimes hidden
In the linen—so said Gliddon.
Hieroglyphics he translated,
Mysteries elucidated,
You'd have sworn the Theban learned,
Had himself been long interned,
And had risen, a mummy knowing,
For the simple sake of showing
Modern Athens all the history
Of each Theban mystery.

One Athenian modest trembled
As, before the crowd assembled,
He remark'd the mummy's stature
Rather tall for female nature.
Gliddon had an explanation
Nearly ready for narration,
But, ere he'd begun his answer,
Said another, "She's a man, sir."
Consternation, ladies blushing,
Beaux confused, disposed for rushing,
Off, without a moment waiting;
For 'twas fixed, beyond debating
That the unroll'd priestess tender
Was not of the female gender!
Gliddon for a moment falter'd
But his visage soon was alter'd,
For he saw a dawning notion
That would settle the commotion.
"Gentlemen and ladies," said he,
"This had surely been a lady,
But the blundering undertakers,
Or the blundering coffin makers
In the Theban shops of mummies,
Proved themselves a set of dummies,
And misplac'd the lady's body
By this base-born, male tom-noddy."

Great applause this statement greeted
From the "folks" around him seated;
'Twas a genuine Boston notion,
Thus to settle the commotion.
All abused'd the mummy bakers,
Stupid Theban undertakers,
For their blundering egregious
And their treatment sacrilegious
Of the holy priestess' ashes,
And for sending them such trash as
This male mummy, with the label
Of a lady, on the table.
But, in Gliddon's praise they firmer
Drew, and never let a murmur
Breathe against his Theban learning,
And they're thinking now of turning
All their extra cash together
For a amulet fine of leather,
With a suitable inscription,
In the purest of Egyptian,
To attest their admiration
And their wondrous estimation
Of the learned Gliddon's history,
Of this Theban mummy mystery.

The 31 August 1850 issue of the *Christian Register* reported, under the heading "That mummy once more":

> The *Boston Transcript* of August 21st and 23rd, contains a long letter from Mr. Gliddon, telling the whole story, which the latest and complete examinations of papyrus, straps, bandages, &c., &c., have unfolded about his mummy early this summer in Boston. It seems the said mummy was all right, in the right coffin, duly embalmed, the body being that of a priest who died about B.C. 900. The Theban undertakers, in this particular case, were honest; and all suspicion of fraud on their part is unnecessary and unfair. Mr. Gliddon made a slight mistake, before the opening of the coffin, in reading the fragments of the inscription; and so got the notion that the contents was a female body. The frank, manly, good-natured and generous manner in which Mr. G. explains the whole affair and owns his error, should now stop the laugh and satisfy every body.

In spite of this admission and correction of the facts, the mummy mistake would just not go away. On 29 October 1850 the *Daily Columbus Enquirer* published the following:

> Profane epigram—Whoever is responsible for the following will probably expire without the benefit of clergy.
>
> > When Gliddon from the mummy case
> > The wrappings did untwine
> > No priestess was revealed, but la!
> > The manly form divine.
> > Ah! said a wit, who'd paid to see
> > A priestess there unrolled,
> > "He keeps his word, this surely is
> > A dam-sel, for I'm sold."

Another poem, written by A.H.P. of Boston, was published in *The Alta California* of 31 October 1850:

> > The Boston mummy.
> > Humbugs are very much in vogue;
> > And people run, for every rogue
> > Enthusiastically mad—
> > For signs and wonders, always glad
> > To snatch at almost any bait
> > Like fishes; soon they curse their fate,
> > 'Twas rich to hear them stamp and scold,
> > Just after they'd been fairly sold.—
> > The other day, when all had paid
> > To see the famous mummy maid,
> > I heard one of the sold ones singing
> > The song which in my ears is ringing.
> >
> > Parody on the "Old oaken bucket."
> >
> > How dear to my heart are antiquity's treasures
> > Which story-books many present to my view;

How dear are the tokens of so many past pleasures
And legends of giants which valiant Jack slew;
Of ruins all moss-green, by groaning ghosts haunted;
Of Pompey's tall pillar that glorious old pile;
Of the dragons which men have attacked, never daunted;
And even the mummy, that lived by the Nile.
The old shrunken mummy—the wonderful mummy—
The linen-wrapped mummy that lived by the Nile.

A fine lady mummy (for so said the papers,)
Was brought to the city of notions one day.—
A priestess who having deceased, ceased her capers,
But had not been suffered to turn into clay.
How ardent I started and bought me a ticket,
And hastened, with mouth open wide, to the hall,
And saw them take hold of the mummy and stick it,
Boxed up in a coffin in full view of all.
The old shrunken mummy—the wonderful mummy—
The linen-wrapped mummy astonished them all.

How pleasant it was, as the rags tore asunder,
To gaze on her form, on so young-looking yet old;
As each wrapper fell off, 'twas the general wonder
How, packed in such shape, one could ever be cold—
When up stepped the savons, very eager to view
The maid from old Egypt, with visage so wan;
But as soon as the mummification was through,
Lo! The lady turned out to be nought but a man.
Another base mummy—a sneaking young mummy
Had turned out the priestess—and turned out a man.

As late as 1895 the incident was resurrected by the Rev. David Burrell as an object lesson on secret sin:

Here we touch the lowest part of our nature. A dog with a bone sneaks off to a corner of the garden and buries it, watching meanwhile out of the corners of his eyes that none may know his secret. So we bury our darling sins, so we flatter ourselves that none shall ever find us out. An Egyptian princess died four thousand years ago and her body was committed to a company of priests for embalming. They said "let us save ourselves the trouble; it will never be known." So they dipped the body of a common Egyptian into bitumen and placed it in the princess' casket. It was a clever trick; but a few years ago, before a company of scientists at Tremont Temple, gathered together to witness the unswathing of the royal mummy, the bands of byssus were unwound and the fraud perpetrated by those priests, now forty centuries dead, and turned into dust, was detected. There is indeed nothing hidden that shall not be brought to light and that which is done in a corner shall be proclaimed on the housetop.[19]

It seems that everyone remembered the error, but not the true explanation of it. Gliddon packed up his panorama and the mummies and left town, eventually winding up in Philadelphia. On 23 November 1850, underneath a picture

of the coffin and mummy of Got-Mut-As-Anch, Gliddon issued a similar proposal to the one he had issued in Boston.

> Mr. Gliddon proposes to give a course of eight archaeological lectures—seven
> in the lower saloon of the Chinese Museum, and one in the upper, on Monday
> and Friday evenings, at 7½ o'clock, between the 30th of December and the
> 24th of January, provided not less than 200 subscribers be obtained by the 10th
> of December. Two very interesting mummies will be unrolled in the upper
> saloon, on one of those evenings. Referring to the subjoined prospectus of
> subjects, the following are the proposed arrangements:
>
> 1st.—Each subscriber of $3 to the course will be entitled to a reserved seat
> on the opening of the mummies, free of additional charge.
>
> 2d.—Each subscriber will also have the privilege of bringing ladies and chil-
> dren to the entire course (with the same advantages of reserved seats at the
> mummy-opening,) the former at $2 and the latter at $11/2 each. Medical and
> collegiate students, and pupils of schools, will also be admitted at $11/2 each
> for the course, on application through a subscriber.
>
> 3d.—Subscribers will receive especial tickets for each person to the course of
> eight lectures. These tickets to be transferable.
>
> 4th.—Reserved seats at the "mummy-opening" being guaranteed to holders
> of subscribers' tickets, the remaining places to the lectures, on this and all
> other evenings, will be open to the public at 50 cents. No half-price.
>
> 5th.—The cost of the mummies being above $500, and the expenses of rent,
> &c., not less than $500 more, (aside from the labor and outlays encountered
> by Mr. Gliddon in bringing the materials from Europe and Egypt to Philadel-
> phia,) if the number of names on the subscription list reach the amount
> required, the subscriptions will be collected, and, with due announcements
> through the press, the lectures will be given. Should the list fall short, no sub-
> scription will be called for, and the mummies will not be opened.
>
> 6th.—An early answer (not later than the 10th of December) is solicited, in
> order that Mr. Gliddon may be able to judge whether to proceed with public
> announcements of his design.

There followed a list of places where subscribers could sign up, and a
description of the order of the lectures. A "Postscriptum" ends the proposal,
giving the particulars of the attainment of the three mummies A.C. Harris had
procured for him from Egypt and included the following annotations:

> One of them, the embalmed corpse of the Theban priest, Got-Thothi-Aunkh,
> who died in the 10th year of King Orsokon IIId, about 900 B.C., was opened at
> Boston, last June, in the presence of 2000 persons. The amusing equivoque of
> gender that occurred at its opening received satisfactory elucidation in the
> "Letter from Mr. Gliddon about the papyrus found on the Boston mummy,"
> published in the Boston *Evening Transcript,* 21st and 22d August, 1850. A copy
> is appended to the mummy, which lies open to inspection at the "Panorama of
> the Nile."
>
> Pending the transmission of these mummies from Egypt, after he had
> renounced all hope of recovering them, Mr. Gliddon, at the suggestion of Mr.
> Birch, the renowned antiquary of the British Museum, and Mr. David W.
> Nash, a very eminent Egyptologist, purchased from a dealer the only mummy
> procurable last year in London. It is the one figured in the above woodcut. In

the opinion of both of these gentlemen, after a critical examination, as well as Mr. Gliddon's, this mummy has never been taken out of its inner coffin. It had been injured slightly at the foot by the probes of custom-house officers; and since landing in the United States, the stitchings of this coffin, chafed in railroad transportation, have partially given way, but the corpse, with whatever was originally enshrouded in its envelopes, seems to be intact; and there is no doubt that the coffin yields the legends that promise a very curious and valuable specimen of embalming in the person described.

This is the mummy Mr. Gliddon has preserved to be unrolled at his lectures in Philadelphia; together with that of an Egyptian child, probably of the Roman period, obtained by Mr. Harris; the more curious as mummies of children are exceedingly rare in Egypt. None but this one, it is believed, has ever been brought to the United States.[20]

The 16 January 1852 *North American and United States Gazette* announced:

To-morrow evening, our former consul at Cairo, the well-known Egyptian lecturer, Mr. Gliddon, will open two very interesting mummies in the presence of 500 subscribers and of all who choose to witness this instructive entertainment.... We sincerely hope that Mr. Gliddon's laborious devotion will be amply remunerated by a crowded attendance on this highly interesting occasion.

A little bit of whimsey preceded the unrolling, as the mummies were displayed to the public before the event. A collection of gentlemen were inspecting the cases and the illustration thereon, when they were startled to hear a voice issue from the folds of linen which enveloped the body:

"Open the box! Open the box!" said the voice.

"Who are you?" inquired one of the learned Thebans, whose curiosity had gotten the better of his astonishment.

"I am a descendant of the pharaohs," answered the voice within.

"Are you a genuine mummy?"

"Yes, and no mistake; regularly manufactured in Egypt, by some of the first artists."

"Do you come from Ham?"

"Ham—no, I am a better specimen of dried beef."

"What do you want here?"

"Ask yourself; your confounded prying Yankee inquisitiveness has waked me from the slumber of ages."

A thought struck the scientific questioner, and he determined to settle a long mooted question.

"Were the Egyptians black or red men?"

"Red as the knave of hearts."

"What caused the decline of the Egyptian nation?"

"It didn't decline; like the modern Celt, the Egyptian emigrated to Mexico."

"To Mexico?" inquired the doctor.

"Yes; open the box, open the box."

"Then the pyramid at Choluiu is—"

"Exactly; it is nothing else."

"And you are—"

"Bobby."

"Bobby who?" asked the astonished inquirer.

"Bobby Blitz;" and a little man with a peculiar head of hair glided out of the hall and disappeared into the lecture room of the museum. The doctors looked at each other, and the word "sold" was audibly heard coming from the box, as if the dried descendant of Mizraim was laughing in its sleeve at the credulity of science, which could not tell a living ventriloquist from the fried remains of burnt rags and a monkey's skeleton.[21]

There are a number of things going on in this bit of folderol; the topics of race, fake mummies and the possibility of a link between the Egyptians and

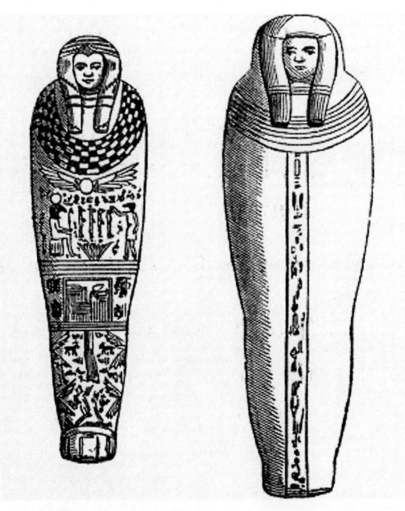

Inner and outer coffins of Got Mus As Anch, the mummy unwrapped by Gliddon in Philadelphia (*Proposal* [Boston: s.n., 1850]. Courtesy American Antiquarian Society).

Mesoamericans are all raised and treated rather cavalierly by the ventriloquist. At the time they were all valid routes for scientific inquiry, and part of the popularity of the unwrappings was to see if any of these could be proven through examination of the ancient bodies. It was a good joke and worked so well that Blitz went on to use a mummy as a prop in a show he presented at the Assembly Building in Philadelphia in 1866.[22]

Gliddon's mummy unrollings in Philadelphia went a bit more smoothly than had the one in Boston—at least there were no surprises. The *North American and United States Gazette* of 18 January 1851 reported on the proceedings:

> The upper saloon of the Chinese Museum was pretty well filled last evening by a very excited and expectant audience, assembled to witness the opening and unrolling of two Egyptian mummies by Mr. Gliddon. After a few introductory remarks, operations were commenced on the mummy of the Egyptian lady, named Got-Mut-As-Anch, daughter of Got-Har-Af-Anch, priest and scribe of the sacred signet in the temple of Amun, at Thebes. The case being first removed by sawing a portion of it apart and ripping up the stitching confining it on the back, the lady was taken out and placed on a table. At the request of Mr. Gliddon, Dr. Henry S. Patterson, aided by Drs. [Wm. R.] Grant and [David] Gilbert, whom he invited to assist him, proceeded to unwrap the bandages with which the corpse was enveloped. The process was attended with no difficulty and little delay, except that required to cut the separate pieces of linen cloth in which the mummy was swathed. In the course of taking off the wrappings a papyrus was found—the book or record of the dead—which was in the hieratic character, or abbreviated hieroglyphics used by the Egyptian priests. It appears to be similar to that found on the mummy recently opened by Mr. Gliddon at Boston. As the body was approached, the clothes were discovered to be more firmly glued together, and of much coarser quality. There was a scarabeus, or sacred beetle found, as usual, on the breast of the mummy, placed there according to the Egyptian superstition, to protect the heart of the dead from demoniacal influence. It was so enveloped in pitch that its particular examination was necessarily postponed. The corpse, when finally reached, was in a perfect state of preservation, excepting that the feet were broken off and a leg above the knee. These injuries were supposed to have been caused by the probes of custom house officers. The work of unrolling the cere clothing being finished, Dr. Patterson stated to the audience that as in all cases being examined the swathing [of] the mummy had been effected by wrapping the body with bandages circularly, then placing pieces of cloth longitudinally, and then filling up the inequalities of the surface with compresses. Excepting the papyrus and scarabeus, nothing was discovered worthy of remark. These, with the bandages, were placed on the front of the stage, where they were subsequently scrutinized by those present.
>
> The process of unrolling the child was next proceeded with; but as it was found, that the cloths, from the great quantity of pitch used, adhered so closely and firmly to the body, that it would have required a mallet and chisel to get them off. The operation was deferred for another time. Mr. Gliddon then observed that he would reserve until next Monday evening a particular examination of the two bodies, as well as the remarks which he deemed it proper and interesting to make in explanation.

The unrolling was elaborated upon in the 29 January 1851 issue of the *Missouri Daily Republican*. If nothing else, Gliddon did know how to put on a good show:

> An audience of about one thousand persons, consisting of ladies, medical, scientific and professional men were present. The back part of the stage was decorated with several mummy cases, outer and inner coffins, some mummies, papyrus and ornaments; among them was the body of a very large and powerful man, which Mr. G. said belonged to John L. Hodge, Esq., of this city, which was partly unwrapped about twenty years ago. From the inscriptions, it was found that his name was Pet-isse, he who belongs to Isis, and that he was a priest of Isis, who died at Thebes, about 1,000 or 1,500 years before Christ....
>
> The child appears to be in good condition, as far as could be seen. It was swathed in linen, with the face painted on the cloth. Mr. Gliddon said the mummies of children are very rare. In all his life he has not seen more than a dozen, and six were in the British Museum. Over five hundred million mummies are supposed to be in Egypt, and it is strange that the bodies of children are rarely found....
>
> The inner coffin of the lady who was about to be removed from the clothes was richly painted and gilded, and covered with figures of various kinds, the lines of which were very vivid. Mr. Gliddon said this inner coffin was composed of a substance technically called cartonnage. It was formed of strips of linen cloth glued together and molded so as to fit the body; it was then sewed together at the back and covered with stucco, from which paintings were made.

The wags still could not resist making a little fun of Gliddon and his unwrappings. The following appeared in the 28 January 1851 issue of *The Cleveland Herald*, which had taken it from the *Cincinnati Gazette*.

> We are advised that the "upper saloon" of the Chinese Museum, Philadelphia, was thronged with an anxious crowd, on the 17th inst., to see Mr. Gliddon undress Miss Got-mut-as-anch, daughter of the Rev. Mr. Got-har-af-anch, a Theban minister who preached some 2,500 years ago—be the same more or less. During that long interval the body has remained "wrapped up in solitude of its own originality," splinted and bandaged like a broken leg. It was expected, says Major Noah, that the little gipsy would look as bright and blooming as a side of sole leather. We trust that the young woman proved to be a woman; for as Mr. Gliddon well knows strange changes of sex sometimes occur in mummy cases. An Egyptian baby, supposed to have been pickled about the time of the Babylonish captivity, was also to be undiapered. As regards the sex of the sucking mummy, Mr. Gliddon is mum. It is surmised however, by several celebrated archaeologist [sic], that it is either a girl or a boy, and that it belongs to the celebrated Theban family of Sarcophagi, nearly related to the Catacombs. There is no doubt that both mummies were of patrician origin, and members of the "upper ten"—known in Nilotic society as "Upper Egypt," to distinguish them from the canaille, or "Lower Egypt."

In 1852, Gliddon was in New Orleans, giving his series of lectures and offering to unwrap his last mummy. The *Daily Picayune* of 27 February 1852 noted:

Opening of a mummy.—This climax of Mr. Gliddon's lectures on Egyptian antiquities will take place this evening at the Lyceum Hall. All the members of the Lyceum will be present, together with the professors of the University of Louisiana. Non-subscribers to the series of lectures will be charged $1 for entrance. The proceeds, it is announced, will be devoted to the exclusive benefit of those highly useful institutions, the Lyceum and the Library. Apart from the mere curiosity to witness the mere operation of unrolling a mummy, which motives will doubtless attract many spectators, the novel and instructive explanations that must accompany it will be an attraction equally powerful and of useful results.

On 29 February 1851 the paper reported:

The great event of the Gliddon lectures took place last night in the presence of a very large audience at Lyceum Hall. The mummy was unrolled. After some explanatory remarks by the lecturer, in which he stated to his audience that the mummy before them had never been unrolled, and that he knew nothing of its history, age, or sex, any more than did the audience. it having been received by him precisely in the state in which they saw it. The mummy was placed in an elevated position, so as to be clearly visible by the whole audience, and the process of unswathing commenced, under the immediate supervision of the medical savons of New Orleans, the faculty of the Medical Department of the University of Louisiana.

The unswathing was performed principally by Drs. Jones, Wedderburn and Chilton, and occupied some half or three quarters of an hour. As swathing after swathing was removed, and the roll, which at first appeared to be of so respectable a size, began to grown smaller and smaller and beautifully less, the audience evidently began to get apprehensive lest the mummy was about to be dissipated into consecutive layers of cloth. At length, however, after removing linen enough to have served the whole household of the ancient Egyptian dame during a lifetime, the savons came to the body of a female, in what was pronounced a "beautiful" state of preservation. The hair, nails, &c. were as distinct and as well preserved as though the spirit had left the earthly tenement but yesterday. From the symmetrical properties of her well-turned limbs we did not hesitate to conclude that body lying before us, when animated by its spiritual habitant, had been a distinguished belle of ancient Egypt—had one day moved about among her peers in their full pride and satisfaction of conscious beauty—had been the object of many an envious glance from her own sex, and of adoratory looks, ill-suppressed sighs, and badly composed sonnets innumerable, of a countless throng of admirers from the opposite. Perhaps she may have intrigued with pharaoh himself, or she may have been the veritable Mrs. Potiphar who so sorely tried the continence of Joseph.

Those who are curious about her history must attend the next lecture, when Mr. Gliddon has promised to divulge all the secrets which an examination of the various swathings, and of any inscription to be found thereon, may disclose. In the mean time we are to rest contented with the fact, that the method of embalming used in her case fixes the period in which she flourished to somewhere between 1500 B.C. and the second or third century after Christ.

The concluding article appeared in the *Daily Picayune* on 1 March 1851:

That mummy again.—Mr. Gliddon last night delivered before the Second Municipal Lyceum his twelfth and last lecture on Egyptology.

The mummy which had been "unrolled" on the evening of the previous lecture lay in state immediately in front of the audience. It is said to be in an uncommonly good state of preservation. Its very dark appearance, as well as the reddish color of the hair on the head, is owing, as the professor informed us, to the bitumen used in embalming. Several letters were read by the professor from gentlemen of the medical faculty of the University, containing the results of their examinations since the mummy was unrolled. They informed us that the mummy was that of a person of middle age. We are sorry to say, however, that neither the researches of the learned professor, nor the industry of the medical savons were able to disclose anything very interesting or satisfactory relative to the life and history of the great "unrolled" or to fix with much certainty the period in which she flourished. It was made sufficiently clear, however, that she lived somewhere between the age of Moses and the Christian era. From a variety of indications the professor thought it highly probable she lived during the Ptolomaic period. He, however, greatly dashed our curiosity on this subject and dissipated our previous speculations by informing us that the mummy before us was that of a person of low condition in life; that she was, in fact not a "lady" but only a "woman." Of course our interest being gone, we shall pursue our speculations no further.... Professor Gliddon concluded his interesting lecture by presenting the mummy to the University of Louisiana, to be placed in the museum of the medical school.

This mummy was given the name "Nefer Atethu" or "Beautiful youth" many years later during a radiological study of her and Got-Thoth-Aunk, who had also been given to the museum in 1851 by Gliddon and Josiah C. Nott. It was also during his sojourn in New Orleans that Gliddon and Nott collaborated on the writing of *Types of Mankind*.[23] In this book, Got-Thoth-Aunk was described as the perfect example of an ancient Egyptian as described in the books of Exodus and Ezekiel.[24]

The two mummies and their coffins were stored in various locations, including a space under the bleachers in the football stadium. They attended three Super Bowl games (and numerous college games) before being rescued, in the mid–1970s, and placed in a somewhat more appropriate setting at the college.[25] According to Samuel Morton's catalogue of skulls, the head of Got-mut-as-Ankh was given to him for that collection. It is not known what happened to the rest of the body, nor to the child's mummy unwrapped in Philadelphia.

On Thursday, 15 December 1864 Professor Henry J. Anderson unwrapped a mummy at the Hall of the Cooper Union Institute as part of the New-York Historical Society's lectures on Egypt series. Tickets were fifty cents.[26] Anderson had obtained the mummy and its coffin on a tour of Egypt in 1848, and donated it to the New-York Historical Society in 1864, and from there it went to the Brooklyn Museum in 1937.[27]

The New York *Evening Post* of 16 December 1864 gave the following description:

The mummy was taken from its coffin, and the ceremony of unrolling was performed by Dr. Weiss, demonstrator of anatomy in University [i.e., Columbia]. The removal of the bandages and wrappers from the body was the work of time. All the cerements were clean and fresh. Finally the skeleton was seen. It was in a good state of preservation. All the soft parts of the body had disappeared, except for some ligaments and muscles, and a small part of the skin ... Dr. Weiss, after a particular investigation, gave it as his opinion that the mummy was that of a very old person.

The *Springfield Daily Union* of 19 December 1864 did not think much of the unwrapping. "A mummy, evidently that of a person of wealth and distinction in his day was unveiled at New York lately under the auspices of the Historical Society, but no discoveries were made."

In 1884 news spread quickly that an Egyptian gentleman named Penpi (and sometimes referred to as Peupi, or Reupi) was on his way to Cornell.[28] The *Brooklyn Eagle* of 26 January 1884 reported under the heading "A distinguished graduate of Cornell:"

If haply the souls of mummies still take an interest in their remains, the late Mr. Penpi, of pious memory, who belonged to the twenty-third Egyptian Dynasty and reposed comfortably for some ages in the necropolis of Thebes must have a good deal to think about at the present time. He must be gratified to find from the letter of the United States Consul at Cairo to president White of Cornell, that he is to leave that port for Liverpool immediately and without wasting time upon the sights of London or even having leisure to call upon his contemporaries in the British Museum, is to come right away to New York. He will probably decline the hospitalities of the ancients of that metropolis and will not ever cross the Brooklyn Bridge. That will not prevent his superior mind from viewing it from his present altitude. Egypt was "some pun'kins" but we doubt if he can recall so big a work as the bridge. But transportation by steam will probably astonish him the most. It must be especially gratifying to the blest shade of a mummy of respectable lineage and proud of his family to find the director of the Museum of Egyptian Antiquities sending his name and former address so precisely to the university which will make him an alumnus after his matriculation. He may be said to have passed his "little go" in transportation. Mr. Penpi need not mind being regarded as an antiquity, for "old fellow" is a term of endearment.

Early in July 1884, Penpi's mummy was unwrapped before an audience of about one hundred and fifty people, at 3 o'clock in the afternoon, as recorded by the 4 July 1884 issue of the *Duluth Daily Tribune* which had copied the account printed in the *Ithaca Journal*:

The mummy was taken from its case [evidently of the same material as the cloth wrappings, but soaked in some gum] and the unwrappings commenced. The bandages which were of a yellowish color about ten feet long and four inches wide, were made of linen and fringed at the ends, they were put on very symmetrically, one layer being crosswise, the next up and down. The head only was uncovered in the presence of the visitors, this was found to be in a good state of preservation, the hair had been shaven closely but on the back of the head a little could be seen, which was of a sandy color; the beard also could be recognized. The face was of medium size with a low forehead, a Roman nose, and rather high cheekbones, altogether a good looking face taking age into consideration.

Those present were asked to look at the mummy as they passed out, an opportunity of which nearly all availed themselves, after this the bandages were taken from the whole body. Between the legs parts of the viscera, which had been taken from the body, were found carefully wrapped in linen cloth. The body was hard and of a dark brown color, five feet and five inches in height, and the nails of the fingers and toes were as perfect as when the body was placed in its narrow limits. A number of small beetles that had bored their way through the case were found among the bandages.

There was something very fascinating, though strange and weird, about this whole ceremony; to think that this man belonged to another race, lived on the other side of this sphere in the days that we are accustomed to call mythological, and that perhaps he may have been personally acquainted with some of the ancients about whom we know, serves to excite the imagination to the utmost limit. It is not probable that when "Penpi" was laid away amid the tears of his friends that the idea came to them that in distant ages his body would be regarded as a curiosity, and that ruthless hands would take him from his case that he might make another specimen for the Cornell Museum.

Penpi is still at Cornell, although not readily recognizable as a mummy, as little remains but his skeleton.[29]

The *New York Times* for 23 January 1887 recorded, under a column headed "Royalty from the Nile":

About a hundred persons, mostly officers of seminaries and colleges, assembled in Suydam Hall Chapel, connected with the [New Brunswick] Theological Seminary, this afternoon, in response to an invitation, and celebrated Washington's birthday by listening to Prof. Lansing talk on "mummification." Then they watched him unwrap a mummy. When he said it was a female mummy, some of the irreverent students suggested that it might be the remains of Martha, the mother of her country; but Prof. Lansing said the mummy was that of a royal priestess of the nineteenth dynasty, B.C. 1400. She was about contemporaneous with Moses, and perhaps fished him out from among the bull rushes.... Prof. Lansing was assisted by Dr. Van Vranken of Albany, and Mr. Van Dyke, librarian of the seminary. First was a layer of carefully painted linen, then hundreds of yards of narrow linen bands, with an occasional sheet of linen all yellow with age and smelling of bitumen. At last the royal priestess lay revealed, a black and hideous thing, shriveled to a mere skeleton. Her arms were crossed devoutly on her breast, the muscular tissues and some of the flesh adhered to the bone, but soaked in bitumen. No valuables were found, and no papyrus rolls. The unwrapping occupied two hours, and when through Prof. Lansing and his assistants were covered in yellow dust.

The mummy had come to Prof. Lansing from his father, a missionary in Syria, and Lansing had kept it in a case in his library at home before using it as an illustration to his lecture. This mummy, whose name is Iset Ha, is now on loan to Rutgers, and located in the Geology Hall.[30]

One of the more unusual groups interested in mummy physiognomy were the phrenologists, who believed that bumps and patterns on the skull revealed character traits of their owners. As early as 1851 Fowler and Wells were advertising their Phrenological Cabinet at Clinton Hall, 131 Nassau Street, New York, wherein they had "Skulls and casts from the heads of the most distinguished men that ever lived; also skulls ... from all quarters of the globe—including Egyptian mummies, pirates, robbers, murderers and thieves." Admission was free, and if one wished, one could also have a phrenological examination and chart made, as well as a written description of character based on the consultation, although those services required payment.[31]

By 1855 the cabinet had moved to 380 Broadway, and in the *American Phrenological Journal* for July 1859, Fowler and Wells claimed that they had the "Real Head-Quarters" and that they had added cannibals, Caribs, and Flat-Head Indians to the motley mix of skulls. "On Ethnology" was the title of an article in the January 1864 issue of the *American Phrenological Journal and Life Illustrated*. It was liberally adorned with drawings of mummies, mummy cases and skulls, most of which were from *Types of Mankind*, although two of the drawings were of heads which were part of the cabinet (see ill. pp. 174–175). Those are described thusly:

> The mummy heads now before us are of a dark brown color; the features, where not broken by hard usage, are tolerably well preserved; the hair is mostly gone, but what remains is of a bright red color (though this is not likely to have been its natural hue); the skin is hard and somewhat elastic; the flesh has peeled off in some places, exposing the bone. The face of the male (fig. 3) shows signs of a beard, though but little of it remains. Both the heads emit a strong pitchy odor....
> Phrenologically, these mummy heads present no very remarkable aspect. The size is not far from the average, and they are of fair proportion. They indicate large cautiousness, firmness, approbativeness, conscientiousness, hope and veneration; while the organs in the lower portions are not as large. Intellectually, there is neither an excess nor deficiency in development, but a general evenness prevails. The quality of the organization, judging from the fineness in the texture of the bone is nearly if not quite equal to that of the Egyptians to-day....

As late as 1900, Luther C. Bateman was using the "head of a royal Egyptian mummy" in his phrenological lectures, as evidenced by the notice he placed in the April 1900 issue of *The Phrenological Journal and Science of Health,* that he was selling his "outfit" which had been making one to two hundred dollars a week, and which was worth three thousand dollars, for two hundred and fifty dollars "spot cash."

Unwrappings were not always easily performed as is evidenced by this article in the 1 September 1895 *Daily Inter Ocean* which had cribbed the information from the *Baltimore American*. It concerned the attempted unrolling of the larger of two mummies obtained by John F. Goucher from the National Museum in Cairo and which he had given to the Women's College in Baltimore in 1895:

> It has been Dr. Goucher's intention from some time to make anatomical examinations of the mummies, and yesterday afternoon he made the attempt but it was not successful.... When the mummy proper was lifted from the case

it did not look unlike a large sack covered with pitch. Dr. Goucher went to work on the outside covering with a pair of shears, but he found his task a harder one than he had contracted for. The pitch layer was finally pierced, and then a couple of newspaper men, one armed with a pair of tin-cutting shears, and the other with a screwdriver and a hammer, assisted the doctor in tearing away the next covering. This covering was of linen, and if the bands had not parted from the ravages of twenty centuries, it would have come off in rolls. Most of the upper covering consisted of pads of linen that were placed in various position to give shape to the body.... After these pads were removed, more wrappings were reached. They were wound with great uniformity, and at one place they covered the breast like a pair of suspenders crossed on the back. Under this were broad strips of linen running longitudinally.

All of this was removed with comparative ease. Finally a layer of pitch was reached that looked as if the embalmer had poured a great quantity of it on the body before commencing to the process of winding it up with linen. The substance was as hard as cement, and, after working diligently on it for half an hour, the doctor and his assistants managed to expose the left elbow and also to remove enough of the deposit to show the contour of the right hand. The arms were crossed over the breast. The bone of the elbow glistened white in comparison with the deposit which covered the body, and if there was any skin it had become hardened and was broken off with pitch. Around the neck were a great number of little bandages, and, although Dr. Goucher cut away a great portion, he only succeeded in showing the contour of the head. When the examination had reached this point Dr. Goucher discovered the fact that he had but a few minutes to catch a train for his home in Pikesville, so the examination was brought to an abrupt end.

This mummy became a long-time favorite at Goucher College and is affectionately known as "Boris." It had been on long-term loan to the Baltimore Museum of Art (1938–1971), and also to Johns Hopkins.[32]

Another difficult (and somewhat rowdy) unwrapping will be delineated in the final chapter rather than in this one, as the circumstance surrounding the acquisition of the mummy and its reception fit rather more nicely into that narrative, than they do here. The majority of documented unwrappings in America seem to have been performed more out of scientific curiosity rather than for the purpose of seeking treasure or out of prurient interest, although a few were more spectacle than anatomy or anthropology lessons. The question of ethnicity and race was certainly a highly motivating factor in nineteenth-century examination of mummies, but it was not the only one.

Most of the unrollings were accompanied by lectures illustrative of one or more topics of Egyptology, and were geared to large audiences of interested and intelligent spectators. In many cases the lecturer tried to draw in the audience by references to biblical figures and events, and in that way establish the mummy not just as a curiosity, but as an historical, tangible presence from which to link the present to the past. Many mummies were described as being of high rank, princesses, priestesses, government officials, and the like. Americans did not have much of their own royalty, therefore the chance of seeing some was enticing, even if it were ancient.

What the reactions of audience members were to these sorts of spectacles is not easily discerned, although from comments in the newspapers about the demonstrations, at least some people were a bit disturbed that the remains of a human being had been treated so cavalierly and irreverently. There was enough knowledge of ancient Egyptian funerary belief for some spectators to ponder what would happen to the soul now that the body was away from Egypt. Others looked upon the mummies as mortal object lessons; the figure before them was once human and had the same types of hopes and dreams as the modern spectator had, and that death was, in the end, the same for every person, no matter from what epoch he or she had come.

6

"Better Than Stealing Pennies from the Eyes of Dead Men"

Commercial Exploitation of Mummies in Victorian America

According to a poem on the subject, written in 1952 by Francis Schiller, an employee of the Oxford Paper Company in Rumford, Maine, in the mid 1860s, I. Augustus Stanwood faced a shortage of rags for his paper mill in Maine. Purportedly, while bandaging a cut finger, he remembered hearing or reading that mummies had been burned for fuel in Egypt, and that there was a huge supply of them. He also knew that the mummies were wrapped in many layers of linen, and linen was the best fabric for making paper. He reportedly then imported several tons of mummies into Portland, and had them shipped to Gardiner, where he stripped them of their "clothes" [i.e., wrappings] and made coarse brown wrapping paper from the resultant slurry. This was sold to the local shopkeepers, with supposedly disastrous results. As the poem explains:

> For the cholera bug was hiding in the mummies clothes,
> Why Augustus didn't sterilize, only Heaven knows....[1]

This commemorates one of the more famous (or perhaps it should be "infamous") commercial uses of Egyptian mummies in America during the nineteenth century. In spite of its cleverness, and the probable validity of the basic facts, a great deal of it is incorrect, and belongs in that shady gray area of urban legend, to which hitherto, most such mummy stories have been relegated.

Egyptian mummies were not a new phenomenon to Victorian America. By the 1840s, quite a number of them had been exhibited in museums and traveling shows across the United States. For the most part, they were objects of curiosity and wonder to people—relics of a far away time and place which were only just beginning to be studied in an archaeological way. But there was also an earlier, more gruesome side to the history of modern contact with the ancient Egyptian dead.

Plundering tombs was very nearly an honored national pastime in Egypt. From the time of the first Pharaohs to the present day, the burial places of the rich and famous (and often as not, the poor and not-so-famous) had been

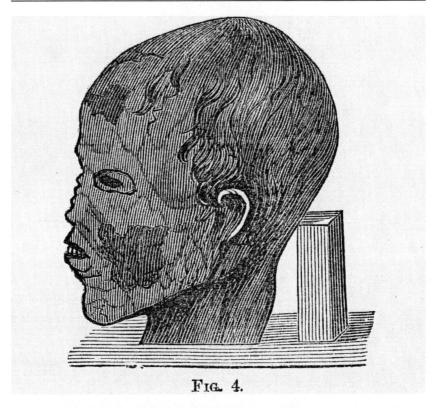

FIG. 4.

Female mummy head in the Phrenological Museum of New York (*American Phrenological Journal and Life Illustrated* [New York, N.Y.], January 1864. Courtesy American Antiquarian Society).

exploited for their treasures. There was a continuous ready market for the gold
and jewels, the aromatics and spices, and other items which could be procured
from the resting places of deceased Egyptians. By the time of the first millen-
nium C.E., even the physical remains of the tombs' occupants were being
exploited. William Brashear gives the following humorous and alliterative
description of the depredations:

> Early Islamic Egypt's clever sons and daughters had discovered a recyclable
> "natural resource" ... mummies! Lying peacefully and innocently about by the
> tens of thousands ... mummies were a convenient source for two valuable
> commodities, the one sartorial (linen), the other sarcophagal ("bitumen").
> Braving the miasmic foul fetor of the millennia—old, musty mausolea, venal
> grave robbers in a grotesque, mocking travesty of the "harrowing of hell" fer-
> reted out and wrested the resting dead denizens from their well-intended, but
> short-lived, eternal repose. In their ghoulish pursuit the pillagers prized out
> the highly prized, doubly precious prey, swiftly and sacrilegiously transform-
> ing the tenebrous tunnels of their forefathers' teeming labyrinthine cenotaphs

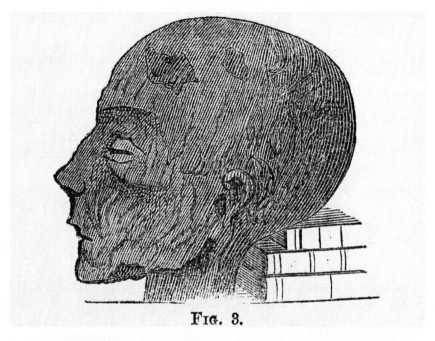

Fig. 3.

Male mummy head in the Phrenological Museum of New York (*American Phreno-logical Journal and Life Illustrated* [New York, N.Y.], January 1864. Courtesy American Antiquarian Society).

into desolate cenotaphs—ancient Anubis' divine devices for defending the deceased proving no match for the wiles of these modern marauders.

Forcing an untimely, unforeseen resurrection on the unsuspecting dead, the grave robbers reascended with their prematurely resurrected prisoners in tow, destined this time not for the empyrean but for a fate far worse than anything either they or their grieving kin ever could have envisioned in their most hideous fantasies of the torments after the tomb. For having once been regurgitated from the ground the departed and now returned dearly beloved were pressed into a loathsomely heinous and abominably repulsive service which in the end would only return them whence they had come, dashing them down again into the ground this time around to be reunited inexorably and irrevocably with the irreconcilable sod. Centuries and millennia ago having already been disemboweled and desiccated, untold *quondam* Satabuses, Thaeses and their progeny, now were not only denuded but, suffering the final ignominy leading up to their ultimate and complete annihilation, dismembered and levigated besides—all for the good of European gullets![2]

As unbelievable as it sounds, for centuries, "mummy" had been one of the staples in the pharmacopoeia of early medicine (see ill. p. 179). It was especially important in American Paracelsian medical philosophy, which advocated the medicinal ingestion of prepared human body parts. As Brashear describes it:

By the +14th c. its use is documented in Christian Europe where such noted physicians and scientists as Vesalius (1514–1564), Paracelsus (1493–1541), Francis Bacon (1561–1626) and Robert Boyle (1627–1691) helped to promulgate its renown. Mummies by the myriads were imported, imbrocated, imbibed and ingested. So great was the demand of "bitumen"-besotted Europeans for the necrotic narcotic that unscrupulous mummymongers, lacking the "genuine" stuff, did not shirk from manufacturing mummy ersatz out of the earthly remains of the more recently deceased and—piling sham(e) upon sham(e)— fobbed off their home-made noxious nostrum, bogus "bitumen," as the bonfide article to slake the cravings of their solvent sarcophagous contemporaries who were all too willing to pay the price if only they could masticate a macerated mummy or chew on a sinewy Sinuhe.[3]

Brashear goes on to note that although "mummia" gradually fell from fashion as more progressive doctors condemned its use, even as late as 1910 the Merck Pharmaceutical Company offered its clients "mumia vera Aegyptica."[4] Indeed, in some specialty shops in America today, it is possible to still procure "mummy powder," although I would not be willing to attest to either its genuiness or efficacy.

Another use for ground up mummies was in the preparation of a lovely shade of dark paint, variously called "Mummy brown" or "Egyptian brown." Frank H. Stauffer reported in 1882 that:

Few persons are aware that veritable Egyptian mummies are ground up into paint. In Europe mummies are used for this purpose—the asphaltum with which they are impregnated being of a quality far superior to that which can elsewhere be obtained, and producing a peculiar brownish tint when made into paint, which is highly prized by distinguished artists. The ancient Egyptians, when they put away their dead, wrapped them in clothes saturated with asphaltum, and could never have realized the fact that ages after they had been laid in the tombs and pyramids along the Nile, their dust would be used in painting pictures in a country then undiscovered, and by artists whose languages were unknown to them.[5]

Putting aside medicines and pigment (both purportedly derived from the desiccated flesh of the mummy), one is left with the sarcophagi (which could be sold to tourists and museums) and the cerements or wrappings in which the bodies were enveloped. These had been doused in ancient times with resins and gums, which served not only to mask any odor of decay, but also to hold the entire ensemble together. Among these aromatics were olibanum, labdanum, issopnax, and ambergris, all of which proved useful in making quantities of incense used in Catholic Church services.[6]

The unguents also had the virtue of rendering mummies, or parts thereof, extremely flammable, which property was demonstrated not only during "archaeological" forays into tombs, but also in popular literature, from H. Rider Haggard's adventure story *She* to the modern day exploits of Indiana Jones. Perhaps the most famous (and most often quoted) of these is the account given by Mark Twain in *Innocents Abroad*, wherein he describes the homely practice of using mummies as fuel for the locomotives which plied the rail line from Cairo to Alexandria: "I shall not speak of the railway, for it is like any other railway—I shall only say that the fuel they use for the locomotive is composed of mummies three thousand years old, purchased by the ton or by the graveyard for that purpose, and that sometimes one hears the profane engineer call out pettishly, "D–n these plebeians, they don't burn worth a cent— pass out a King."[7]

James Silk Buckingham mentioned in 1838, that Egyptian peasants had cut up and burned mummies as fuel, making quite an odor. (He also commented upon using pulverized portions of the bodies to make a dark umber paint and what he termed "momia.")[8]

As early as 1848 articles were appearing in newspapers about the use of mummies as fuel on the rail lines, as evinced in this story from the 1 February 1848 issue of the *Wachusett Star*:

> The powers of Europe, are about to build a railroad across a part of Egypt, to facilitate communication to India. Fuel is by no means abundant in that part of the world and to obviate the difficulty, a bold schemer has proposed to use the mummies that fill those gigantic and mysterious sepulchers, for fuel to drive the locomotives! The cerements in which they are wrapped are first to be taken off and sent to France, where they will be used as material for making newspaper. [Author's note—see more on this topic further on in the chapter].... Think of a Sesostris or pharaoh, disturbed at last from the balsalmic eternity of asphaltum, myrrh, and frankincense in which he has slept ten thousand years, and crammed into the capacious and fiery maw of a locomotive to become the means of dragging a train of Englishmen, Frenchmen and Yankees across his own kingdom.

A small item in the *Daily Standard* (Syracuse, New York) on 27 September 1859 reads: "Egypt has 300 miles of railroad. On the first locomotive run, mummies were used as fuel, making a hot fire. The supply of mummies is said to be almost inexhaustible, and are used by the cord."

An article in the 3 December 1859 *Scientific American* reports the following:

> Fuel for Egyptian locomotives.—There are now over 300 miles of railroads in Egypt. A foreign correspondent gravely states that, on some of these lines, the engine-stokers burn "mummies" for fuel, that the latter make a very hot fire, and that, as the supply is almost inexhaustible, they are used by the "cord." The firemen of these engines must have no *tender* [pun intended] feelings for departed greatness. What a destiny for the Egyptian kings! Think of your body being carefully preserved for three thousand years, and then used to "fire up" a locomotive! "To what base uses do we come at last!"

The paper historian Dard Hunter relates a story from Professor David Stanwood, son of the aforementioned Augustus Stanwood from the opening poem, which states that the elder Stanwood's only competition for Egyptian rags was the Egyptian railroad. "For during a ten-year period the locomotives of Egypt made use of no other fuel than that furnished by the well-wrapped, compact mummies."[9]

One of the more common arguments which is always advanced against this practice is that bodies are notoriously difficult to burn, and even in crematoria it requires a very high heat and a long period of time. This analogy falls apart when one considers that such bodies are fresh and full of moisture, while Egyptian mummies are thoroughly dessicated, and, moreover, many are covered in highly flammable resins and other dried oleaginous unctions. It might also be considered that the mummified bodies of animals, especially if enclosed in cartonnage, would make a nice, compact fuel.

While this has no direct bearing upon mummies in America, it does serve to point out the relative disregard in which the ancient Egyptians were held by the modern inhabitants of that country. Thus they would have no compunction against using the mummies for whatever purposes would generate income.

Prior to the "invention" of using wood pulp processes to make inexpensive paper, almost all American paper was made from rags of linen or cotton. During Colonial times this was not much of an issue; but as the demand for paper rose steadily in the eighteenth century, the supply of rags diminished. There are numerous pleadings from newspaper publishers around the time of the Revolution for people to save their rags for the paper makers. In 1776, the Massachusetts General Court appointed official rag collectors for each population center in order to make sure none of the precious supply was overlooked.[10] Legislation was enacted, which persevered through 1812, exempting skilled papermakers from military service.[11]

The following advertisement of Moses Johnson, a New Hampshire bookseller and newspaper proprietor, in the 22 March 1792 issue of *The Cheshire Advertiser* offered particular inducements to his customers if they would save rags:

> Moses Johnson informs all little misses, and others his customers, that he receives all kinds of cotton or linen rags and flatters himself they will be encouraged to save them when they are informed ½ lb of rags will buy a primer or story book, one yard of ribbon, two thimbles, two rings, twelve good needles, two strings of beads, one penknife, nine rows of pins—4 lb will buy a pair of handsome buckles, or the famous history of Robinson Crusoe who lived 28 years on an uninhabited island.

In 1804, the American Company of Booksellers offered a $50 gold medal prize for the greatest quantity of paper made from something other than rags, and a $20 medal for wrapping paper.[12]

The paper shortage impacted not only America, but also England. The search for a substitute for rags which would be economical and easily obtainable was on. By 1800 as many as one hundred thirty-five substitutes had been suggested by paper making experimenters, including asbestos, thistles, potatoes, linden leaves, St. John's wort, corn husks, cabbage stalks and cattails.[13] In

ENGLISH MUMMY-PILL FACTORY.

A humorous depiction of a fictitious London mummy pill factory (James Ewing Cooley, *American in Egypt with Ramblers through Arabia Petræ and the Holy Land during the Year 1839 and 1840* [New York: D. Appleton & Company, 1842]).

1700 Chancellor Robert R. Livingston held a patent on papermaking improvement based on utilizing the alga frog spittle. Other United States patents involved seaweed, seagrass, and straw.[14] Horseradish and bleached, desiccated cow manure were also proposed.[15] By 1719 a French scientist, Rene Antoine Ferchault de Reaumur, had conceived of the idea of using wood to make paper, purportedly by watching the actions of wasps in building their nests. Mathias Koops, in 1800, published a book in London, of which he claimed a part was printed on paper made from wood. He was ahead of his time, and it would not be until 1867, when a paper mill in Stockbridge, Massachusetts, made paper from groundwood pulp. The first newspaper printed on the stuff came out the following year in New York. It was not very good paper, but it was the beginning of the end of sole reliance on rags for paper manufacture in America.[16]

Of course the Japanese had been making paper from beaten mulberry bark for years; and Egyptian papyrus had made from a type of reed, long before the advent of Jesus Christ. Neither of these methods proved very feasible for "modern" papermakers. Although all sorts of substitutions were tried, rags still remained the chief source for fibre for paper. The demand for an alternative was so strong that in 1855, The London *Times* offered a prize of £1,000 for the discovery of another source of fibre for papermaking.[17]

The antithesis to this was to find new sources for rags. Papermakers turned to continental Europe for their supplies. Rags were imported into the United States from about twenty different countries, but the bulk came from Italy—twelve million pounds in 1852 alone, and twenty-four million pounds in 1854.[18]

The idea of using mummy wrappings to make paper was not a new idea. Abd al-Latif, a physician in Baghdad in the late twelfth century is supposed to have originated the idea. He wrote, in a text concerning the thieving habits of the Bedouins:

> There are, however, circumstances which really contribute to strengthen their covetousness.... They occasionally discover, underground, vast caverns of very solid construction, containing an immense number of corpses, deposited there at some very distant period. The corpses are enveloped in winding-sheets of hempen cloth; for some of them, more than a thousand yards have been employed.... The Bedouins, the Arabs established on the cultivated lands, and all those who employ themselves in search of these sepulchral caves, carry away the winding sheets, and every thing which continues to possess a sufficient consistency; these they employ in making dresses, or sell to the manufacturers of paper, who use them in the fabric of paper for the grocers.[19]

In 1825, as recorded in the 10 December issue of the *Independent Chronicle & Boston Patriot*:

> It is intended to build a paper mill on the banks of the Nile, and to manufacture writing paper on a small scale. The Pacha it appears regards the contents of the ancient pyramids and tombs as among the resources of the country; for after a few questions about cotton and hemp rags, he enquired whether the wrappings of mummies would not make good paper.

To many people, the idea of making paper slurry out of mummy cloth was not so far-fetched. There is no absolute date at which the practice started, but Joel Munsell, a well-known and prolific Albany, New York printer and publisher, who had the habit of clipping articles of interest to him from newspapers and magazines, and pasting them in scrapbooks, which would later become the source material for his *Chronology of the Origin and Progress of Paper and Paper-Making*, reported that in 1850, Great Britain imported 23 tons of mummy rags.[20]

The impetus for this hitherto untapped source of rags may have come from the urgings of Dr. Isaiah Deck, who, as early as 1847, was a strong advocate for making use of the vast amount of mummy linen available from the occupants of the tombs of Egypt.[21] Deck was a curious man, an adventurer at heart, who had first gone to Egypt in 1847 to hunt for Cleopatra's lost emerald mines. His father had known Giovanni Belzoni, and Deck had a piece of mummy linen from one of the mummies uncovered by that quondam archaeologist. While searching for evidences of the lost mines, Deck could not help but notice there was a plethora of mummies and mummy parts which turned up in communal burial sites, commonly called "mummy pits."[22]

> So numerous are they in some localities out of the usual beaten tracks of most travelers, that after the periodical storms whole acres may be seen stripped of the sand, and leaving fragments and limbs exposed in such plenty and variety that the wanderer would be impressed with the idea that he was in the studio of a Frankenstein, in an extensive line of business, and the lamented Warburton expresses with much gusto "the erratic Frank at his impromptu breakfast, may boil his coffee and cook his kid steak over an aromatic fire kindled with the spiced bosom of an Oriental princess."

Deck did some calculations, and made an extraordinary proposal, that of turning mummy wrappings into paper, which was first published in *Spettatore Egiziano,* a newspaper under the proprietorship of Abbas Pasha in Cairo.[23]

An anonymous poem concerning this proposal was published in England in *Punch* 29 May 1847, and republished in America in the 3 July issue of *Littel's Living Age* under the heading "Musings on Mummy-Paper":

> Oh shades of Memnon!
> Cheops and Ramses, shake in your cere-cloths!
> Save smoke-dried pashas of true Eastern phlegm,
> None
> Can read, unmoved, the end of all your glory.
> Announced in the Grand Cairo *Spettatore;*
> How in the place of mere cloths
>   Of woolen, linen, cotton
>   More or less rotten,
> As made at Manchester, and sold by every draper,
> They're going to take the bier-cloths,
> That wrap the sons and daughters of old Nile,
> From gilded kings to rough-dressed rank and file,
> And turn them into paper!
> We're not told, in the *Egyptian Spectator,*
> What daring speculator
> Conceived the notion; but I'd make a bet he grew
> Up to the thought from watching Dr. Pettigrew ...
> But yet, methinks, the venerable sheets,
> In which have slept, their long, millennial night,
> Those who once trod Theban or Memphian streets,
> Should not receive the vulgar black and white,
> Impressed by common types on common reams;
> No-mummy-paper should record the dreams
> Of those who'd have society rolled back into the track
> Which the world left five hundred years ago—
> The lovers of the stont status quo.

Selections from this proposal were reprinted in American newspapers in 1847. One of these was *The Friend* for 7 July 1847, and claimed its origin in an unnamed "English paper":

> Mummy scrip from Egypt.—Speculation has taken a new turn respecting the mummies of Egypt. Formerly the question was, Why were they made? The more utilitarian spirit of the present day inquires, What can be made of them? It is actually proposed to strip them of their manifold wrappers of sumptuous linen, in order that the cloth may be manufactured into paper, for the profit of the Pasha's government! The details are given in an article of *Lo Spettatore Egisiano,* an Italian newspaper recently started in Grand Cairo, and conducted with great zeal and ability.
>
> The writer, whose proposal had been already laid before the government, sets out by assuming, that embalming was practiced in Egypt for at least twenty-one centuries, that is from the death of Joseph to the birth of Christ. Allowing thirty-two years to a generation, the population (7,000,000) must

have renewed about sixty and a half times during the twenty-one centuries, That is to say, four hundred and twenty millions of bodies must have been mummified in that period. Estimating the cloth employed in wrapping them up at two kilograms (four pounds) per mummy, there would be a total of eight hundred and forty million kilograms, or 8,400,000 metrical quintals of cloth which may be used for the manufacture of paper. Now supposing that even one half of this quantity has been destroyed by the Arabs and others, let us ask what value may be assigned to the remaining 4,200,000 metrical quintals.

"Here," says the ingenious speculator, "it is necessary to observe, that the cloth which encloses the mummies is all of the finest linen; and everybody knows how superior the paper manufactured from yarn is to that made from other substances. The rags that serve for the preparation of paper are now sold in France at the rate of 200 piastres (50f.) per metrical quintal. Subtracting from this sum 100 piastres for expenses, or rather more, to keep always below an impossible *minimum*, there will nevertheless remain a total of 420,000,000 piastres, or 105,000,000 f., or 21,000,000 dollars. Only admitting the half of this result, viz., 10,500,000 dollars, every one will agree that this industrial resource, reduced to its very lowest proportions, would, nevertheless, yield an immense profit to His Highness the Pasha of Egypt."

On 10 July 1847 *Literary World* reported:

MUMMY CLOTHS—*Le Spettatore Egiziano* (Cairo newspaper) enters into a long calculation of the number of mummies which must have been embalmed and deposited in crypts, pits, sepulchral chambers, &c. during the existence of Ancient Egypt as a great and populous country; and proposes that Mahomet Pasha should allow their clothing to become an article of extended commerce in the linen trade, valued at least at ten millions and a half of dollars!! The digging up of this treasure, it is further calculated, would bring to light jewels and other materials of archaeological price.

Scientific American, on 19 June 1847, took a more frivolous attitude: "Mehemet Ali has found a new source of revenue, in the fine linen in which the immense deposits of mummies are wrapped, by applying it to the manufacture of paper. Calculations founded upon mummy statistics, make the linen swathings of the ancient Egyptians worth $21,000,000. This is better than stealing pennies from the eyes of dead men."

The *Cold Water Fountain*, a temperance newspaper, published at Gardiner, Maine, ran this article in its 17 December 1847 issue:

Mummy cloths for paper. The latest idea of the Pacha of Egypt for a new source of revenue is the conversion of the cloth which covers the bodies of the dead into paper, to be sold to add to the treasury. It is estimated that from the year 2097 B.C. to the year 1, of our era, four hundred and twenty millions of Egyptians have died in the "Valley of the Nile." All these millions were embalmed, and all wrapped more or less fully in linen, furnishing 8,400,000 metrical quintals of cloth which may be used for the manufacture of paper. This calculation does not include the land of Ethiopia, nor the three centuries that elapsed before Egypt began to bury its dead with spices, &c. And, as the value of the resuscitated wrappings, the estimate is as follows:—

"The cloth which encloses the mummies is all of the finest linen; and every body knows how superior the paper manufactured from linen is to that manufactured from other substances. The rags that serve for the preparation of paper are now sold in France at the rate of £70 per metrical quintal. Subtracting from the sum 100 piastres for expenses, there will nevertheless remain a total of 320,000,000 piastres, or 21,000,000 dollars, (about £4,000,000 sterling,) only admitting the half of this result, 10,500,000 dollars, every one will agree that this industrial resource, reduced to its very lowest proportions, would, nevertheless, yield an immense profit to the government of His Highness, the Pacha of Egypt."

The *Tri-Weekly Ohio Statesman* of 17 July 1847 printed this rebuttal of the entire idea under the headline "Mummy cloth paper:"

Mr. Gliddon, our authority on Egyptian matters, has written a letter to Park Benjamin, of the "American Mail," in which he says the project of making paper out of "mummy cloths, from which the Pacha of Egypt was to reap four millions of dollars, is all Cairo claptrap." ...

In 1838 Mr. Gliddon carried out from this country [i.e., Egypt] materials, samples, &c. for the conversion of all Nilotic materials into paper.... In the list of those proposed was the one now suggested, mummy cloths; which, on investigation, were proved to be utterly valueless for the object in view, from the following causes: laying aside the fact, that granting that 500,000,000 bodies have been "mummified" from first to last, but that of course not a tithe of that amount can remain, after fifteen centuries of ceaseless desecration, yet the expense of exhuming those now left—even in a country where despotism has reduced the wages of labor of able bodied men to five cents a day—would render the undertaking profitless. For the clothes of the few mummies now remaining of the old empire, or pyramidal period, ending with the 12th dynasty, about 2097 B.C., not having been bitumened ... are perfectly rotten, and of course unfit for paper; while those still obtainable from mummies of a later date, i.e., from the beginning of the new empire, 18th dynasty, 1800 B.C., down to Roman days, except those of priests and nobles (which are very rare and inaccessible) are so impregnated with bitumen and are often so completely scorched as to be still more unsuitable for paper.

Sometime after this, Deck left England for New York City, where he found an audience for an expanded version of his paper published in 1855 as part of the *Transactions of the American Institute of the City of New-York, for the year 1854*. In an article entitled "On a Supply of Paper Material from the Mummy Pits of Egypt. By Dr. Isaiah Deck, chemist, etc. New-York." Deck sets forth the following statements and comments:

At a time when the leading journals, and the mass of the reading public of the Old and New World are invoking the aids of their respective governments and scientific investigators to devise some means for remedying the scarcity and increasing price of rags, and those materials hitherto adapted to the manufacture of paper, it is presumed a few practical facts, founded upon the author's experiments and observations in relation to sources of supply of linen for this necessary fabric, for many years will be acceptable, and ultimately available.... I have taken pains to acquire exact paper statistics from the sources within my reach and observation.

A brief summary of these up to the end of 1853 and '54, and upon which calculations for the future may be safely founded, will not be uninteresting here, and prove that the average consumption of paper in the United States, is fully equal to 15 lbs. per head per annum, or three hundred millions of pounds ... to meet this demand. There are in the States about 800 paper mills at work, consuming 405,000,000 lbs of rags, and the imports and exports of the article being pretty nearly equal; the average value of these rags at four cents per pound, being $16,200,000 ... and assuming the present supply of rags to be an average product for years of the imported and home grown, it will, in a few more, at our increasing rate of population, fall far below the actual demand....

The source of supply of rags to which I would direct attention either of companies or private speculators, is from the contents of the mummy pits, tombs and catacombs of ancient Egypt, and having been commissioned during a former mineralogical investigation of the valley of the Nile, and an exploration of Upper Egypt as far as Mount Zalora, to endeavor to discover the long lost emerald quarries of that region ... to report also practically upon this subject, with the facts recent in my memory, I give you the statistical results which I contributed at the time to "Lo Spettatore Egiziano," an Italian newspaper, published in Grand Cairo, and there conducted with great zeal and ability under the patronage of the late viceroy, Abbas Pasha.

The quantities of mummies still preserved in the pits and tombs in the Valley of the Nile from Cairo to Thebes, and in the crypts located in the Arabian and Libyan chain of mountains, appears almost incredible except to those acquainted with those localities.

Deck then reprises his calculation and estimates, and goes on to talk about the quality and quantity of linen available. "It is by no means rare to find above 30 lbs. weight of linen wrappings on mummies; one from the collection of Mr. Davidson yielded, when unraveled, nearly 300 yards, and weighed, when bleached, 32 lbs. A princess, from the late Mr. Pettigrew's collection was swathed in 40 thicknesses, producing 42 yards of the finest texture."

Deck calculates that the supply of cloth would be able to supply the demand in the United States for about 14 years, by which time he thinks it reasonable to conclude that scientific research will have, by that time, come up with a medium for manufacturing paper in which rags would play but a meager part. He goes on to conjecture that human mummies would not be the only source of linen for paper mills:

> The supply of linen rags would not be limited to the mummies of the human species alone; independent of that obtainable from this source, a more than equal quantity could be depended upon from the mummies of the sacred bulls, (symbol of Apis), crocodiles, ibides and cats, which last animals occupied a high position in their domestic theology, symbolizing the various phases of the moon in the pupil of the eye contracting and expanding. They were highly cared for by a body of priests ordained especially for their service, were most bountifully fed on a small species of catfish, (silurs, or slyfish) and when dead were spiced, embalmed and swathed in a superior quality of linen, potted in earthen ware jars of quaint feline shapes, and deposited in sepulchers

prepared expressly for them at Sakkarah.... The crocodiles were equally provided for.

Deck also talks about the burning of the bones of the sacred bulls to provide charcoal for refining sugar, and for clarifying the juice and syrup in its manufacture. He thinks it not unreasonable that because of their close proximity to human mummy pits, the human bones might be easily substituted for the animal bones. He points out there is no need for keeping the wrappings, just the skeletons, and that this might prove to be a way to secure rags "at a trifling cost," as they would be thrown away after the bones were extracted. He quotes an historian "as early as Abdalatif, " whom he says records the early use of mummy wrappings for paper manufacture, and describes the kinds of paper he has himself been able to make:

Some specimens of delicate cloth ... I have caused to be manufactured into bank note and writing paper of the finest but toughest material and texture, with some coarser fragments found in nearly equally ancient mummies, and evidently substituted by the embalmers between the folds instead of finer cloth (proving that "cabbaging" is not of modern date) makes a paper of "single or double milled" cartridge kind, equal to that of the most recent rags; and as the Egyptians were but imperfectly acquainted with the art of dyeing, except in the piece, and then only in primitive colors, and not at all with the art of bleaching, the pulp can be readily got up to any degree of whiteness and strength. The latter may be judged of when I state that some bandages, from five and six yards long, have been stripped from mummies their entire length without tearing.

For the important purposes of papier mache the coarser kinds of fragmentary rags may be used with great advantage. Indeed, so well is this property known to the Arabs always in attendance on the traveler, that they supply him with a sort of impromptu pulp from the boiled and beaten rags to take impressions of the hieroglyphs from the monuments; when hardened they can be rolled up in sheets for transport and future reference.

Once he finished extolling the virtues of the rags, he turned his attention to other by-products of the de-mummification process:

The question of "will it pay?" may be readily answered by assuming the value of the rags to be from 4 to 6 cents per pound; in the United States this is considerably under the market estimate of fine linen rags; the cost of purchasing, collecting and transportation would be under 3 cents, while on the other hand the substances used in the process of embalming would be far more valuable than the swathing envelopes; aromatic gums of the rarest and most expensive qualities, and such as are now used in preparing the costliest incenses for the ceremonies of the Catholic Church, I speak of olibanum, labdanum, issopnax, ambergris, &c. These and other resins of an equally rare species, were employed in embalming the superior class of mummies, and can be readily separated from the animal remains and the cloth, by solution and distillation, while the varieties of bitumens, employed in the inferior mummies, could be made equally serviceable for varnishes, illuminating and machinery oils. At the same time the animal remains can be manufactured into soap (they are too dry for glue or gelatin); the alkali or soda necessary for the purpose, existing in abundance in the natron lakes ... and the bones are convertible into animal charcoal or guano.

Deck also does not dismiss the possibility of relics and "antiquarian curiosities" whose value in resale to collectors could offset any cost in digging out the mummies. He ends his dissertation with a bit of humor:

> I think it not *outre* on the imagination to predict that a Rosseau, Abelard and Heloise of the next generation may transcribe their amorous epistles on "ivory satin," once the chemisettes enveloping the bosom of Joseph's fair temptress, or a sheet of the "New-York Times" be issued on the indestructible shroud of Moses' fairer (Pharaoh) stepmother ... and I would ask them whether it is not preferable to employ the clean and sound linen wrappings from a virgin mummy to the dubious rags collected from the loathsome persons of the Lazaroni, who swarm the quays of the chief seaports of Italy and Spain, and are equally the pest and annoyance of travelers in the interior, and from which source more than four-fifths of the present raw material for paper is obtained ... I have samples of the wrapping and paper which I shall present to the American Institute, and shall be happy to afford further personal information.

Signed and dated: "Isaiah Deck, M.D., 113, Nassau Street, N.Y. March, 1855."

Given the choice between rags which were strongly implied to have come from diseased, if not in fact leprous, persons, and rags which had been contaminated only with sand, Deck felt that manufacturers could only make one decision—to import mummy wrappings to make paper.[24] Deck does not say where he made his paper specimens or what happened to them after he made them; although he did offer them to the American Institute, there is no indication they ever received them.

Joel Munsell recorded the following item for 1855: "Egyptian rags did not make an appearance in this country until the present year, when a cargo of 1215 bales arrived, and were purchased by J. Priestly & Co. at 4 and 3⅜ cents a pound on six and eight months time. The bill amounted to $25,000.—Paper trade reporter."[25]

There is no further note to say where that cargo of rags went once J. Priestly & Co. had bought them, but it is not beyond possibility than some of them found their way to upstate New York.

On 31 July 1856 the Syracuse *Daily Standard* informed its readers that their familiar daily newspaper was not its usual self: "Rags from Egypt.— Our daily is now printed on paper made from rags imported directly from the land of the Pharaohs, on the banks of the Nile. They were imported by Mr. G.W. Ryan, the veteran paper manufacturer at Marcellus Falls, in this country, and he thinks them quite as good as the general run of English and French rags." Munsell's *Chronology* duly reports this, with an added fillip: "1856. The Syracuse *Standard* boasted that its issue was printed on paper made from rags imported directly from the land of the Pharaohs, on the banks of the Nile. These were said to have been stripped from the mummies."[26]

Scientific American of 9 August 1856 also reports on this sensation: "The wrappings of mummies. A newspaper came to us yesterday from Syracuse, New York, made from rags imported directly from Egypt, and which had once wrapped within their folds the mummified remains of the descendants of Mizraim." The *Daily Standard* for 19 August 1856 cribbed the following from *The Albany Journal*:

> An Onondaga county man, worshipful of the golden Eagle and not of the Egyptian Ibis, has put upon the market "paper made from the wrappings of mummies." Could anything better illustrate the practical character of this age, and the intense materialism of America?
>
> With an intense materialism that shears right through sentiment, and world's ideas and usages, this American sees fibre in all the mummied dead of Egypt. He would not ask for nor accept moral instruction, political teaching, artistic suggestions, or historical learning from the preserved and garnered generations of the rulers, warriors, architects, and mechanics of the foremost state of the Old World. It is fibre he wants, and nothing but fibre. He would pass the cerements of Cleopatra through a paper mill as quick as he would the shirt of Winnebago. Pharaoh would be to him but so many reams of "demy," "commercial post," or "satin note," He would not question him about the first fugitive slave law, nor the Nile granite quarries, nor the Pyramids. He would curtly ask him for his fibre, and would inform him that his mill was idle, while he delayed producing his fibre. If Potiphar's wife tendered to his ear a whispered confession, he would interrupt her with a directive—"your fibre, Madame, if you please, the mill is idle."

On 4 November 1856, under the heading, "The Rags and Paper Business," the New York *Tribune* reported that paper manufacturers in the United States were running short on domestic rags, and needed to import them in order to keep making paper:

> The Custom-House books show that the rags come from Alexandria, Smyrna, Trieste, Leghorn, Genoa, Ancona, Palermo, Messina, Actinia, Hamburg, Bremen, Great Britain, Madeira and Havana. It is within a very short time that rags have come from the Nile, and now it is quite a business. About two and a quarter millions of pounds have come to New York from Alexandria last year.... In Smyrna the sorting, washing and drying of the rags is done by government contract, and the bales thus made up of assorted articles are so marked that the manufacturers know the quality of the articles, as numbers one, two and three.

Sometime during this period, a paper mill in Broadalbin, New York, was purportedly making paper from mummies. According to the reminiscences of Dr. Myron K. White, who had worked as a young man in that paper mill from about 1855 to 1860, the mill received great bundles of old mummy wrappings which still retained the form of the bodies which had formed their cores. He recalled that when the workmen tried to straighten out this "cocoon" the linen sprang back into its tightly rolled shape."[27]

In 1858 the *Daily Standard* reported that a Boston importer had bought forty thousand pounds of linen rags "said to be taken from Egyptian [sic] mummies," which yielded thirteen thousand pounds of sand when threshed.[28]

Although there is no indication as to the final destinations of these imported rags, the paper mill market is clearly the front runner in any claims upon these cargoes. And while only some of the statements specifically refer to rags taken from mummies or to mummy cloth, perhaps the articles which mentioned only "Egyptian rags," were trying to spare their readers from the grisly (or as Dard Hunter puts it, "grewsome") reality of the fabrics' source.

In 1859 the Chelsea Manufacturing Company at Greenville (Norwich, Connecticut) advertised in a broadside which was printed for the Norwich Jubilee celebration: "This paper is made by the Chelsea Manufacturing Company, Greenville, Conn., the largest paper manufactory in the world. The material of which it is made, was brought from Egypt. It was taken from ancient tombs where it had been used in embalming mummies"[29] (see ill. pp. 190–191). *The Norwich Jubilee*, a souvenir book published by John W. Stedman at the same time, boasted that the book was entirely a Norwich product, and that the paper upon which it was printed had come from the Chelsea mills. As it is contemporaneous with the broadside, it is almost certainly printed on "mummy paper."[30]

The idea was spreading in the United States—first in New York, then in Boston and Connecticut, and finally as far away as Gardiner, Maine. In 1858, a correspondent from the *Journal of Commerce* who was visiting the Great Falls Mill in Gardiner complained about the smell of the rags. He noted in the *Northern Home Journal* of 12 August 1858:

> Yesterday I visited, in company with Mayor Woods, of Gardiner, the two principal paper factories, and I was astonished in looking at the millions of pounds of rags piled up in warehouses or spread over acres of ground to find that a portion of them had arrived from Alexandria, in Egypt. They were the most disagreeable odiferous old clothes that I have ever had the misfortune to smell. This, doubtless, was owing to the fact that a part of them were in a damaged state. The Egyptian rags had been collected from all the corners of the Pacha's dominions—from the living and the dead. How many cast-off garments of howadjis and hadjis; how many tons of big, loose, Turkish, ragged breeches; and how many head pieces in the shape of old doffed turbans, the deponent sayeth not. But the most singular and the cleanest division of the whole filthy mess came not from the limbs of the present generation of travelers—pilgrims, peasants, soldiers and sailors of Egypt—but were the plundered wrappings of men, bulls, crocodiles and cats, torn from the respectable defunct members of the same.
>
> What a scene to call up the grim past! And what a desecration too, to take the garments of pharaohs, Rameses, and of sacred bulls, holy crocodiles, and pious cats, and mingling them with the vulgar unmentionables of the shave-pated herd of modern Egyptians, to ship them to the other side of the world—to a land which Ptolemy's map had no room for—there to grind them up to the music of the cogwheels and the falls of the Cobbossee Contee.
>
> How little did the religious old Egyptians think that they were piling away stores for the future cash accounts of Turkomans, and that the linen folds

which so carefully bandaged their holy dead, should one day make highly calendared paper. Mummy cloth as well as old rags from Italy (how do they manage to produce so many rags there!) are ground up and come forth mingled in fond embrace and in the purest white. It has been estimated that some of the Egyptian rags contain about 40 percent dust and dirt. The dusts doubtless consists of many fine particles of pharaoh's embalmed subjects, but not a few of the modern rags seem to have been spread upon the sands at the periodical overflow of the Nile, and received a deposit of the fine earth that has been washed down from the mountains of Abyssinia. This adds to the weight, but Yankees will not be sold twice in this manner.[31]

The Wisconsin Weekly Free Democrat observed on 18 August 1858: "At two of the principal paper factories at Gardiner, Me., paper is made from the rags of mummies, recently arrived from Alexandria, Egypt. A correspondent of the New York Journal of Commerce says the New York Ledger, the Boston Courier, and the Boston Journal use this paper" (see ill. p. 193).

Isaac Augustus Stanwood had been involved with the paper industry for many years (see ill. p. 194). In 1865 he moved to Gardiner, where he started a paper mill in partnership with William Towar, near the Great Falls mill on the Cobbossee Contee. Known as the Cobbossee Mill, it was situated at Dam #5.[32] Great Fall's mill was above him, at Dam #6[33] (see ill. p. 195). Cobbossee Mill was a one-machine mill, which made "bogus manila paper."[34] According to reminiscences by his son David, Stanwood had serious difficulties in obtaining rags for his mill during the Civil War. He imported several shiploads of mummies; threw the wrappings and the papyrus filler into his machinery, and from the resultant slurry made a coarse brown paper, which he then sold to shopkeepers, grocers, and butchers who used it for wrapping paper. According to the younger Stanwood, the rags were blamed for a cholera epidemic in the town.[35]

Stanwood purportedly had his own agent in Cairo, with whom he dealt, and a gang of women who did the actual stripping of the linen from the mummy bodies.[36] Another version of the story has Stanwood haunting the docks in Portland for rags, and then sharing a mug of ale with a sea captain, discussing the tantalizing prospects of importing mummies to rectify the rag shortage. Stanwood and the captain struck a deal and months later, Stanwood had a shipload of mummies on his hands. He had to store them in a cool, dry place to keep them from rotting, and so he kept them in pits dug on property he owned, ten miles southwest of Portland. He kept the location of these pits a secret, of course. He only used a portion of his supply, and so to recoup his investment, he tried to sell the mummies but no one wanted them. The secret of their location died with Stanwood.[37] Yet another version of the story states that the mummies themselves were burned after their disrobing.[38]

Stanwood died on 4 March 1914. His extensive obituary in the New York Herald of 6 March 1914 mentions the infamous mummy rags:

He entered the paper manufacturing business with his father at an early age. That was when paper was made from rags and the industry had grown to such an extent that the manufacturers were forced to import their supplies. Large importations of mummy clothes were shipped here from Egypt and also rags from Italy. Because the health authorities were lax in those days the germs carried by the rags caused epidemics of cholera, it was said, among the rag sorters in the mills through the country.... It was to remedy this evil that Mr. Stanwood started to experiment with wood as a material for making paper.

In 1864, a Boston entrepreneur named Samuel Dennis Warren bought the Copsecook Paper Mill begun in 1852 by the Great Falls Company on the Cobbossee Contee (see ill. p. 193). Warren, known as "Dennis" to his family, was not just a papermaker, but also a rag merchant. He was, in fact, an early pioneer in the large-scale importation of rags into the United States, and actually made more money from the fibre business than he did in papermaking.[39]

Rags were unloaded on the docks in Portland, Maine, and then hauled by the wagonload to Warren's other manufactory, Cumberland Mills, in Westbrook. One of the storehouses for the rags was on the island between the bridges of the Presumpscot River where the mills were situated.[40]

The rags came from Japan, Belgium, and Sweden, but most of them came from Italy and Egypt. The ones from Egypt were taken from Egyptian mummies. According to Warren's son Fiske, Warren wanted "to convert dirty useless rags [from the Old World] into clean, useful paper."[40]

The Cumberland Mills (formerly Congin Paper Mill) at Westbrook made brown and manila paper from old bags and jute butts for the Portland market. But in 1864, Warren, seeing more opportunity, bought the mill in Gardiner in order to manufacture newsprint from bleached cotton and linen for the lucrative Boston paper market.

The rags were brought to the mills where they were sorted, shredded and retted. The smell associated in particular with the rags from Egypt, brought suspicion onto Warren, and the miasma was blamed for several outbreaks of "pestilence." The smell was described as an "unpleasant wet paper bag smell" and Warren's son Samuel was said to have often tried to convince his friends that the smell had nothing at all to do with mummy rags.[42] In 1874, the Cumberland Mills were one of the first to experiment with "soda pulp," and by 1904, were using almost no rags for their paper manufactures, although the company continued to import Japanese rags in big Maine square-riggers well into the 1890s.[43]

Around 1927, a Warren scion was supposedly approached by a salesman who wanted to cheaply unload between five and ten thousand pounds of rags which were at the Portland docks. The fast-talking salesman gave away some

Opposite: Broadside of the order of celebration for the Norwich, Connecticut, Jubilee, which clearly states the paper on which it was printed had been made from the stripped wrappings of Egyptian mummies (*Bi-Centennial Celebration, Norwich, September 7, and 8, 1858* [(Norwich, Conn.): Manning Perry & Co., (1858)]. Courtesy Brown University Library).

BI-CENTENNIAL CELEBRATION,

Norwich, September 7, and 8, 1859.

MANNING, PERRY & CO.,

Steam Book and Job Printers,

Chapman's Block, Franklin Square.

Publishers of the "Norwich Morning Bulletin," (daily,) and "Eastern Bulletin," (weekly.)

HYMN.

FOR THE BI-CENTENNIAL ANNIVERSARY OF THE SETTLEMENT OF NORWICH, CONN.

To be sung in the tune of Old Hundred.

We praise the God who guides our feet
 Back to this sacred spot of earth,—
With filial gratitude to greet
 Our Mother, on her day of birth.

We praise Him for these cultured glades
 Redeem'd from thorns and savage sway,—
For rock, and stream, and woven shades
 That charm'd our childhood's cloudless day.

We praise Him for the happy homes,
 The prosperous marts that thronging rise,
The peaceful academic domes,—
 The church-spires pointing to the skies.

We praise Him for the righteous dead,—
 Who have their course so nobly spent,
And o'er their race rich-luster shed
 When through Heaven's open gate they went.

We praise Him for the wondrous change
 The last two hundred years have wrought,
For His blest Gospel's glorious range
 Of faith and hope and holy thought:—

And as the past with joy is bright,
 So may the unborn future prove,—
And wrap thee in new robes of light,
 Sweet Land !—the Mother of our love.

L. HUNTLEY SIGOURNEY.

CHELSEA MANUFACTURING COMPANY.

This paper is made by the CHELSEA MANUFACTURING COMPANY, Greeneville, Conn.,

THE LARGEST PAPER MANUFACTORY IN THE WORLD.

The material of which it is made, was brought from EGYPT. It was taken from the ancient tombs where it had been used in embalming mummies. A part of the process of manufacturing is exhibited in the procession. The daily production of the Company's mills is about 14,000 pounds.

samples, and the Warren Company's chemists worked a full day to try and find a solvent which would dissolve the gum with which the cloth samples were impregnated, and failed. Without a way to remove the sticky substance, the rags were useless. Confronted with this fact, the salesman admitted that the rags were, in fact, mummy cloth. The unnamed Warren refused to buy them, as he felt there was no way to inexpensively remove the gum; he was also afraid of the adverse publicity which using mummies for paper would bring. The sample was then purportedly buried "somewhere around Gardiner."[44] Nothing further was said about the fate of the bales of mummy wrappings left languishing on the Portland docks.

In 1874, H.R. Richards was summoned from Boston to Gardiner to take control of the family paper business there. The mills had originally been established by his wife Laura's grandfather Gardiner (for whom the town was named) and had been managed by Francis Richards throughout that time.[45] The Richards Mill was located at Dam #7, just above S.D. Warren's mill and the mills of Hollingsworth & Whitney (which had formerly been I. A. Stanwood's mill)[46] (see ill. p. 196).

Laura wrote about her remembrances of the paper trade in Gardiner:

> In those years paper-making went through the greatest of its many revolutions. The day of wood pulp was dawning; the day of rags was drawing to a close; and with it—or so it seemed—the romance of the ancient trade.
>   Linen clippings, "domestics," "Blue Egyptian." The old names bring back the old memories.... I see those other rooms, where the ragpickers toiled over their multicolored heaps, in an air thick with dust and lint.... "Blue Egyptian" were what their name implies—indigo cotton rags, dirty and odiferous, yet with an aroma all their own. There was no knowing what you might find in them.... Once a bale was received containing clothing of such a fine quality and so little worn that suspicion was instantly aroused, and the bale set carefully aside till inquiry should be made. Not so carefully, though, but that a few "hands" peeped, handled and appropriated some of the "good" clothes. The smallpox epidemic that followed it is not yet forgotten.[47]

Maine was not the only area of the country using mummy cloth for papermaking. In 1862 Ayer & Co. of Lowell, Massachusetts (manufacturers of patent medicines, particularly Ayer's Cherry Pectoral and Cherry Drops), received a cargo of rags in exchange for a shipment of their medicine (see ill. p. 198). According to an article in the *Davenport Daily Gazette* of 8 August (cribbed from the *Daily Evening Journal*), the rags were:

> Evidently gathered from all classes and quarters of the Pacha's dominions—the cast off garments of Hadjis and Howadjies—white linen turbans, loose breeches, and flowing robes. Not the least part of their bulk is cloth in which the bodies were embalmed and wound for preservation three thousand years ago. They are now to be made into paper for Ayer's Almanacs, and thus, after having wrapped the dead for thirty centuries, are used to warn the living from the narrow house which they have so long inhabited, and to which, in spite of all our guards and cautions, we must surely go.

Paper Mills, Gardiner, Me.

View of the Gardiner paper mills from the river side (*Papermills, Gardiner, Me.* [Gardiner, Me.: s.n., n.d.]).

Munsell's *Chronology* shows this entry for 1866:

> The editor of the *Bunker Hill Aurora* said, that a few Sundays before, he heard a clergyman, in illustrating a point in his discourse, state that during the late war, a New York merchant, at Alexandria, in Egypt, having occasion to furnish a ship with a freight homeward, was led, partly through fear of pirates, to load her with mummies from the famous Egyptian catacombs. On arriving here, the strange cargo was sold to a paper manufacturer in Connecticut, who threw the whole mass, the linen cerement, the bitumen, and the poor remains of humanity, into the hopper, and had them ground to powder.

"And," added the speaker, "the words I am now reading to you, are written on some of this paper."[48]

Harrison Elliott, repeating and commenting on this "traditional story," makes the observation that although the use of clay as a filler in papermaking was of comparatively modern usage, here was a man who made use of a different sort of "clay" in his work. Elliott says "The thought occurs that this might be a better disposition of human clay than that afforded by cremation which reduces it to unknown ashes, a wasteful process.... This phase of the human element in papermaking, man serving as filler, has possibilities."[49]

It is highly unlikely that the bodies ever made it to America. There was a thriving business in Alexandria involving separating the cloth from the bodies—the fabric going into the international rag trade and the corporeal remnants being ground up for fertilizer. Villiers Stuart wrote in 1879 of the scattered mummies and mummy parts which he saw in the crocodile catacombs (and which applied equally as well to human bodies):

I enquired how it came that the mummies had all been disturbed and scattered about; they told me that a great number had been taken away by the Viceroy, but that the greatest destruction had been caused by a German speculator, who, about three years ago, came and employed men to bring out the mummies wholesale; he stripped them of their bandages, and freighted a large barge with them as rags for the papermills; the bones of men and reptiles alike he carried off to make superphosphate of, so that the poor Egyptian who took such pains to find a resting-place where they might never be disturbed, have been applied as manure to the ground, and will be eaten in the shape of bread grown from this strangely compounded superphosphate.[50]

An anonymous author penned, in the 7 July 1881 *Waukesha Freeman:*

Of all the queer flours we have heard of, says an exchange, mummy flour is the queerest, and yet it is actually an article of commerce in Egypt. With an iconoclasm which "out-yanks the Yankee" the inhabitants of Egypt have been dragging forth the mummies which have lain for centuries in the catacombs and grinding them into powder. This "mummy flour" is shipped to Europe for fertilizers.

Yet another use for the bodies was reported by the 22 November 1879 *Mountain Democrat.* "The mummy crop of Egypt is running short and the price is going up since it was found they make good lamp-black." There was no need to transport the bodies at all—they had already been extracted for other use. Besides, no respectable ship captain would want to carry so much "dead weight" which would bring him much less profit than transporting just the rags.

In 1869, an unnamed contributor to *Eighty Years' Progress of the United States* penned the following comments:

The use of cotton for clothing has become so general so as to have an important influence upon the supply of rags. It has to a considerable extent superseded linen. When cotton cloth has been much worn, it is of little value for pulp, since the

I. Augustus Stanwood, of Gardiner, Maine, entrepreneur and papermaker who imported mummy wrappings to use in making coarse brown wrapping paper (*National Cyclopedia of American Biography* [New York: James T. White & Co., 1910]. Courtesy American Antiquarian Society).

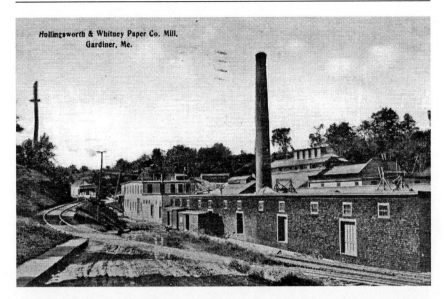

Hollingsworth & Whitney Paper Co. Mill,
Gardiner, Me.

Hollingsworth and Whitney papermill, formerly the mill owned by I. Augustus Stanwood, a single vat mill, which made bogus manila paper from mummy wrappings. This mill is still standing, although no longer in use (Hollingsworth & Whitney Paper Co. Mill, Gardiner, Me. [Gardiner, Me.: s.n., n.d.]).

paper made from it will hardly bear its own weight. To remedy this, imported rags, which are supposed to be about 80 per cent. linen, are mixed with the domestic cotton rags, giving the paper a strength and fullness it would not otherwise have. The best qualities of writing and printing papers contain 30 to 50 per cent of linen, which is obtained derived from abroad.... Some twenty years since, after the great revulsion of 1837, cotton was so cheap that large quantities were manufactured into paper. It is generally to dear for that purpose. Some years since the project was started of importing the mummy wrappers from Egypt, to convert them into paper. Old Mehemet Ali, who was chief manufacturer in his own dominions, stopped the project, by forbidding and monopolizing that valuable material for his own mills. A curious thing that, that the clothing which swathed dead Egyptians, three to four thousand years since, should now be the medium of knowledge in this nineteenth century.[51]

The 27 June 1877 *Waukesha Democrat* announced that a consignment of mummies from Egypt had been shipped to New Haven on a sailing vessel, as stock for a paper mill. On 7 November 1882 *The Oshkosh Daily Northwestern* reported:

A Milwaukee paper says: a day or two ago a large shipment of "mummy cloth" passed through the city, consigned to one of the paper mills at Appleton. It seems curious that the cloth with which dead Egyptians were prepared for the eternal sleep thousands of years ago should come to light in this age of civilization and find its way into interior Wisconsin to be converted into ordinary linen paper. A vast quantity of this ancient material is used by the Appleton mills.

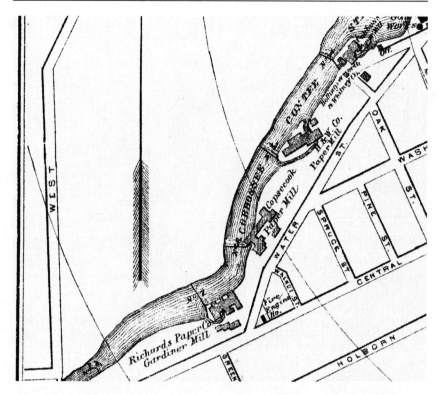

Map of the Cobbossee Conte stream, showing (from left to right) Richards' Mill, S.D. Warren's Mill, and Hollingsworth & Whitney Mill (formerly Stanwood & Towar's Mill). These mills used Egyptian mummy rags to manufacture paper during the latter half of the 1800s (*Colby's Atlas of the State of Maine*, 4th ed. [Houlton, Me.: Colby & Stuart, 1888]).

The Seymour Paper Company, of Windsor Locks, Connecticut, made mummy paper all through the 1880s. The company used Egyptian rags almost exclusively. These rags were shipped to New York and New Haven in sailing boats and tramp steamers in lots of between five and ten thousand tons. To ensure an ample supply of these rags, Charles E. O'Hara, Sr., went to Alexandria in 1881 and built a large plant for sorting and cleaning the rags before shipment to America. The majority of sorters were women and children, who sat amidst piles of rags and sorted them by color. O'Hara had the rags boiled before shipment as it reduced the amount of sand, dirt, grease and foreign impurities and left only the cloth. As labor was much cheaper in Alexandria than in Connecticut, it made sound economic sense to do as much as possible in Egypt. The company could sort between two hundred and five hundred tons of rags a month, and boil and process about one hundred tons a week.

As early as 1879 the Treasury Department halted direct imports of rags, especially from the Mediterranean area, and ports on the Black Sea. Ships conveying such items were to be isolated, and they and their cargoes had to be thoroughly ventilated and disinfected. This had to be certified by health inspectors before the ships could continue to ports in New York, Massachusetts and Maine. These actions were taken in order to protect American citizens from cholera, plague, smallpox and yellow fever, all of which were claimed to be contained within the rags imported for paper making. But a steady increase in the cases of cholera among paper mill workers, particularly rag sorters, in 1883, resulted in the United States Treasury Department halting of all rag importations in 1884. O'Hara railed against this order, explaining that the women and children sorted, played and slept in the piles of rags without contracting cholera or indeed any other illness. And that his boiling of the rags for four to five hours would certainly thoroughly clean them and make them safe.

O'Hara also went on to defend the general cleanliness of the Egyptian rags (a large percentage of which were gathered from mummies) and pointed out that cholera was epidemic in India, especially Bombay, and that the government didn't seem to be concerned about rags coming from that country, only from Egypt where there was no apparent danger. Nevertheless, Egyptian rags came under the interdict, and the Seymour Company could only continue to sort and boil their rags, and hope for the ban to be lifted before they ran out of storage space.[52]

In 1884 the Treasury Department issued a special circular specifically addressing the importation and disinfecting processes for rags originating in Egypt. This all had to take place in Egypt, after which the consul-general at Cairo would issue a certificate attesting to the place and process and the rags would then be allowed to be shipped to the American ports.[53] The largest effect this had on the paper industry was a huge rise in the cost of paper at the time the rags were quarantined, as many mills still depended wholly on rags at that time and could not keep their prices low. Afterwards, when importation resumed, prices sank to new levels, and a great deal of money was made and lost in rag speculation.[54]

A note in the 17 February 1884 *Brooklyn Eagle* states:

> Upward of $10,000,000 worth of rags is imported every year. Curiously, one of the the chief exporting ports is Alexandria, Egypt, whence comes the best rags, possessing a better average texture than the others. Much of the Egyptian rag crop is made up of linen mummy cloths, which, having served as burial robes for thousands of years, are now gathered in by the impecunious Arab, who adds to his scanty store by disposing of them at a good figure to American and English dealers. So you who write upon fine stationery may, perchance, be using in another form, the last garment of some Egyptian king.

The idea of contact with mummies or their wrappings causing disease was not a new idea. Benjamin Franklin wrote of some physicians in London, in 1763 or 1764, who had been taken ill of malignant fevers and died, after having

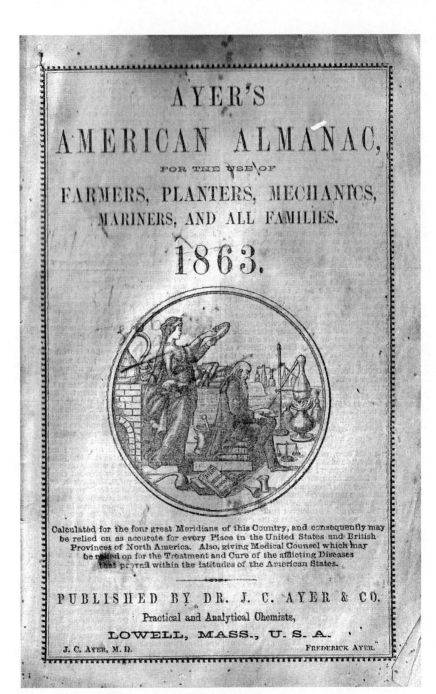

AYER'S
AMERICAN ALMANAC,

FOR THE USE OF

FARMERS, PLANTERS, MECHANICS, MARINERS, AND ALL FAMILIES.

1863.

Calculated for the four great Meridians of this Country, and consequently may be relied on as accurate for every Place in the United States and British Provinces of North America. Also, giving Medical Counsel which may be relied on for the Treatment and Cure of the afflicting Diseases that prevail within the latitudes of the American States.

PUBLISHED BY DR. J. C. AYER & CO.

Practical and Analytical Chemists,

LOWELL, MASS., U. S. A.

J. C. AYER, M. D.   FREDERICK AYER.

This edition of *Ayer's American Almanac* was almost certainly printed on paper made from the mummy rags imported in 1862 (*Ayer's American Almanac, for the Use of Farmers, Planters, Mechanics, Mariners, and All Families,* 1863 [Lowell, Mass.: J.C. Ayer & Co., (1862)]).

attended the dissection of an Egyptian mummy. Opinions differed as to what had actually caused the fever, with at least some of the doctors thinking the infection had been embalmed with the body, and others suspecting the same embalmment had destroyed the illness and the men had died from something else altogether.[55]

In 1874 the public was warned against the consumption of "Golden Drip," a breakfast syrup for pancakes and the like, in articles such as this one which appeared in *The Wellsboro Agitator* of 3 March 1874:

> For behold you, it has been discovered that the elegant, beautiful delicious-looking syrup known as the "Golden Drip" is made of what? Why of rags and muriatic acid! The rags of commerce, the common rags from the papermills, are taken by the skillful chemist and treated with muriatic acid, and from the results this golden drip syrup is made. Imagine the horror which attended this discovery! Rags from Turkey, from the backs of the leprosy-stricken people of the Bosporus—rags from the backs of the filthy lazzaroni of Italy, and rags even from the mummies of Egypt—sweltered through a chemical process, and coming on our tables as Golden Drip.

And in May and June 1877 persons who engaged in the practice of pica were warned by the newspapers (this example is from *The Perry Chief* of 14 June 1877):

> People who make a habit of chewing paper are herby warned not to use postal cards for mastication purposes. During the letting of the contract for printing them last week, it was developed that the linen rags from which the cards are made are mostly imported from Egypt, and are obtained by stripping mummies. Many tons of mummy wrappings are imported every year by American paper manufacturers.[56]

Of course we know much more now about germ theory, and modern medicine has proven that the cholera morbus germ cannot survive very long in open air, and yellow fever and plague cannot be caught from infected clothing, but are instead spread by the actions of mosquitoes and fleas. Smallpox is the only disease which could conceivably be spread by infected cloth, and there were few epidemics of that reported around the mills. It is more likely than not that crowded and unsanitary living conditions in the papermaking towns were the cause of the increase in cholera cases in New England during this time. Not knowing any better, the people in the towns who were affected had to blame something, and mummy cloth was a good target for their worries and fears.

Mummy cloth was not just used for making paper. An article in the 13 May 1890 Waukesha *Evening Journal* (taken from the *Philadelphia Record*) reports:

> From 1860 to 1870 the rage for paper collars stretched across the sea and Egyptian dudes attired themselves in the new gads and gallivanted around the pyramids with the daughters of the people. It is said that so great was the fashion of paper collars in Egypt during this period that the muslin wrappers

around some of the defunct kings were sent to Holyoke, Mass., where they were utilized for the muslin lining of the collars. The records show that the Holyoke paper manufactory received 15,000 yards of these mummy wrappers for this purpose.

There were two manufactories in Holyoke at the time which made paper collars; Franklin Paper Company (founded 1866) and Hampden Paper Company (later Albion Paper Company, founded 1862).[57]

There is as yet, no type of physical or chemical analysis which would prove, or disprove, the mummy paper story. Chemical testing would only reveal that the paper was made from linen. Carbon-14 requires destruction by burning of the sample, and also depends, as does DNA testing on a "pure sample," which, given the circumstances surrounding the manufacture of paper, is impossible. The addition of rags from different centuries would be enough to throw off the Carbon-14 dates and make them unreliable. DNA testing would show that the materials in the paper had come into contact with humans at some point, but the physical processes of making paper (heating, beating, rolling, etc.) would probably have a deleterious effect on any DNA present and so obviate any data obtainable.

As for me, I believe I have seen and touched mummy paper. I own a copy of the *Norwich Jubilee* book, and of the *Ayer's American Almanac*. The paper looks, feels and smells like any other rag paper from the time period. I have no qualms about handling it, although some house guests do cringe and touch it gingerly, if at all. There is probably much more of it extant than anyone will ever know, or be able to prove.

Bloodgood H. Cutter, in his *The Long Island Farmer's Poems* (New York, 1886) penned the following lines in his poem "Pyramid" which seem to sum up the whole concept of mummy as commodity:

> This grave-yard of the Egyptian race,
> Is yet a very solemn place;
> Millions on millions of their dead
> Lie 'neath the ground whereon I tread.
>
> They have taken the bodies, I've heard say,
> For fuel on the great railway;
> For cooking too, have used this fuel,
> Though to us this seems very cruel.
>
> Dismal and solemn was this scene.
> The end of their "life's fitful dream";
> Egypt's great pride lay there in dust,
> To come to that we really must."

7

"No Stiff Has Ever Gone Over This Road Without a Death Certificate"

Egyptian Mummies and the American Public

"Mummies as bric-a-brac" read the headline in the 16 August 1882 Boston *Congregationalist*, in an article copied from *Harper's Magazine*:

> The modern traveler is not content to collect merely beads and funereal statuettes and such small game. He must bring home an ancient Egyptian in *properia persona*. The amount of business done of late years in this grim kind of bric-a-brac has been very considerable. A foreign agent and wine merchant of Cairo assured me that when I returned from the second cataract in 1874, that he had that very season "passed" and shipped no less than eighteen Theban mummies; and many other agents were most likely equally busy and equally successful. Amenhotep III, artfully stowed away inside a crocodile, or Hatasu rolled up in the folds of a sketching-tent, may have easily have slipped by the Alexandria Customs House by one of these gentlemen. Mummies, however, are expensive hobbies, only to be indulged in by the wealthy. From £60 to £100 was at that time the average price of a full sized specimen, while £10 to £12 was asked for a baby.... The ordinary mummy sold to the ordinary tourist is of quite another class. He belonged in his day to the lesser nobility; that is to say, he was an architect, a sacred scribe, a civil or military official. Such mummies, ranging chiefly from the twenty-first to the twenty-sixth dynasties, form the staple of the Theban trade.

In the latter half of the nineteenth century, industrialization and the growth of cites produced families of wealth, and more and more Americans began to tour the world. Egypt was one of those destinations, and although there were still strictures on the exportation of mummies, this did not deter intrepid travelers from bringing back souvenirs. An unusual gift of such relics was recorded in the 8 October 1892 *Stevens Point Journal* which reported upon an unnamed Tioga girl who had returned from abroad with a mummy's hand and foot, a philopena gift from a young admirer. Philopena was a game of forfeits wherein if two people found a double nut in a shell, usually an almond, upon meeting the next time, they would call out a "philopena." The first to do so could demand a present from the other. These gifts ranged from silly to elaborate and often took the form of books. In this case the young gentleman involved decided to be original, and for a few piastres, managed to provide a most unusual forfeit.

John A. Wilson, a photographer who had been present at the opening of the mummy cache in 1881 at Deir el Bahri, and who had documented the historic occasion, wrote the following description of the mummy trade, as quoted from the May *Century Illustrated Monthly Magazine* in the 3 May 1887 *Daily Northwestern*:

> In a line of tombs beyond the Rameseum lived four sturdy Arabs named Abd-el-Rassoul. They supplied guides and donkeys to tourists who desired to visit the ruins of Thebes, and sold them genuine and spurious antiquities. When they found a mummy, it being forbidden by law to sell it, the head and hands and feet were wrenched off and sold on the sly, and the torso was kicked about the ruined temples until the jackals came and carried it away. I purchased a head and hand of one of the brothers amid the dark shadows of the temple at Querneh.

Under a headline "The Mummy as Fad," the *Arizona Weekly Journal Miner* of 7 February 1894 lamented, in an article it had copied from Rae's *Modern Egypt*:

> American visitors to Egypt are accounted the best patrons of Egyptian body snatchers. They are glad to return home with a mummy; they are proud to have their friends see it unrolled; they bury their own dead with surprising care, placing them in caskets within splendid tombs.... A cemetery in America is generally the most beautiful adjunct to a city. Would not the cultured citizens of Boston shudder if told that Mount Auburn would be treated as a mine in which shafts are sunk and levels driven to discover human remains and bring them to the surface, there to be sold to strangers from beyond the sea in quest of curiosities, or else to be put on exhibtion at home.

Many of the mummies thus purchased wound up in museums of one sort or another, not to be dissected but to serve as visible remains of long-ago cultures. Whether this intent was always followed, can be somewhat debatable. The 10 January 1876 *Milwaukee Daily Sentinel* reported the following San Francisco New Year's celebration by the City Guards:

> Beneath a crimson canopy, and shrouded with an American flag, lay all that was left of a once living Egyptian—in fact, a mummy. The corpse was appropriately dressed in black and white, and the ghastly expression of the mask that covered its face horrified all.... Each member as he entered the room, was respectfully led up to the bier, and, as with uncovered head he viewed the remains, a strange, weird sound rose in the air, like the wailings of a soul plunged into outer darkness.... The funeral musicians were about fifteen in number, and were presided over by Paul Scott, who led the band with a devil's fiddle of gigantic proportions, manufactured from a grocery size oil can. The rest of the band manipulated imps' fiddles of every size and shape, from a percussion cap box to the oil can above mentioned. These notes were varied by tin horns.... At half-past 11 the various members of the company, in uniform, formed a line, and after marching several times around the Armory were briefly addressed by Mayor Bryant, who wished them all success in their

organization. They then, with arms reversed, marched out of the armory, escorting the mummy. This was borne by six pall-bearers, and followed by a crowd of mourners in plug-hats ornamented with flags and bearing the emblem "76" in large figures. The company was led by the captain, with a sword dressed with crepe, and under his guidance they marched up Post Street to Powell, thence down Post and into the square, where the line was again formed. Here, with mournful solemnity, the body was deposited upon the grass, and the funeral sermon, delivered by Mr. Penniman, as follows:

Comrades, once more we meet to pay the last solemn tribute to a departed year. which is exemplified by the noble form which lies motionless before us, in silence, and at rest. It is perhaps unnecessary to express the many changes from better to worse, the great and continued misfortunes, through which he has, with indomitable energy, safely passed, to be cut down, alas, in the prime of manhood, and to become, what you now see before you, a piece of lifeless greatness. His was a character that is seldom our lot to look upon, so gentle his temperament, so chivalrous his spirit, and, added to this, his great personal beauty. I could enumerate myriads of acts of the most unbounded generosity of which the world knew nothing. His was a modest and retiring disposition, and of him I can only say "We shall ne'er see his like again."

After the address a salute of five or six rattling volleys of musketry were fired over the corpse, which was then touched with a lighted candle. By some peculiar process of embalming, a large quantity of gunpowder had been placed in the body, and when touched by the fire it went off with a tremendous report. The echo of this had scarcely died away before the two guns of the National Guard bellowed out their salute, and the deep-toned bell of Trinity Church rang out above the heads of the assemblage, proclaiming that '75 was a thing of the past and '76 reigned in its stead.

The crowd then adjourned to the armory where a banquet of sandwiches, coffee, and a few hundred gallons of whiskey and beer awaited them. The latter, however, owing to the strict temperance principles of the company, were principally imbibed by the outsiders.

The provenance of this poor unfortunate mummy has not as yet been uncovered, and it is fairly certain to expect that none of it remained after the celebration.

During the 1870s and 1880s, the students at Mount Union College in Alliance, Ohio, had two mascots—a stuffed gorilla, and an Egyptian mummy. Both were part of the college's museum collections, and President Orville Nelson Hartshorn, ever mindful of the advertising value of the museum, was more than willing to lend one or both artifacts to any fair or exposition which desired an "educational exhibit" from Mount Union College. Exhibits were sent as far away as Jamestown, New York. In 1874 Hartshorn sent parts of the collection to the Exposition at Louisville, Kentucky; in 1875 to the Pittsburgh Exposition; and in 1876 to the Centennial Celebration at Philadelphia. Hartshorn was also usually able to convince the fairs' organizers to pay freightage and build the exhibition platforms.[1] Mount Union College came in for its share of ribbing on the subject. An Alliance newspaper reported "Mount Union has a full lay representation at the Pittsburgh Conference this week. Professor Chapman, the Gorilla, and the Mummy."

Students were very fond of these unusual exhibitions, as exemplified by one student's letter in the early 1880s: "If I should fail to attend commencement, please extend my heartfelt regards to Doctor [President Hartshorn] and the Mummy, to Moulton [a student] and the Gorilla." The mummy even crept into student doggerel written for the college *Annual* in the 1880s: "To the mummy, the much abused mummy; the mummy transported on shoulders and cart; child of the pharaoh, pride of the Doctor, to thee I render my glory and art."

The mummy was always subject to being the butt of pranks. Word would go out "The mummy is dead again" and the hunt for the body would be on. The student kidnappers would send cryptic messages to the faculty and when finally its resting place was discovered, would follow the body in procession back to the college, displaying mock grief, and presenting a "funeral scene rarely witnessed."[2] Sadly, this mummy proved to be, in the end, a disappointment, for when it was finally x-rayed (after the New York World's Fair) only the head, a hand and the two feet proved to be human. The rest was two-by-fours, nailed firmly and wrapped very tightly.[3] Whether this was done in Egypt or after the mummy came to America is not clear.

Mummies and colleges were not always a good mix, as the following article from the *Daily Inter Ocean* of 7 September 1891 (which had copied it from the 27 August issue of the *Washington Post*) reveals. Under headlines of "A Mummy's Night Off," "Lively Scenes Caused by a Deceased Egyptian," "Out with Four Students," "Stampede in the Negro Section of Washington," and "Passengers Suddenly Decide to Walk and Bar-tenders Forget to Charge for Drinks," the following story of student high jinks at Columbian College in Washington, D.C., unfolded:

> Four fun-bent students having in their possession Prf. Fristoe's mummy, created no little excitement Tuesday night. Prf. Fristoe values the mummy very highly, and for years it has been kept in a glass case at Columbian University, where the medical students could view it. Perhaps there is no finer body in existence and the janitors of the building have been instructed for years past to keep a close watch on the Professor's pet.
>
> The Professor did not appear to fear the law students and the janitors were not disposed to believe that they would steal it. Tuesday, however, four young men of the law department concocted a plan to give the mummy a night's outing. At night they entered the building, and told the janitor there were certain books they wished to get. Three of them repaired to the room in which the mummy was kept while the other member of the conspirators entertained the janitor. The hideous-looking mummy was taken from the glass case, and with the aid of a rope which one of the young men had secreted around his body beneath his coat was lowered from a window to the rear yard.
>
> The young men gathered up a few books and departed from the building, the janitor suspecting nothing. After walking down the street the young men returned and secured the mummy, which they succeeded in getting out of the yard without being detected. To get as far away from the university as possible and in the quickest way was their first aim.

Going around to Fourteenth Street, they boarded a car, trying to conceal the grinning mummy as much as possible, but several of the passengers caught sight of it, and they stopped the car immediately, getting off as if there was a sudden outbreak of small-pox or yellow fever. Of course the young men enjoyed the fun, and one of them who was something of a ventriloquist began to make the mummy talk. This settled it. The remaining passengers vacated the car, and the young men and the mummy had it all to themselves until the junction of Pennsylvania Avenue and Seventh Street was reached, when ten or a dozen persons boarded the car, but one by one they dropped off when they saw the mummy, which by this time had a hat and coat on.

The conductor told the young men that they must either throw the thing out or get off the car themselves; but they had no idea of parting company with the mummy, and stopped the car, and after making the ticket puncher shake hands with their pet, got off the car. They entered a saloon near the National Hotel and ordered beer, at the same time placing the mummy on the counter.

"Mine Godt, my frients, vot is dot?" exclaimed the dispenser of liquids as he gazed on the mummy. "You tinks dis vos a grabe-yard?"

Then the mummy began to talk and in less than two seconds the rotund figure of the saloonist made a hasty exit through the rear door leaving the young men in full possession of the place. Mr. Barringer in the absence of the proprietor served the drinks to his companions and then the saloon was vacated. A Chinese laundry was next visited and One Lung and some of his friends soon discovered that they had pressing business in other sections of the city and did not tarry to ask for "washee tickets."

It was late in the night before the Celestials ventured back into the laundry and then it was in company with a policeman. Opposite Carson's Hotel a large crowd of colored people had assembled, but when the young men passed holding between them the mummy the walk was soon cleared and rumors that the "night doctors" were on the warpath spread rapidly. If there is anything in the world a majority of colored people are shaky on it is the body-snatchers, and the appearance of the young men with the mummy was a little more than they could stand. As they proceeded down the street people stopped and looked at the strange sight and wondered what medical college would get the "stiff." Opposite Twelfth Street the young men crawled into a hack, but when the driver saw the mummy he jumped off his box and raised a scene. He wanted it distinctly understood that he was not hauling dead people. A great deal more that the regular fare was offered the cabby, but he refused to turn a wheel, and when he got a good look at the mummy and heard it begin to sing "Down in the cold, cold ground" he dropped his whip and made 2:40 time down D Street. Several cabmen were tried, but the young men could not get one of them to haul them. Before they left the cab-stand there was not a vehicle there. They had succeeded in clearing them out completely, and finding no further amusement there they made a flank movement to F Street where several saloons were visited. One of the bartenders was so badly frightened that he fainted and as he fell he cut his head against the edge of the counter.

Just as the young men came out of the saloon door a colored girl ran up against the mummy. There was a scream resembling that of a lost soul, and she sank to the pavement shouting "Oh, dem night doctors!" Fortunately an alley was conveniently near and into this the young men took refuge until the excitement subsided, when they quietly walked out and made straight for a saloon near Weleker's. Here cocktails were ordered, but the bartender was so badly frightened that he served beer and refused to accept pay. He begged piteously for the young men to leave the saloon, but they did not depart until several rounds of beer had gone down their throttles. The mummy couldn't drink, but several straight ten-cent cigars were stuck into his mouth as he was straightened up to the bar. Several private residences were then visited, and finally the mummy was laid to rest under Mr. Kirkland's bed, and the boys sat up telling ghost stories until the sun was up.

Last night Prf. Fristoe's pet was quietly slipped back into the glass case at the university and when he discovers that the boys have had it out on a lark there will be trouble.

By the late 1880s and early 1890s, mummies were "dirt cheap" as reported by the 12 January 1888 *Elyria Democrat* which quoted Dr. J.A.S. Grant Bey, of Cairo, who attributed the reduction in cost to the takeover of Egypt by the English, as well as to recent discoveries of large deposits of mummies. The price had dropped to ten or twenty dollars apiece, depending on the state of preservation. The doctor also revealed that more mummies were being sold to museum agents than to scientists.

In the early 1880s the necropolis at Akhmim was unearthed by an Italian archaeologist. Thousands of mummies were discovered, many of them in beautifully painted coffins.[4] The following narrative is taken from the unpublished memoirs of John Romich Alexander, and details the extraordinary tale of how some of the Akhmim mummies came to America.

A dozen or so of the mummies from Akhmim were opened and sent for sale at Assiut. Presbyterian missionaries John Romich Alexander, and John Giffen (an 1871 graduate of Westminster College) went to view them, and finding them to be good specimens, they bought four of the most beautiful, which were in highly ornamented coffins, for the price of about eight dollars apiece. The two missionaries felt that mummies would be handsome additions to the collections of several Presbyterian Colleges, in order to enhance their museums of history and science.

One, a priestess of the temple at Akhmim, was given to the college at Assiut; Romich then desired to give one to his *alma mater*, and the two missionaries decided to give one each to Erskine College, in Due West, S.C., and to the College of Wooster in Ohio. As Alexander and his wife and children were due on furlough, he agreed to accompany the mummies to New York and to get them shipped off to their respective destinations.

The mummies were crated up, sent off to Cairo, examined and sealed by the Department of Antiquities. From thence they went to Alexandria, where they passed customs, and were then placed as part of the Alexander's luggage aboard ship, bound for Liverpool. At Liverpool the family and their baggage transferred to a Cunard liner, and headed off to New York. Alexander was under the impression the mummies would be treated as luggage, and was quite distressed to discover that the purser soon came around, demanding that freight had to be paid on the three crates.

Terribly ill with seasickness, as were his wife and children, Alexander plunged into despair over this unexpected development. He had not brought much money with him and did not have enough to pay the fifteen dollars demanded by the purser. He languished in the lounge, worried about his mummies and his family. His wife had bravely gone on deck and found that their fellow passengers were interested in helping her out. Many were interested in the children, but one, Charles Arbuthnot of Pittsburgh, was more interested in the missionary. Arbuthnot had been a good supporter of the Presbyterian Church, and had annually contributed money to their mission board, even though he himself had left the church. He was a kindly man, and his gentle manner and considerations soon had Alexander confessing his problems. Arbuthnot told him not to worry, and the next day gave Alexander's wife twenty-five dollars to buy something for the children in New York, and to pay for the freight on the mummies. Alexander, his family and the mummies reached New York in peace.

They had been in Egypt for ten years, and this was their first trip home. They disembarked and waited for their luggage. Soon all the passengers and baggage had been unloaded, but there was no sign of the mummies. The missionary appealed to the Customs officer, but was told that as it was late, nothing more could be done until the next day. Bright and early Alexander went to the wharf and anxiously watched every box and crate as it was unloaded. There was no sign of the mummies. At lunch time everything came to a temporary halt, and finally, at about four in the afternoon, the precious cases were finally on the dock.

There was, however, no customs officer present, and Alexander was told he'd have to carry the mummies to the Customs House, which was several miles distant. He hired a cart, and headed quickly for the office, where he was told there was no duty on mummies. However, the officers had never seen a mummy and were curious, so the missionary unsealed one of the cases and gave a short lecture. This delayed him long enough that by the time he got to the Pennsylvania Railway freight office, it was closed. The carter was anxious to get paid and get home, but there was not much Alexander could do. He couldn't take the mummies back to the hotel, and there was no other place to store them. One of the freight office employees finally agreed that Alexander could leave the mummies in the outer enclosure of the office, where they could be guarded by the night watchmen. With no other choice, Alexander agreed. The carter helped unload the mummies and went home, and the missionary headed back to his hotel and a restorative bath.

The next day he managed to have two of the mummies shipped without problems, the ones to Wooster and Westminster. However, the third mummy, destined for Due West, South Carolina, presented a fresh problem. The Pennsylvania line could not ship this mummy, it had to go out from the Southern Road station. This was on the other side of town, and so another carter had to be hired, and Alexander trotted off the get his last crate sent so that he and his family could begin their much awaited furlough.

However, the agent at this terminal was not disposed to handle something of which he had never ever heard nor seen. In vain Alexander argued he had already shipped off two mummies on another line, but the agent would have none of it.

> "A mummy, what is that?"
> "A dead Egyptian," the missionary explained.
> "Do you mean to say that you have a dead body in that box?"
> "Yes."
> "Well, I won't receive it."
> "Why not? I have just shipped two by the Pennsylvania Road."
> "How do I know how long it has been dead?"

The agent actually sniffed at the box.

> "This person may have died of some infectious disease and shipping it may spread the disease all along the line!"
> "Oh, don't be afraid. The mummy has been dead for 2500 or 3000 years. It's as dry as punk and won't infect anybody."
> "See here.... Are you crazy or just kidding me? If that is a dead body where is the death certificate? No 'stiff' has ever gone over this road without a death certificate and this one is not going unless you produce a certificate of its death. Take it to the Health Office."

Alexander was beside himself. He had brought the thing safely from Egypt and was not about to throw away a perfectly good mummy because of the obstinacy of the station agent. He demanded to know where the man's superior was, and was told. The agent grudgingly allowed the mummy to remain while Alexander went off, grumbling silently about the culture and mentality of some railway officials. He had not gone far when he was hailed by a passing gentleman, named Mr. Torrey, who had come looking for him.

Torrey had come into the city to meet the Alexanders, who had brought his young niece from Cairo with them. Upon learning of all the difficulties with the mummies, he had gone to see what he could do to help. Torrey listened to the entire story and could not help but laugh at the absurdity of the whole affair. He accompanied Alexander back to the freight office where he bearded the agent in his den. The man kept insisting that Alexander had to be crazy to want to ship a dead body to a college in South Carolina. Torrey could hardly contain his amusement, and finally showed the agent the seals of the Egyptian Antiquities Department, assuring him that there was no danger whatsoever of disease from the mummy. He gave the agent his card and took the responsibility for the shipping on himself. The mummy duly went to Erskine College, Torrey went back to Pennsylvania with his niece, and the Alexanders at last headed for a well-deserved rest with their families in Ohio.[5]

The Westminster College mummy, Pesed, spent the next hundred or so years living a life, as it were, which would have been totally unfamiliar to her. In 1886 she was the chief attraction of the Greenville Citizen's Hose Company Exposition. She was moved from building to building on campus, and sometimes languished in unused storage rooms. She was decapitated at some point, and gained the unsavory reputation of spending unchaperoned nights in dormitory rooms. Finally, in the mid–1980s, Pesed's dignity was restored, and she became the centerpiece of the Westminster College museum[6] (see ill. pp. 210, 212).

The College of Wooster mummy was exhibited in the Wooster Administration building before the 1901 fire which destroyed the building and caused the mummy to suffer some minor burns. It was then moved to different locations, being in the biology building (Scovel Hall) in 1922, and was finally settled in the art museum in the mid–1960s.[7]

Erskine College received a letter from John Giffen telling them of their arriving gift:

> You may tell Dr. Grier that I have gotten an Egyptian damsel, some two or three thousand years old, as far as Alexandria, on her way to Due West. I trust he will be able to so modify the rule of the college excluding females as to admit this lady to the institution. I don't think there is any danger of any of the boys falling in love with her as to neglect their lessons, and she has such old-fashioned, staid and quiet habits, that I do not imagine she will give him the least trouble. She is the daughter of a rich priest, but, still, we will have to ask free admittance, though she may have some treasure sticking to the folds of her quaint gown.

Iset Kheb was an attraction of Erskine College, attracting visitors not only from the student body but also from the surrounding community, where much of the travel of that population was largely confined to attendance at church, or visiting the county courthouse.[8] She was unfortunately burned in the great fire of 28 January 1892 which completely destroyed the main college building.[9]

Not all colleges were as careful with their ancient charges as they might have been. The 14 October 1886 *Washington Post* reported a grisly story from Pittsburgh:

> The remains of a woman were found in an oak box at the Allegheny "dump" near the end of the Union Bridge, at 10 o'clock this morning. The dump is used for the deposit of ashes and filth, and it is supposed that the box was left there by an ash hauler some time this morning. The lid of the box had been broken off by the jar the box received when it fell and its contents had rolled out. The body was nude and in an advanced stage of decomposition. On the box were the labels of the Pacific Mail Steamship Company and the New York authorities of Allegheny City are inclined to think the body was shipped from Europe, but no definite information has been learned in regard to it. An investigation is now in progress.
>
> Later.—The mystery has been solved. Some years ago a mummy was sent to the ex-president of the Pittsburgh Female College. The mummy was mutilated by rats and it was ordered to be removed. This was done by a colored ash-hauler, who thought he was doing the proper thing in disposing of it in the way he did. The mummy is probably 3,000 years old.[10]

The mummy of Pesed, excavated at Akhmim, and brought to America by Presbyterian missionary John Romich Alexander. Presented to Westminster College (courtesy Westminster College Cultural Artifacts Collection).

In 1896, Evanston, Illinois, was the macabre scene of a mummy uprising right out of the pages of fantasy. Dr. Phillips, of Northwestern University, had been at great pains to obtain some Egyptian "princesses." These had arrived during the summer and were placed by Dr. Phillips in his cellar, while he went away on his vacation. When he returned, he found chaos. One of the mummies had stuck her leg out of her coffin. Another had burst her wrappings and was swollen beyond imagination. A third body appeared to have thrown aside its cerements and rolled, naked, a distance from its coffin. Skeletons had moved and seemingly intermingled their parts, and were no longer laid out in the neat rows Dr. Phillips had arranged before his departure. The humid Chicago summer was a far cry from the dry deserts near the Nile. The poor mummies had suffered dreadfully from their move, and had to be taken to an upper floor and laid in the sun, where they gradually shrank back to their former state.[11]

In 1894 James Henry Breasted became the first American to receive a PhD in the new field of Egyptology (from Berlin), and became the first professor of Egyptology in the United States, at the University of Chicago. The University had been a center for Near Eastern Studies since 1891, just after the Haskell Oriental Museum (later the Oriental Institute) was founded at the University. While on his honeymoon in Egypt, he took the opportunity to copy inscriptions and also acquire artifacts for the University. His wife, Frances, wrote in a letter dated 15 January 1895, that her husband had purchased four Egyptian mummies, after haggling over the price for three quarters of a day. The mummies were then carried by camel back to the honeymoon houseboat and stored under the marriage bunk. Frances noted that their unusual traveling companions did not cause them to lose any sleep.[12] One of these mummies was a toothless old man from Akhmim named Petosiris; another was the mummy of a boy from the Roman period.[13] In 1897, according to the Lima, Ohio *Times Democrat* of 29 October, Breasted acquired another mummy for the Oriental Institute collection, that of Mery, a priestess of Hathor.

Breasted was one of the few "professionals" to have been involved in the mummy trade up to this point. Americans had been slow to embrace the study of foreign histories and culture—they had too much of their own nation to explore and study. Caves such as Mammoth Cave produced naturally dessicated Native American human remains which were being unearthed and studied. The attitude of many Americans still seemed to be "why look at Egyptian mummies when we have our own?"

However, mummies were still often the souvenir of choice when an intrepid American traveler visited Egypt, even though the Department of Antiquities was very strict about which mummies could be let out of the country. Royal and other exalted personages, and/or mummies which had jewelry and other valuables were kept by the Antiquities Department.[14]

In the 1880s Emil Brugsch became more liberal in his disposition of mummies to museum and private collectors. *The Milwaukee Sentinel* of 5 April 1886 records the following about Bookwalter's mummy, which he had purchased from Brugsch at the Boulaq Museum:

> The mummy of an Egyptian princess is one of the most interesting objects in the collection.... So wonderfully preserved are the features of the princess that it is thought that any one who knew her in life would be able to recognize her as embalmed. The old girl's body and face are as black as night and look tough and leathery. The features are sharp and the head narrow. The flesh is considerable shrunken and the chin is very sharp. The row of front teeth are exposed to view and look like a circle of pearls. The tongue protrudes slightly and looks like a piece of thin black sole leather. In the case is a gilt mask, something like those worn at masquerade balls, which were put over the faces of the embalmed bodies. The three hundred layers of cloth used in the embalming process, and making a covering about three inches thick, are cut from one side of the body to show the embalming process. The mummy is placed in a magnificent sarcophagus, wrought in gilt and colors, and with designs showing the royal asp on the cover. The age of the princess is over 2,500 years.

The "princess," Hathor Neb Tau I, was loaned to the Cincinnati Museum Association before 1893, and from thence to the Cincinnati Art Museum.[15]

Despite the loosening of the restrictions, it still was not all that easy to get a mummy, as is shown by an article in *The Davenport Leader* of 14 April 1896:

> A letter received today from Hon. C.A. Ficke by the Davenport Academy of Natural Sciences announces that he has purchased and shipped a fine Egyptian mummy of the 20th dynasty.
>
> This is a great surprise to the academy and at the same time a matter of great rejoicing. These mummies are hard to get. It takes a great amount of red tape and an order from the Boulaack museum to get a mummy out of Egypt. Mr. Ficke is a member of the Davenport Academy of Natural Sciences and when he went away he took letters to the Boulaack museum. The British Museum is also making explanations [sic] in Egypt at this time and his friends here think that he got the mummy through the combined efforts of the letters and the British Museum.

All of Davenport anxiously awaited the arrival of this treasure. On 11 May 1896 the *Davenport Leader* announced "The mummy here." It had arrived on the Chicago Rock Island & Pacific Railroad, and was being unpacked at noon at the Academy. On 12 May the *Davenport Daily Republican* described the opening:

> The outer box and contents weighed 350 pounds. After removing the top and one side of the box, which was well lined with hay to prevent breakage of its precious burden, the inner case was disclosed to view. It was a coffin-shaped cedar box measuring six feet in length and twenty-one inches across. The bottom is broad and intended by the designer to be used as a standard. The top bears an image of a face and the casket is covered with Egyptian figures and hieroglyphics upon the black stained background. The lid was removed and the mummy carefully lifted out onto the floor. It was evidence to all present that it was the body of a woman. It is five feet five and a half inches in height and proportioned small in other respects. The body and face could not be seen as the manner of preservation practiced in those ancient days was complete and well

executed. The face and head were enclosed in a hood or mask upon which a pretty face is painted. The body is covered with what looks to be a continuous bandage of linen which has been thoroughly saturated with spices to prevent action by the elements. The artistic arrangements of the layers of the bandage and the manner in which it and the hood cover the whole body show what pains these people of the past took in properly preserving their dead royalty.

As with so many mummies, this was perceived to be an "ancient member of an Egyptian royal family ... from the twentieth dynasty." The mummy still resides at the institution, now called the Putnam Museum of History and Natural Science.

The enthusiasm for mummy collecting seemed to transcend social and educational boundaries, interesting all strata of society. Colleges, museums and libraries seemed to be the chief benefactors of the importations, but as was alluded to at the beginning of the chapter, private collectors were not immune to the allure of the mummified ancients. Adolph Sutro, wealthy philanthropist and future mayor of San Francisco, purchased a collection of artifacts in Egypt. Among the collection, as recorded by the 11 April 1885 *New York Times,* were "Several mummies, one of a lady who died 3,800 years ago. There is one mummy head that is in so perfect a condition that the little ringlets of hair are plainly visible on the skull. There are several very perfect hands and feet. One hand still retains the long, well-shaped nails and on the wrist a beaded bracelet."

The 20 March 1886 *St. Louis Globe Democrat* gives a few more details.

> There were four of them, all in their coffins, with the lids raised and supported above them. One of these was "half unrolled." ... The poor one lies in a single poor coffin, and the rich or royal one is incased in three separate caskets, one within another.
> On the top of the coffin lid are crossed hands and a face and head carved in

The face on the coffin of the mummy of Pesed, one of the mummies from Akhmim (courtesy Westminster College Cultural Artifacts Collection).

the wood of the coffin—possibly the origin of the skull and crossbones. The man is distinguished from the woman by an irregular black line drawn along one cheek to indicate a beard. It looks as though it might have been made with a stick dipped in tar.

One of these mummies—the one enclosed in three coffins—looks precisely like a photograph of the mummy of Princess Isinikheb, of the court of King Monkhoprieri, in the twentieth dynasty, and, therefore, must have been a woman of lofty rank—possibly a princess of the royal blood—a daughter of the pharaohs she might have been ... [there was] a promiscuous assortment of heads, hands and feet. The crumbling cloth had dropped away—or been removed—and around the ankles and wrists of some of them were strings of beads.

The unknown author of this description described his reactions. "A 'creeping' cold sensation came upon me, I was fascinated. A genuine Egyptian mummy I had never seen before, and here was one nearly 4,000 years old. It makes one feel kind of queer to be suddenly brought into so ancient a presence—to stand and gaze upon a form that was animate with life's loves and hates, hopes and fears, 4,000 years ago!"

Sutro installed his collection on the grounds of his house and allowed people to view it. In 1895–1896 he built a fantastic bathing spot for the city of San Francisco, and transferred his museum there. Sutro Baths changed hands several times, becoming a skating rink under the ownership of his grandson Adolph G. Sutro, and an amusement park under the auspices of George K. Whitney. The mummies and mummy parts were transferred as well, but along the way two of the mummies, and the feet and hands seem to have disappeared. The Baths were slated for destruction in 1966; and Whitney was persuaded to donate the collection to San Francisco State University, which obtained it in 1972. Pride of the collection is the triple nested set of coffins and mummy of Nes-Per-N-Nub. A second mummy and the two heads also reside in the collection.[16]

In 1890, The *New York Times* of 9 September reported:

Herman Frank, during a tour through Egypt some months since, purchased two mummies and shipped them to Milwaukee to be placed in the public museum there. The mummies cost $500 each and to protect the infant mummy industry of this country something like $100 each was added to the value in the Custom House. The people of Cleopatra's country could not stand the rigorous climate of Wisconsin, and when the case was opened here it was discovered that one mummy had returned to dust according to the divine law.

The *McKean Democrat* of 7 November 1890 claimed the mummies had cost $2,500 and $400 more was paid in duty, money which Frank was now seeking to recover from the federal government.

The 9 February 1891 issue of *The Philadelphia Inquirer* reported on the immense collection of antiquities which August Hohl, a Philadelphia pharmacist, kept on display at his place of business on the northeast corner of Fourth and Girard Streets. During the previous summer, Hohl had traveled to Egypt and brought back a mummy "which he dug up with his own hands" and which he unwrapped himself. He claimed that the mummy had been found at the "Tomb of Kings, near Thebes, on the Upper Nile, where so many interesting discoveries have been made in late years by French and English Egyptologists."

In early 1891 the city of Tacoma was on tenterhooks, awaiting the arrival of a mummy belonging to Allen C. Mason of that city. On 6 April 1891 the *Tacoma Daily* News announced the Mr. Mason was home and had bought a "royal mummy." Mason described his curio as:

> The most splendid thing I purchased was a royal Egyptian mummy. He is a fine one, and is put up in an elegant case covered with paintings and hieroglyphics made 2000 years before Christ. There is also a marvelous inside case which has never been opened, I propose to bring this mummy to light in Tacoma 3,900 years after it was sealed up. I had the legend on the outside case translated by Prof. Sayce, an Egyptian scholar at Oxford College. He gave the mummy's date; also his name, which is Aukh-Unofei. His mummyship is particularly valuable as a work of art. The various colors of the case, including red, crimson, scarlet and blue are clear and sharp. Prof. Sayce put the mummy in about the twentieth dynasty, bringing his life 1500 to 2500 years before the Christian era. I had to have him shipped back by way of the Indian and Pacific oceans, which will bring him here sometime in June.

The 29 June 1891 issue of the same paper bore the following headline and story:

> Finest of his race. Mr. Mason arranges to exhibit his 3500 year old mummy.
> Allen C. Mason today received the bill of lading for his Egyptian mummy which will arrive in Portland next week on the steamship *Batavia*, via China. His mummyship is 3500 years old and was the best specimen of the royal dynasty which governed Egypt four thousand years ago, that Mr. Mason could find while there on his recent tour around the world. It cost him $225 in Cairo, being the most expensive mummy in the market and including freight which represents an outlay of $350 when it reaches Tacoma. It will be the second real mummy ever brought to the Pacific coast.
> Mr. Mason has generously given Mr. W.P. Hopping, his popular bookkeeper, the privilege of exhibiting the mummy at some central place during the summer for the benefit of Mason Chapel, in the North end, the proceeds to be applied towards liquidating the church's indebtedness.

The claim that this was the only the second mummy was not true. The Pacific Museum of Anatomy in San Francisco had five mummies in 1865, Adolph Sutro had brought in several in the 1880s and Jeremiah Lynch imported some more in 1890. Nor can the pathetic mummy who served in the 1875–76 San Francisco New Year's celebration be ignored. Mason's mummy was, however, the first to have been brought to the Pacific Northwest.

The *Morning Olympian* of 11 July 1891 announced that:

> Allen C. Mason opened his 3500-year-old mummy at 1 o'clock this afternoon in the presence of his office staff, the officers of the Mason Mortgage and Loan Company and representatives of the press.

His mummyship was takes from two fine cases covered with hieroglyphics in 20 minutes, and opened his eyes to the light for the first time in nearly 4,000 years, with a smile upon his features.

There followed an imaginary interview with the mummy, much in the same manner as Poe's earlier story "Some Words with a Mummy."

The mummy gave his name as Ankh-Unnofi, son of Ma Nen-Thinsfri, son of the lady Te-Tau, and said that he was a prophet of Min. He further explained that Mason had bought him in Luxor, but that he had originally come from Abydos, from a tunnel in the rocks, excavated by a team of excavators working for the German consul.

"Perhaps you do not know, sir," he said, "that the Egyptian government allows these excavations to proceed only where the guards are present and that half the antiquities go to the Egyptian Museum at Cairo. Such is the fact, and all over Egypt American, English and native explorers are now searching for old relics. The government will not allow us dummies [sic] to go out of the country without permission of the curator at the Cairo Museum, which Mr. Mason secured with considerable trouble."

The imaginary conversation then turned to the mummy's admiration of the pretty girls he was hoping to meet while on exhibtion for the chapel, and he decried the rough handling he had received during his travels.

I have had an "awful" trip, to use an expression I hear the young ladies use so often. I was tumbled and jerked about from Egypt to Cairo, then to Yokohama and across to a little Oregon town called Portland, and thence up to here. The baggage-smashers used me very roughly. My cases were cracked, one ear knocked off, my nose injured, and, worst of all, my legs were broken squarely off. They pain me very much, though Dr. Reeves has set them nicely.

The mummy didn't care much for Tacoma water, complaining it was "too flat," thought there were not enough boards of Public Works, and was not very complimentary towards the fire department. After that it lapsed into silence for the rest of the examination of its coffins.

The exhibition for the benefit of Mason Chapel was abetted by Gross Bros., owners of the block on Railroad Street, where the mummy was to be exhibited beginning on 15 July 1891. Admission was 15 cents for adults and 10 cents for children, all the proceeds to go to the chapel. The exhibition was accompanied by over one thousand Kodak views of Mason's trip around the world.[17]

In 1897 Mason suffered financial reverses, as described in the 14 May *Tacoma Daily News*: "Sells his mummy. Allen C. Mason has sold his Egyptian mummy, his Chinese gods, and a lot of other curiosities he collected some years ago on his trip around the world to the Safety Investment Company, in satisfaction of a mortgage held by that company against him. The bill of sale has been filed in the auditor's offices." Mason eventually bought the mummy back, and donated it to the Washington State Historical Society where it was exhibited until 1959 when it was loaned to the University of Puget Sound for use in biology courses. In 1983, the mummy was returned to the Historical Society, where it remains.[18]

Collecting curiosities was not limited to men, as is shown by this article in the 8 November 1899 *Middletown Daily Press*: "Miss Adelaide Olcott, of Wurstboro, has just added a couple of mummies' hands, which are 3,000 years old, to her collections. She has now over 3,000 curiosities and specimens of fancy and other works in her museum." The importation of mummies accelerated in the last years of the nineteenth century, and although the proliferation would seem to have familiarized the majority of residents of the States with the curiosities, there were still a few problematic issues which cropped up and were not easily solved.

The *Tacoma Daily News* of 15 May 1894 recorded that an auditor was called upon to make out a bill of sale which disposed of "one woman, head, dress and bust." When the clerk calmed down, he noted further that the bill of sale also included one mummy, a skull, an electric eel and a set of shark jaws. From this he deduced that some museum or collection was the object of the bill of sale, and duly recorded the transaction of H.D. Crickmore in favor of Louisa F. Crickmore in the sum of $50.

On 3 April 1894 the *Davenport Daily Leader* reported on an unusual dilemma in New York City:

> Some weeks ago the furniture house of Thoesen Bros. at 803 Third Avenue, was destroyed by fire. The workmen in clearing away the ruins unearthed three boxes. Each box was found to contain a lead casket covered with Egyptian characters.
>
> In each casket was a shriveled up mummy. Now under the laws of the state of New York it becomes the duty of a coroner to impanel a jury, hold an inquest, and if possible, discover the name of the deceased, inquiring diligently into the cause of death. Inasmuch as the gentlemen whose mortal remains now figure before Coroner Fitzpatrick as the mummies belonging to the Ptolemy family and assisted at the laying of the cornerstone ceremonies when the first of the pyramids was projected, several thousand years B.C., the jury may find itself unable to assign the true cause of death.
>
> But should it come to pass that the jury decides that death was the result of violence the dilemma will be transferred to the shoulders of the sheriff, who must under the law make an effort to apprehend and bring to justice the party or parties guilty of the crime.

An earlier inquest story was mentioned in the chapter on mummy exhibitions, and antedates this one by a decade and a half. It is difficult to know if the story is real, but at least parts of it may be true. The April date makes it slightly more suspect that it is meant as a joke. However, as with the earlier one, it is included inasmuch as it does mention specific mummies.

In the *Cazenovia Republican* for 24 January 1895 appeared a headline, "The Mummy at the Public Library":

> The Egyptian mummy given the Public Library of this village by Mr. R.J. Hubbard has been placed in the Egyptian room of that building and will be first

exhibited to the public on Thursday, Jan. 31. The sights of the museum are of course free, but on this interesting occasion the members of the art class, inspired by a desire to help the library and interest the public in the same, will serve a tea at the library building, at the low price of ten cents, the proceeds to go entirely to the library fund. It is hoped that an unusually large amount of our citizens will be present and that the tea, so generously provided by the art class, will be largely patronized.

According to his travel diary for March 1894, Hubbard bought the mummy from Mr. Costi B. Bochorides, and that gentleman also unrolled another mummy for Hubbard but nothing was found upon it. "The skull is to go home among my treasures," Hubbard recorded. The mummy was sent by Wells, Fargo & Co. at a total cost of £21.15.[19]

The 7 February 1895 *Cazenovia Republican* reported on the "Mummy Tea":

The mummy tea held at the Library House Thursday afternoon was a great success socially and financially. Everyone seemed to want to make the acquaintance of the embalmed lady in whose honor the tea was given, and of course one could hardly feel like declining refreshments after having satisfied their curiosity; so the dimes kept dropping-in, until they amounted to over $35. Of this sum $26.40 was cleared for the library.

The mummy rests in the bottom of a new glass case in one of the upper rooms of the house, and to the disappointment of many people is not entirely unwrapped. It seems that after the embalming process was finished, a hollow mask of a substance resembling paper-mache, and large enough to cover the head and shoulders of the deceased, was slipped into position, and below this, narrow strips of cloth were wound around the body and back over the mask itself. Those windings were then covered with other windings of wider cloth, until the body became quite bulky, when it was placed in its coffin and laid away. In this case, all the wrappings except the first layer had been removed, exposing the mask, but not the face. The face of the mask is gilded, and the gilding and painting is as fresh, apparently, after the lapse of 2,000 years, as it was when first put on. The strips of cloth with which it is wound are yellow with age, and are wound on in exactly the same pattern as the familiar log cabin bed quilt—another illustration of the fact that there is nothing new under the sun.

The reason for retaining some of the coverings to the mummy was explained by the appearance of a skull on another shelf—all that remained of another mummy unrolled in Mr. Hubbard's presence last year, the other parts of the body having crumbled on exposure to the air.

The mummy, know as "Hen" after the partial hieroglyphic remains of her name, is still in residence at the Cazenovia Public Library.[20]

In 1896, the Rev. H. Allen Tupper, formerly minister of the Seventh Baptist Church in Baltimore, toured Egypt. While there he was approached by a Bedouin Arab who mysteriously informed the good Reverend that he had the mummy of a baby to sell. Concerned about running afoul of the Antiquities Service, Tupper purchased the little mummy and found that it could be fitted easily into his valise, wherein it traveled safely through the rest of his trip and back to Baltimore. Tupper intended to write a book for children about life in ancient Egypt, but it is not know if he ever accomplished that goal.[21] Nor is it known what happened to the baby mummy.

Mrs. Elise Braun, theosophist pastor of the Progressive Spiritual Church, in St. Paul, was quite distraught over the fate of the mummies being imported into the United States, and claimed they were "cruelly mistreated." As quoted in the *Milwaukee Sentinel* of 3 January 1896, Mrs. Braun said:

> If only those poor things were on sale, and I only had money enough, I would purchase them and end their sufferings by incineration. The lowest form of astral life still exists in these poor old "physicals," and as a result they have been suffering for thousands of years. The lowest astral does not leave the body of flesh and blood until it has entirely returned to its original condition—dust. When a physical is embalmed disintegration is prevented and the astral cannot take its flight.

Some mummies were acquired as rewards for services rendered by diplomats while on duty in Egypt, or through the various machinations of the United States consuls. One of the earliest of these was Jeremiah George Harris, who had gone to sea as a purser on a United States man-of-war in Egyptian waters in 1860. While he was there he met the Khedive and members of his household. One day, while he was walking with a member of the staff, the man was attacked. Harris, who happened to be very strong, managed to vanquish the ruffians, and was promptly offered a reward.

Harris laughingly requested a mummy, and was informed that it was prohibited to remove these objects under penalty of death. Nevertheless, the man told Harris he would honor the request. Harris did not believe it, and was quite astonished to have a boat pull up to his ship as they were about to leave. On board was a bundle directed to Harris, who did not open it until he returned to port in Boston. The bundle proved to contain not one, but six mummies. The best was singled out and sent off to the Tennessee Historical Society, of which Harris was a member. During the Civil War, the Society suspended active operations, and the collections were removed to a private house, far from the dangers of war. Various stories were circulated about depredations made to the mummy by invading Union forces, but none have been proven. The mummy now resides in the Tennessee State Museum. A brochure from the late 1950s shows a mummy, hands positioned on its thighs, almost entirely unwrapped. It was stripped in New York before being sent to the museum. The mummy is male, aged about 30, and is about 3,600 years old.[22]

The 2 August 1888 *Albany Evening Journal* reported upon one of the more intriguing cases of diplomatic mummy enterprise. In 1876 Samuel Sullivan "Sunset" Cox, United States minister to Turkey, wrote a book entitled *Why We Laugh*. The Khedive of Egypt read it and heartily enjoyed it. When Cox visited the potentate shortly after he had read the book, the Egyptian said: "I enjoyed your book exceedingly. And now I propose to present you with something as dry as your book, I will give you two mummies." One was destined for the National Museum of Natural History at the Smithsonian in Washington. Frank George described the mummy in his column "Washington Gossip" for the 20 July 1886 *Bismarck Daily Tribune*, which also ran a drawing of the mummy and its outer anthropoid coffin (see ill. p. 223). The coffin exterior is plain, while the mummy is enclosed in what appears to be painted cartonnage. According to George, the mummy:

> Lies flat on its back in its shell in a big glass case, just to the left of the rotunda of the museum.... The mummy proper has a mummy box almost two inches thick, which fits around it almost like a glove.... The casket is some light wood. It is painted dark green, and is as carefully made as though chiseled out by a sculptor. The mummy is five feet six inches long, and it is exceedingly well preserved. The arms were pressed close to the side and you see nothing of their outline through the wrappings, which are wound tightly around the body from head to foot. This mummy, while not of royal birth, must have been a great dignitary. The body is covered with hieroglyphics and paintings in gold. The face is covered with gold leaf, and a mask of green cement is pasted over it.

The 5 August 1888 *Troy Northern Budget* chronicled the circumstances of the second mummy:

> Mr. Cox accepted the offering with due thankfulness and brought both mummies home with him. They were not the most agreeable companions du voyage, but they made no complaints at scant quarters and were never late at dinner....
>
> When he arrived at home, Mr. Cox sent one of the mummies to the Smithsonian Institute, at Washington, where it now is. The other was consigned to the tender mercies of a storage-house keeper in New York City, to be kept until called for. There were a good many calls for it, but Mr. Cox held back until he could assure himself perfectly that his ancient ward should receive a good home. Finally he was persuaded to give a refusal of it to a Cincinnati man. Then the Rev. Dr. H.C. Farrar, director of the George West Museum at Round Lake heard of the treasure and at once began to sue for it.

It was not so easy to persuade Cox to sell it, even with the help of assorted politicians and museum directors, but finally the mummy arrived in the village, an occasion of great spectacle and entertainment:

> It was about 3 o'clock Wednesday afternoon last when two workmen lugged the mummy box from the Museum to the covered pavilion known as the auditorium.... The singers were in their seats, a group of thirty or forty pretty girls. Those in the front row jumped up and screamed "oh!" when the strange box was put at their feet. Those in the rear rows uttered a subdued "oh!" out of sympathy, and then they all became very still and blushed. Everybody in the community was in the main part of the auditorium except the singers and a few prominently identified with the summer school. Among the latter were Dr. Farrar, Bishop J.P. Newman, the Rev. Dr. William Griffen, president of the association, Professor J.G. Lansing, and ex-senator C.L. MacArthur of Troy.
>
> As the mummy entered the building, the organist played something lively,

and afterwards the choir of pretty girls sang a hymn, beginning "AWAKE! AWAKE!" all of which the silent guest took in without a smile.

There followed a prayer, and address by the bishop, and a short lecture on embalming by Dr. Lansing, who then put on an old coat and scarf, and with the aid of some of the school professors, tipped the box upright and took off the cover.

> There stood revealed in the coffin a shapeless figure about four feet nine inches high, all covered over with what looked like chamois skin. It was really the linen with which the ancient Egyptians bandaged their dead after the process of embalming had been completed. There were many layers of the linen, and the first came off easily. Those nearest the body were tied down and well nigh immovable. While the exterior bandages were being stripped off, an enterprising photographer caught a view of the work. In the picture Dr. Newman and Professor Lansing were represented as supporting the mummy....
>
> To get at, and remove the interior bandages the hapless mummy was laid upon a table. Some of the professors yanked and pulled with their fingers while Professor Lansing jabbed viciously at the remains with a bright new carving knife. As the work went on the pretty girls in the choir hid their little noses behind handkerchiefs and some of the men standing about said "paugh!" and looked homesick. Several small boys ran upon the platform and made off with stray pieces of the linen bandages until an indignant doctor of divinity chased them away. The head of the mummy was uncovered first, and it was fond to contain a complete set of perfect teeth. The mummy was that of a woman as the Egyptologist present had determined from certain peculiarities in the hieroglyphic inscriptions on the lid of the coffin. The remains were uncovered as far as the waist when the mummy was made to sit for another picture. Then the work was abandoned until the scientists of the school could be by themselves in the museum. Inasmuch as it was certain that the lady had lived during the twenty-second dynasty, Dr. Farrar decided that her name must have been Thothmea, after the kings Thothmes of that time. Professor Lansing said with a smile that her name was probably not Thothmea, and that she was not a very extraordinary woman, anyway, except for her well preserved old age.... The coffin here is poor, and the embalming badly done.[23]

The 2 August 1888 *Albany Evening Journal* added the fillip that the feet, which had broken off during transportation, hung only by the wrappings, and that during Lansing's work, one of the ankle bones "as dry as tinder" fell and rolled on the platform. It was also reported by the paper that there was little evidence of hair, and the skull was very brittle. One of the ribs had gotten dislodged, and the hands rested upon the thighs, palms downward (see ill. p. 226).

Tothmea (as she became better known) resided at the West Museum until it closed in 1919. Thereafter she resided in the care of the undertaker, Mr. Garnsey. In 1939 J. Franklin Clute loaned her to the Schenectady Museum, where she stayed until 1978 when she returned to the Village of Round Lake. In 1983 the mummy's disintegration had progressed to such a degree that she could no longer be displayed. Clute's daughter, Inez Swell, took charge of the mummy in 1984, and shortly thereafter Kathy Kuznia reported that it was now residing in her basement. Tothmea was purchased by the Rosicrucian Museum in San Jose, California in 1987, and then transferred in 1995 to their Egyptian Museum in Curitiba, Brazil, where she remains.[24]

Jeremiah Lynch, with the help of United States consul-general Eugene Schuyler was able to acquire a princess of the twenty-fourth dynasty and two male mummies, all excavated at Girgeh. They were sent down to Cairo in a barge loaded with loose wheat. Brugsch Bey translated the coffins and allowed them to leave the country. They traveled to Alexandria by rail and thence to San Francisco where the princess, dubbed "Lady Isis," was donated to the Bohemian Club. The second went to a valued friend, and Lynch kept the third. Eventually the two male mummies were given to the Midwinter Memorial Museum (later Golden Gate Park Museum), where they were destroyed when the walls of the museum crashed inwards during the earthquake of 1906. Lady Isis also was destroyed during the quake, when fire swept the Bohemian Club.[25]

Brugsch Bay may have been mistaken in his coffin reading, as the 29 December 1890 *Galveston Daily News* cites an article from the *Alta California* that Lynch had given a mummy to fellow newspaper editor, John P. Young (of the *San Francisco Chronicle*), who had loaned it to the Mining Bureau Museum in San Francisco. A Professor Brooks, of the Cairo Museum, translated the inscription as "Hateson, vestal virgin and priestess in the temple of Amun-Ra." The article mentions that the mummy was unusually tall for a woman, which may help explain the confusion. There is no indication in Lynch's own story of Lady Isis that he acquired four mummies in 1890, and so Hateson must be one of the two other mummies, and was destroyed in the earthquake.

It is also possible that Lynch was mistaken in the mummies having been destroyed, for the Fine Arts Museums of San Francisco, successor to the M.H. DeYoung Museum which had arisen from the ruins of the Golden Gate Park Museum, has mummies named "Hatason" and Thoth, High Priest of Isis. Hatason had been on loan to the Rosicrucian Museum in San Jose.[26] Thoth, or more formally, Iret-net-Hor-irw, was loaned several times to the Haggin Museum, from December 1944 through May 1945, when it was billed as the "mummy of a bishop who died 3500 years ago"; again in March 1950; and then sometime again before 1964.[27] It is now at the Legion of Honor Museum.

In 1894 the National Museum was the recipient of seven mummies in coffins, a gift from the Khedive. Each case had a carved portrait of its owner and one was described by *The Penny Press* of 17 February as of "heroic size." According to the newspapers, the occupant of this coffin was described as "The great lady of Ashron." It is not known what happened to these seven mummies, as the only pre–1900 mummy claimed to be extant in the collections of the National Museum of Natural History is the one sent by Cox.[28]

In 1897, Judge Alexander Watkins Terrell, who had served as a diplomat in a dispute between the United States and Egypt during his service from 1893 to 1897 as U.S. minister plenipotentiary to the Ottoman Empire under Presi-

THE NEW MUMMY AT THE NATIONAL MUSEUM.

This drawing of the mummy case and mummy which Samuel Cox brought for the National Museum of Natural History (Smithsonian) appeared in numerous newspapers along with the story of the mummy's acquisition (Newspaper clipping, unknown newspaper).

dent Grover Cleveland, was allowed to return to his home in Austin with a recently excavated mummy. From him the mummy went to his daughter and her husband (Dr. M.M. Smith), and they were persuaded by Mrs. M.L. La Moreaux (President of the Texas Anthropological Association) to donate the mummy to them. It was exhibited at the Texas State Fair in 1908, and remained on exhibition at the Fair Park Museum until 1913, when it was returned to LaMoreux. The Association disbanded in 1913, and the mummy was donated to Southern Methodist University in 1915. In 1926 it became part of the A.V. Lane Museum, and went with that collection to Southern Methodist University's Bridwell Library in 1950. The mummy has been identified as "Princess Hatashesu," a daughter of Rameses II. She is in a cypress wood and carton-nage mummy case which has been heavily restored.[29]

Mrs. Robert Rutherford, of Houston, kept in the yard of her home on the corner of Jefferson Avenue and San Jacinto Street a large collection of objects originally amassed by her brother, John Cardwell, minister to Egypt under Grover Cleveland's first administration. His exceptionally favored standing in the country enabled him to make a collection of relics and antiquities which was almost unparalleled by any other American at that time. After his death the collections were acquired by Mrs. Rutherford, who built in her yard a house measuring twenty by thirty feet for the express purpose of displaying them. The articles were displayed on glass shelves and upon the walls, and included several mummies.[30]

Not all generous would-be donors found their efforts acceptable, as the 9 January 1890 *Davenport Morning Tribune* recorded, quoting an article from the *Albany Express*:

> A jilted maiden. When ex-mayor John Boyd Thacher was touring Egypt he chanced to observe in a museum at Boulak a finely preserved mummy of a young girl. So perfect was the retention of all that had been tenderly laid away in those mighty mausoleums of the Nile country that the outlines of the flowery garlands which had wreathed about her fair form 2,000 years before were still easily discernable. Remembering the Albany Historical and Art Association with its embryo museum on the corner of State and Hawk Street, our generous fellow townsman at once, after some patient negotiation, succeeded in purchasing the mummy. Leaving his new acquisition to be called for, the ex-mayor journeyed on, but had not altogether abandoned the region before he heard that the Historical and Art Association, finding the local populace unappreciative and disinclined either to have their higher tastes cultivated or to support the institutions so carefully planned and provided for, had retired from business.
>
> The energetic ex-mayor was in a quandary. He did not want to stretch his hospitality to the extent of inviting even an attractive maiden mummy to take a permanent seat at his fireside, be she never so undemonstrative and self-possessed. Moreover, he didn't feel like bringing her carefully over and turning her loose upon the street, for as he parenthetically remarked "there are enough mummies in Albany as it is." Ultimately he was able without much trouble, for the museum authorities had repented of their bargain, to recall his mummy.

The mummies referred to in Thacher's comment doubtless refer to the members of the state government! Poor Albany, losing out on such a chance to have a mummy of quality.

While mummies may have been more common during the latter half of the century, there was still a general lack of understanding among most people as to what part the mummy played in ancient Egyptian religion. The goal of the most enlightened museum curators was to provide some sort of artistic and cultural connection to these ancient beings, but for many people, mummies were still nothing more than curiosities, and not a few doubted that the mummies were real at all.

One of the most vexing issues throughout the nineteenth-century was the continuing debate over whether or not the mummies brought back by travelers were genuine. Early mummy entrepreneurs collected depositions from doctors and learned professors attesting to the authenticity of their dead Egyptians. But the public remained skeptical, and numerous newspaper columns appeared throughout the century decrying the manufacturing of fake mummies. A few late specimens of this *caveat emptor* type of warning are included below.

An article in the *Collector* of 1 October 1890 insisted:

> Of course, when a man finds himself consumed by an uncontrollable vocation to collect mummies—whether they be those of Egyptian kings, Peruvian Incas, sacred bulls or sanctified cats—he has a right to demand the genuine article. However, as it does not add appreciably to the pleasure of enlightenment of the world to make a public show of corpse or carrion, the actual genuineness of the mummy does not much matter, as long as the owner believes it to be genuine.

The New York Times of 2 June 1888 repeated a story from the *Portland Oregonian* of 26 May:

> A gentleman who has just returned from an extended foreign tour was asked yesterday why he had not brought home from Egypt, among other curios, a mummy. He said there was a great deal of fraud in the mummy business. Persons purchasing mummies, of course, like to get them as well preserved and natural-looking as possible, and as those found are generally in a more or less dilapidated condition, vendors have engaged in the business of manufacturing bogus mummies. They bargain with tramps, beggars, and such people for their defunct carcasses, paying therefore a sum sufficient to make their remaining days short and sweet. These fellows are preserved and pickled and then smoked till they are good imitations of the genuine mummy. Whole rows of these articles can be seen in smokehouses at once. When sufficiently dry they are wrapped in mummy cloth and sold, to Americans chiefly, bringing a high price.

The alleged sources of bogus mummies ranged from Egypt (at Alexandria), to France, and even the United States (Connecticut, Birmingham and California being only three of many such places mentioned.) Museums all over the world were urged to carefully examine their mummies to prove their

The mummy Tothmea, at her unwrapping at the Round Lake Museum. From left to right: unidentified, Tothmea, Captain Rogers, Professor J.G. Lansing, Bishop John Newman (unprovenanced copy of a photograph).

authenticity. Sadly, some did not pass the test, including a large number in the Berlin Museum.[31]

Even if long dead and inanimate, mummies sometimes served oddly useful purposes not in keeping with their usual circumstances of exhibition and display. The *Brooklyn Eagle* of 8 April 1898 reported on some hapless thieves who just happened to pick the wrong house to rob. Dr. Charles E. West lived in a handsome brownstone mansion on Pierrepont Street, which was fearsomely guarded by a massive front door and iron gate leading to the cellar door. One morning the servants awoke to find that in spite of the precautions, the house had been entered and all of the valuable silver in the house spread out upon the dining room table. Only some of the silver and a small amount of money from the cook's pocketbook had been taken and speculation was that the thieves had been startled by the "grewsome looking mummy case" on the landing leading into the parlor and had fled in sheer terror from the unaccustomed sight. The occupant of the coffin, none the worse for its experience, was later loaned out for a charitable party as was mentioned in a previous chapter. Its subsequent whereabouts have not as yet been ascertained.

Dr. James Douglas, who had been instrumental in helping the Niagara Falls Museum procure some of its mummies, also had two of his own which he had unwrapped before the Literary and Historical Society of Quebec in 1865. Douglas had lived in Quebec for nearly fifty years as a well-respected surgeon and advocate of the mentally ill (after being run out of Auburn, New York, for the crime of body snatching, in order to procure specimens for dissection). In 1875 he moved to Phoenixville, Pennsylvania, to live with his son. The old stone house in Phoenixville had a glazed veranda on which Douglas displayed the mummies and coffins. The mummies were popularly supposed to be ancestors, and inspired such awe that although burglaries were common in the area, the house was never broken into.[32]

One mummy was that of a youth, humpbacked and lame. The second was a male of the 18th dynasty in a handsome mummy case. The body was little more than that of a skeleton, and it had suffered a severely fractured skull prior to death.[33] The disposition of these mummies has not been ascertained.

Perhaps the most poignant mummy story, and the one with which I will end my narrative, is the tale of the baby mummy of

Dr. James Douglas, M.D. Helped obtain mummies for the Niagara Falls Museum and also kept two of his own on his front veranda (James Douglas, *Journals and Reminiscences of James Douglas, M.D.*, ed. the Rev. James Douglas [New York: Privately Printed, 1910]).

A plain slate gravestone amid a plethora of Egyptian revival monuments identifies the location of the buried ashes of Prince Amun-her kepeshef, aged three years (photograph by author).

Middlebury, Vermont. The story begins around 1886, when Henry Sheldon, searching for artifacts to display in his Museum in Middlebury, met up with some Spanish traders in New York City, who had a mummy to sell. They had gotten it in Cairo from a group of Arab grave robbers.

Sheldon purchased the mummy and brought it to Vermont, where the New England weather had a deleterious effect on the poor little body. After Sheldon's death, when the coffin started to disintegrate, someone stored the prince in the attic.[34] In 1945, the curator, Florence Abbott, and George Walcott Mead, one of the Trustees, found the remains and determined that the mummy was in such disrepair it would have to be discarded. Mead, for many years a staunch member of the Episcopal Church, was a gentleman of the old school who believed in fundamental decencies. "This," he declared, "was once a human being. It is fitting and proper that it should have a Christian burial."

Mead took the mummy and its coffin to the Logan House, where Leonard Zeeman cremated the remains. Mead dug a hole in his family plot in the old West Cemetery and poured in the ashes, all except for a small handful, which he tossed to the winds. No one asked for a burial permit, and no one demanded a death certificate. Mead erected a marker for the lad, at the top of which is a cross, because the burial is in a Christian cemetery. There is also an ankh, the Egyptian hieroglyph for life, and a little bird, symbolizing the soul of the deceased. The prince's names and the names of his parents and date of birth were translated from inscriptions on the coffin and verified by experts in New York before the coffin and its occupant were immolated.[35] And so, to this day, one can see in Old West Cemetery (a graveyard adorned with Egyptian revival monuments such as pyramids, obelisks, and urns) a small, plain, dark, slate stone, which reads: "Ashes of Amun-Her-Kepeshef-Ef, aged 2 years, son of Sen Wosret 3rd, King of Egypt and his wife Hathor-Hotpe 1883 B.C."[36] (see ill. p. 228).

The original title of this book was to be *From Eternity to Here*, because the ancient Egyptians believed that after death they would journey to the Western Lands and spend their eternities living the good life and performing such services as the gods required. I doubt that any of them could have ever imagined winding up this far west, or ending up in such wildly diverse types of service.

Appendices

Appendix 1. Catalogue of Pre-1901 References to Mummies in America Not Mentioned in the Text

Agassiz, Louis—unwrapped a mummy at Harvard "a few years ago," according to an article on the unwrapping of Penpi (*Duluth Daily Tribune* [Duluth, Minn.], 4 July 1884); also unwrapped a mummy in Boston (*Duluth News Tribune* [Duluth, Minn.], 2 July 1893).

Army Medical Museum mummies—mentioned in an article about the collapse of the Ford's Theatre building where the museum had been quartered (*Decatur Weekly Republican* [Decatur, Ill.], 15 June 1893).

Art Institute of Chicago—mummy mentioned as being in the collection prior to 1894 (Kirkland, Joseph, *The Story of Chicago* [Chicago: Dibble Pub. Co., 1894], 268).

Ashland (Wis.) mummy—"an alleged Egyptian mummy" exhibited at an unknown venue in the city (*Daily Northwestern* [Oshkosh, Wis.], 16 August 1897).

Autopsy mummy—depicted as being the subject of an autopsy by four medical students in a circa 1890s photograph. Acquired originally in West Virginia and may depict West Virginia University in Morgantown. (Offered on eBay, 10/31/2001).

Baggerly, H. C.—mummy's head, mentioned in a 1879 article on the Hillsdale College Museum, as being part of the Baggerly collection, but no longer extant. Possibly destroyed in a fire in 1873 or 1910 (Anthony L. Swineheart, "Hillsdale College Museum, Est. 1874," [article on-line]; available from; http://www.hills dale.edu/academics/bio/Swinehart/ CollegeMuseum/Home/Main.html; accessed 2/27/2002; Swinehart, e-mail correspondence with the author, 1/22/2003).

Bay View Association mummy—polydactyl male child from the Roman period, donated to the association in the late 1800s by Miss Hattie M. Connor, of Cairo. Acquired by the Kelsey Museum, Ann Arbor, Mich., in 1971 (Janet Richards and Terry Wilfong, "Kelsey Mummy Encounters Modern Medicine" in *Kelsey Museum Newsletter* [Spring 2002] [journal on-line]; available from; http://www.lsa.umich.edu/kelsey/research/Pub lications/spring2002/mummy1.html; accessed 8/19/2005).

Bennett, Louis—female mummy, Menne, supposedly a princess of the 12th Dynasty, found near the pyramid of Hwara; given to the Glen Island Natural History Museum, 1897 (*New York Times*, 6 August 1897; *Brooklyn Eagle* [New York, N.Y.], 6 August, 1897).

Boston Society of Natural History mummies—number unknown (R.L. Midgley, *Sights in Boston and Suburbs* [Boston and Cambridge: James Munroe and Company, 1857, 102]; This was the precursor to the Museum of Fine Arts. They had at least two heads which were given to the Peabody Museum at Harvard (Peabody Museum of American Archeology and Ethnology, *Fourteenth Annual Report* [Cambridge (Mass.):

Printed by order of the Trustees, 1881],
10). They also had the mummies from
the *Peregrine,* before transferring them
to the Peabody Museum at Harvard
(Wolfe, entries PER001; PER002).

Bridgeport Historical Society—male
mummy, Pa Ib., a gift from the American consul in Cairo to Nancy Fish Barnum in 1892 or 3 (*Daily Gazette and
Bulletin* [Williamsport, Pa.], 9 August
1895); The Bridgeport Historical Society became the Barnum Museum and
Pa Ib is still residing there (*Barnum Museum,* [publication on-line]; available
from; http://www.barnum-museum.org/
core.htm; accessed 8/10/2008).

**California Mid-Winter Exposition
mummy**—"Maggie," a Ptolemaic
"princess" (possibly from Akhmim)
brought from Cairo in 1895 for the exhibition, sold to Nathan Joseph, a private collector, who loaned it to the
Golden Gate Park Museum where it remained on display until 1910. It was then
purchased by Donald O. Boudeman and
donated by him to the Kalamazoo Museum. ("Maggie the Mummy," in *Hobbies* 53 [June 1948]: 141; Paula Metzner
"Hidden Treasure; Uncovering the Secrets of an Egyptian Coffin," [article on-
line]; available from; www.kalamazoo
museum.org; accessed 1/24/2005; Metzner, e-mail correspondence with the
author, 1/24/2005).

Clarke, Robert—mummy acquired before
1885, donated to Cincinnati Society of
Natural History, 1885 (Cincinnati Soci-
ety of Natural History, *Journal of the
Cincinnati Society of Natural History* 7
[January 1885]: 173).

Clifton, L. B.—female mummy, brought
before 1891. When bandages were all removed, weighed only 18 pounds ("A
Talk about the Water," in *The Macon
Telegraph* [Macon, Ga.], 14 June 1891).

Clinton Hall—auction sale of an undisclosed number of mummies in New
York, provenance unknown (*Burlington Hawk-Eye* [Burlington, Iowa], 28
September 1876).

Coleman, Lyman—mummy of a child, a

woman's mummified hand, and a small
mummified pet, given in 1858 to Yale,
by Coleman, an 1817 Yale graduate.
Consigned in their shipping case, to a
remote attic, where they lay moldering
away until 1908, when Dr. G.G. Mac-
Curdy, the curator of the Peabody Museum, re-discovered them. The mummy
is now a prized part of the Peabody Museum's extensive collection of Egyptian
artifacts (*New York Times,* 8 March
1908).

Cooper Medical College mummy—an
unnamed "chantress of Amon," dated
to Late Pharaonic Period (or later) acquired before 1900 and given to Jane
Stanford, who donated it to Stanford
University. (Diane Manuel, "How to
Handle a Mummy: Verrrry Carefully,
Art Museum Curators Agree" in *Stanford On-line Report* [journal on-line];
available from; http://news-service.stan
ford.edu/news/1998/september23/mum
my923.html; accessed 2/24/2007).

Cranium Club—"a mummy from Egypt,
which beats the Kentucky mummy all
to rags" (*Salem Gazette* [Salem, Mass.],
1 April 1817); Considering the date and
the farcical assemblage of exhibits associated with this object, probably not
real.

Dead Sea Expedition mummies—supposedly two large cases of mummies, probably purchased from a Beirut bazaar,
collected by Lieut. William Lynch, in
command of the *Supply* (Andrew C.A.
Jampoler, *Sailors in the Holy Land; The
1848 Expedition to the Dead Sea and the
Search for Sodom and Gomorroah* [An-
napolis, Md.: Naval Institute Press,
2005], 245); newspaper and magazine
accounts mention one mummy (*Waukesha Democrat* [Waukesha, Wis.], 9 January 1849; "Dead Sea Expedition," in
Niles National Register [Baltimore, Md.]
74, no. 1935 [20 December 1848]: 385).
This may have been given to the Naval
Lyceum Museum [*q.v.*]).

Dental Museum mummy—jaw with teeth
taken from the desert near Sakkara for
a dental museum in New York. The

teeth came from one of four mummies in coffins which had been destroyed as "entertainment" on the orders of an unnamed viceroy (*The Friend* [Salem, Mass.], 1 October 1870).

Depew, Chauncey Mitchell—had an Egyptian mummy in his New York home (*The Galveston Daily News* [Galveston, Tex.], 10 April 1889).

European Museum mummy—a Philadelphia museum which in 1858 had a hydrocephalic female mummy (Kimball, 82–83).

Field Museum of Natural History mummies—at least two of this extensive collection of mummies arrived in the United States before 1900; Udja-ren-es, originally thought to be female, but radiologically proven to be male, who arrived in 1894 ("The Trail of Invisible Light: A Century of Medical Imaging," in *University of Iowa Health Care* [journal on-line]; available from; http://www.uihealthcare.com/depts/medmuseum/galleryexhibits/trailoflight/06egyptianmummy.html; accessed 2/23/2008); and the mummy originally exhibited by Charles F. Gunther cited in text).

Forshey, Caleb G.—attended the unwrapping of an unknown mummy in New Orleans, circa 1870. Forshey, a Texas man, identified grains of wheat in the mummy wrappings (*Galveston Tri-Weekly News* [Galveston, Tex.], 16 November 1870).

G.W. Scovill & Co. mummy—illustration of a mummy case used in an advertisement for G.W. Scovill & Co.'s furniture store in Decatur, Ill. Not discernable if an actual mummy was used for advertising purposes (*Decatur Review* [Decatur, Ill.], 25 November 1891); similar cut used for a differing advertisement on 23 October 1891 for Hutchin mummy (*q.v.*).

Gray, Asa—five mummy heads, donated to Peabody Museum of American Archeology and Ethnology, 1870 (Peabody Museum of American Archeology and Ethnology, *Third Annual Report of the Trustees of the Peabody Museum of*

American Archæology and Ethnology ... [Boston: Press of A.A. Kingman, 1870], 11).

Greene, Joseph C.—had a mummy "certified to be a High Priest of Thebes" donated to the Buffalo Historical Society (*Buffalo Historical Society Publications* [Buffalo, N.Y.: Buffalo Historical Society, 1896], v. 4, 424–425).

Greenwood, John—"two curious Egyptian mummies" imported before 1860, given in 1860 to the Peabody Museum of American Archæology and Ethnology (Josiah Quincy, *The History of Harvard University* [Boston: Crosby, Nichols, Lee & Co., 1860], 492).

Hamrick, Graham—two fake mummies, female cadavers from the West Virginia Hospital for the Insane; experiments to see if the ancients' method of preservation could be duplicated. Now on display in the bathroom of the Barbour County Historical Museum, in Philippi, West Virginia ("Mummies of the Insane" in *Roadside America* [website online]; available from; http://www.roadsideamerica.com/attract/WVPHImum.html, accessed 3/30/2008).

Hebbard, William Wallace—Boston lecturer, delivered a lecture in New York at the Young Men's Christian Association, 1867; exhibited "mummies" during the lecture (*Brooklyn Eagle* [New York, N.Y.], 16 March 1867).

Heinz, Henry John—had a mummy in his Pittsburgh home before 1897; it was later exhibited on Heinz Pier at Atlantic City (*Kansas City Star* [Kansas City, Mo.], 31 January 1897; Robert C. Alberts, "The Good Provider," in *American Heritage Magazine* [journal online]; available from; http://www.americanheritage.com/articles/magazine/ah/1972/2/1972_2_26.shtml; accessed 7/7/2006).

Hirsch, Marcus—owner of a New York curiosity shop, who had a mummy in a showcase which was destroyed in a vandalism fire in 1891, by Alfred Madden, who claimed he was intoxicated at the time of the incident. The case and mummy were valued at $25 (*Brooklyn Eagle* [New York, N.Y.], 24 December 1891).

Hutchin mummy—illustration of a mummy case used in an advertisement for Walter Hutchin's shoe store in Decatur, Ill. Not discernable if an actual mummy was used for advertising purposes (*Decatur Review* [Decatur, Ill.], 23 October 1891); similar cut used for a differing advertisement on 25 November 1891 for G.W. Scovill & Co., (*q.v.*).

Lippincott, Son & Co. mummies—arrived New York Custom House; Lippincott, Son & Co. won the consignment. The mummies were excavated from Memphis and Thebes; viewed by Anglo-Egyptian Club, London, who offered to buy some of them, but they were to be sold only as a lot. Number of mummies is not known but at least several, "from kings down to hewers of wood and drawers of water" were sent to an unspecified New York destination (*Philadelphia Inquirer*, 13 December 1891).

Lowell mummy—"The artificial theatre is here; the circus is here; the mummy is here, and the pedlars have come in a caravan"—announcement in the 18 July 1828 *Freedom's Journal* (New York, N.Y.), which cribbed from an as yet unlocated issue of the *Lowell Journal*. This may be the same as the "Belzoni mummy" which was cited in the text. It could also be Turner's or Lee's mummy.

Lowell, John, Jr.—sent home several mummies from his trip to Egypt in the 1830s, but they had disappeared from the collection by the time it was presented to the Museum of Fine Arts, Boston, in 1874 (Edward Weeks, *The Lowells and Their Institute* [Boston and Toronto: Little, Brown & Co., 1966], 26).

Lowry, Thomas—of Minneapolis; had least two mummies, brought in 1886, one of which was pronounced by Amelia B. Edwards to be a "princess" named Amenhotep. The mummy was unwrapped in July 1891 and discovered to be a "man of above the average size, with powerful hands and a wonderful

frame." This mummy was loaned to the Minneapolis Public Library (*The Atchison Champion* [Atchison, Kan.], 18 July 1891; *Minneapolis Tribune* [Minneapolis, Minn.], 2 June 1935).

McCauley, Edward—amateur Egyptologist who did a drawing of Charles Huffnagle's mummy case on exhibition at Memorial Hall, Philadelphia (cited in text); may have had a mummy of his own (Jonathan Elias, undated telephone conversation with the author).

McKenzie, Dr. and Mrs. H.B.—gave "quite an enjoyable mummy party" at their Henrietta, Texas home in 1891 (*Dallas Morning News* [Dallas, Tex.] 14 December1891). Not known if this were an unwrapping, or if, indeed, actually featured any genuine Egyptian mummies.

Meinecke, Adolph and Ferdinand—two mummies from Akhmim, Djed-Hor (Tja Hir) and Padi-Heru, purchased in 1887, donated to St. Louis Public Museum (*The Milwaukee Sentinel* [Milwaukee, Wis.], 19 September 1887; "Museum Scans Mummies for Clues to Past" in *St. Paul Pioneer Press* [St. Paul, Minn.], 25 June 2006).

Mills, Joseph J.—female mummy, Ta'an, purchased in the 1880s from the Government Museum in Cairo; presented in 1889 to Joseph Moore Museum, Earlham College ("Joseph Moore Museum" [publication on-line]; available from; http://www.earlham.edu/josephmooremuseum/content/history.html, accessed 8/28/2008).

Naval Lyceum Museum mummies—later the Naval Academy Museum, which had two female mummies, one possibly the gift from the Dead Sea expedition (*q.v.*) and one given by George Gliddon in 1840, as well as some animal mummies. One of the mummies was described as five feet or less high, enveloped in a white cloth painted with hieroglyphics in dark colors, some of which had been cut away to expose the body. The right hand rests upon the left elbow, it had lost an eye and the lower jaw was sunken in a "constant grin" (*Brooklyn Eagle* [New York, N.Y.], 18 December 1846; 28 May 1853; 4 November 1871; 7 August 1872; 10 June 1877; 1 August 1886; 6 November 1892; *New York Times*, 8 December 1852).

New Orleans Universal Exposition and World's Fair mummies (also called the World Cotton Centennial Exposition)—unknown number of mummies (both Egyptian and native North/South American) to be displayed by "the Bureau of Ethnology" in 1884 (*Telegraph and Messenger* [Macon, Ga.], 6 September 1884).

New York collector—had a mummy hand with a valuable ring on it; leased house to a family while he went to Europe, when he returned, hand had been given to the children as a plaything and been mutilated to get the ring off, which was sold for 10 cents and a stick of candy (*San Antonio Daily Express* [San Antonio, Tex.], 11 July 1888).

New York Customs House mummies— unknown number of mummies, allowed to enter duty free in 1887 (*The Wheeling Register* [Wheeling, W. Va.], 29 March 1887).

New York photographer—mummy of "Assa Sheffer" sold to an unnamed New York photographer for $45 in 1880 by Leavitt's Auction Rooms (*New York Times*, 27 May 1880).

Nye, Bill—newspaper columnist and humorist who claimed to have had a mummy which crumbled to dust when exposed to air. Probably not a real mummy ("Mummies from Egypt and from the Bowery," in *Wheeling Sunday Register* [Wheeling, W. Va.], 1 July 1888).

Old Albany Museum mummy—owned by Henry T. Meech, exhibited a mummy, date unknown, but probably circa 1830 ("Interesting and Important People of Albany Rural Cemetery" [article on-line]; available from; http://www.albanyruralcemetery.org/albrur/notable.html; accessed 3/28/2008).

Parsons, Charles—two mummies, Henut-Wedjebu (14th cent. B.C.E.); Pet Menekh

(300 B.C.E.); purchased in Egypt prior to 1896, donated to the Washington University Gallery of Art in 1896; loaned to the St. Louis Art Museum, but now returned to Washington University (Alex Fak, "WU Gallery displays Egyptian Mummies" in *Student Life News* [journal on-line]; available from; http://local host:123/HLPage?pg=http%3A//www.st udlife.cpm/99-00/99_09_07/news/egy ptian08.html&; accessed 1/18/2002).

Peabody Museum of American Archæology and Ethnology mummies—had "two curious Egyptian mummies from John Greenwood (*q.v.*); five heads from Asa Gray (*q.v.*) and two heads and the *Peregrine* mummies (mentioned in the text) from the Boston Society of Natural History (*q.v.*). Also purchased a mummied head and foot from the tombs at Memphis, 1881 (Peabody Museum of American Archæology and Ethnology, *Fourteenth Annual Report...*, 32).

Public Stores mummies—Brooklyn, N.Y.; two mummies from tombs at Karnak, importers questioned whether they had to pay duty, inasmuch as the consignee was an unnamed museum (*Brooklyn Eagle* [New York, N.Y.] 22 May 1898; *New York Times*, 22 May 1898).

Redling, L.—from Norwalk, Ohio, donated in 1863 a piece of a mummy found at Thebes to the Firelands Historical Society (*The Norwalk Reflector* [Norwalk, Ohio], 23 June 1863).

Rominger, H. V.—Moravian minister of Crawford, Neb., who acquired a mummy from the royal burial ground at Thebes in 1885, and presented it to the University of Nebraska State Museum sometime before 1899. The museum also has two other Egyptian mummies (*Nebraska State Journal* [Lincoln, Neb.], 20 January 1899; "Division of Anthropology—University of Nebraska State Museum" [article on-line]; available from; http://www.musem.unl.edu/research/anthropology/about.htlm; accessed 1/9/2003).

Saint Louis Museum mummy—run by Albert Koch, mummy was advertised in

1836. Koch sold the entire museum in 1841 to W.S. McPherson of New Orleans (John Francis McDermott, "Dr. Koch's Wonderful Fossils," in the *Bulletin of the Missouri Historical Society* 4 no. 4 [July 1948]: 249).

Saint Paul Railroad Baggage Dept.—female mummy, returned as "unclaimed baggage" in 1894. Was to be included in the sale of unclaimed baggage 4 Jan. 1896 (*The Milwaukee Journal* [Milwaukee, Wis.], 21 December 1895).

Salina Man—probably male, purchased as a curiosity. Possibly not real, butt of a political joke (*The Emporia Daily Gazette* [Emporia, Kan.], 29 May 1895).

Sarles, Maria C.—presented an Egyptian mummy at her graduation from Packer Institute, 1880 (*Brooklyn Eagle* [New York, N.Y.], 13 June 1880).

Sarony, Napoleon—mummy and case, collected by Sarony, sold at auction by American Art Galleries, April 1896 ("The Napoleon Sarony Sale" in *New York Times*, 1 April 1896).

Schenley Park Museum and Library mummies—two mummies and cases purchased by Andrew Carnegie in Cairo for the museum. Ten feet high, stated "not unlikely to be ancient kings of Egypt" (*Philadelphia Inquirer*, 1 May 1894). At least one is now part of the Carnegie Museum of Natural History collection, which contains several other mummies, including a child and some heads (Wolfe, entries SPM001, SPM002).

Shaw, W. J.—"An old Egyptian mummy and highly decorated coffin," sold for $45, by G.A. Levitt & Co., May 1880 ("Selling off curiosities," in *The New York Times*, 26, 27 May 1880).

Silver, Mrs. John A.—female Ptolemaic mummy from Akhmim, given to her by her uncle, U.S. Consul Frederick C. Penfield, around 1895. She donated it to Hobart College in 1897 ("The mummy of the Archives of the Warren Hunting Smith Library" [article on-line]; available from; http://academic.hws.edu/library/archives/pdfs/mummy.asp; accessed 3/28/2008).

Skelly, Peter—Tanet-pahekau, female child mummy given prior to 1896 by a friend who was a museum official in Cairo, donated to College of the Holy Cross in Worcester, Mass. (*Sunday Telegram* [Worcester, Mass.], 9 April 2000).

Spinster of the upper ten mummy—possibly spurious. "A spinster of the upper ten recently purchased at the Philadelphia Exposition an Egyptian mummy. She said it would seem better to have a man around, even if he was a little advanced in life and somewhat withered" (*Brooklyn Eagle* [New York, N.Y.], 31 March 1877).

Stanford, Leland, Jr.—collected two mummies during his trips between 1880 and 1884 (excavated by Brugsch Bey of the Gizeh Museum). The mummies became part of the collection at Leland Stanford Junior University (Leland Stanford Junior University, *Ninth Annual Register 1899–1900* [Stanford, Calif.: Published by the University, 1900], 27).

Stearns, Frederick—Detroit pharmaceutical manufacturer who donated "mummies" to the Detroit Institute of Arts in 1890 (*The Detroit Institute of Arts* [website on-line]; available from; http://www.dia.org/collections/ancient/anci entindex.html; accessed 8/19/2004).

Sunday-School Assembly mummy—exhibited at the Sunday-School assembly on Lake Chautauqua, in August 1874 (*Independent* [New York, N.Y.], 20 August 1874).

Taylor, William M.—Presbyterian minister of North Beaver Township, Pa., had a mummy's hand (*Biographical Sketches of Leading Citizens of Lawrence County Pennsylvania.* [Buffalo, NY: Biographical Publishing Company, 1897], 459).

Union Depot mummy—transferred from one freight car to another on 14 October 1881 in Decatur, Ill. Supposedly destined for the St. Louis Museum (*Decatur Daily Review* [Decatur, Ill.], 15 October 1881).

Unknown Hermann, Mo., dentist—purchased a child mummy around the turn of the century. Family presented it to the St. Louis Science Center in 1895 (Diane Toroian Keaggy, "St. Louis Science Center Unveils Child Mummy" [article on-line]; available from; http://www.stltoday.com/stltodat/entertainment/storeis.nsf.vististlouis/story/071BF3EE65; accessed 3/22/2007).

Unknown (Augusta, Me.)—supposedly exhibited circa 1849, resulting in a judge asking, "is the durned critter still alive?" (*Saturday Evening Post* [Philadelphia, Pa.], 25 August 1849). Spawned a number of variations in the story and locations of the incident. This may be based on an actual exhibition which has not as yet been referenced.

Unknown mummies (Boston, Mass.)—notice of forty packages of Egyptian antiquities including three mummies and a stuffed crocodile had lately arrived in Boston (*The Adams Sentinel* [Gettysburg, Pa.], 11 January 1836).

Unknown mummy (Columbus, Ohio)—supposedly 284 years old. Possibly a joke; exhibited circa 1878 (*Georgia Weekly Telegraph* [Macon, Ga.], 30 April 1878).

Unknown mummy (Council Bluffs, Iowa)—supposedly exhibited by a man on the streets of Council Bluffs, Iowa, 1894 (*Morning World-Herald* [Omaha, Neb.], 5 December 1894).

Unknown mummies (U.S.)—Seven mummies for which $1,756 was paid in duty in 1886. Purportedly the coroners wanted to perform autopsies, but the cost would have bankrupted the showman who imported them. The article claimed they ought to have been imported as "guano" to escape the high duty (*San Antonio Daily Express* [San Antonio, Tex.], 2 December 1886).

Unknown "Princess mummy"—an Egyptian mummy supposed to be that of a princess, disclosed a "curious cheat" when unrolled. "The priests who did the embalmment probably spoiled the body intrusted [*sic*] to them and for it substituted that of an ordinary Negro man" (*Christian Recorder* [Philadelphia, Pa.],

17 January 1895). This may be a "filler" based on the Gliddon unwrapping in 1850, or may also be related to the Amelia Edwards unwrapping story.

Vassar College mummy—Male, Shep-en-Min, from Akhmim, purchased in London in the 1890s by a "pair of Classics professors." The mummy is the son of Pahat, the mummy at the Berkshire Museum, originally obtained from Ward's Scientific Establishment (*q.v.*) ("Wrapped up in History," in *Vassar; The Alumni Quarterly* 104 no. 1 [Winter 2007] [journal on-line]; available from; http://www.aavc.vassar.edu/vq/articles/features-winter07-treasure, accessed 4/11/2008; Jenny Lee, "Mummy gets CT Scan At Facility" [article on-line]; available from; http://www.poughkeepsiejournal.com/apps/pbcs.dll/article?AID=/20080409/NEWS01/804090325&template=printart; accessed 4/11/2008).

Walters, Henry—mummy acquired before 1900, given as part of collection of the Walters Art Museum in Baltimore (Holly Selby, "Ancient Art in a New Light," SunSpot [journal on-line]; available from; http://www.sunspot.net/entertainment/galleriesmuseums/bal-as.walters14oct.14story?coll=b; accessed 12/18/2001).

Ward's Natural Science Establishment mummy—Pahat (Ptolemaic period, Akhmim), acquired from the Government Museum of Egyptian Antiquities in 1899. Sold in 1903 to The Berkshire Athenaeum, now the Berkshire Museum, Pittsfield, Mass. (Kathryn J. Beebe, Registrar, The Berkshire Museum [Pittsfield, Mass.], e-mail correspondence with the author, 1/27/2003).

Wesleyan University mummy—purchased somewhere in Egypt in the 1880s by James Van Benschoten, and shipped back to Middletown, Connecticut, where it became part of the Natural History Museum at Wesleyan University. It was relegated to an attic in the 1950s but rediscovered and examined in the 1970s (Stephen L. Dyson, "The Mummy of Middletown," in *Archaeology* 32 [September 1979]: 57–59).

Wig mummy—mummy head examined by an unnamed naturalist, who discovered what had been thought to be rolls of hair, but which later proved to be a wig ("Mechanical and Scientific" in *St. Joseph Herald* [St. Joseph, Mo.], 25 January 1879).

Wood, Horatio G.—Purchased by Wood, when U.S. consul, from a Bedouin sheik in the desert outside of Cairo in 1887. Purchased from him for $200 in 1893 by the Charleston Museum. Dates from the Roman period (William A. Gardener and Charles Griffin, "A Paleopathologic Exercise—The Charleston Museum Mummy," in *The Journal of the South Carolina Medical Association* 67 no. 6 [June 1871]: 269–270).

X-rayed mummy—unknown hand, purchased by a woman from a fakir in Thebes. Was told it was fake, had it x-rayed and proven to be real (*Salt-Lake Semi Weekly Tribune* [Salt Lake City, Utah], 12 January 1897).

Zorayda Castle (St. Augustine, Fl.)—foot only, brought by Franklin Smith, circa 1883 ("Zorayda Castle," in *Castles of the United States* [website on-line; available from; (http://www.dupontcastle.com/castles/zorayda.htm]; accessed 9/23/2004).

Appendix 2. Suggestions for Further Reading

Biographical

Many of the sources cited in the notes and bibliography contain biographical material.

Bolton, Ethel Stanwood. *A History of the Stanwood Family in America*. Boston: Rockwell and Churchill Press, 1899.

Cooper, Alan R. "Colonel Wood's Museum; A Study in the Development of the Early Chicago Stage" Thesis, Roosevelt University, 1974.

Dawson, Warren R., and Eric P. Uphill. *Who Was Who in Egyptology*. 2nd. rev. ed. London : Egypt Exploration Society, 1972.

Larkin Thorndike Lee Collection, Phillips Library, Peabody Essex Museum, Salem, Mass.

Larkin Turner Collection, G.W. Blunt White Library, Mystic Seaport Mystic, Conn.

Peterson, H. Donal. "Antonio Lebolo; Excavator of the Book of Abraham." *Brigham Young University Studies* 32, no. 3 (Summer 1991).

Peterson, H. Donal. *The Story of the Book of Abraham: Mummies, Manuscripts and Mormonism*. Salt Lake City: Deseret Book Company, 1995.

Warren, Edward. *Life of John Collins Warren, M.D.* Boston: Ticknor and Fields, 1860.

Weigle, Anastasia S. *A Presence in the Community: The Warren Family Legacy*. Westbrook, Maine: Warren Memorial Foundation, 2000.

Who Was Who in American Art. Madison, CT: Sound View Press, 1999.

Egyptology and Travel

Fagan, Brian M. *The Rape of the Nile*. New York: Charles Scribner's Sons, c. 1975.

Field, James A. *America and the Mediterranean World, 1776–1882*. Princeton, N.J.: Princeton University Press, 1969.

Finnie, David H. *Pioneers East*. Cambridge, Mass.: Harvard University Press, 1967.

Irwin, John T. *American Hieroglyphs*. Baltimore: Johns Hopkins University Press, 1980.

Reid, Donald Malcolm. *Whose Pharaohs?* Berkeley: University of California Press, 1997.

Wilson, John A. *Signs and Wonders upon Pharaoh.* Chicago: University of Chicago Press, 1964.

Egyptomania and Mummymania

Day, Jasmine. *The Mummy's Curse.* London: Routledge, 2006.

MacDonald, Sally, and Michael Rice, ed. *Consuming Ancient Egypt.* London: UCL Press, 2003.

Ethnology and Race

Campbell, John. *Negro-mania.* Philadelphia: Campbell & Powers, 1851.

Dain, Bruce. *A Hideous Monster of the Mind.* Cambridge, Mass.: Harvard University Press, 2002.

Nott, Josiah Clark and George R. Gliddon. *Types of Mankind or, Ethnological Researches.* Philadelphia: J.B. Lippincott, Grambo & Co., 1854.

Sappol, Michael. *A Traffic of Dead Bodies.* Princeton: Princeton University Press, 2002.

Trafton, Scott. *Egypt Land.* Durham: Duke University Press, 2004.

Mormons and Mormonism

Brooke, John L. *Refiner's Fire.* Cambridge, Mass.: Cambridge University Press, 1994.

Christensen, Ross T., ed. *Mummies, Scrolls, and the Book of Abraham.* Provo, Utah: Brigham Young University, 1968.

Gee, John. *Guide to the Joseph Smith Papyri.* Provo, Utah: FARMS, c. 2000.

Johanson, Jerald R. *Enoch's Zion, Joseph's Zion, and Future Zion.* Bountiful, Utah: Horizon Publishers, 2003.

Larsen, Charles M. *By His Own Hand upon Papyrus; A New Look at the Joseph Smith Papers.* Rev. ed. Grand Rapids, Mich.: Institute for Religious Research, 1992.

Marquardt, H. Michael. *Rise of Mormonism.* Longwood, Fla.: Xulon Press, 2005.

Peterson, H. Donal. "Antonio Lebolo; Excavator of the Book of Abraham." *Brigham Young University Studies 32,* no. 3 (Summer 1991).

Terry, Keith, and Walter Whipple. *From the Dust of Decades; A Saga of the Papyri and Mummies.* Salt Lake City: Bookcraft, 1968.

Mummies and Mummification

Aufderheide, Arthur C. *Scientific Study of Mummies.* Cambridge: Cambridge University Press, 2003.

Brier, Bob, *Egyptian Mummies.* New York: William Morrow, 1994.

Brier, Bob. *Encyclopedia of Mummies.* New York: Checkmark Books, 1998.

Ikram, Salima, and Aidan Dodson. *Mummy in Ancient Egypt; Equipping the Dead for Eternity.* New York: Thames and Hudson, 1998.

Pringle, Heather. *Mummy Congress.* New York: Hyperion, 2001.

Mummy as Medicine

Aesculapian Register 1, no. 15 (September 23, 1824).

Gordon-Grube, Karen. "Evidence of Medicinal Cannibalism in Puritan New England: 'Mummy' and Related Remedies in Edward Taylor's 'Dispensatory.'" *Early American Literature* 28, no. 3 (1993).

Kirtley, William Lawton. "Using 'Mummy' in Medicine; A Case Study of Efficacy and Change in Therapeutics from Dioscorides to the Twentieth Century." A.B. thesis, Harvard University, 1997.

Quigley, Christine. *The Corpse; A History.* Jefferson, N.C.: McFarland, 1996.

Reichman, Edward. "The Impact of Medieval Medicine On Medical Halacha: Mumia." *Pioneers in Jewish Medical Ethics,* ed. Fred Rosner. Northvale, N.J.: Jason Aronson, 1997.

Sugg, Richard. "Good Physic But Bad Food: Early Modern Attitudes to Medical Cannibalism and Its Suppliers." *Social History of Medicine* 19, no. 2 (August 2006).

Museums, Circuses and Sideshows

Conn, Steven. *Museums and American Intellectual Life, 1876–1926.* Chicago: University of Chicago Press, 1998.

Dennett, Andrea Stulman. *Weird and Wonderful; The Dime Museum in America.* New York: New York University Press, 1997.

Taylor, James, and Kathleen Kochter. *James Taylor's "Shocked and Amazed!" On and Off the Midway.* Guilford, Conn.: Lyons Press, 2002.

Appendix 3. Notes on the Coffins of the First Mummies Brought to America

The notes on the coffin of Padihershef are from Joyce Haynes, *Padihershef: The Egyptian Mummy* (Springfield, Mass.: George Walter Vincent Smith Art Museum, 1985), p. 22.

1. Padihershef (Massachusetts General Hospital Mummy)

The proper names of the mummy and his parents all date from the late period (730–332 B.C.) The particular spelling of the name of the god Osiris is present in non-royal inscriptions after only after 730 B.C., thus establishing the oldest possible date for the coffin.

The iconography of the deceased standing before an upright snake followed by a group of gods is not documented until Dynasty XXV (730–656 B.C.) The faience bead net on the body was common during the Saiite period but not thereafter. The wooden anthropoid coffin is well represented from Dynasty XX (1797–1085 B.C.) until the beginning of the XXVI Dynasty (663–525 B.C.). An early Dynasty XXVI date seems probable.

(John Taylor, of the British Museum, in an e-mail to me on 9 September 2005 stated "I would put him a little earlier, perhaps about 680 B.C. (25th Dynasty), on the evidence of the style of his coffins.")

The following notes are from e-mail correspondence with John Taylor, Department of Ancient Egypt and Sudan, The British Museum on 9 September 2005.

2. Larkin Turner's Mummy

The style of the coffin is typical of the 22nd Dynasty: no arms or hands; stole painted on the collar (a legacy of the late 21st/early 22nd Dynasty coffins—cf. Larkin Lee's mummy, below); simple decoration of the lid, with winged ram-headed scarab beetle and single column of inscription. On the drawing the hieroglyphs have been rendered pretty accurately, so that most of the text can be read: "An offering which the king gives to Re-Horakhty, the great god, lord of heaven, to Atum ... and to

Anubis, lord of the sacred land, that they might give ... provisions ... alabaster jars and clothing to the Osiris Djedkhonsuiue-fankh [or Djedkhonsuiuesankh], justified."

The spelling of the name is not entirely clear. Depending on whether it contains an 'f' or an 's' it would belong to a man or a woman, respectively. The face of the coffin seems to be beardless, and the description of the mummy states that it is female, so perhaps we are dealing with a woman here—but I cannot be sure. The style of the coffin is in accord with the Theban provenance given in the description.

3. Large Coffin of the Peregrine Mummies

Probably 21st Dynasty on the evidence of the large collar, the crossed arms and the division of the lower part of the lid into narrow zones filled with small images, many of them winged figures.

4. Small Coffin of the Peregrine Mummies

Seems to be an inner coffin of the 25th or 26th Dynasty. This is suggested by the absence of hands or arms, the inclusion of a rectangular pedestal under the feet, and the general design of the lid, with collar, single large winged figure on breast (probably the goddess Nut), a horizontal band of figures (probably the weighing of the heart and presentation of the deceased to gods: cf. Padihershef's coffin), then a tripartite arrangement of images and texts—in the centre a vignette of the mummy lying on a bier, with columns of text below; at each side a series of deities standing in compartments.

5. Larkin Thorndike Lee's Mummy

The image of the coffin is well done (only the inscriptions are illegible), and it is clearly of the late 21st or early 22nd Dynasty. The very large collar, which completely covers the crossed arms is typical of this period, as is the depiction of a stole or red leather band around the neck and crossing on the breast. The manner in which the stole passes beneath a pectoral ornament with symmetrical images of scarabs etc. is also very characteristic. The iconography of the wig, with decorative bands across the lappets, is appropriate for a female, as is the face without ears or false beard. The rounded features at the ends of the wig lappets are stylized depictions of female breasts. The provenance is pretty certainly Thebes (as indicated in the caption); most of the coffins of this type are from the Theban necropolis, though it is more likely to be from the non-royal cemeteries than from the "King's [*sic*] Tombs." This particular type of coffin has been studied in detail by Rene van Walsem, *The Coffin of Djedmonthuiufankh in the National Museum of Antiquities at Leiden* (Leiden, 1997). He lists over 120 coffin-ensembles of this kind, but does not seem to know of this specimen.

The following information is also from John Taylor and was communicated in a letter to the author dated 24 November 2005.

6. "Blockhead Mummy" (Peale's Mummy)

Most likely of Roman date (for other examples see Gottfried Hamernik, "Ägyptologische Sammlung des Landesmusems zur Fundgeschichte und Datierung Eines Ägyptischen Mumiesarges im Landesmuseum Kärnten," in *Sonderdruck Aus Rudolfinum: Jahrbuch des Landesmuseums Kärnten 2002* (Klagenfurt, 2003), 185–198.)

This includes numerous examples of this type of coffin in European museums, including a double coffin for twins.

There is very little known about how the drawings were done or who did them (except for the bills for the engravings of Padihershef's outer coffin, which were inserted in Chapter 1.) We know that the original of Padihershef's coffin illustration was a metal engraving, and that a woodblock engraving was made from that—otherwise it would not have appeared in the press notices. In order for the illustration of the coffin to be printed in the newspapers, it had to be a relief print—metal engravings are intaglio prints and will not print in a set up of type. We also know that at some point a stereotype was made from the wood engraving. This involved making a mold from the wood engraving, using papier mache or gutta percha or a similar material, and then filling the mold with lead which then produced a plate containing the relief image. Numerous copies of the image could thus be obtained and distributed to various newspapers. Indeed one of the verifying factors that the illustration of Padihershef's coffin is a stereotype, is that it appeared on the same day in different newspapers. If you examine the images of the coffin carefully, you can discern that the metal engraving is much more precise and finely done.

There are no records for the artists who drew any of the other coffin pictures, although it is possible Ethan Allen Greenwood, who was an artist of some renown, did the drawings for Turner's mummy and the Peregrine mummies. If he did, there is nothing in his extant records which details the process. Owing to the clarity of the hieroglyphics and illustrations, at a time when the iconography of both was meager, it is possible that a device such as a camera lucida was used to prepare the drawings. Needless to say the engravers had to be extremely precise—in a wood block the areas which are to show up as black must be raised and the areas which are to show up as white must be cut away, and it is quite remarkable that the illustrations are as accurate and readable as they are.

Unfortunately none of the coffin pictures are in color, nor are their colors mentioned except in the case of the face of Padihershef's coffin (remarked upon as being red). All of the coffins, except for Turner's mummy, were originally brightly painted, in yellow, red, blue, green, black and white. Turner's mummy's coffin was painted black and the decorated strip down the front was probably gilt, or at least painted yellow to imitate gilt. (The ancient Egyptians believed in sympathetic magic. If two things were similar, then they could be the same. Gold is yellow and so if one can't afford real gold, one uses yellow paint, which then magically becomes gold.) From the surviving inner and outer coffins of Padihershef we can at least imagine how splendid the other early coffins, now lost, appeared.

Appendix 4. Spreading the News

I referred early on in this book to "scissors and paste pot editors." Because newspapers could be sent for free to other newspaper editors, news was copied from one place to another, often with startling rapidity. In some cases the originating source of the news was noted, but in many cases, it was not. Throughout the nineteenth century, mummies were *news*, and reports of them circulated wildly and widely. In most cases I tried to cite the "hometown" newspaper where a mummy event occurred, but when I did not, it was because I did not have at hand the originating title, but used instead, one of the numerous reprints.

The following is an example of a news story spreading and being reprinted all over the country (and I am sure I haven't gotten *all* the instances where it showed up). It's the story of Ward Nicholas Boylston's mummy, first published in the

Boston paper *Columbian Sentinel* on 16 May 1818. I've listed the dates, newspapers and towns below. All dates are 1818:

16 May—*Columbian Centinel* (Boston, Mass.)

19 May—*Boston Recorder* (Boston, Mass.)

19 May—*New-Hampshire Gazette* (Portsmouth, N.H.)

19 May—*Newburyport Herald* (Newburyport, Mass.)

19 May—*Rhode Island American ...* (Providence, R.I.)

20 May—*Massachusetts Spy, or Worcester Gazette* (Worcester, Mass.)

20 May—*Poulson's American Daily Advertiser* (Philadelphia, Pa.)

22 May—*Lancaster Journal* (Lancaster, Pa.)

23 May—*Farmer's Cabinet* (Amherst, N.H.)

23 May—*Portsmouth Oracle* (Portsmouth, N.H.)

23 May—*City of Washington Gazette* (Washington, D.C.)

25 May—*Baltimore Patriot & Mercantile Advertiser* (Baltimore, Md.)

25 May—*National Messenger* (Georgetown, D.C.)

25 May—*Spirit of the Times & Carlisle Gazette* (Carlisle, Pa.)

26 May—*Connecticut Herald* (New Haven, Conn.)

27 May—*Christian Messenger* (Middlebury, Vt.)

27 May—*Norwich Courier* (Norwich, Conn.)

28 May—*Bangor Weekly Register* (Bangor, Me.)

29 May—*Alexandria Gazette & Daily Advertiser* (Alexandria, Va.)

30 May—*Berks and Schuylkill Journal* (Reading, Pa.)

30 May—*New York Columbian* (New York, N.Y.)

2 June—*Columbian Gazette* (Utica, N.Y.)

4 June—*Hampden Federalist* (Springfield, Mass.)

5 June—*New Bedford Mercury* (New Bedford, Mass.)

8 June—*Watch-Tower* (Cooperstown, N.Y.)

9 June—*Reflector* (Milledgeville, Ga.)

10 June—*Rutland Herald* (Rutland, Vt.)

12 June—*Albany Argus* (Albany, N.Y.)

12 June—*Northern Sentinel* (Burlington, Vt.)

12 June—*Weekly Recorder* (Chillicothe, Ohio)

13 June—*Plattsburgh Republican* (Plattsburgh, N.Y.)

13 June—*Ulster Plebian* (Ulster, N.Y.)

20 June—*Portsmouth Oracle* (repeated) (Portsmouth, N.H.)

1 August—*Weekly Visitor and Ladies' Museum* (New York, N.Y.)

Quite obviously the arrival of this mummy was newsworthy for the note attesting to its arrival to have disseminated so quickly and over such distances in a time when the news was carried in "hard copy" by post riders and not transmitted electronically.

Chapter Notes

Chapter 1

1. *Boston Daily Advertiser* (Boston, Mass.), 26 April 1823.

2. George E. Gifford, "The Case of the Ether Dome Mummy," *Harvard Medical Alumni Bulletin* (March–April 1977): 6.

3. Charles Coulston Gillespie and Michael Dewachter, eds., *The Monuments of Egypt* (Old Saybrook, Conn.: Konecky & Konecky, 1987): 1, (47).

4. Edwin Wolf, "The Library Company of Philadelphia, America's First Museum," *The Magazine Antiques* 120, no. 2 (August, 1981): 349–350.

5. Doddridge, Joseph, *Notes on the Settlement and Indian Wars of the Western Parts of Virginia and Pennsylvania, From 1763 to 1783, Inclusive* (Albany: Joel Munsell, 1876), 72 f I.

6. Manuscript note by an unknown person in the Library Company of Philadelphia's copy of John Fanning Watson's *Extra-illustrated Autograph Manuscript of "Annals of Philadelphia,"* verso #AM1758Lab. 1069.F.I. (The manuscript is an unpaged scrapbook of notes, illustrations and ephemera collected by Watson as research for his book.) The note appears adjacent to an engraving of the coffin of Padihershef, beneath notes from Watson, which are quoted elsewhere. The note reads, in its entirety: "This is a mistake. A number of Egyptian mummies were imported by I. (or J.) Germon about 1800 but he not meeting with ready sale for them they were stored in Dock Street below 3d until 1832 when in repairing premises they were discovered by the workers. They had been there so long as to have been forgotten. The workmen not knowing their value in the curiosity to see what they were destroyed most of them. One is or was lately preserved in a private family in Southwark. Aug. 1848." John Germon was listed as a silversmith in the Philadelphia city directory for 1820.

7. "From the Minutes of the Board of Trustees of the University of Pennsylvania, July 2, 1816," *William and Mary Quarterly* 1st ser. 23, no. 1 (July 1914): 48–49.

8. *The National Gazette and Literary Register* (Philadelphia, Pa.), 14 June 1820.

9. John Collins Warren, "Description of an Egyptian Mummy, Presented to the Massachusetts General Hospital, With an Account of the Operation of Embalming, in Ancient and Modern Times," *Boston Journal of Philosophy and the Arts* 1 (1823): 284–285.

10. American Antiquarian Society, *Donations to the American Antiquarian Society with Names of its Benefactors, 1813–1849,* American Antiquarian Society Archives (Worcester, Mass.), 122, 133.

11. Harvard University, Warren Anatomical Museum, *A Descriptive Catalogue of the Warren Anatomical Museum,* J.B.S. Jackson, comp. (Boston: A. Williams and Company, 1870), 700.

12. Kathryn Hammond Baker, Manager Special Collections, Francis A. Countway Library of Medicine, Cambridge, Mass., e-mail correspondence with the author, 2 August 2007.

13. Charles Coleman Sellers, *Mr. Peale's Museum* (New York: W.W. Norton & Company, 1980), 241.

14. *Daily National Intelligencer* (Washington, D.C.), 2 June 1820; *The Republican Compiler* (Gettysburg, Pa.), 14 June 1820.

15. Ibid.

16. Some representative examples occurs in the *Louisiana Advertiser* (New Orleans, La.), 31 July 1820; *New England Galaxy & Masonic Magazine* (Boston, Mass.), 30 June 1820; *The National Gazette and Literary Register* (Philadelphia, Pa.), 7, 10, 14 June 1820; *Baltimore Patriot & Mercantile Advertiser* (Baltimore, Md.), 8 June 1820; *Daily National Intelligencer* (Washington, D.C.), 2 June 1820; *American* (New York, N.Y.), 12 June 1820.

17. Louis Leonard Tucker, "'Ohio Show-Shop'; The Western Museum of Cincinnati 1820–1867," in *A Cabinet of Curiosities; Five Episodes in the Evolution of American Museums* (Charlottesville: University Press of Virginia, 1967), 76.

18. Ibid., 80–81.

19. Ibid., 81, 83.

20. Ibid., 79.

21. Warren, "Description of an Egyptian Mummy," 164–165.

22. Massachusetts General Hospital, Board of Trustees, Records, 4 May 1823, Massachusetts General Hospital Archives and Special Collections, Boston.

23. N.I. Bowditch, *A History of the Massachusetts General Hospital to August 5, 1851. Second Edition with Continuations to 1872* (Boston, 1872), 63.

24. Massachusetts General Hospital, Board of Trustees, Records, 18 May 1823, Massachusetts General Hospital Archives and Special Collections, Boston.

25. Massachusetts General Hospital Archives and Special Collections, Boston. Miscellaneous file of bills and receipts pertaining to Padihershef. Bill from H. Williams to Dr. Warren, dated 25 June 1823. On 15 August 1825, the Massachusetts General Hospital reimbursed Warren for this expense. Warren used the drawings to have plates made for his articles. Woodblocks and stereotype plates for the newspaper articles were also probably made up from these drawings. Unfortunately the nature of Mr. Williams' "preparations" is not noted.

26. Massachusetts General Hospital Archives and Special Collections, Boston. Miscellaneous file of bills and receipts relating to Padihershef. A page of accounts with Nathan Hale, beginning 21 May 1823 and ending 20 March (1824).

27. Massachusetts General Hospital Archives and Special Collections, Boston. Miscellaneous file of bills and receipts pertaining to Padihershef. This bill was dated 23 May 1823. According to a note on the reverse of the bill, it was not paid until 20 January 1825!

28. Edward Warren, *The Life of John Collins Warren, M.D.* (Boston: Ticknor & Fields, 1860), 208.

29. John Collins Warren, *Description of an Egyptian Mummy, Presented to the Massachusetts General Hospital* (Boston: Cummings, Hillyard & Company, 1823), 1.

30. Massachusetts General Hospital Archives and Special Collections, Boston. Miscellaneous file of bills and receipts relating to Padihershef. This bill is marked on the reverse "T. Smith's bill. Pd. De 6, 1823 no. 66."

31. *The Christian Journal and Literary Register* (New York, N.Y.) 7, no. 11 (November 1823): 351.

32. Warren, "Description of an Egyptian Mummy," 273–279.

33. Massachusetts General Hospital Archives and Special Collections, Boston. Miscellaneous file of bills and receipts relating to Padihershef. Bill to Ballard and White, May 21, 1823. The cost of advertising in *the Boston Patriot & Mercantile Advertiser* was $28.87. The bill was paid on 31 October 1823.

34. Massachusetts General Hospital Archives and Special Collections. Boston. Miscellaneous files of bills and receipts relating to Padihershef. Memo from Gideon Snow, dated 26 May 1823.

35. William Slade, "Journal" in Leslie L. Luther, *Moravia and Its Past and Adjoining Townships* (Indianapolis, Ind.: Frederic Luther Company, 1966), 427, 439–440.

36. Massachusetts General Hospital. Board of Trustees. Records. 16 September 1823. Massachusetts General Hospital Archives and Special Collections, Boston.

37. Massachusetts General Hospital, Board of Trustees, Records, 7 October 1823, Massachusetts General Hospital Archives and Special Collections, Boston.

38. Massachusetts General Hospital Archives and Special Collections, Boston. Miscellaneous file of bills and receipts relating to Padihershef. A page of accounts with Nathan Hale, beginning 21 May 1823 and ending 20 March (1824).

39. R. Jackson Wilson, "Thebes to Springfield; The Travels of an Egyptian Mummy" in *Padihershef the Egyptian Mummy* (Springfield, Mass.: The Springfield Library and Museums Association, 1984), 30.

40. George E. Gifford, "The Case of the Ether Dome Mummy," in *Harvard Medical Alumni Bulletin* (March-April 1977), 9.

41. Massachusetts General Hospital Archives and Special Collections, Boston. Miscellaneous file of bills and receipts relating to Padihershef. Ledger page dated 27 October 1823.

42. George D. Odell, *Annals of the New York Stage* (New York: Columbia University Press, 1928), vol. 3, 113.

43. John Cumming, *Description of an Egyptian Mummy, Now Exhibiting in This City* (New York: W. Grattan, 1823), (title page).

44. Ibid., 1–2.

45. Ibid., 3–4.

46. Massachusetts General Hospital Archives and Special Collections, Boston. Miscellaneous file of bills and receipts relating to Padihershef. Letter dated 6 December 1823.

47. Agnes M. Bondurant, *Poe's Richmond* (Richmond, 1942), 142.

48. Watson manuscript and scrapbook, n.p.

49. "Mummies" in *The Evergreen* (Philadelphia: American Sunday School Union, 1837), plate facing 107.

50. Charles Willson Peale, *The Selected Papers of Charles Willson Peale and His Family*, ed. Lillian B. Miller (New Haven: Yale University Press, 1983–1996), vol. 4, 416–417. Letter from Charles Willson Peale to Coleman Sellers. Peale gives the amount as $600; in reality it was $650.

51. William T. Alderson, ed., *Mermaids, Mummies and Mastodons: The Emergence of the*

American Museum (Baltimore: Baltimore City Life Museum, 1992), 60.

52. Peale, 437.

53. Wilson, 31.

54. Nathaniel Ingersoll Bowditch, *A History of the Massachusetts General Hospital (To August 5, 1851). 2nd. ed., With a Continuation to 1872* (Boston: Printed by the Trustees from the Bowditch Fund, 1872), 68.

55. Massachusetts General Hospital, Board of Trustees, *Minutes,* Massachusetts General Hospital Archives and Special Collections, Boston, vol. 2, 259.

56. Gifford, 7.

57. I. Hayward. *Chronology of the Mummy—Padi-hershef and the Two Coffins,* typescript, Massachusetts General Hospital Archives and Special Collections Boston.

58. Ibid.

59. Bowditch, 69.

Chapter 2

1. Thomas Larkin Turner. *"Biography of Turner, Larkin, b. 1781,"* Larkin Turner Collection, G.W. Blunt White Library, Mystic Seaport, Mystic, Conn.

2. Ethan Allen Greenwood, *"Extracts From the Journals of Ethan A. Greenwood": Portrait Painter and Museum Proprietor,* ed. Georgia Brady Barnhill (Worcester, Mass.: American Antiquarian Society, 1993), 167.

3. *Egyptian Mummy From the Catacombs at Thebes* (Boston: E.G. House, 1824?.

4. *Egyptian Mummy to be Exhibited at (blank)"* (Boston?, 1824?), 1–8.

5. Greenwood, 174.

6. Ibid., 175.

7. Karl Bernard, Duke of Saxe-Weimar-Eisenbach, *Travels through North America, During the Years 1825 and 1826* (Philadelphia: Carey, Lea & Carey, 1828), 38.

8. *Three Mummies from Egypt at the New-England Museum, 76, Court-Street, Boston* (Boston, Mass., 1825), 1)

9. *Rare curiosities.* No place of publication or printer are noted on the broadsheet. The various letters and testimonials are all dated 30 November 1827.

10. Walter K. Watkins, "The New England Museum and the Home of Art in Boston," in *The Bostonian Society Publications,* by the Bostonian Society (Boston, 1927): (series 2) 2, 127–128.

11. *History of the Boston Museum,* (article on-line); available from http://www.emerson.edu.majestic/history /Bos_Museum_History.html; accessed 18 September 2002.

12. Boston Museum and Gallery of Fine Arts, *Catalogue of the Paintings, Marble and Plaster Statuary and Engravings Comprised in the Collection of the Boston Museum and Gallery of Fine Arts, Corner of Tremont and Bromfield Streets, Together with a Descriptive Sketch of the Institution and Its Collection* (Boston: William White & H.P. Lewis, 1842), 24.

13. *History of the Boston Museum;* S.J. Wolfe, *Egyptian Mummies in America Database,* (unpublished electronic resource), entries PMA001, PMA002.

14. Agnes Lynch Starrett, *Through One Hundred and Fifty Years: The University of Pittsburgh* (Pittsburgh: University of Pittsburgh Press, 1937), 89.

15. The pamphlet included an article from *The Minerva,* n.s., 22, no. 1 (4 September 1824).

16. *Egyptian Mummy, With Its Sarcophagus* (New York: E. Conrad, 1824), 8)

17. *Works of the Old World, the Wonder of the New* (New York?: E. Conrad, printer, 1824), 1–6.

18. Ebenezer Fisk (New York) letter to Larkin T. Lee (Beverly, Mass.), 11 January 1825, Larkin Thorndike Lee Collection, Phillips Library, Peabody Essex Museum, Salem, Mass.

19. *Vital records of Beverly, Massachusetts, To the End of the Year 1849* (Topsfield, Mass.: Topsfield Historical Society, 1906–1907), vol. 2, 488.

20. Ebenezer Fisk (New York?), letter to John Dike (Beverly, Mass.), 25 October 1825, Larkin Thorndike Lee Collection, Phillips Library, Peabody Essex Museum, Salem, Mass.

21. Ebenezer Fisk (New York) letter to Robert Rantoul (Beverly, Mass.), 9 December 1825, Larkin Thorndike Lee Collection, Phillips Library, Peabody Essex Museum, Salem, Mass

22. *A History of Trenton, 1679–1829; Two Hundred and Fifty Years of a Notable Town with Links to Four Centuries* (Princeton: Princeton University Press, 1829), 30.

23. Ebenezer Fisk (New York) letter to (unknown) (Beverly, Mass.) undated note, but probably late December 1825, Larkin Thorndike Lee Collection, Phillips Library, Peabody Essex Museum, Salem, Mass.

Chapter 3

1. Lillian B. Miller, ed., *The Selected Papers of Charles Willson Peale and His Family* (New Haven: Yale University Press, 1996), 4: 517.

2. *Egyptian Mummy* (Ithaca, N.Y.: A.P. Searing & Company, 1827), 1–8.

3. Ibid.

4. H. Perry Smith, ed., *History of The City of Buffalo and Erie County; With Illustrations and Biographical Sketches of Some of Its Prominent Men and Pioneer*, (Syracuse, N.Y.: D. Mason & Company, 1884), 542.

5. "The Law," in *The Ariel; a Semimonthly Literary and Miscellaneous Gazette* 3, no. 13 (Oct. 17, 1829), 99; "Trover for a Mummy," in *American Jurist and Law Magazine* 2, no. 4 (October 1829): 400–402.

6. Winfred E. Howe, *A History of the Metropolitan Museum of Art* (New York: Gilliss Press, 1913–46), vol. 1, 75–78.

7. L.P. Gratacap, "Formative Museum Period," in *Science* n.s., 14, no. 344 (2 August 1901): 173–174.

8. Barnum's American Museum, *Catalogue or Guide Book of Barnum's American Museum New York* (New York: Published for the proprietor, undated), 88, 94.

9. Walt Whitman, *New York Dissected* (New York: Rufus Rockwell Wilson, 1936), 28–29.

10. Henry Abbott, *Catalogue of a Collection of Egyptian Antiquities; the Property of Henry Abbott, M.D., Now Exhibiting at the Stuyvesant Institute, no. 629 Broadway, New York* (New York: Printed for the Proprietor by J.W. Watson, 1853), 1–72; The New-York Historical Society has the original visitor register for the Abbott Museum.

11. Whitman, 28, 31, 37–38.

12. R.W.G. Vail, *Knickerbocker Birthday; A Sesqui-Centennial History of the New-York Historical Society, 1804–1954* (New York: New-York Historical Society, 1954), 109–111.

13. W.S.W. Ruschenberger, *A Notice of the Origin, Progress, and Present Condition of the Academy of Natural Sciences of Philadelphia* (Philadelphia: T.K. and P.G. Collins, 1852), 33.

14. Academy of Natural Sciences, *Proceedings of the Academy of Natural Sciences of Philadelphia. 1858* (Philadelphia: Printed for the Academy, 1859), 5.

15. Tom Avril, "Mummy Mystery," *Philadelphia Inquirer* (22 May 2006) (journal on-line); available from http://www.philly.com/mid/inquirer/news/local/14636650.htm; accessed 30 May 2006.

16. Col. Joseph H. Wood's Museum and Art Gallery, *Synoptical Catalogue of Col. Joseph H. Wood's Museum and Art Gallery, N.W. Cor. Ninth and Arch, Philadelphia* (Philadelphia, Pa.: J. Moore & Sons, 1872), 15; *Philadelphia Inquirer* (Philadelphia, Pa.), 2 September 1881; *Georgia Weekly Telegraph* (Macon, Ga.),10 March 1882.

17. National Institute, *A Popular Catalogue of the Extraordinary Curiosities of the National Institute, Arranged in the Building Belonging to the Patent Offic0e* (Washington, D.C.: Alfred Hunter, 1855), (11), 49–50.

18. Grossman, Edwina Booth, *Edwin Booth: Recollections by His Daughter, Edwina Booth Grossman; and Letters to Her and to His Friends* (New York: Century Company, 1894), 96.

19. Curtis M. Hinsley, *Savages and Scientists; The Smithsonian Institution and the Development of American Anthropology, 1846–1910* (Washington, D.C.: Smithsonian Institute Press, 1981), 17, 19.

20. William Jones Rhees, *An Account of the Smithsonian Institution, Its Founder, Building, Operations, Et* (Washington, D.C.: T. McGill, 1857), 84.

21. David R. Hunt, Collections Manager, Division of Physical Anthropology, National Museum of Natural History, e-mail correspondence with the author, 16 and 17 January 2007.

22. Museum of Fine Arts, Boston *Collections Database* (on-line database); available from http://www.mfa.org/collections/sub.asp?key=20&subkey=6; accessed 29 July 2004.

23. Ibid.

24. *American National Biography On-line* (subscription database on-line); available from http://www.and.org/articale/10/10-02260; accessed 20 August 2004.

25. (Charles Frederick Gunther), *Chicago's Royal Princess of the Ancient Pharaohs* (Chicago, 1886?), 1–3.

26. *American National Biography On-line.*

27. Wolfe, entries CFG001, LPM001, FMN0 22.

28. Ibid., entries MMA004, PEM006, PM S006, UNR001.

29. *Philadelphia Inquirer* (Philadelphia, Pa.) 8 December 1895; *New York Times* (New York, N.Y.) 30 March 1887; Deborah Winkler, Assistant Director & Registrar, Reading Public Museum, e-mail correspondence with the author, 27 September 2001.

30. Gretchen Worden, Director of the Mutter Museum, Philadelphia, e-mail correspondence with the author, 16 January 2002.

31. Michael Sappol, "Morbid Curiosity"; The Decline and Fall of the Popular Anatomical Museum, " in *Common-Place* 14:2 Jan. 2004 (journal on-line); available from http://www.common-place.org/vol-04/no-02/sappol/; accessed 7 August 2006.

32. Pacific Museum of Anatomy and Natural Science, *Hand-book & Descriptive Catalogue of the Pacific Museum of Anatomy and Natural Science, Now Open at the Eureka Theatre* (San Francisco, 1865?), 44.

33. *Social Violence and Conflict in San Francisco; A Chronology of the American Era.* (pub-

lication on-line); available from http://www.
notfrisCompanycom/colmatales/sfviol.html;
accessed 17 February 2008.

34. Great Chicago Museum, *Great Chicago
Museum Catalogue* (Chicago: Blakely Marsh,
1885), 20.

35. American Museum cartes de visite
(Electronic Images) on e-Bay (Electronic Resource); accessed 9 August 2005 and 16 March
2006.

36. *New Hampshire Sentinel* (Keene, N.H.),
17 July 1851; *Milwaukee Daily Sentinel* (Milwaukee, Wis.), 11 July 1853.

37. Rosalie Maggio, *How They Said It; Wise
and Witty Letters from the Famous and Infamous* (Paramus, N.J.: Prentice Hall, 2000),
(232).

38. *P.T. Barnum's Museum, Menagerie,
Caravan and Hippodrome* (New York?: P.T.
Barnum, between 1871 and 1881?), 1.

39. *How Ti Ameny Net Came to the University of Richmond*,; available from *http://her-
mes.richmond.edu/tiameny/TAN-UR.html*; accessed 7 April 2000; "Saving the Mummy," in
Richmond Now, (journal on-line); available
from http://oncampus.richmond.edu/news/
richmondnow/2007/05/mummy.html; accessed
28 June 1007; J.S. Ingram, *The Centennial Exposition Described and Illustrated* (Philadelphia: Hubbard Bros., 1876), 721–722.

40. Ibid.

41. Ben Truman, *History of the World's Fair*
(Chicago: E.G. Morse & Company, 1893), 555.

42. "Cairo Going to San Francisco," *Macon
Telegraph* (Macon, Ga.), 26 December 1893;
Edward F. Wente, "Who Was Who among the
Royal Mummies" (article on-line); available
from http://oi.uchicago.edu/research/pubs/
nn/win95_wente.html (accessed 21 February
2008); "Tumult in Cairo Street," in *Morning
World Herald* (Omaha, Neb.), 3 November
1898.

43. "Pharaoh and the World's Fair,"
Chicago Daily Tribune (Chicago, Ill.), 9 March
1890; "Cleopatra's Bones for Sale," *Macon
Telegraph* (Macon, Ga.), 9 June 1890.

44. Donald Malcolm Reid, *Whose Pharaohs?
Archaeology, Museums, and Egyptian National
Identity from Napoleon to World War I* (Berkeley: University of California Press, 2005), 55–
57.

45. *Report of the Christmas Bazaar, Held
under the Auspices of the Ladies' Hospital Relief
Association, From December 14 to December 22,
Iinclusive at Corinthian Hall, Rochester, N.Y.*
(Rochester (N.Y.): Newton & Andrews, 1863).

46. *Brooklyn Eagle* (New York, N.Y.), 2
March 1859; William Prime, *Boat Life in Egypt
and Nubia* (New York: Harper and Brothers,
1874).

47. "A Course of Six Lectures on the 'Bible
Lands' ..." (Washington, D., (between 1859
and 1870?), (1) (undated broadside from the
collections of the Library of Congress).

Chapter 4

1. James R. Clark, *The Story of The Pearl of
Great Price* (Salt Lake City: Bookcraft, 1962),
62–63, 73–75. The quotations from the *History of the Church* are as reported in Clark's
book.

2. Ibid.

3. Clark, 77.

4. H. Donal Peterson, *The Story of the Book
of Abraham; Mummies, Manuscripts and Mormonism* (Salt Lake City: Deseret Book Company, 1995), 36–37. The depth of the research
carried out by the Mormon Church in this
matter is incredibly detailed and takes up several chapters in Peterson's book. Peterson gives
an almost overwhelming amount of evidence
tracing Lebolo's whereabouts in Egypt and in
Europe during the time period 1817 through
1830, as well as listing all of the documents and
papers pertinent to the establishment of what
is at the present time believed to the most correct and accurate account of Lebolo's colorful
life.

5. Ibid., 47.

6. Ibid., 48–51.

7. Ibid., 65.

8. Peterson, 69–70, 79.

9. Brian M. Fagan, *The Rape of the Nile;
Tomb Robbers, Tourists and Archaeologists in
Egypt* (New York: Charles Scribners' Sons,
1975), 258.

10. Peterson, 65.

11. Ibid., 67. Drovetti served as France's
Consul-General from 1803 to 1814, and again
from 1820 to 1829.

12. Ibid., 70–71.

13. Ibid., 73.

14. Ibid., 75.

15. Ibid., 76

16. Ibid., 77.

17. Ibid., 80.

18. Ibid., 83–85.

19. Ibid., 87. Most records from the Treasury Department, which might have contained
further information, were destroyed by fire in
1833.

20. Ibid., 88–89.

21. Ibid., 169–174,

22. Ibid., 88–89, 107–108, 169–176

23. N.L. Nelson, "The Book of Abraham,"
The Academic Review 1, no. 6 (March 1885): 46.

24. Samuel George Morton, *Catalogue of*

the Skulls of Man, and the Inferior Animals, in the Collection of Samuel George Morton (Philadelphia: Turner & Fisher, 1840), 7, 9.

25. Ibid., "Observations on Egyptian Ethnography. Derived from Anatomy, History, and the Monuments," in *Transactions* (American Philosophical Society) 9 (Philadelphia, 1846), 124.

26. E.A. Wallis Budge, *The Mummy; A History of the Extraordinary Practices of Ancient Egypt* (New York: Bell Publishing Company, 1989), 177–179

27. Samuel George Morton, *Crania Ægyptiaca; or, Observations on Egyptian Ethnography, Derived From Anatomy, History and the Monuments* (Philadelphia: John Pennington; London: Madden & Company, 1844), Plate X.

28. "Egyptian Antiquities," *Times and Seasons* 3 (2 May 1833): 774.

29. Peterson, 94.

30. Brian L. Smith and Philip R. Webb, "Mystery of the Mummies: An Update on the Joseph Smith Collection," *RSC Newsletter* 20, no. 2 (2005): 3.

31. Ibid., 3.

32. Stephen M. Archer, *Junius Brutus Booth; Theatrical Prometheus* (Carbondale, Ill.: Southern Illinois University Press, c. 1992), 129.

33. Grossman, 96.

34. Smith and Webb, 3.

35. Asia Booth Clarke, *Booth Memorials. Passages, Incidents, and Anecdotes in the Life of Junius Brutus Booth (the Elder)* (New York: Carleton, 1865), 110.

36. Peterson, 97.

37. Friend Palmer, *Early Days in Detroit; Papers Written by General Friend Palmer, of Detroit, Being His Personal Reminiscences of Important Events and Descriptions of the City for over Eighty Years* (Detroit: Hunt & June, 1906), 330, 342, 452, 702.

38. Peterson, 97.

39. Ibid., 97.

40. Ibid., 1, 3–4.

41. "Egyptian Antiquities," *Times and Seasons* 3 (2 May 1842): 774.

42. Peterson, 3.

43. Jay M. Todd, *The Saga of the Book of Abraham* (Salt Lake City: Deseret Book Company, 1969), 159.

44. Peterson, 6, 8.

45. Ibid., 6, 8.

46. Ibid., 125.

47. Ibid., 125.

28. Clark, 73.

49. Peterson, 123–124, 127.

50. *Cleveland Herald and Gazette*, as quoted by the *Western Reserve Chronicle* (Warren, Ohio), 30 January 1838.

51. Peterson, 137–138, 140–141, 191–192

52. Ibid., 193.

53. Ibid., 193.

54. Ibid., 193, 198.

55. Ibid., 193, 198.

56. Charlotte Haven, "A Girl's Letters from Nauvoo," *Overland Monthly* (December 1890): 623–624.

57. LaFayette Knight letter to James H. and Sharon Fellows, December 21, 1843, MS 2362, LDS Archives.

58. Peterson, 200.

59. Christopher G. Crary, *Pioneer and Personal Reminiscences* (Marshalltown, Ia.: Marshall Printing Co, 1893), 33.

60. Mary Ann Hubbard, *Family Memories* (Chicago: R.R. Donnelley and Sons Company, 1912), 100–101.

61. Peterson, 195–197.

62. Peter A. Clayton, *Chronicles of the Pharaohs; The Reign-by-Reign Record of the Rulers and Dynasties of Ancient Egypt* (London and New York: Thames and Hudson, 1994), 196.

63. Budge, 55–58.

64. Todd, 315–316.

65. Clayton, 174, 176.

66. Todd, 317–318.

67. Clayton, 172.

68. Peterson, 53–62. This is one of the better sources of all the arguments for and against the identification of the tomb from which Lebolo took the mummies. Other studies are reported in Ross T. Christensen, ed. *Mummies, Scrolls, and the Book of Abraham* (Provo, Utah: Brigham Young University, 1968).

69. Ibid., 199–203.

70. Ibid., 199–203.

71. Todd, 290, 291.

72. Ibid., 290, 291.

73. *Guide to the Chicago Museum* (Chicago: Evening Journal Book & Job Press, 1863), 1–2.

74. *Guide to the Chicago Museum*, 1–2.

75. Austin H. Clark and Leila G. Forbes, "Science in Chicago," *Scientific Monthly* 36, no. 6 (June 1933): 562.

76. Col. Joseph H. Wood's Museum and Art Gallery, *Synoptical Catalogue of Col. Joseph H. Wood's Museum and Art Gallery, N.W. Cor. Ninth and Arch, Philadelphia.* (Philadelphia, Pa.: Printed for the Proprietor, J. Moore & Sons, 1872), 3–8.

77. Stanley B. Kimball, "New Light on Old Egyptian Mummies 1848–1871," *Dialogue, A Journal of Mormon Thought* 16, no. 4 (Winter 1983): 70.

78. Chicago Museum, *Complete Guide to the Chicago Museum* (Chicago): Evening Journal Book and Job Print., 1868), 1.

79. Chicago Museum, *Guide to the Chicago Museum* (Chicago: Evening Journal Book & Job Press, 1863), 12.

80. Kimball, 79.

81. Peterson, 215.

82. Ibid., 215.

83. Joseph Jackson, *Encyclopedia of Philadelphia* (Harrisburg, Pa.: National Historical Association, 1931–1933), vol. 3, 917.

84. Col. Joseph H. Wood's Museum and Art Gallery, 15.

85. Kimball, 80, f. 15, 83, f. 21.

86. *Niagara Falls Museum!* (Niagara Falls, Canada, 1878), (1).

87. "One Museum—Many Homes," *Cataract News* 1, no. 1 (1993): 4.

88. "What Is a Museum Without Artifacts?" *Cataract News* 1, no. 1 (1993): 2; *For Sale by Auction at Niagara Falls, on Wednesday, May 1st, 1878, at 12 O'Clock "Barnett's Niagara Falls Museum Property."* (Ontario?: Thomas Barnett, 1878), 2.

89. James Douglas and James Douglas, Jr. "Excerpt from 'Honeymoon on the Nile' 1881 (?)," photocopy of an original manuscript in the possession of William Jamieson, unpaged.

90. William Howard Russell, *My Diary North and South* (Boston: T.O.H.P. Burnham; New York: O.S. Felt, 1863), 363.

91. *Niagara Falls Museum!* 1.

92. Peterson, vii-viii, 247.

93. Gayle Gibson, "Names Matter," *KMT* 11m no. 4 (Winter 2000–2001): 20.

94. "Brief History of the Niagara Falls Museum," in *Niagara Falls Museum* (website online); available from; http://www.niagaramuseum.com/museum_history.htm; accessed 8 September 2008.

95. Gibson, 20, 18.

96. Louis Grigoroff, *Educational Booklet of the Niagara Falls Museum* (Niagara Falls: Niagara Falls Museum, ca. 1961), 13, 15–16.

97. "The Mummies," "The Coffins," "Artifacts," *The Egyptian Museum* (website online); available at http://www.egptianmuseum.com; accessed 1 March 2008.

98. Gibson, 22.

Chapter 5

1. Bob Brier, *Egyptian Mummies; Unraveling the Secrets of an Ancient Art* (New York: William Morrow, 1994), 149–173.

2. *Three Mummies from Thebes at the New-England Museum* (Boston, Mass., 1825?), 1.

3. David Marks, *Memoir of David Marks, Minister of the Gospel*, ed. Marilla Marks (Dover, N.H.: Free-Will Baptist Printing Establishment, 1846), 398.

4. Samantha Taylor Long, "Rubens Peale's New York Museum and Gallery of Fine Arts and Its Place in the First Seventy-Five Years of Museum History in the United States" (M.A. thesis, University of Houston, 1998), 83, 110–111.

5. J. Aitken Meigs, *Catalogue of Human Crania in the Collection of the Academy of Natural Sciences of Philadelphia* (Philadelphia: J.B. Lippincott, 1857, 3.

6. Morton, *Crania Ægyptiaca*, 1–19.

7. Guido Lombardi, "Egyptian Mummies at Tulane University: An Anthropological Study" (M.A. thesis, Tulane University, 1999), 52–54.

8. Morton, *Catalogue of the Skulls of Man,* 7, 9.

9. Warren R. Dawson and Eric P. Uphill, *Who Was Who in Egyptology*, 2nd rev. ed. (London: The Egypt Exploration Society, 1972), 117.

10. Vivian, Cassandra, "George Gliddon in America," paper delivered at the Conference on Travellers in Egypt and the Ancient Near East, Manchester University (England), July 11–14, 2005, unpaged.

11. Dawson and Uphill, 67.

12. Vivian, n.p.

13. George Robbins Gliddon, *Transparent Panorama of the Nile* (New York, 1849), 1.

14. George Robbins Gliddon, *Hand-book to the American Panorama of the Nile* (London: James Madden, 1849), 25.

15. *Proposal* (Boston, Mass., 1850), 1.

16. "Unrolling a Mummy," in *Peter Parley's Thousand and One Stories of Fact and Fancy, Wit and Humor, Rhyme, Reason, and Romance,* ed. S.G. Goodrich (New York: James Miller, 1857), 121–127.

17. John Lloyd Stevens, *Incidents of Travel in Egypt, Arabia Petræ, and the Holy Land,* ed. Victor Wolfgang von Hagen (San Francisco: Chronicle, 1991), xxviii-xxix, f.11.

18. Donald Grant Mitchell, *The Lorgnette; Or, Studies of the Town. By an Opera Goer,* 2nd ed. (New York: Stringer and Townsend, 1850), 101–102.

19. James Burrell, *"The Morning Cometh." Talks for the Times* (New York: American Tract Society, 1895), 76–77.

20. *Proposal: Printed For Private Circulation among Mr. Gliddon's Friends* (Philadelphia, 1850), 1–3.

21. "Gliddon's Mummy vs. Blitz," *Spirit of the Times* 21, no. 2 (1 March 1851), 20.

22. *The Philadelphia Inquirer* (Philadelphia, Pa.), 27 January 1866.

23. Lombardi, 18, 11–12.

24. Josiah Nott and George R. Gliddon, *Type of Mankind* (Philadelphia: Lippincott, Grambo & Company, 1854), 428–429.

25. Heather Pringle, *The Mummy Congress; Science, Obsession, and the Everlasting Dead* (New York: Theia, 2001), 170.

26. *New-York Historical Society. Lectures on Egypt: 1864* (New York: New-York Historical Society, 1864), 1).

27. Aidan Dodson and Wendy Raver, "Dr. Anderson's Mummy," *KMT* 14, no. 3 (Fall 2003): (39)–43.

28. *New York Times* (New York, N.Y.), 26 January 1884; *Scientific American* (New York, N.Y.), 19 July 1884.

29. Courtney Pott, "Anthropology Collection Features Mummies," *Cornell Daily Sun* 4 (April 2003) (journal on-line); available from http://cornelldailysun.com/articled/8310/; accessed 4 April 2003.

30. "Unwrapping the Egyptian Mummy," *St. Louis Globe-Democrat* (26 February 1887); Chris Dela Cruz, "Mysterious Mummy Lays in Geology Hall" *Daily Targum,* 20 Oct. 2005 (journal on-line); available from http://media.www.dailytargum.com/media/storage/paper168/news/2005/10/28/PageOne/Mysterious.Mummy.Lays.In.Geology.Hall-1037715.shtml; accessed 15 January 2008.

31. *New York Daily Times* (New York, N.Y.), 20 September 1851.

32. "Boris Is Back," in *Goucher Library News* 33 (September 1988): 1; Elizabeth S. North, "Mummy Meets Computer," *Goucher Quarterly* 66, no.4 (Summer 1988): 14.

Chapter 6

1. John J. Leane, "When Mummies Made Paper in Maine," *Yankee,* February 1971, 112, 31.

2. William Brashear, "Egyptian Papyrus Then, Chinese Paper Today (or: Of Mummies in Maine and Tea From Cathay)," *Archiv fur Payprusforschung, Akten des 21. Internationalen Papyrologenkongresses, Berlin, 1995,* B. 3, 1997, 124.

3. Ibid., 124–125.

4. Ibid., n. 37.

5. Frank H. Stauffer, *The Queer, the Quaint, the Quizzical: A Cabinet for the Curious* (Philadelphia: Robert A. Tripple, 1882), 174–175.

6. Leah Hager Cohen, *Glass, Paper, Beans; Revelations on the Nature and Value of Ordinary Things* (New York: Doubleday/Currency, 1997), 104.

7. Mark Twain, *Innocents Abroad; or, The New Pilgrim's Progress* (Hartford, Conn.: American Publishing Company, 1869), 632.

8. James Silk Buckingham, *Notes of the Buckingham Lectures: Embracing Sketches of the Geography, Antiquities, and Present Condition of Egypt and Palestine* (New York: Leavitt, Lord & Company, 1838), 103–104.

9. Dard Hunter, *Papermaking; The History and Technique of an Ancient Craft* (New York: Alfred A. Knopf, 1943), 287–288.

10. Rebecca Rupp, *Red Oaks and Black Birches; The Science and Lore of Trees* (Pownal, Vt.: Storey Communications, 1990), 232–233.

11. Edmund H. Fulling, "Botanical Aspects of the Paper-Pulp and Tanning Industries in the United States; An Economic and Historical Survey," in *Fifty Years of Botany,* ed. William Campbell Steere (New York: McGraw Hill Book Company, 1958), 510.

12. Joel Munsell, *Chronology of the Origin and Progress of Paper and Paper-Making* (Albany: J. Munsell, 1876), 60.

13. Francis W. Dolloff and Roy L. Perkinson, "History of Paper," in *How To Care For Works of Art on Paper* (Boston, Mass.: Museum of Fine Arts, 1985) (electronic notebook on-line); available from; www.noteaccess.com/MATERIALS/historyP.htm; accessed 8 November 2001.

14. Fulling, 511.

15. Nicholson Baker, *Double Fold; Libraries and the Assault on Paper* (New York: Random House, 2001), 57.

16. Dolloff, 3. Many other paper companies claim this crown, including several mills in Gardiner and Cumberland Mills, Maine.

17. Joseph A. Dane, "The Curse of the Mummy Paper," *Printing History* 17, no. 2 (1995), 19.

18. Baker, 56.

19. Dane, 19, 24, n. 11, 12.

20. Munsell, 120.

21. Baker, 59.

22. Isaiah Deck, "On a Supply of Paper Material from the Mummy Pits of Egypt," in *Transactions of the American Institute of the City of New-York, For the Year 1854* (Albany: Van Benthuysen, 1855), 83, 85, 87, 91–92.

23. Regrettably, no extant issues of this paper have as yet turned up.

24. Deck, 83–85, 87–89, 91, 93.

25. Munsell, vi.

26. Ibid., 149.

27. Hunter, *Papermaking,* note at bottom of p. 288. This reminiscence was reported to Hunter second-hand, from a Mrs. John Rumsey, who had read about the paper-making experiments in the 22 December issue of the Syracuse *Post-Standard,* and who had been told the story by Dr. Waite, who was a friend of her father's.

28. Baker, 62. Baker does not give a date for this newspaper item.

29. *Bi-Centennial Celebration, Norwich, September 7, and 8, 1859* (Norwich, Conn.: Manning, Perry & Company, 1859).

30. *Norwich Jubilee: A Report of the Celebration at Norwich, Connecticut, on the Two Hundredth Anniversary of the Settlement of the Town, September 7th and 8th, 1859* (Norwich, Conn.: John W. Stedman, 1859), iv.

31. *Northern Home Journal* (Gardiner, Me.), 12 August 1858.

32. "Cobbossee Stream Busy Place in 1800's," in *Daily Kennebec Journal* (Gardiner, Me.), 30 July 1930.

33. *The City of Gardiner, U.S.A.* (Gardiner, Me., 1896), 75.

34. *Illustrated History of Kennebec County, Maine, 1625–1892*, ed. Henry D. Kingsbury (New York: H.W. Blake & Company, 1892), 615–617.

35. Hunter, *Papermaking*, 287.

36. Dard Hunter, *Story of Early Paper* (exhibition catalogue, 1950), 8–9.

37. Jeff Ferguson, "Mummy Treasure of Maine," in an unknown journal September–October 1974, no page given. This is from the clippings file at the Gardiner Public Library. Another nebulous source which reiterates much from Hunter is Michael Pollack "Mummies Rags Were Once the Rage That Provided Us the Printed Page," in *Printing Impressions* 21, no. 7 (December 1978): 60–61.

38. "Maine Mummy History Unwrapped," *Maine Antique Digest* (April 1997), unpaged.

39. Lyman Horace Weeks, *A History of Paper Manufacturing in the United States, 1690–1916* (New York: Lockwood Trade Journal Company, 1916), 322. Weeks states 1854. According to several researchers at the Westbrook Historical Society (who declined to be identified), Warren bought the Gardiner Mills in 1864, not 1854.

40. *History of S.D. Warren Company, 1854–1954* (Portland, Me.: Anthoensen Press, 1954), 27, 33.

41. Martin Green, *The Mount Vernon Street Warrens; A Boston Story, 1860–1910* (New York, 1989), 23, 24, 27, 29. According to historians at the Westbrook Historical Society, Green's account contains numerous egregious errors. Green states that the mill in Westbrook made white paper and the mills in Gardiner made brown. I have reversed this in the text to conform to the findings of the Westbrook Historical Society, as given to me in an e-mail correspondence dated 26 June 2003 with one of the researchers who declined to be identified. Green also misnamed the mill as the "Androscoggin Mills" when in fact it was the Congin Paper Mill.

42. *History of S.D. Warren Company*, 34–35.

43. *A Day's Work*, ed. William Henry Bunting (Gardiner, Me.: Tilbury House, 1997–2000), vol. 2, 94.

44. Harold Boyle, "S.D. Warren and the Mummies," in *Best of Boyle* (Portland, Me., 1980), 34–35.

45. Laura E. Richards, *Stepping Westward* (New York: D. Appleton and Company, 1931), 168.

46. *City of Gardiner, Maine*, 36, 76.

47. Richards, 291, 293–294.

48. Munsell, 198.

49. Harrison Elliott, "Connecticut's First Papermaker," in *Papermaker* 19, no. 2 (1950): 43.

50. Villiers Stuart, *Nile Gleanings Concerning the Ethnology, History and Art of Ancient Egypt as Revealed by Egyptian Paintings and Bas-Reliefs* (London: John Murray, 1879), 90; also: Bob Kinsey, Interview with the author, 19 July 2006. Kinsey had been general manager of the former Hollingsworth & Whitney paper mill and had looked for years for evidence of mummy paper. When he retired he went to Egypt and while in Alexandria, asked the tour guides about it. They replied they were not supposed to talk about it, but he elicited from them the information that as the rail line was being laid from Cairo to Alexandria, the engineers kept uncovering vast repositories of human and animal mummies. The smaller ones were burned as fuel in the locomotives and the larger wrapped ones went to Alexandria where there was a thriving industry in the separation of cloth from bodies. The cloth was shipped into the international rag trade and the bodies were ground up for fertilizer and sent chiefly to England for the rose gardens.

51. *Eighty Years' Progress of the United States* (Hartford: L. Stebbins, 1869), 293.

52. Charles E. O'Hara, "Egyptian Rags," *Superior Facts* 3, no. 6 (December, 1931): 11–12

53. United States. Treasury Department, *Circular, Importation of Rags from Egypt* (Washington D.C: U.S.G.P.O., 1884), 1.

54. O'Hara, 11.

55. Benjamin Franklin, *The Posthumous and Other Writings of Benjamin Franklin*, William Temple Franklin, ed. (London: Henry Colburn, 1819), vol. 2, 300.

56. *Perry Chief* (Perry, Iowa), 14 June 1877; *Stevens Point Journal* (Stevens Point, Wis.), 9 June 1877.

57. Weeks, 283.

Chapter 7

1. Newell Yost Osborne, *A Select School; The History of Mount Union College and an Account of a Unique Educational Experiment, Scio*

College (Mount Union, Ohio: Mount Union College,1967), 371–375.

2. Ibid.

3. Ibid.

4. Sam Farmerie, *Pesed Reports.* (publication on-line); available from *http://www.west minster.edu/about/mummy/report.cfm*; accessed 7 September 2008.

5. John Romich Alexander, *Knowest Thou Yesterday?* (unpublished manuscript), 890–897.

6. Farmerie, *Pesed Reports.*

7. College of Wooster Museum accession form, 1979. Photocopy from the Archives, College of Wooster, Wooster, Ohio.

8. Ralph E. Grier, *Legends of Erskine College* (Due West, S.C, n.d.), 7–8.

9. "Erskine is Ready to Receive Her," in *Messenger* (Due West, S.C.), 16 July 1885.

10. "Mummy in a Box," in *Washington Post* (Washington, D.C.), 14 October 1886.

11. "Uprising of Mummies," in *Washington Post* (Washington, D.C.), 15 November 1896.

12. *The Oriental Institute—In the Beginning* (website on-line); available from; http://www.oi-uchicago.edu/OI/INFO/OIBH/OI_Early_History.html, accessed 1/23/2003.

13. *Mummy Museums,* (website on-line); available from; http://www.mummytombs.com/museums/continent.namerica.us.il.htm, accessed 6/27/2007.

14. "Egyptian mummies," *Helena Independent* (Helena, Mont.), 21 November 1877.

15. Cincinnati Museum Association, *Catalogue of Objects Loaned by Mr. John W. Bookwalter, to the Cincinnati Museum Association* (Cincinnati: F. Bradley Co, 1893), 12. The booklet has a cover title: *Catalogue of the Bookwalter Collection of the Art Museum, Cincinnati.*

16. *Adolph Sutro's City,* (website on-line); available from: http://www.historysmith.com/Adolph.html, accessed 24 April 2008; "The Sutro Egyptian Collection," (website on-line); available from: http://www.sfsu.edu/~muse umst/sutro/; accessed 22 January 2003; Adrienne Terhert, "Mummy Mania" in *Golden Age Xpress* (journal on-line); available from; http://xpress.sfsu.edu/archives/life/003407.html; accessed 24 April 2008.

17. *Tacoma Daily News* (Tacoma, Wash.),14 July, 18 August 1891.

18. Ray Lyle, *Ankh Unnofi; A Viewing Guide to the Washington State Historical Society's Egyptian Mummy* (Tacoma, Wash.: Washington State Historical Society, 1985), iii.

19. James Robert Hubbard, *Diary* (unpublished manuscript in the Cazenovia Public Library), entries for 9–14 March 1894.

20. Rick Moriarty, "Mummy's a Maiden with Perfect Posture," in *Syracuse Post-Standard* (Syracuse, N.Y.), 6 June 1984.

21. "Brought the Baby Mummy in a Bag," *New York Times* (New York, N.Y.), 20 June 1896.

22. "Story of a Mummy," *Godey's Lady's Book* 95 (September 1877), 265; W. Woodford Clayton, *History of Davidson County, Tennessee, with Illustrations and Biographical Sketches of Its Prominent Men and Pioneers* (Philadelphia: J.W. Lewis & Company, 1880), 300; *Tennessee State Museum Nashville* (Nashville, Tenn.: Tennessee State Museum, 1956?), 2; Dan E. Pomeroy, Chief Curator & Director of Collections, Tennessee State Museum, e-mail correspondence with the author 11 September 2001.

23. Mary Hesson, David J. Rogowski and Marianne Comfort, *Round Lake; Little Village in the Grove* (Round Lake, N.Y.: Round Lake Publications, 1998), 28–29.

24. "Princess Tothmea," photocopy of undated information from Village of Round Lake; Charles Hillinger, "At 3500, She's All Wrapped up in California," *New York Times*, 31 May 1988; "Museum from Curitiba Houses Egyptian Mummy" in Brazil-Arab News Agency (website on-line); available from; http://www.anba.com.br/ingles/noticia.php?id=15392; accessed 24 April 2008.

25. Lynch, Jeremiah, *Lady Isis in Bohemia* (San Francisco: Printed for J. Lynch by Taylor, Nass and Taylor, 1914), 3–4.

26. Carl Nolte, "High-Tech Peek under Mummy's Wraps," *San Francisco Chronicle* (journal on-line); available from; http://www.sfgate.com/c/a/2000/05/13/MN8507.DTL; accessed 21 April 2008.

27. *Haggin Museum History Collection* (website on-line); available from; http://haggin museum.org/collections_history.htm; accessed 18 August 2003.

28. Hunt, correspondence.

29. "The A.V. Lane Collection; an On-line Exhibition" (article on-line); available from; http://www.smu.edu/bridwell/specialcollec tions/avlane/avlaneexhibit.htm; accessed 3/28/2008; Eric White, Curator of Special Collections Bridwell library, e-mail correspondence with the author 22 August 2003.

30. "Collection of Antiquities," in *Dallas Morning News* (Dallas, Tex.), 13 October 1896; L.E. Daniell, comp. *Personnel of the Texas State Government* (Austin: Smith, Hicks & Jones, 1889), 111.

31. *Brooklyn Eagle* (New York, N.Y.), 7 August 1872, 11 July 1900); "Manufactured Mummies," in *Christian Observer* 94, no. 33 (8 August 1900), 2; "Manufactures Antiquities," in *New York Times,* 21 June 1896; *Evening Demo-*

crat (Warren, Pa.), 13 August 1895; "Mummy Factories," *Reno Evening Gazette* (Reno, Nev.), 23 October 1891.

32. James Douglas, *Journals and Reminiscences of James Douglas, M.D.*, ed. the Rev. James Douglas (New York: Privately Printed, 1910), 128–131, 253.

33. Ibid., "On Two Mummies from Thebes in Egypt," in *Transactions of the Literary and Historical Society of Quebec Session of 1864–1865*, n.s., pt. 3 (Quebec: Hunter, Rose & Company, 1865), 108, 110–111.

34. William Hazlett Upson, "The Mummy of Middlebury," *Vermont Quarterly*, 19 (January 1951), 22.

35. Upson, 23.

36. Ace Croll and Jenny Reilly, *The Middlebury Mummy* (Middlebury, Vt.: Henry Sheldon Museum, n.d.), 1.

Bibliography

Monographs and Articles

Abbott, Henry. *Catalogue of a Collection of Egyptian Antiquities; the Property of Henry Abbott, M.D., Now Exhibiting at the Stuyvesant Institute, no. 629 Broadway, New York*. New York: Printed for the Proprietor by J.W. Watson, 1853.

Academy of Natural Sciences. *Proceedings of the Academy of Natural Sciences of Philadelphia. 1858*. Philadelphia: Printed for the Academy, 1859.

Alderson, William T., ed., *Mermaids, Mummies and Mastodons: The Emergence of the American Museum*. Baltimore: Baltimore City Life Museum, 1992.

Archer, Stephen M. *Junius Brutus Booth; Theatrical Prometheus*. Carbondale: Southern Illinois University Press, 1992.

Ayer's American Almanac, for the Use of Farmers, Planters, Mechanics, Mariners, and All Families. 1863. Lowell, Mass.: J.C. Ayer & Co., 1862.

Baker, Nicholson. *Double Fold; Libraries and the Assault on Paper*. New York: Random House, 2001.

Barnum's American Museum. *Catalogue or Guide Book of Barnum's American Museum New York*. New York: Published for the proprietor, n.d.

Bi-Centennial Celebration, Norwich, September 7, and 8, 1859. Norwich, Conn.: Manning, Perry & Co., 1859.

Biographical Sketches of Leading Citizens of Lawrence County, Pennsylvania. Buffalo, NY: Biographical Publishing Company, 1897.

Bondurant, Agnes M. *Poe's Richmond*. Richmond, 1942.

"Boris Is Back." *Goucher Library News* 33 (September 1988): 1.

Boston Museum and Gallery of Fine Arts. *Catalogue of the Paintings, Marble and Plaster Statuary and Engravings Comprised in the Collection of the Boston Museum and Gallery of Fine Arts, Corner of Tremont and Bromfield Streets, Together with a Descriptive Sketch of the Institution and Its Collection*. Boston: William White & H.P. Lewis, 1842.

Bowditch, Nathaniel Ingersoll. *A History of the Massachusetts General Hospital to August 5, 1851. Second Edition with Continuations to 1872*. Boston: Printed by the Trustees from the Bowditch Fund, 1872.

Bowen, Abel. *Bowen's Picture of Boston*, or, *The Citizen's and Stranger's Guide to the Metropolis of Massachusetts*. Boston: Lilly, Wait & Co., 1833.

Boyle, Harold. "S.D. Warren and the Mummies." *Best of Boyle*. Portland, Me.: The author, 1980.

Brashear, William. "Egyptian Papyrus Then, Chinese Paper Today (or: Of Mummies in Maine and Tea from Cathay.)" *Archiv fur Payprusforschung, Akten des 21. Internationalen Papyrologenkongresses, Berlin, 1995* (B. 3, 1997): 113–141.

Brier, Bob. *Egyptian Mummies; Unraveling the Secrets of an Ancient Art*. New York: William Morrow, 1994.

Buckingham, James Silk. *Notes of the Buckingham Lectures: Embracing Sketches of the Geography, Antiquities, and Present Condition of Egypt and Palestine*. New York: Leavitt, Lord & Co., 1838.

Budge, E.A. Wallis. *The Mummy; A History of the Extraordinary Practices of Ancient Egypt*. New York: Bell Publishing Co., 1989.

Buffalo Historical Society. *Buffalo Historical Society Publications*. Vol. 4. Buffalo, N.Y.: Buffalo Historical Society, 1896.

Burrell, James. "The Morning Cometh." *Talks for the Times*. New York: American Tract Society, 1895.

Chicago Museum. *A Complete Guide to the Chicago Museum*. Chicago: Evening Journal Book and Job Press, 1868.

_____. *A Guide to the Chicago Museum.* Chicago: Evening Journal Book & Job Press, 1863.

Cincinnati Museum Association. *Catalogue of Objects Loaned by Mr. John W. Bookwalter, to the Cincinnati Museum Association.* Cincinnati: C.F. Bradley Co., 1893.

Cincinnati Society of Natural History. *Journal of the Cincinnati Society of Natural History* 7 (January1885).

City of Gardiner, U.S.A. Gardiner, Me.: s.n., 1896.

Clark, Austin H., and Leila G. Forbes. "Science in Chicago." *Scientific Monthly* 36, no. 6 (June 1933): 556–567.

Clark, James R. *The Story of the Pearl of Great Price.* Salt Lake City: Bookcraft, 1962.

Clayton, Peter A. *Chronicles of the Pharaohs; The Reign-by-Reign Record of the Rulers and Dynasties of Ancient Egypt.* London and New York: Thames and Hudson, 1994.

Clayton, W. Woodford. *History of Davidson County, Tennessee, With Illustrations and Biographical Sketches of Its Prominent Men and Pioneers.* Philadelphia: J.W. Lewis & Co., 1880.

Cohen, Leah Hager. *Glass, Paper, Beans; Revelations on the Nature and Value of Ordinary Things.* New York: Doubleday/Currency, 1997.

Colby's Atlas of the State of Maine. 4th ed. Houlton, Me.: Colby & Stuart, 1888.

Col. Joseph H. Wood's Museum and Art Gallery. *Synoptical Catalogue of Col. Joseph H. Wood's Museum and Art Gallery, N.W. Cor. Ninth and Arch, Philadelphia.* Philadelphia, Pa.: Printed for the Proprietor, J. Moore & Sons, 1872.

Cooley, James Ewing. *American in Egypt with Ramblers through Arabia Petræ and the Holy Land during the Year 1839 and 1840.* New York: D. Appleton, 1842.

Course of Six Lectures on the "Bible Lands." Washington, D.C.: s.n., between 1859 and 1870?.

Crary, Christopher G. *Pioneer and Personal Reminiscences.* Marshalltown, Ia.: Marshall Printing Co., 1893.

Cumming, John. *Description of an Egyptian Mummy, Now Exhibiting in This City.* New York: W. Grattan, [1823].

Cutter, Bloodgood H. "Pyramid." *The Long Island Farmer's Poems. Lines Written on the "Quaker City" Excursion to Palestine and Other Poems.* New York: N. Tibbals & Sons, 1886, 113–126.

Dane, Joseph A. "The Curse of the Mummy Paper." *Printing History* 17 no. 2 (1995): 18–25.

Daniell, L.E. *Personnel of the Texas State Government.* Austin: Smith, Hicks & Jones, 1889.

Dawson, Warren R., and Eric P. Uphill. *Who Was Who in Egyptology.* 2nd rev. ed. London: Egypt Exploration Society, 1972.

Day's Work. Edited by William Henry Bunting. Gardiner, Me.: Tilbury House, 1997–2000.

Deck, Isaiah. "On a Supply of Paper Material from the Mummy Pits of Egypt." *Transactions of the American Institute of the City of New-York, For the Year 1854.* Albany: C. Van Benthuysen, (1855): 83–93.

Delafield, John. *An Inquiry into the Origin of the Antiquities of America.* New York: J.C. Colt, 1839.

Doddridge, Joseph. *Notes on the Settlement and Indian Wars of the Western Parts of Virginia and Pennsylvania, From 1763 to 1783, Inclusive.* Albany, N.Y.: Joel Munsell, 1876.

Dodson, Aidan, and Wendy Raver. "Dr. Anderson's Mummy." *KMT* 14, no. 3 (Fall 2003): 39–43.

Douglas, James. "On Two Mummies from Thebes in Egypt." *Transactions of the Literary and Historical Society of Quebec. Session of 1864–1865* n.s., pt. 3 (Quebec: Hunter, Rose & Co., 1865): 108–112.

Douglas, James. *Journals and Reminiscences of James Douglas, M.D.* Edited by the Rev. James Douglas. New York: Privately Printed, 1910.

Dyson, Stephen L. "The Mummy of Middletown." *Archaeology* 32 (September 1979): 57–59.

Egyptian Mummy from the Catacombs at Thebes. Boston: E.G. House, 1824?

Egyptian Mummy to be Exhibited at [blank]. Boston, 1824.

Egyptian Mummy, With Its Sarcophagus. New York: E. Conrad, 1824.

Egyptian Mummy. Ithaca, N.Y.: A.P. Searing & Co., printers, 1827.

Egyptian Mummy. New York: Wm. Grattan, 1823.

Eighty Years' Progress of the United States. Hartford: L. Stebbins, 1869.

Elliott, Harrison. "Connecticut's First Papermaker." *The Papermaker* 19, no. 2 (1950): 41–43.

Fagan, Brian M. *The Rape of the Nile; Tomb Robbers, Tourists and Archaeologists in Egypt.* New York: Scribner, 1975.

Ferguson, Jeff. "Mummy Treasure of Maine." Unidentified journal (September–October 1974): n.p.

For Sale by Auction at Niagara Falls, on Wednesday, May 1st, 1878, at 12 O'clock. "Barnett's Niagara Falls Museum Property." Ontario: Thomas Barnett, 1878.

Franklin, Benjamin. *The Posthumous and Other Writings of Benjamin Franklin.* Edited by William Temple Franklin. London: Henry Colburn, 1819.

"From the Minutes of the Board of Trustees of the University of Pennsylvania, July 2, 1816." *William and Mary Quarterly* 1st ser., 23, no. 1 (July 1914): 48–49.

Fulling, Edmund H. "Botanical Aspects of the Paper-Pulp and Tanning Industries in the United States; An Economic and Historical Survey." *American Journal of Botany* 43, no. 8 (October 1956): 621–634. Republished in *Fifty Years of Botany.* Edited by William Campbell Steere. New York: McGraw-Hill, 1958.

Gardiner, Me. Hollingsworth and Whitney and Warren Paper Mills. Gardiner, Me.: C.H. Beane, n.d.

Gardiner, Me. New Dam, S.D. Warren Paper Mills. Gardiner, Me..: C.H. Beane, n.d.

Gardner, William A., and Charles Griffin, "A Paleopathologic Exercise—The Charleston Museum Mummy." *Journal of the South Carolina Medical Association* 67, no. 6 (June 1871): 269–270.

General Ossipumphneferu. Chicago: Curteich, n.d.

Gifford, George E. "The Case of the Ether Dome Mummy." *Harvard Medical Alumni Bulletin* (March–April 1977): 5–14.

Gillespie, Charles Coulston, and Michael Dewachter, eds. *The Monuments of Egypt.* Old Saybrook, Conn.: Konecky & Konecky, 1987.

Gliddon, George Robbins. *Hand-Book to the American Panorama of the Nile.* London: James Madden, 1849.

_____. *Proposal.* Boston, Mass.: s.n., 1850.

_____. *Proposal: Printed for Private Circulation among Mr. Gliddon's Friends.* Philadelphia: s.n., 1850.

_____. *Transparent Panorama of the Nile.* New York: s.n., 1849.

Gratacap, L. P. "Formative Museum Period." *Science* n.s., 14, no. 344 (August 2, 1901).

Great Chicago Museum. *Great Chicago Museum Catalogue.* Chicago: Blakely Marsh, 1885.

Great Fire in Chicago, October 9, 1871. Chicago: Lovejoy & Foster, 1871.

Green, Martin. *The Mount Vernon Street Warrens; A Boston Story, 1860–1910.* New York, 1989.

Greenwood, Ethan Allen. "'Extracts from the Journals of Ethan A. Greenwood': Portrait Painter and Museum Proprietor." Edited by Georgia Brady Barnhill. *Proceedings of the American Antiquarian Society* 103, no. 1 (April 1993). Reprint. Worcester, Mass: American Antiquarian Society, 1993, 91–178.

Grier, Ralph E. Grier. *Legends of Erskine College.* Due West, S.C.: n.d.

Grossman, Edwina Booth, *Edwin Booth: Recollections By His Daughter, Edwina Booth Grossman; And Letters to Her and to His Friends.* New York: Century Col., 1894.

Gunther, Charles Frederick. *Chicago's Royal Princess of the Ancient Pharaohs.* Chicago: s.n., 1886?

Gunther's Confectionary 212 State St. Chicago. Chicago: s.n, n.d.

Hamernik, Gottfried. "Ägyptologische Sammlung des Landesmusems zur Fundgeschichte und Datierung Eines Ägyptischen Mumiesarges im Landesmuseum Kärnten." *Sonderdruck Aus Rudolfinum: Jahrbuch des Landesmuseums Kärnten 2002.* Klagenfurt, 2003, 185–198.

Haven, Charlotte. "A Girl's Letters from Nauvoo." *Overland Monthly,* (December 1890), 616–638.

Haynes, Joyce. *Padihershef: The Egyptian Mummy.* Springfield, Mass.: George Walter Vincent Smith Art Museum, 1985.

Hesson, Mary, David J. Rogowski, and Marianne Comfort. *Round Lake; Little Village in the Grove.* Round Lake, N.Y.: Round Lake Publications, 1998.

Hinsley, Curtis M. *Savages and Scientists;*

The Smithsonian Institution and the Development of American Anthropology
1846–1910. Washington, D.C.: Smithsonian Institute Press, 1981.

History of S.D. Warren Company, 1854–1954.
Portland, Me.: Anthoensen Press, 1954.

*History of Trenton, 1679–1829; Two Hundred
and Fifty Years of a Notable Town with
Links to Four Centuries.* Princeton, N.J.:
Princeton University Press, 1829.

*Hollingsworth & Whitney Paper Co. Mill,
Gardiner, Me.* Gardiner, Me.: s.n., n.d.

Howe, Winfred E. *A History of the Metropolitan Museum of Art.* New York: Gilliss
Press, 1913–46.

Hubbard, Mary Ann Hubbard. *Family
Memories.* Chicago: R.R. Donnelley, 1912.

Hunter, Dard. *Papermaking; The History
and Technique of an Ancient Craft.* New
York: Alfred A. Knopf, 1943.

_____. *Story of Early Paper.* s.n.: s.l., 1950.

*Illustrated History of Kennebec County,
Maine, 1625–1892.* Edited by Henry D.
Kingsbury. New York: H.W. Blake & Co.,
1892.

Ingram, J. S. *The Centennial Exposition Described and Illustrated.* Philadelphia:
Hubbard Bros., 1876.

Jackson, J. B. S., comp. *A Descriptive Catalogue of the Warren Anatomical Museum.*
Boston: A. Williams and Company, 1870.

Jackson, Joseph. *Encyclopedia of Philadelphia.* Harrisburg, Pa.: National Historical
Association, 1931–1933.

Jampolar, Andrew C.A. *Sailors in the Holy
Land; The 1848 Expedition to the Dead Sea
and the Search for Sodom and Gomorroah.*
Annapolis, Md.: Naval Institute Press,
2005.

Karl Bernard, Duke of Saxe-Weimar-
Eisenbach. *Travels through North Amer-
ica, During the years 1825 and 1826.*
Philadelphia: Carey, Lea & Carey, 1828.

Kirkland, Joseph. *The Story of Chicago.*
Chicago: Dibble Pub. Co., 1894.

"Law." *The Ariel; Aa Semimonthly Literary
and Miscellaneous Gazette* 3:13 (October
17, 1829): 99.

Leane, John J. "When Mummies Made
Paper in Maine." *Yankee,* February 1971,
112, 115.

Leland Stanford Junior University. *Ninth
Annual Register 1899–1900.* Stanford,
Calif.: Published by the University, 1900.

Lombardi, Guido. "Egyptian Mummies at

Tulane University: An Anthropological
Study." M.A. thesis, Tulane University,
1999.

Long, Samantha Taylor. "Rubens Peale's
New York Museum and Gallery of Fine
Arts and Its Place in the First Seventy-
Five Years of Museum History in the
United States." M.A. thesis, University of
Houston, 1998.

Luther, Leslie L. *Moravia and Its Past and
Adjoining Townships,* Indianapolis: Frederic Luther Co., 1966.

Lyle, Ray. *Ankh Unnofi; A Viewing Guide to
the Washington State Historical Society's
Egyptian Mummy.* Tacoma: Washington
State Historical Society, 1985.

Lynch, Jeremiah. *Lady Isis in Bohemia.* San
Francisco: Printed for J. Lynch by Taylor, Nass and Taylor, 1914.

"Maggie the Mummy." *Hobbies* 53 (June
1948): 141.

Maggio, Rosalie. *How They Said It; Wise and
Witty Letters From the Famous and Infamous.* Paramus, N.J.: Prentice Hall, 2000.

"Maine Mummy History Unwrapped."
Maine Antique Digest, April 1997, unpaged.

Marks, David. *Memoir of David Marks,
Minister of the Gospel.* Edited by Marilla
Marks. Dover, N.H.: Free-Will Baptist
Printing Establishment, 1846.

McDermott, Francis. "Dr. Koch's Wonderful Fossils." *Bulletin* (Missouri Historical
Society) 4, no. 4 (July 1948): 233–250.

*Medical Dissertations Read at the Annual
Meeting of the Massachusetts Medical Society.* Boston: Press of the Daily Advertiser, 1829.

Meigs, J. Aitken. *Catalogue of Human Crania in the Collection of the Academy of
Natural Sciences of Philadelphia.* Philadelphia: J.B. Lippincott, 1857.

Midgley, R.L. *Sights in Boston and Suburbs.*
Boston and Cambridge: James Munroe
and Company, 1857.

Miller, Lillian B., ed., *The Selected Papers of
Charles Willson Peale and His Family.*
New Haven: Yale University Press, 1996.

Mitchell, Donald Grant. *The Lorgnette; Or,
Studies of the Town. By an Opera Goer.*
2nd ed. New York: Printed for Stringer
and Townsend, 1850.

Morton, Samuel George. *Catalogue of the
Skulls of Man, and the Inferior Animals, in
the Collection of Samuel George Morton.*

Philadelphia: Printed by Turner & Fisher, 1840.

_____. *Crania Ægyptiaca; or, Observations on Egyptian Ethnography, Derived from Anatomy, History and the Monuments.* Philadelphia: John Pennington; London: Madden & Co., 1844.

_____. "Observations on Egyptian Ethnography. Derived from Anatomy, History, and the Monuments." *Transactions* (American Philosophical Society) 9 (1846): 93–159.

"Mummies." *The Evergreen.* Philadelphia: American Sunday School Union, 1837, 107–114 and plate facing 106.

Munsell, Joel. *Chronology of the Origin and Progress of Paper and Paper-Making* Albany, N.Y.: J. Munsell, 1876.

National Cyclopedia of American Biography. New York: James T. White & Co., 1910.

National Institute. *A Popular Catalogue of the Extraordinary Curiosities of the National Institute, Arranged in the Building Belonging to the Patent Office.* Washington, D.C.: Alfred Hunter, 1855.

Nelson, N. L. "The Book of Abraham." *The Academic Review* 1, no. 6 (March 1885): 46.

New-York Historical Society. Lectures on Egypt: 1864. New York: New-York Historical Society, 1864].

Niagara Falls Museum! Niagara Falls: s.n., 1878.

Niagara Falls Museum. *Visit Our Niagara Falls Museum Tower and Art Gallery.* Niagara Falls, N.Y.: Niagara Falls Museum, between 1901 and 1928?

North, Elizabeth S. "Mummy Meets Computer." *Goucher Quarterly* 66, no. 4 (Summer 1988): 14.

Norwich Jubilee.: A Report of the Celebration at Norwich, Connecticut, on the Two Hundredth Anniversary of the Settlement of the Town, September 7th and 8th, 1859, Norwich, Conn.: John W. Stedman, 1859.

Nott, Josiah C., and George R. Gliddon. *Types of Mankind.* Philadelphia: Lippincott, Grambo & Co., 1854.

O'Hara, Charles E. "Egyptian Rags." *Superior Facts* 3, no. 6 (December 1931): 11–12.

Odell, George C. D. *Annals of the New York Stage.* New York: Columbia University Press, 1928.

"One Museum—Many Homes." *Cataract News* 1, no. 1 (1993): 4.

P.T. Barnum's Museum, Menagerie, Caravan and Hippodrome. New York?: P.T. Barnum, between 1871 and 1881?.

Pacific Museum of Anatomy and Natural Science. *Hand-book and Descriptive Catalogue of the Pacific Museum of Anatomy and Natural Science, Now Open at the Eureka Theatre.* San Francisco: s.n., 1865?

Palmer, Friend. *Early Days in Detroit; Papers Written by General Friend Palmer, of Detroit, Being His Personal Reminiscences of Important Events and Descriptions of the City for over Eighty Years.* Detroit: Hunt & June, 1906.

Papermills, Gardiner, Me. Gardiner, Me.: s.n., n.d.

Peabody Museum of American Archæology and Ethnology. *Fourteenth Annual Report.* Cambridge, Mass.: Printed by order of the Trustees, 1881.

_____. *Third Annual Report of the Trustees of the Peabody Museum of American Archæology and Ethnology.* Boston: Boston Press of A.A. Kingman, 1870.

Peale, Charles Willson. *The Selected Papers of Charles Willson Peale and His Family.* Edited by Lillian B. Miller. New Haven: Yale University Press, 1983–1996.

Peterson, H. Donal. *The Story of the Book of Abraham; Mummies, Manuscripts and Mormonism.* Salt Lake City: Deseret Book Company, 1995.

Pollock, Michael. "Mummies Rags Were Once the Rage That Provided Us the Printed Page." *Printing Impressions* 21, no. 7 (December 1978): 60–61.

Prime, William C. *Boat Life in Egypt and Nubia.* New York: Harper and Brothers, 1874.

Pringle, Heather. *The Mummy Congress; Science, Obsession, and the Everlasting Dead.* New York: Theia, 2001.

Quincy, Josiah. *The History of Harvard University.* Boston: Crosby, Nichols, Lee & Co., 1860.

Rare Curiosities. United States, 1827?

Reid, Donald Malcolm. *Whose Pharaohs? Archaeology, Museums, and Egyptian National Identity from Napoleon to World War I.* Berkeley: University of California Press, 2005.

Report of the Christmas Bazaar, Held under the Auspices of the Ladies' Hospital Relief Association, From December 14 to December 22, Inclusive at Corinthian Hall,

Rochester, N.Y. Rochester: Newton & Andrews, 1863.

Rhees, William Jones Rhees. *An Account of the Smithsonian Institution, Its Founder, Building, Operations, Etc.* Washington, D.C.: T. McGill, 1857.

Richards, Laura E. *Stepping Westward.* New York: D. Appleton, 1931.

Rupp, Rebecca. *Red Oaks and Black Birches; The Science and Lore of Trees.* Pownal, Vt.: Storey Communications, 1990.

Ruschenberger, S. W. *A Notice of the Origin, Progress, and Present Condition of the Academy of Natural Sciences of Philadelphia.* Philadelphia: T.K. and P.G. Collins, 1852.

Russell, William Howard. *My Diary North and South.* Boston: T.O.H.P. Burnham; New York: O.S. Felt, 1863.

S.D. Warren's Paper Mills, Westbrook, Me. Westbrook, Me.: J.D. Brigham, n.d.

Sellers, Charles Coleman. *Mr. Peale's Museum.* New York: W.W. Norton, 1980.

Smith, Brian L., and Philip R. Webb. "Mystery of the Mummies: An Update on the Joseph Smith Collection." *RSC Newsletter* 20, no. 2 (2005): 1–5.

Smith, H. Perry, ed. *History of the City of Buffalo and Erie County; With Illustrations and Biographical Sketches of Some of Its Prominent Men and Pioneers.* Syracuse, N.Y.: D. Mason & Co., 1884.

Starrett, Agnes Lynch. *Through One Hundred and Fifty Years: The University of Pittsburgh.* Pittsburgh: University of Pittsburgh Press, 1937.

Stauffer, Frank H. *The Queer, the Quaint, the Quizzical: A Cabinet for the Curious.* Philadelphia: Robert A. Tripple, 1882.

Stevens, John Lloyd. *Incidents of Travel in Egypt, Arabia Petræ, and the Holy Land.* Edited by Victor Wolfgang von Hagen. San Francisco: Chronicle, 1991.

"Story of a Mummy." *Godey's Lady's Book* 95 (September 1877): 265.

Stuart, Villiers. *Nile Gleanings Concerning the Ethnology, History and Art of Ancient Egypt as Revealed by Egyptian Paintings and Bas-reliefs.* London: John Murray, 1879.

Tennessee State Museum Nashville. Nashville: The Museum, ca. 1956.

Three Mummies from Egypt at the New-England Museum, 76, Court-Street, Boston. Boston: s.n., 1825.

Todd, Jay M. *The Saga of the Book of Abraham.* Salt Lake City: Deseret Book Company, 1969.

"Trover for a Mummy." *American Jurist and Law Magazine* 2, no. 4 (October 1829): 400–402.

Truman, Ben C. *History of the World's Fair.* Chicago: E.G. Morse & Co., 1893.

Tucker, Louis Leonard Tucker. "'Ohio Show-Shop'; The Western Museum of Cincinnati 1820–1867." *A Cabinet of Curiosities; Five Episodes in the Evolution of American Museums.* Charlottesville: University Press of Virginia, 1967: 73–105.

Twain, Mark. *The Innocents Abroad; Or, The New Pilgrim's Progress.* Hartford, Conn.: American Publishing Co., 1869.

United States. Treasury Department. *Circular. Importation of Rage from Egypt.* Washington, D.C.: U.S.G.P.O., 1884.

"Unrolling a Mummy." *Peter Parley's Thousand and One Stories of Fact and Fancy, Wit and Humor, Rhyme, Reason, and Romance.* Edited by S.G. Goodrich. New York: James Miller, 1857.

Upson, William Hazlett. "The Mummy of Middlebury." *Ford Times* (December 1950): 19–21. Reprint. *Vermont Quarterly* 19, no. 1 (January 1951): 22–23.

Vail, R. W. G. *Knickerbocker Birthday; A Sesqui-Centennial History of the New-York Historical Society, 1804–1954.* New York: New-York Historical Society, 1954.

Views in Chicago and Vicinity before and after the Fire. Chicago: P.B. Greene, 1871.

Vital Records of Beverly, Massachusetts, to the End of the Year 1849. Topsfield, Mass.: Topsfield Historical Society, 1906–19.

Warren, Edward. *The Life of John Collins Warren, M.D.* Boston: Ticknor & Fields, 1860.

Warren, John Collins. *Description of an Egyptian Mummy, Presented to the Massachusetts General Hospital.* Boston: Cummings, Hillyard & Co., 1823.

_____. "Description of an Egyptian Mummy, Presented to the Massachusetts General Hospital wth an Account of the Operation of Embalming, in Ancient and Modern Times." *Boston Journal of Philosophy and the Arts* 1 (May 1823–May 1824): 184–179, 269–287.

Watkins, Walter K. "The New England Museum and the Home of Art in Boston." *The Bostonian Society Publications.* 2nd series: 2. Boston: Bostonian Society, 1917, 101–130.

Weeks, Edward. *The Lowells and Their Institute.* Boston: Little, Brown, 1966.

Weeks, Lyman Horace. *A History of Paper Manufacturing in the United States, 1690–1916.* New York: Lockwood Trade Journal Co., 1916.

"What Is a Museum without Artifacts?" *Cataract News* 1, no. 11 (1993): 2.

Whitman, Walt. *New York Dissected.* New York: Rufus Rockwell Wilson, 1936.

Wilson, R. Jackson. "Thebes to Springfield; the Travels of an Egyptian Mummy." *Padihershef the Egyptian Mummy.* Springfield, Mass.: Springfield Library and Museums Association, 1984, 29–35.

Wolf, Edwin. "The Library Company of Philadelphia, America's First Museum." *The Magazine of Antiques* 120, no. 2 (August 1981): 349–350.

Works of the Old World, the Wonder of the New. New York?: E. Conrad, printer, 1824.

Serial Publications

Aberdeen Weekly News (Aberdeen, S.D.). 9 October 1891.

Adams Sentinel (Gettysburg, Pa.). 13 March 1832; 11 January 1836.

Albany Argus (Albany, N.Y.). 12 June 1818; 13 August, 1824.

Albany Evening Journal (Albany, N.Y.). 2 August 1888.

Alexandria Gazette & Daily Advertiser (Alexandria, Va.). 29 May 1818.

Alta California (San Francisco, Calif.). 31 October 1850.

American (New York, N.Y.). 12 June 1820.

American and Commercial Daily Advertiser (Baltimore, Md.). 15 June 1824.

American Phrenological Journal (New York, N.Y.). July 1859.

American Phrenological Journal and Life Illustrated (New York, N.Y.). January 1864.

American Statesman & City Register (Boston, Mass.). 17 June 1824.

Ans Messenger (Athens, Ohio). 16 December 1880.

Appleton's Journal (New York, N.Y.) 13 June 1874.

Arizona Weekly Journal Miner (Prescott, Ariz.). 7 February 1894.

Atchison Champion (Atchison, Kan.). 18 July 1891.

Atkinson's Saturday Evening Post (Philadelphia, Pa.). 13 April 1833.

Atlanta Constitution (Atlanta, Ga.). 5 October 1875; 18 May 1883; 31 March 1889.

Atlantic Monthly (Boston, Mass.). May 1873.

Augusta Chronicle (Augusta, Ga.). 6, 10, 17 March 1824.

Aurora and Franklin Gazette (Philadelphia, Pa.). 3 May 1826.

Aurora General Advertiser (Philadelphia, Pa.) 26 April 1824.

Baltimore American and Commercial Daily Advertiser (Baltimore, Md.). 20 July–16 August 1833.

Baltimore Gazette and Daily Advertiser (Baltimore, Md.). 20 July–16 August 1833.

Baltimore Patriot (Baltimore, Md.) 28 May, 18, 22, 23, 30 June, 14, 22 July 1824; 9 February 1827;16–27 March 1829; 8 July 1830.

Baltimore Patriot & Mercantile Advertiser (Baltimore, Md.). 25 May 1818; 8 June 1820.

Bangor Weekly Register (Bangor, Me.) 28 May 1818.

Barre Patriot (Barre, Mass.). 14 June 1850.

Bee (New Orleans, La.). 28 April 1834.

Berks and Schuylkill Journal (Reading, Pa.). 30 May 1818; 11 June 1825.

Bismarck Daily Tribune (Bismarck, N.D.). 20 July 1886; 14 February 1896.

Boston Commercial Gazette (Boston, Mass.). 18 January, 23 May 1824; 30 January–13 March 1827.

Boston Courier (Boston, Mass.). 16 July 1840.

Boston Daily Advertiser (Boston, Mass.). 26 April, 3 May, 25 December 1823; 26 November 1838; 22 May 1873.

Boston Daily Atlas (Boston, Mass.) 7, 11 June 1850.

Boston Medical Intelligencer (Boston, Mass.). 12 July 1825.

Boston Patriot & Mercantile Advertiser (Boston, Mass.). 21 May 1823.

Boston Recorder (Boston, Mass.). 19, 31 May 1823.

Boston Weekly Magazine (Boston, Mass.) 1 December 1838.

Brooklyn Eagle (Brooklyn, N.Y.). 18 December 1846; 9 March 28 May 1853; 2 March 1859; 16 March 1867; 10 December 1869; 4 November 1871; 7 August 1872; 27 September 1873; 31 March, 10 June 1877; 13

June 1880; 26 January 1884; 1 August 1886; 12 August 1888; 19 October 1890; 24 December 1891; 6 November 1892; 8 April, 22 May, 11 December 1898; 11 July 1900.

Burlington Hawk-Eye (Burlington, Iowa). 28 September 1876.

Cazenovia Republican (Cazenovia, N.Y.). 24 January, 7 February 1895.

Century Illustrated Monthly Magazine (New York, N.Y.). May 1887.

Chatuaquan (Jamestown, N.Y.). July 1885.

Cheshire Advertiser (Keene, N.H.). 22 March 1792

Chicago Daily Tribune (Chicago, Ill.). 17 July 1876; 9 March 1890.).

Chicago Times (Chicago, Ill.). 3 September, 26 October 1863.

Chicago Tribune (Chicago, Ill.). 6 July, 10 August 1864.

Christian Advocate and Journal (New York, N.Y.). 13 March 1835.

Christian Journal and Literary Register (New York, N.Y.). November 1823; January 1825.

Christian Messenger (Middlebury, Vt.) 27 May 1818.

Christian Observer (Louisville, Ky.) 8 August 1900.

Christian Recorder (Philadelphia, Pa.).17 January 1895.

Christian Register (Boston, Mass.). 9 May, 13 June 1823; 18 May, 15 June, 31, August 1850.

Cincinnati Advertiser and Ohio Phoenix (Cincinnati, Ohio). 25 December 1833.

Cincinnati Emporium (Cincinnati, Ohio). 11 November 1824.

Cincinnati Journal and Western Luminary (Cincinnati, Ohio) 25 August 1835.

Cincinnati Literary Gazette (Cincinnati, Ohio). 13 March 1824.

City Gazette and Commercial Daily Advertiser (Charleston, S.C.). 24 January 1824.

City of Washington Gazette (Washington, D.C.) 23 May 1818.

Cleveland Daily Advertiser (Cleveland, Ohio). 26 March 1835.

Cleveland Herald (Cleveland, Ohio). 28 January 1852.

Cleveland Whig (Cleveland, Ohio). 27 March, 31 July 1835.

Cold Water Fountain (Gardiner, Me.). 17 December 1847

Collector (New York, N.Y.). 1 October 1890.

Columbian Centinel (Boston, Mass.). 16 May 1818; 7, 21, 28 May, 23 August-17, September 1823.

Columbian Centinal American Federalist (Boston, Mass.). 11 February 1824.

Columbian Gazette (Utica, N.Y.) 2 June 1818.

Congregationalist (Boston, Mass.). 16 August 1882.

Connecticut Herald (New Haven, Conn.) 26 May 1818.

Connecticut Mirror (Hartford, Conn.) 14 February 1829.

Daily Chronicle (Philadelphia, Pa.). 3 April 1833.

Daily Columbus Enquirer (Columbus, Ohio). 29 October 1850.

Daily Evening Transcript (Boston, Mass.) 3, 5, 7 June 1850.

Daily Free Democrat (Milwaukee, Wis.). 1 August 1853.

Daily Gazette and Bulletin (Williamsport, Pa.). 9 August 1895.

Daily Inter Ocean (Chicago, Ill.). 7 September 1891; 1 September 1895.

Daily Kennebec Journal (Gardiner, Me.) 30 July, 1930.

Daily Louisville Public Advertiser (Louisville, Ky.). 10 January, 18 February, 16, April 1834.

Daily Missouri Democrat (Saint Louis, Mo.). 2 August 1856; 13 May 1857; 3 July 1863.

Daily Missouri Republican (Saint Louis, Mo.). 7 May 1841.

Daily National Intelligencer (Washington, D.C.). 2 June 1820; 15 January1829.

Daily News (San Jose, Calif.). 26 September 1886.

Daily Northwestern (Oshkosh, Wis.). 3 May 1887; 19 April 1895; 16 August 1897.

Daily Picayune (New Orleans, La.). 27, 29 February, 1 March 1852.

Daily Review (Decatur, Ill.). 15 October 1881.

Daily Standard (Syracuse, N.Y.). 31 July, 19 August 1856; 27 September 1859.

Daily Sun (Columbus, Ga.) 17 November 1872.

Dallas Morning News (Dallas, Tex.). 5 May 1887; 19 October, 14 December 1891; 5 May 1893; 13 October 1896.

Davenport Daily Gazette (Davenport, Iowa). 6 August 1862.

Davenport Daily Leader (Davenport, Iowa). 2 April 1894

Davenport Daily Republican (Davenport, Iowa). 12 May 1896.

Davenport Gazette (Davenport, Iowa). 15 September 1886.

Davenport Leader (Davenport, Iowa). 14 April 1896.

Davenport Morning Tribune (Davenport, Iowa). 9 January 1890.

Decatur Daily Republican (Decatur, Ill.). 10 April 1893.

Decatur Review (Decatur, Ill.). 23 October, 26 November 1891.

Decatur Weekly Republican (Decatur, Ill.). 15 June 1893.

Duluth Daily Tribune (Duluth, Minn.). 4 July 1884.

Duluth News Tribune (Duluth, Minn.). 2 July, 1893.

Eastern Argus (Portland, Me.: Daily). 22 June 1824.

Eastern Argus (Portland, Me.: Weekly). 29 June, 5, 12 July 1824.

Elyria Democrat (Elyria, Ohio). 12 January 1888.

Emporia Daily Gazette (Emporia, Kan.). 23 April, 29 May 1895.

Essex Register (Salem, Mass.) 29 March 1824.

Evening Democrat (Warren, Pa.). 17, 18 August 1893; 13 August 1895.

Evening Gazette (St. Louis, Mo.). 16 May 1844.

Evening Journal (Waukesha, Wis.). 13 May 1890

Evening News (Lincoln, Neb.). 7 May 1892.

Evening Post (New York, N.Y.). 16 December 1864.

Farmer's Cabinet (Amherst, N.H.) 23 May 1818.

Fitchburg Daily Sentinel (Fitchburg, Mass.). 27 July 1894.

Focus (Louisville, Ky.). 5 June 1827.

Fort Wayne Daily Sentinel (Fort Wayne, Ind.). 27 June 1871.

Fort Wayne Gazette (Fort Wayne, Ind.). 21, 23 February 1890.

Frank Leslie's Popular Monthly (New York, N.Y.). December 1889.

Freedom's Journal (New York, N.Y.). 18 July 1828.

Friend [Salem, Mass.]. 1 October 1870.

Friend; A Religious and Literary Journal (Philadelphia, Pa.). 25 July 1840; 7 July 1847.

Friends' Review (Philadelphia, Pa.) 25 December 1847.

Galaxy (New York, N.Y.). July 1869.

Galveston Daily News (Galveston, Tex.). 10 April 1889; 29 December 1890.

Galveston Tri-Weekly News (Galveston, Tex.) 16 November 1870.

Gazette and Bulletin (Williamsport, Pa.) 21 February 1882.

Gazetteer (Philadelphia, Pa.). 5 May, 22 December 1824.

Genesee Farmer and Gardener's Journal (Rochester, N.Y.). 21 March 1832

Georgia Weekly Telegraph and Georgia Journal & Messenger (Macon, Ga.). 30 April 1878; 10 March 1882.

Georgian (Savannah, Ga.) 25, 27 March 1824.

Green Bay Advocate (Green Bay, Wis.). 2 February 1848.

Hagerstown Mail (Hagerstown, Pa.). 5 December 1828; 27 April 1838.

Hampden Federalist (Springfield, Mass.). 4 June 1818.

Hampshire Gazette (Northampton, Mass.). 19 May 1824.

Harper's Weekly (New York, N.Y.). 29 July 1865.

Hartford Courant (Hartford, Conn.). 8 August 1894.

Hartford Daily Courant (Hartford, Conn.). 29 May, 17 June 1850.

Helena Independent (Helena, Mont.). 21 November 1877.

Herald (Syracuse, N.Y.). 26 July 1895.

Home Journal (New York, N.Y.). 29 June 1850.

Hornellsville Daily Tribune (Hornellsville, N.Y.). 22 December, 1893; May 1894

Hornellsville Weekly Tribune (Hornells-ville, N.Y). 22 December 1893.

Independent (New York, N.Y.). 24 November 1853; 20 August 1874.

Independent Chronicle and Boston Patriot (Boston, Mass.). 21 February, 29 May 1824; 10 December 1825.

Independent Inquirer and Commercial Advertiser (Providence, R.I.) 12, 16 September , 7 October 1824.

Indiana Progress (Indiana, Pa.). 2 November 1892.

Janesville Gazette (Janesville, Wis.). 7 November 1874.

Kansas City Star (Kansas City, Mo.). 12 April 1895; 31 January1897.

Knoxville Journal (Knoxville, Tenn.). 25, 28 April, 4 May 1889.

Lancaster Journal (Lancaster, Pa.) 22 May 1818. 30 August 1833.

Literary World (New York, N.Y.). 10 July 1847.

Littell's Living Age (Boston, Mass.). 3 July 1847.

Little Rock Daily Republican (Little Rock, Ark.). 16 October 1872.

Louisiana Advertiser (New Orleans, La.). 31 July 1820.

Lowell Daily Sun (Lowell, Mass.). 6, 9, 13 August 1894.

Lycoming Gazette (Williamsport, Pa.). 6 May 1829.

Lynn Mirror (Lynn, Mass.). 7 June 1828.

Macon Telegraph (Macon, Ga.). 9 June 1890; 14 June 1891; 20, 26 December 1893.

Macon Telegraph and Messenger (Macon, Ga.). 24 July 1881.

Marshfield Times (Marshfield, Wis.). 30 June 1893.

Massachusetts Spy, or Worcester Gazette (Worcester, Mass.) 20 May 1818.

McKean Democrat (Smethport, Pa.). 7 November 1890.

Mercantile Advertiser (New York, N.Y.) 15 February 1826; 7 January 1827.

Messenger (Due West, S.C.). 16 July 1885.

Middlesex Gazette (Middletown, Conn.). 25 April 1827.

Middletown Daily Argus (Middletown, N.Y.) 28 May 1894.

Middletown Daily Press (Middletown, N.Y.). 8 November 1899.

Milwaukee Daily Sentinel (Milwaukee, Wis.) 11 July 1853; 10 January 1876.

Milwaukee Journal (Milwaukee, Wis.). 21 December 1895.

Milwaukee Sentinel (Milwaukee, Wis.). 5 April 1886; 19 September 1887; 3 January 1896.

Minerva; or Literary, Entertaining, and Scientific Journal (New York, N.Y.). 25 October 1823.

Minneapolis Tribune (Minneapolis, Minn.). 2 June 1935.

Miscellaneous Cabinet (Schenectady, N.Y.). 8 November 1823–3 January 1824.

Missouri Daily Republican (Saint Louis, Mo.). 29 January 1852.

Morning Olympian (Olympia, Wash.) 11 July 1891.

Morning World Herald (Omaha, Neb.). 3 November 1898.

Mountain Democrat (Placerville, Calif.). 22 November 1879.

National Advocate (New York, N.Y.). 11 November 1823.

National Gazette and Literary Register (Philadelphia, Pa.) 7, 10, 14 June 1820.

National Messenger (Georgetown, D.C.) 25 May 1818.

Nebraska State Journal (Lincoln, Neb.). 20 January 1899.

New Bedford Mercury (New Bedford, Mass.) 5 June 1818.

New Hampshire Gazette (Portsmouth, N.H.). 19 May 1818, 27 April 1824.

New Hampshire Patriot and State Gazette (Concord, N.H.). 16 May 1850.

New Hampshire Sentinel (Keene, N.H.). 17 July 1851.

New York Clipper (New York, N.Y.). 8 April 1871.

New York Columbian (New York, N.Y.).

New York Commercial Advertiser (New York, N.Y.) 26 January, 21, 24 February, 5, 12, 13 March 1832.

New York Daily Times (New York, N.Y). 20 September 1851; 24 October 1853.

New York Evangelist (New York, N.Y.). 25 October 1886.

New York Evening Post (New York, N.Y.). 10 August 1824; 14 February, 2 March 1826.; 7 January 1827.

New York Herald (New York, N.Y.). 6 March 1914.

New York Mirror (New York, N.Y.). 7 February 1824; 22 September 1827.

New York Statesman (New York, N.Y.). 12 July 1824.

New York Times (New York. N.Y.). 8 December 1852; 26, 27 May 1880; 26 January 1884; 26, 28 June 1885; 11 April 1885; 23 January, 18 February, 30 March 1887; 2 June 1888; 9 September 1890; 1 April, 20, 21 June 1896; 6 August 1897; 22 May 1898; 8 March 1908; 31 May 1988.

Newburyport Herald (Newburyport, Mass.). 19 May, 1818, 6 April 1824.

New-England Galaxy (Boston, Mass.). 30 May 1823; 27 February 1824.

New-England Galaxy and Masonic Magazine (Boston, Mass.). 30 June 1820.

Newport Mercury (Newport, R.I.) 11 September 1824.

New-York American (New York, N.Y.). 24 February 1825.

Niagara Falls Museum News (Niagara Falls, Canada). September 1960.

Niles National Register (Baltimore, Md.). 6 June 1818; 20 December 1848.

North American and Daily Advertiser (Philadelphia, Pa.). 22 July 1840.

North American and United States Gazette (Philadelphia, Pa.). 16, 18 January 1852

North Star (Rochester, N.Y.). 27 June 1850.

Northern Home Journal (Gardiner, Me.). 12 August 1858.

Northern Sentinel (Burlington, Vt.) 12 June 1818.

Norwalk Reflector (Norwalk, Ohio). 23 June 1863.

Norwich Courier (Norwich, Conn.). 27 May 1818; 15 June 1825.

Omaha World Herald (Omaha, Neb.) 18 April 1893; 5 December 1894.

Oshkosh Daily Northwestern (Oshkosh, Wis.). 7 November 1882.

P.T. Barnum's Advance Courier (New York, NY). 1873.

Painesville Telegraph (Painesville, Ohio). 27 March 1835.

Penny Press (Minneapolis, Minn.). 18 November 1896.

Perry Chief (Perry, Iowa). 14 June 1877.

Philadelphia Daily Chronicle (Philadelphia, Pa.). 20 May 1833

Philadelphia Daily Intelligencer (Philadelphia, Pa.) 9 April 1833.

Philadelphia Gazette (Philadelphia, Pa.) 10 May–3 June 1833.

Philadelphia Inquirer (Philadelphia, Pa.). 27 January 1866; 9 February, 13 December 1891; 12 March 1893; 1, 3, 6 May 1894; 8 December 1895.

Philadelphia Pennsylvanian (Philadelphia, Pa.) 16 April 1833.

Philadelphia Saturday Courier (Philadelphia, Pa.). 25 May 1833)

Philadelphia U.S. Gazette (Philadelphia, Pa.). 3–23 April 1833.

Philadelphia U.S. Gazette for the Country (Philadelphia, Pa.). 8 April 1833.

Phrenological Journal and Science of Health (New York, N.Y.) April 1900.

Pittsburgh Gazette (Pittsburgh, Pa.). 1 January 1830.

Pittsfield Sun (Pittsfield, Mass.). 20 June 1850.

Plattsburgh Republican (Plattsburgh, N.Y.). 13 June 1818.

Portland Oregonian (Portland, Or.). 26 May 1888.

Portsmouth Journal and Rockingham Gazette (Portsmouth, N.H.). 1 November 1828.

Portsmouth Journal of Literature and Politics (Portsmouth, N.H.). 17, 24 April 1824.

Portsmouth Oracle (Portsmouth, N.H.). 23 May , 20 June 1818.

Portsmouth Times (Portsmouth, Ohio). 20 October 1892.

Poulson's American Daily Advertiser (Philadelphia, Pa.). 4 April 1817; 20 May 1818, 19 April 1824.

Prairie City Index (Prairie City, Iowa). 6 September 1872.

Providence Gazette (Providence, R.I.). 23 June, 1 September 1824.

Providence Patriot (Providence, R.I.). 24 January, 1 September 1824.

Puck (San Francisco, Calif.). November 1865.

Punch (London). 29 May 1847.

Quincy Whig (Quincy, Ill.) 17 October 1840.

Reflector (Milledgeville, Ga.) 9 June 1818.

Reno Evening Gazette (Reno, Nev.) 23 October 1891.

Republican Compiler (Gettysburg, Pa.). 14 June 1820.

Rhode Island American (Providence, R.I.) 19 May 1818; 31 August 1824; 10 June 1825.

Rochester Daily Advertiser (Rochester, N.Y.). 18 August–13 October 1827.

Rocky Mountain News (Denver, Colo.). 21 April 1889.

Rutland Herald (Rutland, Vt.). 10 June 1818; 1 January 1828.

St. Joseph Herald (Saint Joseph, Mo.). 25 January 1879.

St. Louis Globe Democrat (Saint Louis, Mo.). 20 March 1886; 26 February 1887.

St. Paul Pioneer Press (Saint Paul, Minn.) 25 June 2006.

Salem Daily News (Salem, Ohio). 10 March 1894.

Salem Gazette (Salem, Mass.). 1 April 1817; 6 May 1823; 23 March, 1 April 1824.

Salt-Lake Semi Weekly Tribune (Salt Lake City, Utah). 12 January 1897.

San Antonio Daily Express (San Antonio, Tex.). 2 December 1886; 11 July 1888.

Sandusky Daily Register (Sandusky, Ohio). 3, 12 June 1891.

Saratoga Sentinel (Saratoga, N.Y.). 8 August 1828.

Saturday Courier (Philadelphia, Pa.). 20 April 1833.

Saturday Evening Post (Philadelphia, Pa.). 7 June 1823; 24 April, 10 July 1824; 7 May 1825; 22 August 1829; 25 August 1849.

Savannah Georgian (Savannah, Ga.) 4 February 1827.

Scientific American (New York, N.Y.). 19 June, 1847; 18 May, 22 June 1850; 9 August 1856; 3 December 1859; 19 July 1884.

Spirit of the Times (New York, N.Y.). 1 March 1851.

Spirit of the Times & Carlisle Gazette (Carlisle, Pa.). 25 May 1818.

Springfield Daily Union (Springfield, Mass.). 19 December 1864.

State (Clemson, S.C.). 10 November 1897.

Stevens Point Journal (Stevens Point, Wis.). 8 October 1892.

Sunday Telegram (Worcester, Mass.). 9 April 2000.

Supplement to the Courant (Hartford, Conn.). 29 August 1840.

Syracuse Post-Standard (Syracuse, N.Y.). 6 June 1984.

Syracuse Standard (Syracuse, N.Y.). 31 January 1886.

Tacoma Daily News (Tacoma, Wash.). 6 April, 29 June, 14 July, 18 August, 26 August 1891; 15 May 1894; 14 May 1897.

Telegraph and Messenger (Macon, Ga.). 6 September 1884.

Texas Siftings (Austin, Tex.). 19 April 1884.

Times (New York, N.Y.). 14 July 1865

Times and Seasons (Commerce, Ill.). 2 May 1833; 2 May 1842.

Times Democrat (Lima, Ohio). 29 October 1897.

Tribune (New York, N.Y.). 4 November 1856

Tri-Weekly Ohio Statesman (Columbus, Ohio) 17 July 1847.

Troy Northern Budget (Troy, N.Y.). 5 August 1888.

Ulster Plebian (Ulster, N.Y.) 13 June 1818

United States Gazette (Philadelphia, Pa.). 19 February 1829.

Vermont Republican and American Yeoman (Windsor, Vt.). 8 February 1828.

Wachusett Star (Barre, Mass.), 1 February 1848.

Washington Post (Washington, D.C.). 14 October, 1886; 27 August 1891; 15 November 1896.

Watch-Tower (Cooperstown, N.Y.). 8 June 1818; 26 February 1827.

Waukesha Democrat (Waukesha, Wis.). 9 January 1849; 27 June 1877.

Waukesha Freeman (Waukesha, Wis.)., 7 July 1881.

Weekly Recorder (Chillicothe, Ohio) 12 June 1818.

Weekly Visitor and Ladies' Museum (New York, N.Y.) 1 August 1818.

Wellsboro Agitator (Wellsboro, Pa.). 3 March 1874.

Western Reserve Chronicle (Warren, Ohio) 30 January 1838.

Wheeling Daily Register (Wheeling, W. Va.). 23 April 1878.

Wheeling Register (Wheeling, W. Va.). 29 September 1879; 29 March 1887.

Wheeling Sunday Register (Wheeling, W. Va.). 1 July 1888.

Wisconsin Express (Madison, Wis.). 9 July 1850.

Wisconsin Weekly Free Democrat (Milwaukee, Wis.). 18 August 1858.

Zion's Herald (Boston, Mass.). 29 May 1823.

Manuscripts and Letters

American Antiquarian Society, *Donations to the American Antiquarian Society with Names of its Benefactors, 1813–1849*, American Antiquarian Society Archives (Worcester, Mass.), 122, 133.

Baker, Kathryn Hammond, Manager Special Collections, Francis A. Countway Library of Medicine, Cambridge, Mass. E-mail correspondence with the author, 2 August 2007.

Beebe, Kathryn J., Registrar, The Berkshire Museum, Pittsfield, Mass.. E-mail correspondence with the author, 27 January 2003.

College of Wooster Museum accession form, 1979. Photocopy from the Archives, College of Wooster, Wooster, Ohio. Obtained from Sam Farmerie, 2004.

Croll, Ace and Jenny Reilly. *The Middlebury Mummy*. Unpublished fact sheet, Henry Sheldon Museum, Middlebury, Vt.

Douglas, James and James Douglas, Jr. "Excerpt from 'Honeymoon on the Nile' 1881(?)." Photocopy of an original typescript in the possession of William Jamieson, Niagara Falls, N.Y.

Elias, Jonathan, Director, Akhmim Consortium. Undated telephone conversation with the author.

Fisk, Ebenezer (New York). Letter to Larkin T. Lee (Beverly, Mass.) 11 January 1825. Larkin Thorndike Lee Collection, Phillips Library, Peabody Essex Museum, Salem, Mass.

_____. Letter to Robert Rantoul (Beverly, Mass.) 9 December 1825. Larkin Thorndike Lee Collection, Phillips Library, Peabody Essex Museum, Salem, Mass.

_____. Note to [unknown] (Beverly, Mass.). Undated, but probably late December 1825. Larkin Thorndike Lee Collection, Phillips Library, Peabody Essex Museum, Salem, Mass.

Hayward, I. "Chronology of the Mummy—Padi-hershef and the Two Coffins." Typescript Massachusetts General Hospital Archives and Special Collections. Boston.

Hubbard, James Robert "Diary." Unpublished manuscript, Cazenovia Public Library, Cazenovia, N.Y.

Hunt, David R. Hunt, Collections Manager, Division of Physical Anthropology, National Museum of Natural History, e-mail correspondence with the author, 16 and 17 January 2007.

Kinsey, Robert, retired general manager of papermills in Gardiner, Me. Interview with the author, 19 July 2006.

Knight, LaFayette, letter to James H. and Sharon Fellows, 21 December 1843, MS 2362, Church of Latter Day Saint Archives, Salt Lake City, Utah.

Massachusetts General Hospital. Board of Trustees. "Records." Massachusetts General Hospital Archives and Special Collections. Boston. Massachusetts General Hospital. Board of Trustees. "Minutes." Massachusetts General Hospital Archives and Special Collections. Boston.

Metzner, Paula, Collections Manager, Kalamazoo Valley Museum. E-mail correspondence with the author, 24 January 2005.

Pomeroy, Dan E., Chief Curator and Director of Collections, Tennessee State Museum. E-mail correspondence with the author 11 September 2001.

"Princess Tothmea." Photocopy of undated information from Village of Round Lake Historical Society, Round Lake, N.Y.

Smith, Ebenezer (New York?) letter to John Dike (Beverly, Mass.) 25 October 1825, Larkin Thorndike Lee Collection, Phillips Library, Peabody Essex Museum, Salem, Mass.

Swinehart, Anthony L., Director, Hillsdale College Museum. E-mail correspondence with the author, 22 January 2003.

Taylor, John, Department of Ancient Egypt and Sudan, The British Museum. E-mail correspondence with the author, 9 September 2005.

_____. Letter to the author, 11 November 2005.

Turner, Thomas Larkin . "Biography of Turner, Larkin, b. 1781." Larkin Turner Collection, G.W. Blunt White Library, Mystic Seaport, Mystic, Conn.

Vivian, Cassandra. "George Gliddon in America." Paper delivered at the Conference on Travellers in Egypt and the Ancient Near East, Manchester University (England), 11–14 July, 2005.

Watson, John Fanning. "Extra-illustrated Autograph Manuscript of 'Annals of Philadelphia.'" Library Company of Philadelphia, Philadelphia, Pa.

White, Eric, Curator of Special Collections, Bridwell Library, Southern Methodist University, e-mail correspondence, with the author, 22 August 2003.

Winkler, Deborah, Assistant Director and Registrar, Reading Public Museum, Reading, Pa. E-mail correspondence with the author 27 September 2001.

Worden, Gretchen, Director of the Mutter Museum, Philadelphia, Pa. E-mail correspondence with the author, 16 January 2002.

Electronic Resources

A.V. Lane Collection; An On-line Exhibition. Website on-line. Available from http://www.smu.edu/bridwell/specialcollections/avlane/avlaneexhibit.htm.

Adolph Sutro's City. Website on-line. Available from http://www.historysmith.com/Adolph.html

American Museum cartes de visite. Electronic images from articles offered for sale on e-Bay.

American National Biography On-line. Subscription database on-line. Available from http://www.and.org/articale/10/10-02260.

Alberts, Robert C. "The Good Provider." American Heritage Magazine. Journal on-line. Available from http://www.americanheritage.com/articles/magazine/ah/1972/2/1972_2_26.shtml.

Avril, Tom. "Mummy Mystery." Philadelphia Inquirer (22 May 2006). Journal on-line. Available from http://www.philly.com/mid/inquirer/news/local/14636650.htm.

Barnum Museum. Publication on-line. Available from http://www.barnum-museum.org/core.htm.

"Brief History of the Niagara Falls Museum," in *Niagara Falls Museum*. On-line Website on-line. Available from: http://www.niagaramuseum.com/museum_history.htm.

Dela Cruz, Chris. "Mysterious Mummy lays in Geology Hall." *Daily Targum* (20 October 2005). Journal on-line. Available from http://media.www.dailytargum.com/media/storage/paper168/news/2005/10/28/PageOne/Mysterious.Mummy.Lays.In.Geology.Hall-1037715.shtml.

Detroit Institute of Arts. Website on-line. Available from http://www.dia.org/collections/ancient/ancientindex.html.

Division of Anthropology—University of Nebraska State Museum. Publication on-line. Available from http://www-musem.unl.edu/research/anthropology/about.html.

Dolloff, Francis W. and Roy L. Perkinson. "History of Paper." *How to Care for Works of Art on Paper*. Boston, Mass.: Museum of Fine Arts, 1985. Electronic notebook on-line. Available from www.noteaccess.com/MATERIALS/historyP.htm.

Fak, Alex Fak. "WU Gallery displays Egyptian Mummies." *Student Life News*. Journal on-line. Available from http://localhost:123/HLPage?pg=http%3A//www.studlife.cpm/99-00/99_09_07/news/egyptian08.html&.

Farmerie, Sam. *Pesed Reports*. Publication on-line. Available from http://www.westminster.edu/about/mummy/report.cfm.

Haggin Museum History Collection. Website on-line. Available from http://hagginmuseum.org/collections_history.htm.

History of the Boston Museum. Publication on-line. Available from http://www.emerson.edu.majestic/history/Bos_Museum_History.html.

How Ti Ameny Net Came to the University of Richmond. Website on-line. Available from http://hermes.richmond.edu/tiameny/TAN-UR.html.

Interesting and Important People of Albany Rural Cemetery. Article on-line. Available from http://www.albanyruralcemetery.org/albrur/notable.html.

Joseph Moore Museum. Publication on-line.

Available from http://www.earlham.edu/josephmooremuseum/content/history.html.

Keaggy, Diane Toroian. *St. Louis Science Center Unveils Child Mummy*. Publication on-line. Available from http://www.stltoday.com/stltodat/entertainment/storeis.nsf.vististlouis/story/071BF3EE65.

Lee, Jenny. *Mummy gets CT Scan At Facility*. Publication on-line. Available from http://www.poughkeepsiejournal.com/apps/pbcs.dll/article?AID=/20080409/NEWS01/804090325&template=printart

Manuel, Diane. "How to Handle a Mummy: Verrrry Carefully, Art Museum Curators Agree." *Stanford On-line Report* . Journal on-line. Available from http://news-service.stanford.edu/news/1998/september23/mummy923.html.

Metzner, Paula. "Hidden Treasure; Uncovering the Secrets of an Egyptian Coffin." Article on-line. Available from: http://www.kalamazoomuseum.org

"Museum from Curtitibia Houses Egyptian Mummy." Brazil-Arab News Agency Website on-line. Available from http://www.anba.com.br/ingles/noticia.php?id=15392

Museum of Fine Arts, Boston. *Collections Database*. Database on-line. Available from http://www.mfa.org/collections/sub.asp?key=20&subkey=6.

"Mummies of the Insane." *Roadside America*. Website on-line. Available from http://www.roadsideamerica.com/attract/WVPHImum.html.

"Mummy Museums." *Mummytombs*. Website on-line. Available from http://www.mummytombs.com/museums/continent.namerica.us.il.htm.

Mummy of the Archives of the Warren Hunting Smith Library. Publication on-line. Available from http://academic.hws.edu/library/archives/pdfs/mummy.asp.

Nolte, Carl. "High-Tech Peek Under Mummy's Wraps." *The San Francisco Chronicle*. Journal on-line. Available from http://www.sfgate.com/c/a/2000/05/13/MN8507.DTL.

Oriental Institute—In the Beginning. Web site. Available from http://www.oi-uchicago.edu/OI/INFO/OIBH/OI_Early_History.html.

Pott, Courtney. "Anthropology Collection Features Mummies." *Cornell Daily Sun* (4

April 2003. Journal on-line. Available from http://cornelldailysun.com/articled/8310/.

Richards, Janet, and Terry Wilfong. "A Kelsey Mummy Encounters Modern Medicine." *Kelsey Museum Newsletter* (Spring 2002). Journal on-line. Available from http://www.lsa.umich.edu/kelsey/research/Publications/spring2002/mummyl.html.

Sappol, Michael. "'Morbid Curiosity'"; The Decline and Fall of the Popular Anatomical Museum. " *Common-Place* I4:2 January2004). Journal on-line. Available from http://www.common-place.org/vol-04/no-02/sappol/.

"Saving the Mummy." *Richmond Now.* Journal on-line. Available from http://oncampus.richmond.edu/news/richmondnow/2007/05/mummy.html.

Selby, Holly. "Ancient Art in a New Light." *SunSpot.* Journal on-line. Available from http://www.sunspot.net/entertainment/galleriesmuseums/bal-as.walters14October14story?coll=b.

Social Violence and Conflict in San Francisco; A Chronology of the American Era. Article on-line. Available from http://www.notfrisco.com/colmatales/sfviol.html.

Sutro Egyptian Collection. Website on-line. Available from http://www.sfsu.edu/~museumst/sutro/.

Swinehart, Anthony L. *Hillsdale College Museum, Est. 1874.* Publication on-line. Available from http://www.hilssdale.edu/academics/bio/Swinehart/CollegeMuseum/Home/Main.html.

Terhert, Adrienne. "Mummy Mania." *Golden Age Xpress.* Journal on-line. Available from http://xpress.sfsu.edu/archives/life/003407.html.

"Trail of Invisible light: A Century of Medical Imaging." *University of Iowa Health Care.* Journal on-line. Available from http://www.uihealthcare.com/depts/medmuseum/galleryexhibits/trailoflight/06egyptianmummy.html.

Wente, Edward F. *Who Was Who among the Royal Mummies.* Publication on-line. Available from http://oi.uchicago.edu/research/pubs/nn/win95_wente.html.

Wolfe, S. J. *Egyptian Mummies in America Database.* Worcester, Mass., unpublished electronic database.

"Wrapped up in History." *Vassar; The Alumni Quarterly* 104, no. 1 (Winter 2007). Journal on-line. Available from http://www.aavc.vassar.edu/vq/articles/features-winter07-treasure.

"Zorayda Castle," in *Castles of the United States.* Website on-line. Available from http://www.dupontcastle.com/castles/zorayda.htm.

Index

Numbers in **bold italics** refer to pages with illustrations.